Sovereign Stories

University of
Hertfordshire **U H**

Information Hertfordshire

Reference Only

Not For Loan

American Studies: Culture, Society and the Arts

Edited by
Shamoon Zamir

Volume 8

PETER LANG
Oxford· Bern · Berlin · Bruxelles · Frankfurt am Main · New York · Wien

Padraig Kirwan

Sovereign Stories

Aesthetics, Autonomy, and Contemporary Native American Writing

PETER LANG

Oxford· Bern· Berlin · Bruxelles · Frankfurt am Main · New York· Wien

Bibliographic information published by Die Deutsche Nationalbibliothek
Die Deutsche Nationalbibliothek lists this publication in the Deutsche Nationalbiblio-
grafie; detailed bibliographic data is available on the Internet at http://dnb.d-nb.de.

A catalogue record for this book is available from the British Library.

Library of Congress Cataloging-in-Publication Data:

Kirwan, Padraig.
 Sovereign stories : aesthetics, autonomy, and contemporary Native American writing /
Padraig Kirwan.
    pages cm
 Includes bibliographical references and index.
 ISBN 978-3-0343-0203-6 (alk. paper)
 1. American literature--Indian authors--History and criticism. 2. American literature-
-20th century--History and criticism. 3. American literature--21st century--History and
criticism. 4. Politics and literature--United States--History--20th century. 5. Politics and
literature--United States--History--21st century. 6. Indians of North America--Intellectual
life. 7. Indians in literature. 8. Sovereignty in literature. 9. Autonomy in literature. I.
Title.
 PS153.I52K57 2013
 810.9'897--dc23
                              2013023732

Cover image: Star Wallowing Bull, *A Five Star Double Feature* © 2013.

An earlier version of Chapter 4, "'All the Talk and All the Silence': Literary
Aesthetics and Cultural Boundaries in David Treuer's *Little*", appeared in *NOVEL:
A Forum on Fiction* 44.3 (2011), 444–465.

ISSN 1661-4712
ISBN 978-3-0343-0203-6

© Peter Lang AG, International Academic Publishers, Bern 2013
Hochfeldstrasse 32, CH-3012 Bern, Switzerland
info@peterlang.com, www.peterlang.com, www.peterlang.net

This publication has been peer reviewed.

Printed in Germany

For Marion

Contents

Acknowledgments

I would like to thank the Fulbright Commission in Ireland and the Irish Research Council for the Humanities and Social Sciences. I was extremely grateful to receive scholarships from both organizations, and I would like to acknowledge the committee members, administrators, reviewers, and donors who make these awards possible.

Star Wallowing Bull gave me permission to use his fantastic pencil drawing *A Five Star Double Feature* for the cover, and I would like to thank Star for his generosity in doing so.

The folks at Peter Lang, Oxford, especially Hannah Godfrey, were tremendously helpful throughout the process of writing this book and preparing the manuscript.

I would like to thank Sean Walshe and the staff of the Avondale Community College for teaching so many of us about the strength of Irish community and Irish culture. *Go raibh mile maith agaibh.*

I owe a debt of gratitude to the faculty of the School of English, Drama and Film, University College Dublin. Special thanks must go to Ron Callan for his mentorship, collegiality, and friendship over the years. Declan Kiberd, Maria Stuart, and John Brannigan were also superb teachers, and proved to be kind and helpful colleagues when I began my teaching career at UCD.

Elaine Tyler May and Lary May became fast friends when they invited me to visit the University of Minnesota in 2000. I truly appreciated the warm welcome that I got in Minneapolis-St Paul. (I can say "warm" because they wisely advised me to visit before the winter snow arrived!)

Kenneth Lincoln and Joy Harjo supported my application for a Fulbright Scholarship to the University of California, Los Angeles, in 2003, and I wish to thank them both.

The task of writing this book was never a lonely one, and my colleagues in the Department of English & Comparative Literature, Goldsmiths,

University of London, offset the solitariness of the pursuit with count-less conversations and exchanges. In particular, I would like to thank Josh Cohen, Richard Crownshaw, Sarah Barnsley, Caroline Blinder, Tim Parnell, Carole Sweeney, and Gail McDonald for their collegiality, wise counsel, and, most of all, their friendship.

During my time in Goldsmiths I have been fortunate to have students who are passionate about literature. In particular, I would like to thank my English and American Literature students, especially those who opted to take my Indigenous Literature class, thereby electing to hear me lecture more often than they otherwise would have had to! I would also like to acknowledge my graduate students, particularly Robin White.

A very special thanks to LeAnne Howe for graciously accepting the invitation to visit Goldsmiths as part of the Richard Hoggart Lecture Series in 2011, and for her warm friendship ever since.

LeAnne introduced me to some wonderful scholars at two Native American Literature Symposia, and I feel incredibly fortunate to count many of these folks as friends. I would like to thank the Clan Mothers for the warm welcome that they give to international scholars, as well as all of the NALS participants for their advice and shared insight. Special thanks to Scott Andrews, David Carlson, Jill Doerfler, Tol Foster, Gordon Henry Jr., Patrice Hollrah, Jane P. Hafen, Niigaanwewidam James Sinclair, Jesse Peters, Dean Rader, Gwen Westerman, and Theo Van Alst. As well as shar-ing their academic knowledge, NALsters Brian Twenter, Angela Semple, and Royce Freeman also convinced me of the "merits" of social media in 2013, so I guess owe them an extra word of thanks for dragging me into the twenty-first century!

A special word of thanks is due to Stephen O'Neill (National University of Ireland, Maynooth), for his constant camaraderie and good humor. Stephen kindly read earlier drafts of the Introduction and Chapter 6 (any remaining errors are mine). I communicate with Michael O'Sullivan (Nagoya University) and James Byrne (Emerson College, Boston) via email more often than I see them in person, but I value their companionship and camaraderie dearly nevertheless. Anna Hartnell (Birkbeck, University of London) and David Stirrup (University of Kent) have proven to be great sounding boards and great company over the years. *Ar scáth a chéile a mhaireann na daoine.*

I would like to express my heartfelt gratitude to my parents, Nick and Kathleen, who have heard more about the process of writing than they ever needed (or wanted!) to. Thank you so much for your support and love through it all.

Finally, my deepest appreciation goes to my wife, Marion, whose love and friendship makes every day better than the last.

CHAPTER I

Introduction

In 1928 Darcy McNickle made reference to an Indian "map of mind" in a spatially informed figuring of the American Indian intellect. His wonderfully vivid reference was redeployed seven decades later by Louis Owens in *Mixedblood Messages* (1998), when the Choctaw-Cherokee-Irish writer sought to define what he described as a critical "'frontier' [...] where peoples with different culturally expressed identities meet and deal with each other."[1] Owens revisits McNickle's words in order to describe tribal writers' artistic and cultural autonomy in a constructive and affirmative manner, and it is exactly that positive reading of the map as a literary, intellectual, tribal, and critical position that this book favors. It is necessary, nonetheless, to remain conscious at the outset of some of the difficulties that must be circumnavigated in doing so. Specifically, McNickle's explicit reference to Native distinctiveness can be called into question simply because "the notion of an innate Indian consciousness" has, as Maureen Konkle explains, often been "a crucial step in denying Indians political status."[2] Here, the distinction between Native and non-Native cultures was mobilized as a means to exoticize tribal belief systems and devalue the political structures established by tribal communities. At the same time, Owens's idealization of Native people's ability to inhabit an "always shifting frontier space" is problematic for slightly different reasons. Although intended to defy narrative and cultural containment, this space might become limiting in its

1   Louis Owens, *Mixedblood Messages: Literature, Film, Family, Place* (Norman: University of Oklahoma Press, 1998), 52.

2   Maureen Konkle, "Indian Literacy, US Colonialism, and Literary Criticism," in *Postcolonial Theory and the United States: Race, Ethnicity, and Literature*, ed. Amritjit Singh and Peter Schmidt (Jackson: University of Mississippi Press, 2000), 164.

own right, insofar as its unstable, multidirectional, hybridized nature possibly hinders the move to develop tribally specific "conceptual, theoretical,
and methodological discourses [that can] be used in the study of Native
American art, culture and politics."[3]

The complicatedness associated with McNickle's and Owens's concept
of the Indian map of the mind could therefore feed into a particular set of
critical difficulties. For instance, as Konkle points out, "assertions about
Native American consciousness [and] Indians' 'typical' or 'traditional'
characteristics" have been used to suggest that an "'unspeakable contradic-
tion'" exists in Native communities where "'Western' practices or beliefs"
have been adopted or adapted. That is to say, the allusion to distinct spaces
might place Native writers in either the purer cultural, intellectual, and
spiritual space that McNickle seems to identify, or the hybridized frontier
space that Owens subsequently describes. Jana Sequoya Magdaleno calls
this apparent incongruity "the paradoxical injunction entailed by the figure
of the American Indian (that is, if Indian, then not contemporary; hence,
if contemporary, then not Indian)."[4] Thus, Konkle and Magdaleno both
suggest that non-Native commentators have detrimentally applied the
idea of difference in order to fix or locate the indigene, namely by placing
Native peoples in stark "either/or" settings—*either* traditional *or* mixedblood, nationalist *or* hybridized, past *or* present. Even though a decade
has passed since these critics pointed to this particular problem, it is still
the case that any reference to a Native map—be they intellectual, cultural,
political, or otherwise—can, unintentionally, spur debate. In fact, now that
American Indian literary nationalists are attempting to redraw boundary
lines in order to prevent this fixity and to map out their own frameworks
it seems that there is once again the temptation (in some quarters) to portray indigenous writers' sense of difference as an exercise in essentialism

3   Christopher B. Teuton, "Theorizing American Indian Literature: Applying Oral
     Concepts to Written Traditions," in *Reasoning Together: The Native Critics Collective*,
     ed. Craig S. Womack, Daniel Heath Justice, and Christopher B. Teuton (Norman:
     University of Oklahoma Press, 2008), 204.
4   Jane Sequoya Magdaleno, "How (!) is an Indian? A Contest of Stories, Round 2," in
     Postcolonial Theory and the United States, ed. Singh and Schmidt, 284.

and a reductive move, one that both desires an unfeasible return to "'traditional' characteristics" and a causes a critical Balkanization. However, as Gloria Bird once wrote, "differences do not have to be a plague," and literary or critical attempts to chart Native American distinctiveness must not be viewed as a bar to cross-cultural understanding in general, or, more specifically, a non-Native appreciation of the uniqueness of tribal cultures and narratives.[5] In writing this book I aim to recognize both the reality of ethnic and cultural separateness and indigenous writers' familiarity with, use, and subversion of "'Western' practices or beliefs." The latter does not, to my mind, indicate wholesale hybridization or totalized intercultural mixing: on the contrary, indigenous continuance and self-determination are processes that are profoundly concerned with evolving political, social, and artistic structures.

Sovereignty and Story

Sovereignty. Self-determination. Autonomy. Nation. Native American Studies is currently being shaped dramatically by this particular set of terms, and the prevailing discourse aims to interrogate not only various senses of tribal self-determination, but also to re-examine earlier formulations of cultural, spiritual, political, and artistic autonomy. Indeed, the publication of myriad nuanced and substantial works of scholarship focusing on the subject of sovereignty alone is testament to the critical role that definitions of indigenous self-determination and authority play within the field today.[6] Inevitably, perhaps, it is also the case that the definition of the terms

5   Gloria Bird, "Towards a Decolonization of the Mind and Text 1: Leslie Marmon Silko's *Ceremony,*" *Wicazo SA Review* 9.2 (1993), 7.
6   See: Sean Teuton, *Red Land, Red Power: Grounding Knowledge in the American Indian Novel* (Durham, NC: Duke University Press, 2008); Stuart Christie, *Plural Sovereignties and Contemporary Indigenous Literature* (New York: Palgrave Macmillan,

mentioned above, and the application of those terms to any particular set of circumstances in Indian Country is not entirely a straightforward affair. Nor, given the seriousness of the matter in hand, should it be. On the contrary, the values that a state of sovereignty affords a Native individual or tribe are a complex and multifaceted matter, and should be understood as such. For that reason, while it is vital to prioritize the benefits of tribal independence, it is also necessary to take note of the diverse nature of a range of issues that inform current conversations about indigenous homelands, tribal self-government, and various forms of Native sovereignty. Not least among these issues is the degree of usefulness that extremely involved, ostensibly Westernized political terms such as "sovereignty" and "nation" have for Native American communities in the United States today.

Unsurprisingly, Native American authors and scholars have been at the center of the discourse about the efficacy of this term. As members of tribal communities, indigenous writers have sought to examine the structure of tribal self-government, the circumstances that inform cultural and political autonomy, and, above all, the manner in which sovereignty is expressed. In *Sovereign Stories* I aim to examine the fictional and critical narratives created by these authors, and argue that their writing maps out a crucial set of distinct and discernible indigenous spaces—spaces concerned with intellectualism, political and aesthetic sovereignty, tribal consciousness, contemporary Native identity, and life in Indian Country today. This is in keeping with critical readings that interweave notional and concrete definitions of tribal lands, and suggest a methodology that takes into account various territories and places, and does so in a way that aims to enliven existing senses of Native American texts and contexts. Readings of the contemporary Native American novel disclose its engagement with tribal sovereignty and independence and with indigenous writers' bid to "honor the geographic, political, and experiential space[s]" that they come

2009); Ulrike Wiethaus, *Foundations of First People's Sovereignty: History, Education and Culture* (New York: Peter Lang, 2008).

from.[7] In order to do so it is necessary to critically examine the intricate aesthetic figuring of autonomy that occurs within the space of the Native American novel. This book examines the connection between fictional spaces, the extratextual locations that shape them, and critical responses to both. My particular objective is to assess the ways in which a particular set of novels speak not just from, but also of, indigenous worlds, and do so through a distinctive use of narrative style. It is hoped that this approach provides a deeper consideration of the dynamic between Native fiction and current definitions of sovereignty and nation. It is through the investigation of indigenous authors' recurrent interest in various forms of storied location—specifically the literary manifestation of "boundaries and sovereignties"—that a practical interpretative structure framed by extant notions of territory and frontier comes into being.[8] Within that structure it is possible to consider how narrative composition reflects a variety of indigenous autonomies, ranging from land claims and treaty rights to artistic and imaginative forms of individual and communal expression. In order to interrogate issues pertaining to cultural authority, creative freedom, and tribal autonomy, the close textual analyses in this book aim to develop the existing critical frameworks that have informed spatialized readings of Native American fiction. I hope to show that these works present indigenous concerns and reflect indigenous autonomies in an international setting, whether through the literary realism of the Dakotah world visible in Elizabeth Cook-Lynn's *Aurelia: A Crow Creek Trilogy* (1999), or the tribal, corporeal, and geographical spaces on show in such works as LeAnne Howe's *Shell Shaker* (2001), Sherman Alexie's *Face* (2009), or Craig Womack's story "The Song of Roe Náld" (2009). Quite simply, *Sovereign Stories* sets out to track seven indigenous writers' attempts to create liter-

7   Lisa Brooks, "Digging at the Roots: Locating an Ethical, Native Criticism," in *Reasoning Together*, ed. Womack, Heath Justice, and Teuton (Norman: University of Oklahoma Press, 2008), 236.

8   Kathryn Shanley, "'Born from the Need to Say': Boundaries and Sovereignties in Native American Literary and Cultural Studies," in *Native American Literature: Boundaries and Sovereignties*, a special edition of *Paradoxa: Studies in World Literary Genres* (2001), 15.

ary (and sometimes critical) narratives that both reflect and define sites of sovereignty in modern America.

Before that task can begin, it is worth noting that some general, but important, questions spring to mind when the word "sovereignty" is mentioned. For example, we have to question the extent to which the "sovereignty" that Native communities refer to is (dis)similar to other, autonomously defined, international "sovereignties." Who, for instance, guides or regulates supremacy within the various tribal territories? Is it apt to compare a sovereign ruler from the Native community—say, perhaps, the leader of the tribal government—to a head of state such as a president or prime minister, or to search for points of comparison between the offices or roles held by both leaders? Or is tribal sovereignty unrelated to such political structures? Similarly, is it *always* constructive to regard Native lands as sovereign, separate states, or are there occasions when an insistence upon a more deeply imbricated relationship with the federal government of the United States can be of greater benefit to tribes seeking economic or political support? Moreover, can the privileges and rights held by the tribe be exercised, expressed, and protected off the reservation? We need only call to mind James Sheehan's succinct point that "Sovereignty assumes [...] that political power is distinct from other organizations in the community—religious, familial, economic" in order to reveal what might be regarded as an essential point of divergence between Western definitions of dominion and the definitions offered by tribal peoples. The rapacious, political expediencies underlined by Sheehan's definition run contrary to the spiritual and ancestral ties that most folk in Indian Country see as constituent parts of modern-day self-determination.[9] For that reason, it is

9   Craig Womack teases out the various issues surrounding the term "sovereignty" in his essay "Book-Length Native Literary Criticism," in *Reasoning Together*, 74. I agree with Womack's point that even though many Native communities believe the modern "nation-state is inconsistent with Native cultures," the term nevertheless designates indigenous independence, autonomy, and empowerment and, as such, has particular resonances within current discourse. My goal in this book is to link that positive sense of Native self-government to the aesthetic spaces found in recent works of tribal fiction.

not difficult to see why Taiaiake Alfred has argued "'sovereignty' is inappropriate as a political objective for indigenous peoples."[10] Alfred's conclusion is based on the fact that the theological and philosophical arguments that have shaped definitions of sovereignty are European in origin and are therefore irrelevant to the tribal peoples.[11] Notwithstanding the fact that Thomas Jefferson shared a similar conviction—albeit for very different reasons—and argued that an absolute power domiciled in any collaboration between Church and State was "an idea belonging to the other side of the Atlantic," Chief Justice John Marshall had little qualms about adapting the Christian Doctrine of Discovery into United States law. While writing up the Supreme Court's unanimous finding of law in the case of *Johnson v. McIntosh*, Marshall pointed out that "The potentates of the old world found no difficulty in convincing themselves that they made ample compensation to the inhabitants of the new, by bestowing on them civilization and Christianity, in exchange for unlimited independence" (No. 21, 1823).

More importantly, he found that:

> On the establishment of these relations, the rights of the original inhabitants were, in no instance, entirely disregarded, but were necessarily, to a considerable extent, impaired. They were admitted to be the rightful occupants of the soil, with a legal as well as just claim to retain possession of it, and to use it according to their own discretion; but their rights to complete sovereignty, as independent nations, were necessarily diminished and their power to dispose of the soil at their own will, to whomsoever they pleased, was denied by the original fundamental principle, that discovery gave exclusive title to those who made it.

The United States' supreme power in law, which was influenced by (if not a scion of) the Christian Doctrine of Discovery, was consolidated in Marshall's subsequent findings in *Cherokee Nation v. Georgia* and *Worcester*

---

10 Taiaiake Alfred, "Sovereignty," in *Sovereignty Matters: Locations of Contestation and Possibility in Indigenous Struggles for Self-Determination*, ed. Joanne Barker (Lincoln: University of Nebraska Press, 2005), 38.

11 Alfred wonders "how a European term and idea [...] came to be so embedded and important to cultures that had their own systems of government since the time before the term *sovereignty* was invented in Europe" (Barker, *Sovereignty Matters*, p. 39).

v. Georgia. That is to say, Marshall's contention that the tribes had only "diminished" power in the case of *Johnson v. McIntosh* informed his interpretation of them as "domestic dependent nations" who were "under the protection of the United States of America, and of no other power" (in *Cherokee Nation v. Georgia* and *Worcester v. Georgia*). These rulings have dramatically influenced definitions of Indian sovereignty, and Marshall's legal findings frame Indian sovereignty in rather benign terms. The precedent, and the colonial echo, of those earlier determinations can be heard in District Court Judge James Battin's rather cavalier, but ultimately revealing, 1975 declaration that "the blunt fact [...] is that an Indian tribe is sovereign to the extent the United States permits it to be—neither more nor less." In 2011, in its finding on *United States v. Jicarilla Apache Nation*, the Supreme Court "held that the fiduciary exception to the attorney-client privilege does *not* apply to the general trust relationship between the United States and the Indian tribes," simply because the "Government acts not as a private trustee but pursuant to its sovereign interest in the execution of federal law" (No. 10–382).[12] In these cases, tribal sovereignty is but a poor relation to the supreme authority of the federal government, and the tribes have been alarmed—and disarmed—by Supreme Court rulings that opine that Indian sovereignty is trumped by the broader political and legal power that resides within the United States government. Crucially, the tribes have been no less frustrated on occasions when the court has identified a fuller, stronger version of Indian sovereignty, often with the result that cases brought by the tribes are thrown out. For instance, in 1997 the Coeur d'Alene in Idaho

> sought, inter alia, a declaratory judgment establishing its entitlement to the exclusive use and occupancy and the right to quiet enjoyment of the submerged lands, a declaration of the invalidity of all Idaho laws, customs, or usages purporting to regulate

12   A certain wistful irony lies in the fact that one of the greatest legal victories in Indian Country arose out of the Jicarilla Apache's suit against oil and gas companies in New Mexico in 1982. In that case, *Merrion v. Jicarilla Apache*, the court ruled that "sovereign power [...] is an enduring presence that governs all contracts subject to the sovereign's jurisdiction" and cleared the way for tribal taxation by recognizing the Jicarilla Apache's "role as a commercial partner" and "as a sovereign" (No. 80–11, January 25, 1982).

those lands, and a preliminary and permanent injunction prohibiting defendants from taking any action in violation of the Tribe's rights in the lands.

Writing for the majority, Justice Anthony Kennedy found that "'Indian tribes [...] should be accorded the same status as foreign sovereigns, against whom States enjoy Eleventh Amendment immunity."[13] More troubling, perhaps, is the Court's decision in its June 18 2012 finding of law in the case of *Match-E-Be-Nash-She-Wish Band of Pottawatomi Indians v. Patchak* to waive the federal government's sovereign immunity from a respondent's suit. The Court's opinion sets a vital precedence, and could severely impede the Secretary of the Interior's right to hold lands in trust under the Indian Reorganization Act—a right which then allows the tribe to operate a casino under the Indian Gaming Regulatory Act.

In light of historical events and contemporary developments, it is something of a truism to suggest that many indigenous commentators exhibit a healthy skepticism about the term sovereignty itself—a legal and political term informed by a supposed European rationalism that has been adapted to the United States government's somewhat capricious understandings of the term. Indeed, it is hardly any wonder that scholars such as Alfred hold "sovereignty" in very poor esteem. Like Alfred, Joanne Barker has drawn attention to the disastrous outcomes that have arisen as a consequence of a state's supreme right and the catastrophic misuse of power. "Sovereignty," Barker writes, "carries the horrible stench of colonialism. It is incomplete, inaccurate, and troubled."[14] Further, it is important to

---

13   Peter d'Errico, "American Indian Sovereignty: Now You See It, Now You Don't" <http://www.umass. edu/legal/derrico/nowyouseeit.html> accessed June 2, 2012. The Eleventh Amendment can be interpreted a number of ways, and its "jurisprudence has become over the years esoteric and abstruse and the decisions inconsistent": Legal Information Institute <http://www.law.cornell.edu/anncon/ html/amdt11_user. html> accessed September 12, 2012. Despite the perplexed nature of the various rulings handed down in relation to this amendment, it is clear that, in the case of the Coeur d'Alene, the Supreme Court ruled that the tribe were fully autonomous, independent sovereign states, and therefore could not bring suit against any other state.

14   "For Whom Sovereignty Matters," in *Sovereignty Matters*, ed. Barker, 26.

remember that many non-Native commentators with little or no interest in indigenous issues would *also* argue that the various incarnations of
power that the term has sought to define are problematic in nearly every
context. For instance, Dan Philpott has sought to reveal what he calls the
"dysfunctionalities" that "sovereignty gives rise to," and lists three flaws
that he views as being insurmountable and fatal:

> First, its external dimension renders inconceivable international law and a world
> state [...]. Second, the internal dimension of sovereignty, the absolute power of the
> state over the body politic, results in centralism, not pluralism. Third, the supreme
> power of the sovereign state is contrary to the democratic notion of accountability.[15]

In this regard, sovereignty prevents international (or intercultural) dialogue, nurtures centralized rule, and gives way to dictatorial policy. It is
surely necessary, then, to scrutinize tribal sovereignty's basic principles
with a view to redefining the term with an appropriate critical sharpness.
I suggest doing so *not* because the scholarly debate about the definition
of a European or Western version of political sovereignty—its historical
origins, geographical constituency, and pre-eminence—continues to rage
(although the fact that it does is certainly interesting), but because there
are significant questions to be answered about what it means for America's
tribal peoples to have inalienable and supreme authority within a specific
territory. More important, at least to the critical study that I am proposing, is the fact that intellectuals, writers, and scholars, including Alfred and
Barker, are greatly concerned with those questions and with the issue of
indigenous self-determination. My goal, as a result, is to consider the means
by which tribal sovereignty is figured within Native American literature;
"figured" in terms of an identifiable aesthetic style, and "figured out" in
terms of the intellectual, political, and critical discourse.

In doing so, I would also note that contemporary definitions of nationalism give rise to certain challenges for European scholars, and not just for
those of us working in the field of Native American Studies. It has been

---

15   Dan Philpott, "Sovereignty," in *The Stanford Encyclopedia of Philosophy* <http://
     plato.stanford.edu/entries/ sovereignty> accessed March 21 2011.

a long while since Benedict Anderson reminded us that terms such as "nation, nationality, nationalism" have, historically speaking, "proved notoriously difficult to define."[16] We must also be mindful of the fact that "the satisfaction of some [nationalisms] spells the frustration of others."[17] The frustration referred to here has often been a first step toward intolerance, radicalism, and violence, and atrocious acts of ethnic cleansing, military aggression, and terrorism have been carried out in the name of the nation, but rarely in the name of the people. As a result, there is a current "moral debate on nationalism [that] reflects a deep moral tension between solidarity with oppressed national groups on the one hand and repulsion in the face of crimes perpetrated in the name of nationalism on the other."[18] There are other, interconnected, stumbling blocks which complicate any straightforward definition or espousal of the term or celebration of common origin, ethnic identity, and collective self-determination. Intellectually speaking, there is, as David Agnew laments, a tendency to "see the people who subscribe to [nationalism] as cultural dopes," and many commentators remain skeptical of the degree of rationality or functionality that national movements can have in the current moment.[19] Subsequently, the nationalist is often perceived as someone who is mentally sluggish, emotionally over exercised, and/or hopelessly given over to anachronistic gestures. As a somewhat melancholic Irishman I am sure that people have doubtlessly slotted me into one or more of those categories by times. Even where such accusations are successfully disregarded or rebuffed (as in Agnew's essay) and where abject violence under the guise of establishing the national principle is scrupulously avoided, it is still necessary for any discussion of a

---

16   Benedict Anderson, *Imagined Communities: Reflections on the Origins and Spread of Nationalism* (London: Verso, 1991), 3.

17   Ernst Gellner and John Breuilly, *Nations and Nationalisms: New Perspectives on the Past* (Ithaca, NY: Cornell University Press, 2009), 2.

18   Nenad Miscevic, "Nationalism," in *The Stanford Encyclopedia of Philosophy*, ed. Edward N. Zalta (Fall 2008 edition) <http://plato.stanford.edu/archives/fall2008/entries/nationalism> accessed July 7 2009.

19   "Nationalism," in *A Companion to Cultural Geography*, ed. James S. Duncan, Nuala C. Johnson, and Richard H. Schein (London: Blackwell, 2004), 225.

national teleos to involve a comparison of the discreet ways in which diverse national ideals function. What, for instance, is nationalism's relationship to territory in a specific location? To what extent can the individual or community remain nationalist when removed from the land (either by choice or by force)? Is nationalism a political expediency formed in the face of colonial or imperial control, a mindset with ancient and historic roots, or a complex amalgam of both? Are local, distinct versions of nationalism comparable within a global context? All of these questions are in attendance when this complex term is mentioned.

Indigenous and First Nations scholars are challenged by these troubling connotations in much the same way as their European counterparts are. Labrador Métis scholar Kristina Fagan discusses this fact in her wonderfully dextrous examination of Canadian nationalism and literature, and notes that it is hardly "surprising that the idea of nation, which is based on claims to truth, identity, and unity, has largely come to be seen as naïve" in the first instance, or that, in the wake of the resurgence of the far-right, "the idea of nationalism has come to be ethically suspect, widely seen as a way of masking injustice."[20] There are other, more specific, questions surrounding the idea of indigenous nationhood. The first of these concerns competing definitions of nationalism within a given territory; there is, as Fagan points out, a world of difference between Aboriginal nationalism and Canadian nationalism, the latter of which aims to create a sense of "national" cohesion which brings citizens of "different national origins, races, ethnicities, regional identities, [and] religions" together.[21] The distinction between the political nation state and the indigenous nation is brought into even starker relief when the Labrador Métis critic explains that several Aboriginal nations in Canada have government in place *per se*. Importantly, Fagan also recognizes that certain "problems arise when we try to find a definition of nationhood that is appropriate to all Aboriginal

20   "Tewatatha:wi: Aboriginal Nationalism in Taiaiake Alfred's *Peace, Power, Righteousness: An Indigenous Manifesto*," *American Indian Quarterly* 28:1–2 (Winter/Spring 2004), 15.
21   Ibid., 16.

nations."[22] In doing so, her essay not only reveals the difficulty of defining an overarching vision of nationalism that might seem to correspond with various tribal structures in Canada, but it also highlights the challenges facing a literary critic who hopes to conduct a nationalist reading of tribal writing as well. In addition to highlighting the involvedness of nationalism as a term, Fagan's work might also remind us of the need to avoid totalizing or overarching concepts of the nation, and the importance of attending to the specificities of tribal identity.

Yet, in spite of—and quite possibly because of—the significant, often manifest, strain caused by political and philosophical definitions of sovereignty or nationalism in a wider context, several Native commentators, tribal leaders, and artists have found it both enabling and useful to speak about "sovereignty" and "nation," particularly with regard to self-determination and autonomy. It is to these ends that Barker, while acknowledging that supreme autonomy within a territory was once used to troubling colonial ends, points out that sovereignty has been "rearticulated to mean altogether different things by indigenous peoples"; a suggestion that signals the likelihood that various, sometimes contending, definitions of sovereignty are current.[23] Adding considerable value to this line of reasoning is the commonly held proposition that "indigenous sovereignty never departed."[24] Of relevance here is the claim of Harry Charger, a tribal leader of Sans Arc Lakota, that his people "are already sovereign [...]. It is god given: it is our thoughts, our words, our ceremonies. Everything is free."[25] Charger's contention, which appears in *Foundations of First Peoples' Sovereignty* (2008), underscores the belief that Native American sovereignty has long been a distinct phenomenon, separate to and vastly different from its Western counterparts. It is unsurprising, therefore, that in the same collection of essays Ulrike Wiethaus argues: "First Nations' practices of self-determination

22 Ibid., 19.
23 Barker, *Sovereignty Matters*, 26.
24 Christie, *Plural Sovereignties*, 1.
25 Harry Charger, Ione V. Quigley, and Ulrike Wiethaus, "Foundations of Lakota Sovereignty," in *Foundations of First People's Sovereignty: History, Education and Culture*, ed. Ulrike Wiethaus (New York: Peter Lang, 2008), 160.

and politico-philosophical thought have remained in continuous, autonomously defined existence, even if hidden from Euro-American view."[26]

As well as indicating that sovereignty can contain a host of diverse or
separate meanings, Barker's notion of a process of "rearticulat[ion]" usefully
reminds us that although various forms of indigenous sovereignty existed
pre-contact, those same forms continue to be redefined by tribal peoples
today. It is in this sense that Seneca scholar Michelle H. Raheja argues
that while it is most certainly the case that "the term predates European
notions of nation-to-nation political sovereignty" it is also the case that
"indigenous conceptions have now incorporated these non-Native articula-
tions of the term into their definition." This articulation of sovereignty is
slightly different to Charger's, insofar as Raheja suggests that recent definitions of the term itself have intercultural roots. Thus, she concludes, the
"English word *sovereignty* [...] becomes a placeholder for a multitude of
indigenous designations that also takes into account the European origins
of the idea."[27] Craig Womack has similarly drawn attention to the wider
application of the term in the American context: "Sovereignty (by definition government to government relations) has a profound cosmopolitanism
at its core," he writes, and "tribal governments exist in complex relationships
with municipal, state, and federal powers that demand constant movement
between and across borders."[28] However, while this conceptualization is
generous and enriching, it comes close to the kind of "functional plurality"
that Stuart Christie believes will "serve as a valuable tool further enabling
indigenous autonomy."[29] Underpinning these arguments is the key premise
that Native American sovereignty reflects cultural, ethnic, historical, and
political distinctions particular to tribal peoples, while also revealing the
ways in which indigenous communities are simultaneously knowledgeable

---

26   Ibid., 2.
27   Michelle H. Raheja, "Reading Nanook's Smile: Visual Sovereignty, Indigenous
      Revisions of Ethnography, and Atanarjuat (The Fast Runner)" *American Quarterly*
      59.4 (2007), 1163–1164.
28   Craig Womack, "A Single Decade: Book-Length Native Literary Criticism," in
      Reasoning Together (Norman: University of Oklahoma Press, 2008), 37.
29   Christie, *Plural Sovereignties and Contemporary Indigenous Literature*, 4.

of, and conversant with, the countless other meanings that continue to be applied to the term. Subsequently, it can be seen that in each of these critical treatises, tribal sovereignty is introduced in a way that comprehensibly reveals its logic and its reasonableness, announces the more enabling aspects of the term, and circumvents many of the limitations that Philpott finds in Westernized, historical definitions. Emerging from Native definitions of the term as a consequence, then, is a democratic and pluralistic point of view. While it is clear that such designations can, and will, shape and inform wider debates surrounding complex forms of sovereignty in a global context, I would argue that it is far more important to recognize how they reflect the dynamic and intricate fashion in which Native American critics, writers, and communities are currently describing and outlining their own positions. It is just as important to note that indigenous writers—critics and fictionists—are playing a central role in this negotiation of the specificities of Native American sovereignty, and are very often expressing and (re)defining the wider significations and applications of the term. This is not always an easy or straightforward process; the scholarly and creative work examined in this book reflects not only the dexterity and determination of Native writers, but also, by times, latent anxieties about the dilution of tribal sovereignty when it is situated in a Western context.

In the wake of this vigorous working out of tribal sovereignty, it is notable that sovereignty "means different things to different peoples, polities, and First Nations."[30] As a result, it is vital that we use the term judiciously, and remain constantly mindful that varied—but not entirely disparate— versions of indigenous independence often co-exist and overlap within a single sphere. By doing so we will be able to not only understand particular forms of autonomy more fully, but we will also be in a position to form a comparative analysis of the full range of autonomous spaces that tribal peoples have always inhabited and continue to redefine. The value of this critical practice becomes clearer, perhaps, when we consider the nuances

---

30   David E. Wilkins, "Indigenous Self-Determination: A Global Perspective," in *Foundations of First People's Sovereignty: History, Education and Culture* (New York: Peter Lang, 2008). 18.

and shifts in emphasis between cosmopolitan or mixedblood constructivist theories on one hand, and nationalist, materialist readings of Native experiences on the other. By way of example, it is clear that Gerald Vizenor's vision of a liberatory, and somewhat indefinable, indigenous "transmotion" (best defined as a form of "trickster" theory) is, on the face of it, a far cry from the "evaluative claims to normative knowledge" that Sean Teuton and many others (myself included) believe will "better support the philosophical and actual recovery of Indian lands, histories, and identities."[31] Despite substantial differences in critical methodology and political perspective there is, however, an interesting interface between these two versions of tribal sovereignty that must be considered. Vizenor's perception of a "sui generis sovereignty"—which he argues is the result of "native motion and active presence"—appears to be a space not entirely dissimilar to the "dynamic, continuous site of theoretical investigation, evaluation, and revision" that Teuton has persuasively argued will aid tribal people's attempts to reach the "crucial goal of collective tribal self-definition."[32] Indeed, Raheja's definition of "visual sovereignty," described as an "always in motion and [...] inherently contradictory" state, has both notional and material consequences, which are themselves fully revealed in the intertwining of various forms and expressions of indigenous autonomy.

Interestingly, this portrayal of tribal independence also complements Sheehan's broader case that "in order to understand sovereignty we have to examine the relationship [...] between sovereign theory and sovereign practice, between sovereignty as a way of thinking and sovereignty as a way of acting," thereby underwriting the contention that tribal peoples simultaneously invoke *and* also shape existing definitions. Accordingly, I would argue that it is necessary to consider how a range of Native American scholars and fictionists—each working from their own distinct starting

---

31   In his excellent book *Red Land, Red Power*, Teuton argues that "self-identified mixed-blood critics, writing in this zone of the trickster, have been left with little theoretical recourse but subversion. Indeed, they can deconstruct the Western image of the Indian, but, to remain epistemologically consistent, they cannot justify their own normative claims to American Indian identity or history" (14).

32   Ibid., 24.

points and individual methodologies—construct particular versions of tribal and aesthetic sovereignty in a manner that is not only productive and influential but that also support and reflect upon one another. This move is not intended to conflate complex, indigenous conceptualizations of self-autonomy, nor is it a deliberate attempt to take the heat out of the political progress that Teuton and others are currently producing. On the contrary, it aims toward a deeper understanding of both the means by which political movements are supported by the discrete mobilization of spatialized metaphors in both fiction and critical theory, and an appreciation of the ways in which Native American fictionists create multifarious narrative spaces. In looking at those narrative spaces it is important to remember too, as Amanda Cobb counsels, that "[s]overeignty and decolonization are not synonymous terms."[33] For that reason, it is necessary to distinguish between narratives that focus on acts of legal or political reclamation in the face of colonial disruption, and those that concentrate on tribal continuance and pre-colonial sovereignties. Set against this complex background, *Sovereign Stories* aims to tease out the distinctive connotations accruing from Native independence and distinctiveness, and to foreground the work of fiction in marking out various philosophical, political, artistic, and interpretative spaces that are at once open and enabling. My objective, then, is to interrogate *how* Native American fictionists create imaginary realms which, in turn, have extratextual significance. Thus the book is concerned with forging a connection between "rhetorical sovereignty" and the political and legal debates that are taking place in Indian Country at present.[34]

33 Quoted in Daniel Heath Justice, "Kinship Criticism and the Decolonization Imperative," in *Reasoning Together*, 152.

34 Interestingly enough, Christie and Matthew D. Herman both believe that a schism has developed, and that the majority of critics prioritize either constructivist or materialist positions. As a result, Christie aims for a "consensus" between the "autonomy of linguistic signs" and "the autonomy of actual indigenous peoples, places, and the material worlds they inhabit," while Herman seeks out "points of commensurability between theories of nationalism and cosmopolitanism": Christie, *Plural Sovereignties and Contemporary Indigenous Literature*, 4; Matthew D. Herman, "'The Making of Relatives': Sovereignty and Cosmopolitan Democracies," in *Foundations of First People's Sovereignty*, ed. Wiethaus, 38. While I wholeheartedly agree with both scholars

Natives and Nations

Just as it is necessary to excavate the widest possible meaning(s) of Native
American self-determination with regard to sovereignty, thereby paying
attention to the resonances of the term in all of its contexts, it is vital
too that we apprehend the broader meanings that Native writers are currently giving to both functional and figurative reckonings made possible
via tribal nationalism. This task has been made all the more urgent because
many indigenous commentators are unambiguously insisting upon intellectual, imaginative, and political sovereignty. Among the best known of
these voices are Jace Weaver, Craig Womack and Robert Allen Warrior.[35]
Revisiting and very often advancing theories expounded by an earlier
generation of Native critics, these scholars are currently defining tribal

---

that it is of great value to track and examine the relationship between narrative spaces
and actual territories, it is my conviction that a stark and troubling differentiation
between cosmopolitan and nationalist or indigenist positions has, traditionally,
been made by non-Native scholars. For instance, Arnold Krupat's "Nationalism,
Indigenism, Cosmopolitanism: Critical Perspectives on Native American Literatures,"
Centennial Review 42.3 (1998), 622, like his recent discussion of "culturalists" and
"aesthetes" in "Culturalism and its Discontents: David Treuer's *Native American
Fiction: A User's Manual*," *American Indian Quarterly* 33:1 (Winter 2009), 131–160,
and Elvira Pulitano's championing of mixed-blood readings in her work *Toward a
Native American Literary Theory* (Lincoln: University of Nebraska Press, 2004),
have unhelpfully and unnecessarily distorted the field. As a result, I'm not entirely
sure that "consensus" or "commensurability" has been lacking, but argue instead
that there has been a, rather unhelpful, propensity to categorize Native voices and
present subtleties in arguments as evidence of complete disagreement. Accordingly,
I am mindful of the reality that, as Jace Weaver points out, "there is more that unites
[Native critics ...] than divides [them]": *American Indian Literary Nationalism*, ed.
Jace Weaver, Craig S. Womack, and Robert Warrior (Albuquerque: University of
New Mexico Press, 2006), 22.

35   Other voices amongst this group are Amanda Cobb, Lisa Brooks, Malea Powell,
and Scott Lyons. It is vital to note that several non-Native critics support calls for
tribal separatism, and their scholarship has been largely supported by Native critics.
Amongst this second group are James Cox and Maureen Konkle.

sovereignty through their discussion of the critical movement after which their collection of essays, *American Indian Literary Nationalism* (2006), was named.[36] "American Indian Literary Nationalism," Weaver explains, is the "explication of specific Native values, readings, and knowledges" within the fiction itself. In order to strengthen the understanding of this critical paradigm Daniel Heath Justice explains that "[i]ndigenous nationhood" is "[m]ore than simple political independence or the exercise of a distinctive cultural identity"; it is also "an understanding of a common social interdependence within the community."[37] Heath Justice's point resonates here with Benedict Anderson's definition of a nation as "an imagined political community [... one that is] imagined as both inherently limited and sovereign"—not least because tribal nationalism has, as Heath Justice explains, a role to play "on a daily level of governance," and "on the broader stage of international relations [... as well as] in the area of literary and artistic expression."[38] Notably, this conceptualization should assuage, or indeed rejoin, Ernst Gellner and John Breuilly's recently expressed anxiety that "nationalism has not often been [...] sweetly reasonable nor [...] rationally symmetrical."[39] For these scholars, and for many other European commentators, the notion of collective belonging is little more than a myth that ultimately leads to static, exclusionary modes of identity. However, it should be noted that Weaver's vision of "two, three, many separatisms"

---

36 *American Indian Literary Nationalism*, ed. Weaver, Womack, and Warrior. Prior to the publication of this jointly edited work, Warrior's *Tribal Secrets: Recovering American Indian Intellectual Traditions* (Minneapolis: University of Minnesota Press, 1995), Weaver's *That the People Might Live: Native American Literatures and Native American Community* (New York: Oxford University Press, 1997), and his later work *Other Words: American Indian Literature, Law, and Culture* (Norman: University of Oklahoma Press, 2001), along with Womack's *Red on Red: Native American Literary Separatism* (Minneapolis: University of Minnesota Press, 1999) mapped the critical landscape with regard to indigenous autonomy, independence, and separatism.

37 Daniel Heath Justice, "'Go Away Water!' Kinship Criticism and the Decolonization Imperative," in *Reasoning Together*, 151.

38 Anderson, *Imagined Communities*, 6; Heath Justice, *Our Fire Survives the Storm*, 23.

39 *Nations and Nationalism*, 2.

very closely reflects the collectively gratifying and morally sound national ideal that many critics—Gellner and Breuilly included—often suggest is an unattainable model.[40]

How indigenous nationalism functions within a global context and the ability of indigenous peoples to imaginatively express a common ancestry through literature and other forms of expression is important. Of greater significance, perhaps, is the manner in which tribal nationalism is logically, geographically, spiritually, and ideologically distinct from Western nationalisms; ancestrally rooted in tribal stories; and materially enacted in Indian Country today. Even though there is some "common ground" between Native American and European or international nationalisms that can be mobilized to chart paths of shared understanding or negotiate complex political territories, indigenous definitions of sovereignty are uniquely formed and distinctively performed. There is a specific indigenous form of "understanding" that, as Heath Justice explains, arises from "the tribal web of kinship rights and responsibilities that link the People, the land, and the cosmos together."[41] This type of political imagining has resonances with what Elizabeth Cook-Lynn refers to as "nation-specific creativity and political unification in the development, continuation, and defense of a coherent national mythos" in modern America.[42] Indeed, Cook-Lynn's use of the word "mythos" is certainly worth considering. By drawing attention to the fact that the Sioux construct the nation through stories and narratives that are handed down through history, the Crow Creek Sioux author reminds the reader that it is the retelling of these stories *today* that defines the nation, and not some essentialized view of Sioux "essence" that does

40   Despite Weaver's inclusivity, the definition of nationalism is not always that easy. Indeed, recent events in Tahlequah, Oklahoma, might serve as a reminder that tribes can sometimes define the nation in a rather exclusionary and idealizing way; on December 14, 2012, the federal court ruled that descendants of slaves owned by the Cherokee Nation can sue the tribe for restoration of citizenship of that nation, thereby challenging the tribal leadership's definition of the Nation.

41   "Go Away, Water!", 151.

42   Elizabeth Cook-Lynn, *Anti-Indianism in Modern America: A Voice from Tatekeya's Earth* (Champaign: University of Illinois Press, 2007), 35.

so. These descriptions collectively underline the extent to which Native people are, as LeAnne Howe writes, "people of specific landscapes," and they should therefore remind critics that it has always been the case that "specific stories are told about emergence from a specific place."[43] Moreover, international scholars and commentators might do well to consider the ample significations of American Indian separatism for current understandings of place, identity, and social cohesion, given that the accounts provided by Howe, Justice, and others clearly inform Robert H. Wiebe's understanding of nationalism as "the desire among people who believe that they share a common ancestry and a common destiny to live under their own government on land sacred to their history."[44] Despite the conviction shown by the above commentators, the move to outline a critically separate space in which to locate tribally specific methods of reading has met with no small amount of resistance. Frederick Luis Aldama for one argues that scholars of Native American literature often "make the misstep of confusing the fictions they analyze with the real historical, political, and judicial acts that inform the real world *hors texte*." He consequently implores critics to "ask themselves if it is true that the narrative fictions they analyze have the power to mobilize and organize Native people's aspirations and struggles in the world and how they can effect such transformation."[45] Although Aldama's point would appear to be that literature fails to reflect "real" events, his argument might be problematized by those of us who believe that literary scholarship not only comments on (and even precipitates) social and political transformations, but that literature reflects certain tribal contexts. That said, Aldama's question—albeit somewhat paradoxical—may well compel scholars of Native American literature to conduct

---

43 LeAnne Howe, "Blind Bread and the Business of Theory Making, By Embarrassed Grief," in *Reasoning Together*, 333. Howe's essay is, of course, following in the critical tradition established by Vine Deloria Jr., Keith Basso, Simon Ortiz, and countless others.

44 Robert H. Wiebe, *Who We Are: A History of Popular Nationalism* (Princeton, NJ: Princeton University Press, 2002), 5.

45 "Red Matters: Native American Studies, and: Grave Concerns, Trickster Turns: The Novels of Louis Owens" (review), *American Literature* 75.3 (2003), 663–665.

deeper analyses of the relationship between tribal perspectives and tribal fiction, thereby substantiating the claim that fictional form often carries extratextual consequences.

There are other, culturally and racially imbricated, issues surrounding American Indian Nationalism. Particularly exercising the minds of critics and writers is the question of whether or not tribal nationalism is willfully exclusionary or restricted. In a particularly excoriating review of Womack's *Red on Red* (1999) Kenneth Lincoln describes American Indian separatism as a form of "xenophobia," concluding that Natives and non-Natives are "not separate" from one another but are instead "all in this together."[46] Lincoln's line of argument seems to follow Arnold Krupat's earlier reasoning that "Native American written literature [...] is an *intercultural* practice," and therefore "essentialized categories like Native/non-Native [are] an obstacle to real critical work."[47] Krupat, for his part, has revised his opinion over the past decade and now allows that "[c]riticism of Native American literatures [...] proceeds from one or other of [a number of] critical perspectives," that include "nationalist, indigenist, and cosmopolitan." "Each of these perspectives," Krupat concludes, "requires the others to achieve its full discursive effectivity."[48] Despite the critical modification or simple change of tack that accommodates a more inclusive reckoning of Native perspectives, Krupat continues steadfast in his belief that the best prospects for literary study are to be found in the "cosmopolitan" perspective,

---

46   Kenneth Lincoln, "Red Stick Lit Crit," review of Craig S. Womack's *Red on Red: Native American Literary Separatism, Indian Country Today* 26.44. It should be noted that Lincoln was one of the first non-Native scholars to suggest that Native American literatures were deserving of sustained and intelligent scholarly attention and, as Christopher B. Teuton points out, his work *Native American Renaissance* uses "an interdisciplinary methodology based on anthropological, ethnographical, and historical sources" that, at the time of writing, were the best tools with which to read tribal fiction as a culturally specific form when Lincoln was a young scholar (*Reasoning Together*, 201).

47   Arnold Krupat, *The Turn to the Native: Studies in Criticism and Culture* (Lincoln: University of Nebraska Press, 1998), 21 (emphasis added), 9.

48   *Red Matters*, 1, x.

and subsequently prioritizes a form of "cross-cultural translation."[49] Not only is this type of translation in keeping with Krupat's earlier vision of a dialogic that is "constituted by the recognition that 'long-term and persistent processes of cultural hybridization' are ongoing and inevitable," but it judges nationalism's effectiveness in terms of its engagement with cosmopolitanism and intercultural movements.[50] Furthermore, this particularly celebratory assessment of hybridization surely influenced Elvira Pulitano's unfettered acceptance of the basic premise that "a 'pure' or 'authentic' form of Native discourse [...] based on a Native perspective, is simply not possible since Native American narratives are by their very nature heteroglot and hybridized."[51] I will return to these questions elsewhere in the book, especially in Chapter 3.

In light of these readings by non-Native colleagues in the field, it seems appropriate that I outline my own position. *Sovereign Stories* arises out of the conviction that Native American texts are, more often than not, expressions of tribal sovereignty in modern America.[52] Accordingly, the book argues that various types of indigenous narrative (novels, poetry, criticism, and so on) have a shape, form, and style—in sum an aesthetic—that is crucial not only to the *expression* of Native autonomy but is, in fact, a driving force within the *production* of such autonomy as well. My goal is to locate moments of such aesthetic sovereignty within the fiction, poetry and criticism of six tribal authors, and to discuss each work's artistry alongside

49   Ibid., x.

50   Arnold Krupat, "Nationalism, Indigenism, Cosmopolitanism: Critical Perspectives on Native American Literatures," *Centennial Review* 42.3 (1998), 622.

51   Elvira Pulitano, *Toward a Native American Critical Theory*, 13. Indeed, Pulitano cites Vizenor's rejection of "any form of separatism" as evidence of his complicity with Western critical theory, this despite the fact that the writer engages non-Native contexts in order to establish "new theories of *tribal* interpretation" (Pulitano, *Toward a Native American Critical Theory*, 185); Gerald Vizenor, *Manifest Manners: Narratives on Postindian Survivance* (Lincoln: University of Nebraska Press, 1994), 14 (emphasis added).

52   As such, my work builds on the argument put forward by Dean Rader in *Engaged Resistance: American Indian Art, Literature, and Film from Alcatraz to the NMAI* (Austin: University of Texas Press, 2011).

the political, cultural, and social efficacy of each. A large part of my motivation in doing so arises from a personal conviction that fiction, as Neil
Lazarus recently claimed, is "able to recreate the materiality of everyday life
through its density, accumulation of detail, and ability to mediate between
and thread together divergent aspects of reality."[53] The focus of this book is
on questions of self-determination, indigenous artistry, tribal community
and Native authorship as they emerge in Elizabeth Cook-Lynn's *Aurelia*
(1999), Sherman Alexie's *Face* (2009) and *First Indian on the Moon* (1993),
David Treuer's *Little* (1995), Louise Erdrich's *Shadow Tag* (2010), Craig
Womack's *Art as Performance, Story as Criticism* (2009), and Greg Sarris'
Keeping Slug Woman Alive (1993). *Sovereign Stories* is concerned with the
aesthetic, metafictional, and theoretical intervention that each of these
texts make, and with their author's engagement with, and contribution
to, the discussion of tribal sovereignty. As a consequence, questions about
dialogism, hybridization, cosmopolitanism, or (putatively) mixedblood
discourse have no great role to play in the chapters that follow. I should
point out that *Sovereign Stories* does not suggest that those conversations
and topics are no longer of interest; I am mindful that certain scholars,
Native and non-Native alike, continue to operate in that discursive space.
However, I am far more interested in the Native American writer's ability to create a literary narrative that reflects tribal concerns than I am in
intercultural conversation, non-Native "influence," or shared frontiers. In
fact, this book arises out of a conviction that an international audience can
discern, and take heed of, this literature's commentary on tribal separatism
and indigenous rights. The stories studied in the following chapters are
often obfuscatory and challenging, provocative and confrontational, and
I find myself drawn to the type of narrative defiance and foreclosure that
these authors work with throughout their writing. While *Sovereign Stories*
is certainly a response to that challenge, it is my intention to celebrate both
the activist streak in Native American literature, and the moments when
the fiction appears to prioritize tribal concerns.

---

53   *The Postcolonial Unconscious* (Cambridge: Cambridge University Press, 2011), 82.

Furthermore, even though hybridization has proved useful as a theoretical concept, there is also the danger that it can harden into a fixed position. As Gerry Smyth writes, "destabilizing the border" creates a scenario
whereby the Native "'mind' becomes permanently 'hybridized'" and *any*
claim to indigenous distinctiveness is simply eradicated.⁵⁴ Hence, even
though hybridization was once envisaged as a rejoinder to a fixed form of
cultural classification, the theory can harden into a fixed position, virtually compelling continual and obligatory processes of exchange between
Native and non-Native positions. Potentially disserving Owens's conceptualization of a mobile "frontier," this newer, starker version of post-race
identity can, in many circumstances, become an assault on all forms of
tribal autonomy, be they creative, artistic, political, or otherwise. That
assault, in turn, belies the notion that the "in-between" space facilitates an
exchange between equal sites of power, and the "third space" can appear as
a distinctly bounded locale. Here, Native American writers are expected
to inhabit lest their work be labelled essentialized, "narrow"—the gravest
charge that Lincoln, Krupat and Pulitano make against American Indian
nationalists.⁵⁵ Hybridity, as it has been conceived over the last decade,
either underplays or dismisses outright the extent to which indigenous
sovereignty is concerned with what Amanda Cobb calls "the going on
of life."⁵⁶ In other words, there does not seem to be much room for the
continuance or evolution of tribal cultures alongside colonial, European,
or mainstream American traditions where there is the belief that contact automatically, irreparably, or unconditionally results in an intercultural melting pot. Rather than offering yet another consideration of the
intercultural or heteroglot in Native writing, this book addresses the
specificities of narratological engagement with tribal sovereignty and its

---

54   Gerry Smyth, "The Politics of Hybridity: Some Problems with Crossing the Border,"
      in *Comparing Post-Colonial Literatures: Dislocations*, ed. Patricia Murray and Ashok
      Bery (London: Macmillan, 2000), 51. See also Jace Weaver, "Splitting the Earth: First
      Utterances and Pluralist Separatism," in *American Indian Literary Nationalism*, ed.
      Weaver, Womack, and Warrior, 1–89.
55   Homi K. Bhabha, *The Location of Culture* (London: Routledge, 1994), 37.
56   Quoted in Heath Justice, "Go Away, Water!," 152.

various manifestations in the work of Cook-Lynn, Alexie, Treuer, Erdrich, Womack, and Sarris. I suggest that these writers unfold a narrative sovereignty in their work that reflects forms of autonomy at once political, social, cultural, artistic, and, at times, personal. In exploring what might be termed styles of resistance, the interpretative emphases of the following chapters is necessarily on Native forms and cultural traditions. Indeed, this book is mindful of how indigenous communities are involved in an on-going process of (re)defining and enacting their sovereignty as tribal nations, just as Native authors are actively engaged in the interrelated processes of articulating, archiving, and making present that autonomy. While the critical conversation about the narratological expression of indigenous self-determination obviously does not happen in a cultural or racial vacuum—there is no denying the presence of the settler in modern America, just as there is no way of returning to a pre-contact age—the chapters that follow will focus on moments of narrative dissonance, foreclosure, and opposition rather than dialogue. Intended to have a very different orientation, inflection, and effect than those scholarly works that have focused on hybridism in Native studies, this book has been informed by a growing body of criticism by non-Native academics and commentators.[57] In contributing to the study of Native American writing, I am of the conviction that it is crucial, first and foremost, to visualize the critical terrain in a manner that allows us to accept and comprehend the aims of American Indian communities and authors. Thereafter—and *only* thereafter—will we be in a position to enter into an analytic space where non-Native readers and scholars can apprehend, acknowledge, and engage with the distinctive forms of nationalism and sovereignty that currently shape Native American Literary Studies. Consequently, this book seeks to disclose the rich interconnections between sovereign territory

57   See: James Cox, *Muting White Noise: Native American and European American Novel Traditions* (Norman: University of Oklahoma Press, 2005); Elaine Jahner, *Spaces of the Mind: Narrative and Community in the American West* (Lincoln: University of Nebraska Press, 2004); and Stuart Christie, *Plural Sovereignties and Contemporary Indigenous Literature* (New York: Palgrave Macmillan, 2009).

and its textual representations, and to re-focus critical attention on the specificities of those narratological spaces created by indigenous writers and embedded with political, social, or cultural movements.

Novel Spaces:
(Re)mapping Contemporary Native American Fiction

Boundaries, both material *and* imaginative, have become central to Native American Literary Studies. As cultural geographer Juliet Fall explains, "boundary making" is, "an act of power establishing a spatial entity."[58] Scholars working in the area of Native American Literary Studies have much to gain from an examination of the relationship between "boundary making" and the "discernible discourse" through which such acts of territorialization are "made visible", and we would do well to consider "the role [that] boundaries play in the construction of space," the manner in which "shifting territorial discourses enshrine and construct spatial entities," and the extent to which "identities are constructed by symbolic and material boundaries that define Self and Other."[59] I would argue that this sense of space continues to be deeply pertinent to any study of Native American fiction and the construction of attendant criticism. Consequently, this book examines recent conversations concerning control, space, and borders in both, and lays special emphasis on the extent to which Native American writers deal with the efficacies of those distinct borders by creating a spatially informed aesthetics. Rather than conducting a study of landscape traditions, or searching for images of homing and redemptive return within tribal fiction and poetry of the 1990s and 2000s, *Sovereign Stories* concerns itself with the re-evaluation of sovereignty, separatism, and

58 Juliet Fall, *Drawing the Line: Nature, Hybridity, and Politics in Transboundary Spaces* (London: Ashgate, 2005), 5.
59 Ibid.

self-determination that occurred in that time, and links that re-evaluation to both the literature and culture of the authors studied herein.[60] The goal is not to exoticize or corral indigenous writing yet again, but rather to consider the ways in which borders "separat[e] an inside from an outside"—thereby protecting the welfare of communities and writers—while *also* "linking" exterior and interior territories, thereby facilitating conversation.[61] Through my analysis of the "drawing [of] lines"—as Scott Lyons puts it—I will examine several Native American writers' insistence upon a nuanced and balanced understanding of the dynamic that exists not only between tribal and non-tribal cultures but also between the literary traditions of both. Furthermore, I hope to show that the suggestion that American Indian nationalism or separatism are critical movements that reflexively separate

60   Throughout the 1970s and 1980s, a steady stream of literary critics tracked images of "homing in" and landscape within Native American fiction: see William Bevis's "Native American Novels: Homing In," in *Recovering the Word: Essays in Native American Literature*, ed. Brian Swann and Arnold Krupat (Berkeley: University of California Press, 1987), 580–619. While much of this scholarship very cogently (and necessarily) brought an indigenous landscape tradition to the fore, it offered a rather essentialized or stagnant image of plot, metaphor, and characterization as they appear within Native American literature. Consider, for instance, Susan L. Roberson's thesis that "Native American novels are structurally 'incentric, centripetal, converging, contracting' (Bevis 582) allowing [the] author [...] to 'come full circle' (Woodard 146) [... and display a] homing pattern, almost ubiquitous in modern Native novels", in Susan L. Roberson, "Translocations and Transformations: Identity in N. Scott Momaday's *The Ancient Child*," *American Indian Quarterly* 22.1/2 (1998), 31–45. While it is surely a reflection of tribal autonomy that Native characters can return home, the style of critical reading in the 1970s and 1980s quite possibly underplayed the "international and intertribal" movements that Howe argues Natives have always made, and the extent to which those "movements" in turn "reflect a larger worldview that would have been as important in the past as it is in the present" ("Blind Bread and the Business of Theory Making, By Embarrassed Grief," *Reasoning Together*, 330). Moreover, the kind of homecoming that scholars focused on seemed concerned only with the protagonist's "rigid collection of essential truths"; a form of rigidity that, to Sean Teuton's mind, deadens the "dynamic of political awakening and cultural recovery" (*Red Land, Red Power*, 8).

61   Henk Van Houtum, Olivier Kramsch, and Wolfgang Zierhofer, eds, *B/ordering Space* (London: Ashgate, 2005), 2 & 3 (emphasis added).

socially concerned "culturists" from literary aesthetes is misleading.[62] On the contrary, and more accurately, they are movements concerned with the narratological and critical strategies through which Native authors identify and practice their sovereign rights, both as members of the tribal community and as independent artists. Moreover, non-Native scholars—particularly those of us from postcolonial communities and spaces—can embark on critical projects that support indigenous scholars' claims for sovereignty in a wider global community.[63] It is perhaps this inclusive, sensitive form of linkage that David Murray suggested in *Forked Tongues* (1991) when he described a place where conversation between autonomous positions can occur *without* Native positions or identities becoming permanently fixed or eternally hybridized.[64] More recently—as mentioned above—Weaver has called this understanding of bordering and boundary making a form of "pluralist separatism." Here the frame between dissimilar cultural spaces acts as a site of contact *and* as a protective membrane; the construction of border does not deny entry to Native worlds, nor does it obfuscate the non-Native's understanding of those worlds. Instead it brings a much-needed, formative clarity to the field of study. It also reminds, if we need further reminding, that "non-Natives [... *can*] read, engage, and study Native literature" across a "permeable barrier," but should "do so with some respect and a sense of responsibility to Native communit[ies]."[65]

This is, then, a book about territory. But more specifically, it is about why the wider concept of territory and space continues to be one of the main unifying thematic principles within Native American Literary Studies. When the full significance and import of terms like "nation," "sovereignty,"

---

62   Arnold Krupat, "Culturalism and Its Discontents: Native American Fiction and the Current Critical Moment," keynote address at "Native American Studies: Across Time and Space" conference, Johannes Gutenburg University, Mainz, July 12–14 2007.

63   Obviously enough the fiction can be read in accordance to any ethical or critical approach, but it is my choice to adopt this particular one.

64   David Murray, *Forked Tongues: Speech, Writing and Representation in North American Indian Texts* (London: Pinter, 1991).

65   *American Indian Literary Nationalism*, 11.

and "autonomy" are understood within the paradigmatic framework that has recently been constructed by Native writers and intellectuals, it becomes evident that "territory"—both as an extended metaphor *and* as a physical presence—speaks to an array of issues and tendencies within the field. Territory reminds readers of the specific locations from which tribal literatures originate, and is suggestive of both tribal and cultural presences. It also relates to the space of the novel itself, in so far as narrative theory functions along spatialized syntagmatic and hermeneutic axes. It follows that the concept of space indicates not only the degree to which tribal writers are connected to a specific community, but also the development of Native American literature as a discrete and increasingly well-defined area of study. Under these terms, territory comes to denote the aesthetic distinctiveness of indigenous writing, the thematic areas pursued by tribal writers, and a distinct literary terrain. While a number of scholars, both Native and non-Native, have foregrounded the importance of territory as a concept, both as it regulates fictional maneuvers and as it reflects the experiences of tribal communities, readers can occasionally overlook the import of certain spatial realities. As a non-Native reader, I am acutely aware that as analyses of tribal fiction increasingly stem from diverse international zones, it is even more important that non-Native scholars and students are mindful of how we negotiate tribal spaces in our reading of texts by indigenous authors.

As a result, it is necessary to examine not only the association between the landscapes and stories that LeAnne Howe mentions, but also the link between "specific stories [...] specific place[s]" and contemporary tribal fiction. For instance, Robert Dale Parker has suggested that "Indian writers often write about different worlds from those of non-Indian writers."[66] In what might be regarded as a slightly more pragmatic or materialist discussion of the correlation between tribal locations and indigenous expression, Elaine Jahner has provided an absorbing examination of "spatial categories in Siouan languages," thereby revealing how indigenous "narratives [... are]

---

66   Robert Dale Parker, *The Invention of Native American Literature* (Ithaca, NY: Cornell University Press, 2003), 8.

intimately bound up with [...] geographical setting."[67] More importantly, this book has been informed by the work of a number of Native scholars, that when taken together, offers a new critical paradigm for theorizing space in Native writing. One such writer is Lisa Brooks. Her detailed and enlivening attention to early Native American writing in *The Common Pot* has purposefully engaged the methods through which indigenous texts reinvigorate indigenous communities, thereby lending support to processes of land recovery and community activism. Brooks prioritizes the relationality between tribal languages, place, and the book as a physical and philosophical space.[68] All of these ideas and theories are brought to bear in the study of the novels that follows this introduction. Perhaps most notable and interesting, in terms of my own approach to Native American fiction, is Brooks's suggestion that story "operates in particular, tangible spaces" and can be mapped across a "network of writers and texts" and "the historical space they inhabit."[69] This powerful sense of *awikhigawôgan*—the continuing act of writing as a means of creating a worldview—is one that I am particularly taken with, and the critical frame constructed in the Abenaki scholar's work offers a useful interpretative framework through which we might consider the connection between text and indigenous territory(s), aesthetic and materialist spaces, writer and interpreter, text and context. By acknowledging the existence of certain boundaries (particularly those found within the space of the novel) and by comprehending how these borders reflect wider intellectual, political, and historical developments within the Native American community, a deeper understanding of both Native American literary aesthetics and indigenous contexts might be realized.

There other impulses at play, particularly with regard to introducing indigenous texts in international territories. As Diane P. Freedman reminds us, "books" have their own "borders," and therefore I would suggest that

---

67 *Spaces of the Mind: Narrative and Community in the American West* (Lincoln: University of Nebraska Press, 2004), xii.

68 See Lisa Brooks, "Digging at the Roots: Locating an Ethical, Native Criticism," in *Reasoning Together*, 234–264.

69 Lisa Brooks, *The Common Pot: The Recovery of Native Space in the Northeast* (Minneapolis: University of Minnesota Press, 2008), xxii.

fiction quite readily reflects matters of place, land and indigenous presence.[70] Freedman's figuring of the book as a spatially constructed form also echoes Brooks's suggestion that the reader is essentially "entering a place-world and will be compelled to use their minds interactively to try to comprehend" when they read tribal fiction.[71] This examination of textual borders overlaps with Helen May Dennis's line of reasoning in her work *Native American Literature: Toward a Spatialized Theory*, where she examines fictional representations of place and offers an engaging analysis of the spatial dynamic that informs contemporary Native American fiction. The sheer expediency that the metaphor of space and border provides in the attempt to consider complex and productive interactions between novel spaces and the sovereign territories, lands, and nations is readily evident in both of these arguments. In keeping with this sense of the book as a territory itself, the chapters that follow concentrate on various forms of aesthetic sovereignty that are contained within, or suggested by, tribal fiction, and do so in a bid to engage the narratological approaches that may well deconstruct what Raheja calls the "white-generated representations of indigenous people" but, importantly, might also become sites for "locating and advocating for indigenous cultural and political power both within and outside of Western legal jurisprudence."[72] Along these lines, each of the examinations below aim to enter the spaces and territories discussed within the Native American novel, and do so in order to gain a purview not just of the interconnections which join text and context, but also the production and representation of intellectual, narratological, material, and critical spaces.

It is entirely necessary, then, that we note the ways in which contemporary narratological spaces are being charted and new critical territories are being formed. It is crucial, too, that we work through an assortment

---

70 Diane P. Freedman, "Border Crossing as Method and Motif in Contemporary American Writing, or, How Freud Helped Me Case the Joint," in *The Intimate Critique: Autobiographical Literary Criticism*, ed. Diane P. Freedman, Olivia Frey, and Frances Murphy Zauhar (Durham, NC: Duke University Press, 1993), 15.

71 *The Common Pot*, xxv.

72 Raheja, "Reading Nanook's Smile," 1161.

of fictional spaces, paying considerable attention to the wider critical and cultural circumstances that influence them. I mean to do so while also supporting tribal writers' insistence upon artistic, critical, and cultural sovereignty, principally by suggesting that the texts created by Cook-Lynn, Womack, Sarris, and others advocate wider territorial contexts (ideological, physical, narratological, or otherwise). These contexts are not, as others have suggested, in contestation either with each other or with non-Native spaces, but instead offer a range of indigenous perspectives. When considered collectively and cohesively the novels featured in this book illustrate not only the extensive thematic scope evident in the fiction itself, but also the cultural richness of the tribal contexts that they emerge from. As such, each chapter explores the particular ways in which the individual author deploys metaphors of territory through their use of characterization, plot, image, motif, theme, and symbolism. Two of the authors featured in this book—Alexie and Erdrich—are amongst the group described as "the Noble Nine," but their novels warrant (re)examination from the perspective of an American Indian Literary nationalist reading and are freshly appraised here in relation to the fiction of Cook-Lynn, Womack, Treuer, Sarris, and Howe.[73] Each chapter consequently explores the particular means by which the individual author constructs a dynamic narrative form that deploys images and metaphors of territory while also considering the degree to which that artistic deployment of those metaphors is culturally or politically informed.

In the wake of these recent developments, it is evident that there exists considerable scope for interpreting the various nuances that the image of space carries, both in terms of diverse fictional representations of tribal locations, and also recent critical responses. In this sense, an evolving definition of "territory" can be used as the primary metaphor to explore not

73 Daniel Heath Justice, "Seeing (and Reading) Red," in *Indigenizing the Academy: Transforming and Empowering Communities*, ed. Devon Abbott Mihesuah and Angela Cavender Wilson (Lincoln: University of Nebraska Press, 2004), 105. Justice intimates that instead of serving as a compliment to the authors or texts in question, this popularity amounts to a "tokenization" and "privileging" of writers, an act that effectively "reinforce[s] the overculture's assertion that Indians are generally alike."

just indigenous literature's reflection of specific tribal locations, but also
to remind us of the extent to which we all read from *somewhere*—geographically, ideologically, ethnically, theoretically, sometimes tentatively,
sometimes boldly. In keeping with this critical agenda, I want to approach
the work of fiction as a territory or space in and of itself, and do so in a
way that is not merely an exercise in "literary tourism" but is instead an
attempt at gleaning a far more useful and informed sense of the sovereign
territories and tribal nations in question. This book argues, then, that Native
American writers create what Thomas King calls "other ways of imagining
the world," and bring into play spatially informed metaphors in order to
do so.[74] The following chapters examine to what extent Native American
writers produce an "aesthetic sovereignty" that regulates and informs the
discursive spaces that effect not only literary studies, but tribal communities as well.[75] I adopt this approach not least because place of origin, which
clearly interconnects with contemporary definitions of sovereignty and
nation, is a critical part of tribal continuance; one that guarantees the
right to self-government, collective autonomy, and an individual sense of
belonging. In a recent crystallization of the sheer importance that land
and locality have for indigenous peoples on this level, Kathryn Shanley
has drawn attention to geographical specificity, explaining: "[n]othing
defines indigenous peoples more than a belonging to place, a homeland."[76]
It follows that "home" has myriad personal and communal significances,
and that Native concepts of native land can, as Shanley explains, point

74   Thomas King, *The Truth About Stories* (Minneapolis: University of Minnesota Press,
     2005), 110.
75   This move is somewhat similar to Raheja's concern with an artistically framed, indig-
     enously enacted form of resistance, subversion, and-above all-continuance. In exam-
     ining indigenous film making the Seneca scholar examines what she calls "visual
     sovereignty" as "a strategy [that] offers up not only the possibility of engaging and
     deconstructing white-generated representations of indigenous people, but more
     broadly and importantly [...] intervenes in larger discussions of Native American
     sovereignty by locating and advocating for indigenous cultural and political power
     both within and outside of Western legal jurisprudence." I wish to examine a form
     of literary sovereignty or "aesthetic sovereignty" to very similar ends.
76   "'Born from the Need to Say,'" 3.

toward both "self-governance, cultural maintenance, revitalization, and sovereignty (on the collective level)" and act as a dynamic literary signifier that "functions metaphorically to refer to a future place of self-esteem (on the individual level)."

My interest in the connection between art and culture, text and context is, on some level, analogous to Treuer's "concern [...] with how we *read* so-called Native American texts." In particular I share his interest with how

> we interpret Native American fiction in such a way as to take pleasure in the product [... and] interpret it so as to preserve the integrity of the text, the integrity of [... Native] interest and effort, and the integrity of the tradition.[77]

With these words, Treuer reminds us that it is vital that the reader, if they hope to identify the artistic sleight of hand by which the indigenous writer creates diverse literary worlds, must pay close attention to which "traditions and habits of thought have been mobilized and by what means." His point is well made, largely because it explores the relationship between text and context. I do not, however, share Treuer's belief that the majority of scholars working in the field continue to make "sweeping claims about the culturality of a text or the intentionality of the writer."[78] The reductive

---

77 David Treuer, *Native American Fiction: A User's Manual* (Minneapolis, MN: Graywolf, 2006), 4.

78 Ibid., 6. Treuer's essays have caused considerable controversy, largely because of his (I would say, intentionally blithe) claim that Native American literature may not exist at all. Despite this, I believe that his intention was to remind readers that Native fiction is a literary form and should not be approached solely with the intention of gaining information about the tribe. This is, it must be said, a fair point. Similarly, *Native American Fiction* attempts, albeit a little too glibly by times, to form a line of reasoning that asks us *how* indigenous literature reflects tribal contexts aesthetically, and therefore suggests Treuer's frustration with various authors' use of tribal myth as a short-cut to signify Indian presence within the book. For this reason, he does, I believe, reflect Weaver's irritation at "how often [Natives] are complicitous in [the Western] theoretical domination [...] by fetishizing our own cultures" (*That the People Might Live*, 22) or Paula Gunn Allen's difficulty with Silko's decision to speak about Laguna myth in her fiction (see Allen's widely anthologized essay "Special Problems in Teaching Leslie Marmon Silko's *Ceremony*," which first appeared in

modes of reading that *Native American Fiction* aims to confront have, in the main, already been set aside. By the same token, while I concur with Dale Parker's judgment that Native writing produces "many of the same pleasures [...] found in canonical writing," I do not share his anxiety that some commentators, either Native or non-Native, "seek the social apart from the aesthetic."[79] Conversely I would argue that the vast majority of leading researchers are recognizing the need to reach a balanced understanding of the "text's social and aesthetic energies," and are doing so in order to support Native American sovereignty(s).[80] Therefore while this book seeks to undertake an interrogation of literary invention in the vein of Treuer and Dale Parker, it is also concerned with unfolding the deftly formed connections between the aesthetic and the social, rather than putting the accent on the aesthetic alone. If "style creates the convincing semblance of culture on the page," as Treuer insists it does, then I want to deal with the methods by which "style creates the convincing semblance" of sovereignty while simultaneously examining the manner in which tribal sovereignty influences or shapes matters of style. And so, I concentrate my efforts on the methodologies of reading that facilitate the fullest understanding of the connection *between* Native and fiction rather than on "what is gained and what is lost when we" over-emphasize the fiction's "'Native[ness],'" as Treuer does.[81]

American Indian Quarterly 14.4 [1990], 379–386). It is understandable, however, that the strident nature of Treuer's critique, as well as his lack of references to key critical texts, has resulted in some criticism of his work.

79   *The Invention of Native American Literature*, 8 & 18. Womack is cited by Dale Parker as a critic whose work potentially skews methods of reading by conflating the importance of cultural or tribal information above the aesthetic (despite the fact that Womack's creative fiction is both inventive and intercultural).

80   Ibid., 18.

81   *Native American Fiction*, 5.

Marking Territory

Sovereign Stories follows James Cox's lead in "privileging [...] the work of Native scholars and other Native creative writers."[82] Indigenous writers and scholars are leading the way and marking out the territory; it is pointless, not to mention destructive and supercilious, to read Native fiction without first and foremost engaging the scholarship of those best placed to comment on and critique tribal, cultural, and spatial meanings within the fiction itself. Whereas the late Louis Owens emphasizes the possibility for intercultural exchange along the narratological frontier, this book calls attention to the manner in which the border signals indigenous autonomy, thus concentrating on territory as a constructive metaphor that reflects "the [literary] strategies" that Cook-Lynn believes Native writers can use to "defend [their] lands and [themselves] as nations of people."[83] *Sovereign Stories* aims, therefore, to consider the interstices between the ideological "frontier," "fictional territory," and the social and geographical spaces that Native communities inhabit today.[84] My objective, then, is to examine the reverberations caused by the claims of indigenous writers to artistic, political, and cultural sovereignty, and do so by engaging Native American contexts respectfully and meaningfully. As such, this book responds to May Dennis's invitation to scholars to "contribute to a larger sense of community that implicitly supports the current work of Nativist scholars."[85] However, rather than merely offering a "sympathetic, foreign engagement" with Native American fiction by emphasizing "transcultural readings," the chapters that follow directly engage American Indian sovereignty and

---

82 Quoted in *American Indian Literary Nationalism*, ed. Weaver, Womack, and Warrior, 26. This is not to say, however, that my study—or the scholarship it makes use of— ignores or omits salient arguments on the basis of ethnicity or culture. On the contrary I quote the work of several non-Native scholars.

83 *Anti-Indianism*, 154.

84 *Mixedblood Messages*, 46.

85 Helen May Dennis, *Native American Literature: Towards a Spatialized Reading* (London: Routledge, 2007), 1–2.

nationalism, applying current definitions and theories to the work of seven Native American authors—many of whom view the connection between artistic, individual, communal, social, and cultural autonomies quite differently.[86] They do so because, as readers and critics of Native writing, we must find some kind of equilibrium that makes best use of the linkages between an array of fictional landscapes, tangible political positions, and contingent, extensive spaces inhabited by contemporary Native American critics. Such work is all the more important because some critics continue to present the aesthetic and the social as unrelated and even oppositional locations. Even more problematical is a latent critical fondness for interpreting American Indian literary separatism as a movement that radically differentiates between and disconnects a number of spaces: political from artistic, Native from non-Native, mixedblood from traditionalist. These commentators spend their energies contemplating—and conflating—supposed differences of opinion and stance, and focus on divergences more often than they focus on the similarity between the various forms of cultural and creative autonomy locatable in the Native American novel. I am of the conviction that exclusively cross-cultural readings of indigenous literature, even those "sympathetic" to tribal concerns, will ultimately lead to an avoidance of the many difficult questions concerning the ethics of reading, teaching, and researching Native fiction today. And, as Malea Powell (Miami) reminds us, if "scholars convince themselves that they cannot study Indians (i.e., others) from the basis of Indian experience and existence" then they will "distance their work from Indian 'reality.'"[87] *Sovereign Stories* hopes to remain close to that reality at all times and to demonstrate that non-Natives can respectfully and fruitfully navigate the aesthetic and social spaces contained within the contemporary Native American novel. Above all else, the book is about recognizing and celebrating an Indian map of the mind.

86   Contrary to Dennis's reasoning, I would argue that it is vital that we engage and discuss American Indian nationalism rather than steer clear of the debate, or (as Krupat does) perceive indigenous separatism as a split between aesthetics and culture.

87   "Blood and Scholarship: One Mixed Blood's Story," in *Race, Rhetoric, and Composition*, ed. Keith Gilyard (Portsmouth, NH: Boynton/Cook, 1999), 5.

CHAPTER 2

Who's Afraid of Elizabeth Cook-Lynn?
Nationalism and Voice in *Aurelia*

"[I]f I am not going to nation build / I don't need to write"[1]
— ELIZABETH COOK-LYNN

Midway through Elizabeth Cook-Lynn's *Aurelia: A Crow Creek Trilogy* (1999)[2] the omniscient narrator provides an account of contemporary Dakotah history. In doing so, the teller recounts how, in the not so distant past, the tribe "put down their weapons and relinquished their war ponies" before setting "about making new lives in a reconstructed, yet familiar world."[3] This striking image of "a reconstructed, yet familiar world" is fundamental not only to an understanding of *Aurelia*, but is, in fact, something of a leitmotif within Cook-Lynn's writing in general. Indeed, her scholarly essays and fiction are greatly informed by this concept of continuance, and the Crow Creek writer has reiterated, time and again, her straightforward conviction that Native American fiction must be concerned with the creation of a "nation-specific creativity and political unification." That "unification" will, in turn, "guide the development, continuation and defense of a coherent national mythos" she argues.[4] It is

---

1   *Notebooks of Elizabeth Cook-Lynn*, 7.
2   Elizabeth Cook-Lynn, *Aurelia: A Crow Creek Trilogy* (Boulder: University of Colorado Press, 1999).
3   *Aurelia*, 157.
4   Elizabeth Cook-Lynn, *Anti-Indianism in Modern America: A Voice from Tatekeya's Earth* (Champaign: University of Illinois Press, 2007), 35.

hardly surprising then, that the central protagonist of Cook-Lynn's three novel cycle, Aurelia, should be described as "a Dakota Sioux female character, a storyteller and a witness"—a woman who "is neither postcolonial nor postmodern," but is "still committed to the nationalism of her native life."[5] Nor, given Cook-Lynn's interest in creating characters of this type, is it surprising that Craig Womack has drawn attention to her position as "an advocate of nation-specific fiction" or her profound interest in "creative works that recognize the importance of federal Indian policy in both the production and evaluation of such literatures" and "the narration of treaty-protected lands."[6]

The purpose of this chapter, as a result, is to offer a close analysis of *Aurelia* in order to assess the trilogy's specific engagement with what Cook-Lynn describes as the "development, continuation, and defense of a coherent national mythos."[7] By reviewing these novels, it might be possible to gain a broader understanding of interconnectedness between the fictions—most particularly their form and style—and the political and historical issues that the Crow Creek writer concerns herself with. In this way, an examination of this type might possibly reveal the manner in which the "intellect of [indigenous] people expressed in literary art" can, as Cook-Lynn argues, be "examined as the fabric holding a people together."[8] Furthermore, in light of James Stripes's opinion that the aesthetic goals of indigenous fictionists are somewhat challenged by the "Western illusion that art and politics are [somehow] separate," it is perhaps necessary to consider the "aesthetic principles" that Cook-Lynn mobilizes in *Aurelia* in order to discuss the link between fictional storytelling and political principles or cultural efficacies.

5   Ibid., 33.
6   Craig S. Womack, review of *Anti-Indianism in Modern America: A Voice from Tatekeya's Earth* by Elizabeth Cook-Lynn, *American Indian Quarterly* 28.1/2, special issue: "Empowerment Through Literature" (Winter–Spring 2004), 130–141.
7   *Anti-Indianism*, 35.
8   Ibid., 42.

"We Must Make Hard Choices if We Expect the Plot to Keep Moving"

In essence, Cook-Lynn believes that creative fiction by Native American writers should deal directly with "matters of treaty-making, sovereignty as a concept, [and] the nation-to-nation legal status of tribes."[9] To her mind, however, much of the work produced by tribal writers in the United States before the turn of the twenty-first century had failed to do so. Instead, much of the literature and attendant criticism at that time was shaped by what Cook-Lynn characterized as a "cosmopolitan agenda" within Native American Literary Studies. The Crow Creek scholar subsequently suggested that several indigenous authors appear to be more interested in exploring "the tastes and interests of the dominant culture" than they are in considering the possibility of a "nation-specific or culture-specific art."[10] Cook-Lynn's goal, as a result, has been to promote a form of literary criticism that examines "the relationship [between] the modern novel [and] First Nation reality," while also assessing "whether or not these novels can assist in clarifying our tribal-nation sovereign conditions in a postcolonial world."[11] This approach has found considerable currency amongst tribal commentators, and the late Vine Deloria Jr. described Cook-Lynn as "the most insightful Indian essayist of our time."[12] In the final pages of his book *Peace, Power, Righteousness: An Indigenous Manifesto*, Taiaiake Alfred states simply that "Cook-Lynn's uncompromising views point to the true character of indigenous intellectualism and activism."[13]

9   Elizabeth Cook-Lynn, "The Radical Conscience in Native American Studies," *Wicazo Sa Review* 7.2 (Autumn 1991), 11.
10   *Anti-Indianism*, 41.
11   Ibid., 42.
12   Review of *Anti-Indianism in Modern America: A Voice from Tatekeya's Earth* by Elizabeth Cook-Lynn, *Pacific Historical Review* 71.3 (August 2002), 487.
13   Taiaiake Alfred, *Peace, Power, Righteousness: An Indigenous Manifesto* (Oxford: Oxford University Press, 2008), 179.

Yet, there has not always been straightforward adherence to, or acceptance of, the scholar's methodological approach or opinions within the field.
Most notably, Arnold Krupat has suggested that the reasoning behind
Cook-Lynn's call for a "critical discourse that functions in the name of the
people" is both confused and short-sighted.[14] In doing so he draws attention
to what he sees as the countless risks associated with "treating the 'people'
or the 'nation' as a unitary force or indivisible essence."[15] Similarly, in her
work *Toward a Native American Critical Theory*, Elvira Pulitano appraises
Cook-Lynn's "position in the field of Native American Studies" today, and
intimates (albeit indirectly) that the Native scholar is "highly suspicious of
discursive modes that embrace Western theoretical paradigms or notions
of cultural hybridity."[16] The critic also suggests that Cook-Lynn's writing
is effectively an "attack on the [literary and critical] production of mixedblood authors," who, Pulitano believes, are concerned with the production
of an intercultural theoretical space which might enlighten those working
within the field of Native American Literary Studies.[17] In the final event,
Pulitano's greatest difficulty with the "separatist or nationalist perspective"
arises out of her conviction that this critical model "runs the risk [...] of
essentializing Native American discourse, limiting Native Studies in a way
that does not allow the discipline to evolve, and [...] parroting the master's
language, but with the terms reversed and not 'signifying' any difference."[18]

For some, the clash between critics such as Cook-Lynn on one hand
and Krupat and Pulitano on the other is essentially one of ideology. The
discursive tension emanating from this debate centers largely on the question of whether or not one is convinced that tribal nationalists and those
championing indigenous separatism are giving voice to important forms
of Native autonomy, or simply entering into a lamentable and complex

14   Arnold Krupat, "The American Indian Fiction Writers: Cosmopolitanism,
      Nationalism, The Third World, and First Nation Sovereignty," *Red Matters: Native
      American Studies* (University Park: University of Pennsylvania Press, 2002), 9.
15   *Red Matters*, 19.
16   *Toward a Native American Critical Theory*, 60.
17   Ibid., 135.
18   Ibid., 62.

form of reverse racism. Even those who commend Cook-Lynn's greater strategy and her political activism have indirectly queried the terms used by the Crow Creek scholar and others. For instance, Alfred has drawn attention to what he sees as the difficulties with the term sovereignty "as it is currently understood." There is, he argues, a need to "detach the notion of sovereignty from its current legal meaning [...] in the context of the Western understanding of power and relationships."[19] This is largely because "traditional indigenous nationhood stands in sharp contrast to the dominant understanding of 'the state,'" and, more importantly, because "sovereignty is an exclusionary concept rooted in an adversarial and coercive Western notion of power."[20] So, even though Cook-Lynn's commitment to tribal nationhood and indigenous autonomy is certainly commendable, Alfred's careful teasing out of theoretical and philosophical terms possibly reveals a need for exactitude and a judicious use of the terms that Cook-Lynn uses so often. Like Alfred, Womack allows that the Sioux writer, in a bid to "articulate clear-cut definitions" has occasionally framed her beliefs in terms that have been "seen as [being] overly reductive."[21]

As a consequence, there may, then, be a need to revisit a few of the rhetorical and theoretical positions that the Sioux critic has taken. In the collection *Reasoning Together*, Daniel Heath Justice has taken exception to what are, to his mind, Cook-Lynn's rather totalizing notions about identity and tribalism. In particular, he critiques her political and critical stance on mixedbloodedness, and finds that Cook-Lynn focuses "on a purity/assimilation binary" that ultimately conflates "multiraciality with a lack of national spirit."[22] In the same collection, Batchewana First Nations scholar Cheryl Suzack finds that Cook-Lynn relies on "identity categories

---

19 *Peace, Power, Righteousness*, 78.

20 Ibid., 81 & 83.

21 Craig Womack, "A Single Decade: Book-Length Native Literary Criticism between 1986 and 1997," in *Reasoning Together*, 74. Despite allowing for a slight dearth of diplomacy on his Crow Creek colleague's part, Womack goes on to provide a robust defense of Cook-Lynn's main arguments.

22 "'Go Away Water!': Kinship Criticism and the Decolonization Imperative," in *Reasoning Together*, 162.

instituted through federally imposed blood-quantum distinctions, thus lending critical weight to the terms, rather than [...] other categories of social enablement."[23] Meanwhile, Christopher B. Teuton, also writing in *Reasoning Together*, argues that there are three, loosely grouped, developmental categories into which Native American criticism can be gathered, and places Cook-Lynn amidst the "mode-two" scholars—that is, scholars who aim to keep the field focused on "Indians actively committed to supporting the sovereignty of Native nations and cultures."[24] According to Teuton, "mode-three" commentators such as Robert Warrior have moved beyond Cook-Lynn's definition of sovereignty as being solely "the political act of preserving Native national autonomy," and have, instead, "broadened the term to 'intellectual sovereignty' [in order] to refer to a *tribal discourse* that is founded on constructing 'communities and social structures through which those communities exercise political, economic, and spiritual power along with responsibility.'"[25] In this context, Elizabeth Cook-Lynn's important and influential take on tribal autonomy and self-determination might, nevertheless, be said to circulate around a small core of well intentioned but slightly unrefined beliefs. Of course, Sherman Alexie has also taken the Crow Creek Sioux author's vision of contemporary Indian life to task too. In his 1993 poem "In Response to Elizabeth Cook-Lynn's Pronouncement That I One of the New, Angry (Warriors) Kind of like Norman Schwarzkopf and Rush Limbaugh" Alexie challenges Cook-Lynn's suggestion that his work is somehow rootless and therefore valueless.[26] There he describes an encounter between a first-person narrator, who happens to be a poet, and a homeless Yakima man who has read some of the poet's work. At one point the Spokane Coeur d'Alene poet writes: "How easy it would have been to call [the "transient" Indian] by less/than his real name, how easy it would have been/to see him as a white man in Indian skin, how/easy it would have been to make war on him."

---

23 *Reasoning Together*, 174.
24 Ibid., 203.
25 Ibid., 207.
26 *Wicazo Sa Review* 9.2 (Autumn 1993), 9.

In a few short lines Alexie suggests that despite his privileged, cosmopolitan position, the city-based poet continues to have relevance and, more importantly, a specific role within the discourse about contemporary tribal experiences; here, the poet articulates, frames, and perhaps even gives voice to the plight of the homeless Indian, noting his strength and humanity alongside his loss and his (temporary) rootlessness. As well as foregrounding the writer's ability to confront some of the new realities faced by tribal peoples, the poem implicitly suggests that the Yakima man should not be chided for his transience or his alienation from his tribal traditions. Nor, Alexie seems to intimate, should the author be critiqued for speaking about that sense of alienation or speaking to a specific set of indigenous concerns. Moreover, instead of presenting the reader with a long or considered meditation on political or cultural contexts, the poet focuses on the *immediate* circumstance that must be changed within the space of the poem; a reality that renders other pieces of information temporarily irrelevant since the homeless man must be fed *now*. Despite being primarily concerned with the now, Alexie's poem—like so much of his work—reminds us of the long colonial history that has fed into the Yakima man's misfortune. The major difference between this poem and Cook-Lynn's vision of tribal nationalism and traditionalism is its suggestion that Native experiences, voices, and connections can occur not only on spiritual homelands, but also in narrative and geographic locations far away from tribal lands. Thus, in this direct response to Cook-Lynn's criticism of his writing, Alexie appears to imply that his Crow Creek colleague aims to establish a conservative orthodoxy that shapes a narrow and limited vision of modern-day tribal presences. That vision is, Alexie suggests, anachronistic and—ironically enough, given Cook-Lynn's aims—unrealistic, primarily because it fails to accommodate or reflect the fullness of Indian life.

Be that as it may, Cook-Lynn's unambiguous engagement continues to fascinate several critics, and a great deal of the scholarship being produced today either builds on, or takes stock of, her opinions. Moreover, several commentators have underlined the need to search out the nuances that might be found in Cook-Lynn's work, and have called upon critics to begin the arduous task of identifying and working out the ramifications associable with her direct and unforgiving approach to land claims, tribal identity, and literary style/interpretation. In an important essay examining the complex intersection between these things, Sean Teuton points out that Cook-Lynn "objects not to the [issue of] multiheritage" itself, but instead chooses to call into question "the social *views* of mixedbloods, who, she contends, undermine nationhood by providing only self-absorbed narratives of displacement" in their narratives.[27] Therefore, in order to circumvent a distracting and divisive debate about the terms themselves, and in order to remain focused on the interface between indigenous experiences and criticism, Teuton suggests that we "exchange the mixed-blood for the tribal citizen and begin to discuss the merit of particular social values [... and] ethical goals." Womack, meanwhile, goes so far as to argue that Cook-Lynn's "insistence that land redress [...] be regarded as a central tenet of Native literary criticism" might ultimately have the effect of "push[ing] us to examine literature in really fresh, exciting ways."[28]

The anticipation that Cook-Lynn's creative fiction tackles questions of reparation, nationhood and tribal values seems reasonably held in this context, largely because we might expect her to deal with these themes as both an indigenous scholar *and* as a practitioner. The primary question, then, is in what ways, and to what ends, do novels such as *From the River's Edge*, *Circle of Dancers* and *In the Presence of River Gods* reflect a profound interest in "land redress." Beyond that, we might concern ourselves with the possibility that the *Crow Creek Trilogy* might invite "fresh, exciting ways" of interpreting tribal fiction, namely because it reflects a specific set of tribal and aesthetic values and, by so doing, constructs "a survival technique [that is] of major importance in researching and analyzing the hard issues of the day."[29] It is necessary, as a result, to consider the manner in which Elizabeth Cook-Lynn's fictional works interrogate—and comment on—the dynamic interplay that binds the act of "nation build[ing]" to "the

27   Sean Teuton, "The Callout: Writing American Indian Politics," in *Reasoning Together*, 117. Emphasis added.
28   Craig Womack, "A Single Decade: Book-Length Native Literary Criticism between 1986 and 1997," in *Reasoning Together*, 82 & 74.
29   Elizabeth Cook-Lynn, Tom Holm, John Red Horse, and James Riding In, "Reclaiming American Indian Studies," *Wicazo Sa Review* 20.1 (Spring 2005), 171.

act of writing," as well as contemplating the ways in which that interplay has influenced not only recent works of fiction by other Native writers, but also recent developments in literary criticism.

A "Dakotah Aesthetic in Everyday Life"

Comprised of three interlinked texts (*From the River's Edge*, *Circle of Dancers*, and *In the Presence of River Gods*), Cook-Lynn's trilogy *Aurelia* deals with a specific set of themes and issues. Each of the books considers the challenges facing the tribe, and the author confronts harrowing instances of land theft, labyrinthine legal battles, poverty, joblessness, and horrific instances of social and institutional racism. Just as important, or possibly far *more* important, however, is *Aurelia*'s concern with Dakotah senses of *tiospaye* or community. To these ends, the trilogy deals with various questions surrounding "tradition, language, mythology, and politics"—the very questions that Cook-Lynn would have fictionists write about in order to ensure the continuance of tribalism and tribal beliefs in modern America.[30] That sense of continuance is conspicuously absent at the outset, however, and *From the River's Edge* outlines a series of grim and harsh realities from the very beginning; the trilogy opens with the story of John Tatekeya's forty stolen cattle and the flooding of the Dakotah homelands after the damming of the *Mni Sosa* (Missouri) River during the late 1960s. The theft of the cattle and the loss of the land become a metaphor for the many injustices suffered by the people at the hands of white ranchers and federal agents. Further complicating the issue is the somewhat demoralized nature of the tribe at that time, and the book communicates a definite sense that the fabric of the community is slowly being shredded or torn. Tatekeya, "a tall man in his early sixties," laments not only the absence of moral values evident in the federal government's justice system, but also the skewed and odious

30   *Anti-Indianism*, 43.

state of affairs that sees John Big Pipe, a member of the tribe who will later marry Aurelia, giving false testimony during the court hearing about his cattle. However, the wronged farmer is acutely aware that he is himself caught amidst this erosion of the "old, familial bonds of respect for one another, those significant communal codes of behavior as old as the tribes themselves," since his extra-marital affair with the eponymous protagonist, a woman far younger than him, causes tensions within the community.[31] Similarly, at just seventeen Aurelia, who was known for her great beauty and her slightly prepossessed nature, actively chose to make a "deliberate and important alliance" with Tatekeya, and did so in the knowledge that the relationship "would be denounced by her relatives, and [...] would be filled with both pain and joy."[32]

Hence, the trilogy's first installment catalogs instances of turmoil and suffering, and the narrative is formulated in a gloomily realist aesthetic that seems almost relentless by times. The relationship between Tatekeya and Aurelia, although it occasions moments of tenderness and absolute union, arises, in part, out of the "upheaval" and "despair" that the elder partner experiences as a result of having to move his farm to make way for the Oahe dam.[33] That fact is underlined in the novel's final scene when Aurelia, who has just learned that Tatekeya's barn has been torched in reprisal following Sheridan Big Pipe's conviction for cattle rustling, acknowledges "that the flooding of the homelands had to be taken into account in any explanation of her devotion to Tatekeya, and his to her."[34] Over the course of a number of subsequent paragraphs that find Aurelia confronting her mother's loss of tradition and her lover's imminent withdrawal from tribal life, Cook-Lynn's grief stricken protagonist becomes a figure of abject and total loneliness as she attempts to accept the fact that "the wretchedness inflicted upon human beings by other human beings was inseparable from the violation of the earth."[35] This novel ends with the sodden image of the

---

31   *Aurelia*, 70.
32   Ibid., 57.
33   Ibid., 48.
34   Ibid., 138–139.
35   Ibid., 138.

titular character alone, her eyes filled with tears for an unrecoverable past, sat astride her horse on the banks of the Missouri river.

The examination of tribal values continues during the next two books, the action of which is specifically concerned with Aurelia and her journey to become "a storyteller and a witness" of the tribe's history.[36] In *Circle of Dancers*, Cook-Lynn's eponymous protagonist has ended her affair with Tatekeya and fallen in love with Jason Big Pipe, the young man who earlier testified against her previous lover. Although never married, Aurelia and Big Pipe—a returned Vietnam veteran—have a boy together, who they name Blue. This second novella is set during the 1960s and 1970s and focuses on Aurelia's role within the Big Pipe family as well as her interactions with the wider family network. The increased centrality of her voice in this installment has been described by Page Rozelle as a "shift to Aurelia as a character," one that importantly marks a "shift from politics and justice" as central themes in *From the River's Edge*, "to storytelling as both subject and form" in *Circle of Dancers* and *In the Presence of River Gods*.[37] Although the issues of "politics and justice" give way to a closer consideration of what Rozelle believes is a personal "conflict between [Aurelia's] desire to control her own destiny and her role as historian-storyteller in the community," it is still the case that questions of integrity and autonomy shape and inform this book's examination of what Heath Justice describes as "community-in-relationship"—"the ways by which the People understand themselves and their relationships with the rest of the world."[38] As well as revealing traditional Dakotah stories told by Grandma Blue, Harvey Big Pipe and Lewis Grey Iron (who is Harvey's elder brother and therefore Jason's uncle), the second novella in the trilogy narrativizes and catalogs historical and contemporary events that have significant, often unbearable, ongoing consequences for the lives of those living on the Crow Creek Indian reserve.

---

36   Ibid., 133.
37   Page Rozelle, "The Teller and the Tale: History and the Oral Tradition in Elizabeth Cook-Lynn's *Aurelia: A Crow Creek Trilogy*," *American Indian Quarterly*, 25:2, Spring 2001, 204.
38   Daniel Heath Justice, *Our Fire Survives the Storm: A Cherokee Literary History* (Minneapolis: University of Minnesota Press, 2005), 211.

For instance, while teasing out the ill effects accruing from the loss of tribal land, financial impoverishment, and judicial assault, multiple narrators tell stories of Sheridan Big Pipe and Leaper, "a youthful relative" of Harvey Big Pipe. Both men stand accused of murder during the course of the novel.[39] We also learn of the Bureau of Indian Affairs' threat to foreclose on Jason's "farm-ranch program," the stand-off between the FBI and the American Indian Movement at Pine Ridge, the communities' "continuing fight" to save their tribal lands, and the plight of the "dammed" *Mni Sosa*.[40] By the opening lines of *In The Presence of River Gods*, which begins in 1980, it is evident that Aurelia's relationship with Jason is nearing its end: "[they] drove most of the way to Eagle Butte along the river without speaking to one another; she because of a vague dissatisfaction, he because he knew now that he was no longer the extraordinary person with whom she had so much in common." The stifling atmosphere created by the rapidly spoiling marriage is reflected in the weather and the landscape. Surrounded by a "hot August prairie wind [that] was unbearable," the couple endures a silence that the third-person narrator describes as being "as tedious as the land and the sky and the endless highway."[41] This sensation of a stasis, suspension, or deferral is concretized later in the novel when Aurelia is reported as thinking that:

> She was waiting for life after Jason just as she had waited for life before Jason, she was waiting for Grandmother to die or get well, she was waiting for the children to grow up. She was waiting for the Black Hills case to be settled in an ethical way.[42]

The final story is, then, one of ominous expectancy: as well as containing an oppressive vision of life amongst the tribes in South Dakota, this book examines the disintegration of this familial unit.

Aurelia obviously exhibits many of the historicist traits that provide the "social context" in which to "ground the crucial political contentions of our

---

39   *Aurelia*, 229.
40   Ibid., 265, 287 & 324.
41   Ibid.
42   Ibid., 379.

times."[43] Indeed, the main character's commitment to making "the historical past and the contemporary present significant and meaningful" can only be read in terms of what Teuton describes as a work of "tribal realism."[44] The trilogy's sustained engagement with images of time and memory construct a complex narrative in which modern-day life and Dakotah beliefs are imbricated. Rozelle discusses this composite style, noting the manner in which "traditional stories and myths are placed beside the personal and political stories" throughout *Circle of Dancers* and *In the Presence of River Gods*. She also concludes that both forms of "telling" are subsequently "woven into the narrative."[45] Interestingly, James Stripes has drawn attention to Cook-Lynn's conviction that the politics of her first novel, *From the River's Edge*, are "understated and ambivalent," and cites the author's own belief that her work is beset by a certain "ambiguity concerning the Indian rights struggle of politics and land."[46] Rozelle's perception that there is a "shift from politics and justice to storytelling as both subject and form" must be read carefully within this context, largely because the narrative style of the second and third novella may well address what Cook-Lynn describes as the "ambiguity" of the first installment in the trilogy. In other words, it is not just necessary to consider *how* the aesthetic design of the trilogy develops; we must also consider whether that development leads to a more affecting form of political resistance. As a result, it is necessary to bring the images of memory and narrative that Rozelle finds in *Aurelia* into contact with recent conversations regarding tribal nationalism and tribal realism. Doing so can reveal the ways in which the action and form of *Circle of Dancers* and *In the Presence of River Gods* continues, and deepens, what Stripes describes as the Crow Creek Sioux author's "commitment to indigenous sovereignties."[47]

43   Teuton, *Red Land, Red Power*, 15.

44   *Aurelia*, 116; *Red Land, Red Power*, 12.

45   Rozelle, "The Teller and the Tale," 204.

46   James Stripes, "'We Think in Terms of What Is Fair': Justice versus 'Just Compensation' in Elizabeth Cook-Lynn's *From the River's Edge*," *Wicazo Sa Review* 12.1 (Spring 1997), 166.

47   Ibid., 168.

It is also the case that Aurelia appears to be steadily coming "to accept her role as witness, recorder of memory, and carrier of culture" during the course of this final story.[48] Thus, the novel's grim roll-call of death, loss, and justice delayed or denied—which includes the death of Grandma Blue, the suicide of Justin's brother Anthony, the ruling in the legal case *United States v. Sioux Nation*, and the murder of a young Sioux girl by two white boys from a nearby town—is assuaged by a sense of becoming that is connected to Aurelia's newfound responsibility. Although the third-person narrative perspective is employed throughout this one hundred and thirteen page conclusion to the trilogy, she continues to be the main focalizer of the dramatic action. In this, the final book, Cook-Lynn's character is "moving on, taking steps toward someplace unknown."[49] So, even though the narrative has a bleakness and moroseness that seems to intentionally focus on the "hardscrabble" lives endured by the characters (and, for that reason, teeters on being depressing at times), the images of isolation and privation are not only functional and carefully deployed, but they are also contextualized and substantiated. As Aurelia explains to Blue, the Dakotah people "must all get accustomed to alone-ness because that tells us [...] that nothing lasts except the earth [...]. [When] you connect to the alone-ness of the place, acknowledge it, it's like growing up."[50] Above all else, the trilogy is about Aurelia's maturation and her assumption of her place in "the oral narrative poetry transmitted by word of mouth from one singer, one teller of tales, to another."[51] It is crucial to note, however, that despite this unrelenting focus on the more taxing aspects of contemporary Indian life, each of the novels nevertheless opens with a short reverie or preface, in which the author comments in some way on Sioux mythology, times past, contemporary tribal experiences and the manner in which the Sioux "move on in their lives together, communal, mindful, caring deeply about the history they share."[52] For instance, at the

---

48   Rozelle, "The Teller and the Tale," 205.
49   *Aurelia*, 379.
50   Ibid., 373.
51   Ibid., 455.
52   Ibid., 349.

opening of *From the River's Edge* the narrator describes how she watched "the flooding waters of the Missouri River Power Project" cover "trees of a timber stand which had nourished a people for all generations"—an account that effectively pre-empts the trilogy's discussion of the losses suffered by the tribe.[53] "Yet," Aurelia's first-person narration continues, "as your fingertips touch the slick leaves of the milkwood and roll the juicy leaves together, it is easy to believe that this vast region continues to share its destiny with a people who have survived hard winters, invasions, migrations, and transformations unthought of and unpredicted."[54] Near the end of the trilogy, Aurelia attempts to interpret the statement that "even the river has had to learn new ways of being," which is made by an old Sioux treaty man, Reclining Bear, at a meeting convened by the state's Attorney General. In the wake of this comment her nephew by marriage, Philip, feels alienated, lost, and angry, focusing above all on a value system that seems to have vanished with the coming of the colonizer. For her part, Aurelia argues that Reclining Bear is not suggesting that all is lost, but is instead reminding them that the tribe must continue to seek out justice, to accept that the miracle times, the *ohunkaka*, are in the past, and move onwards in a way that simultaneously honors the ancestors *and* guarantees the future.[55] This is a key moment in the novel insofar as Cook-Lynn's narrative is reflecting on matters of oration, tradition, continuance, and nationhood. The late Elaine Jahner's scholarly work *Spaces of the Mind* approaches these issues from a critical perspective, and her study of the oral narratives of the Standing Rock Sioux of North Dakota noted that the performative context that the stories are told in often means that the telling itself becomes a means to oppose any sense of defeatism or hopelessness in the face of colonization.[56] Jahner analyzed several stories told to her by Harry Fast Horse, whose family traveled to the town of Cannon Ball on the banks of the Missouri river as part of Chief Two Bear's band

53   Ibid., 5.
54   Ibid., 5–6.
55   Ibid., 404 & 405.
56   Elaine Jahner, *Spaces of the Mind: Narrative and Community in the American West* (Lincoln: University of Nebraska Press, 2004), 58.

in 1878. In response to one tale about Harry's experiences of being sent to the Indian boarding school at Fort Yates, North Dakota, and his trauma at the hands of assimilationist policy makers, Jahner writes:

> Tales like Harry's [...] may tell about how a young man was destroyed, but people like Harry are able to grasp the strategy at work and turn it into a narrated warning about what to watch for, how to defend oneself. [It] establishes a perspective that situates a critical and knowing witness, it reveals an observer quite capable of telling and analyzing. And that knowing is power. There is nothing defeatist about it.[57]

The narrative structure of *Aurelia* might subsequently be said to demonstrate fiction's ability to frame and retell a particularly crucial set of stories, and to make sense out of them in an ever-changing context. For that reason, it is important that there is also an extended conversation about these questions across the space of the trilogy; even though the 1980 Supreme Court ruling on the historical "theft" of Sioux lands, and the murder of "an Indian woman [...] in Walworth County, South Dakota" that same year are portrayed in the preface to *In the Presence of River Gods*, it is important to note that the reader has been reminded at the very outset—in "Myth and Memory," Part One of *Circle of Dancers*—that "there are myths that still matter."[58] Those myths continue to sustain the people. Accordingly, it can be argued that the trilogy amounts to nothing short of a sustained narratological engagement with both the various historical events that have informed Sioux experiences over the last two centuries—a series of broken treaties, the loss of the Black Hills, governmental relocation projects, the foundation of the American Indian Movement, the siege of Wounded Knee in 1973, and so on—and the spiritual, social, cultural, and even physical continuance of the tribe. In the sum of its parts *Aurelia* is, then, the culmination of Cook-Lynn's engagement with the lived experiences of the tribe, and her stylistic interweaving of historical matters with contemporary realism is ultimately what makes this trilogy so important. As such, this story cycle re-affirms the author's status as a frank and vehement defender of Dakotah

---

57   Ibid.
58   *Aurelia*, 149 & 349.

culture, tradition, and rights, and the trilogy underlines Dakotah *tioyspe* and Cook-Lynn's vision of the Sioux writer.

"Real Humanity in Characterization"

"The car radio plays some jazz and stops for the local news at ten o'clock: 'The winterkill of cattle has been as severe as any time since the turn of the century,' 'The 4-H students from Brainard will visit the Selby School District next month,' 'The Cosy Cup Cafe is closed for remodeling.'" It is with this brief, rather unexceptional, inventory of local events that Cook-Lynn draws her 462-page trilogy to a close. On some level, the concluding sentence is somewhat anti-climactic, since it neither reflects on the heavily effecting political, cultural, and spiritual events that immediately precede it, nor does it attempt to capture the serious tone that the greater part of the trilogy's narrative is soaked in. Indeed, the morning news that Aurelia Blue hears from her car radio while driving home from the county courthouse hardly seems to rank as "news" at all. The conspicuous absence of a *coup de grâce* or narratological fireworks at the very end of the story-cycle is quite telling however, and is in keeping with the starkly realistic nature of Cook-Lynn's overall project. What is most significant then, is the ordinariness associated with our final image of Aurelia—an ordinariness that might initially seem to be at odds with the more dramatic and haunting images that come before it, but is, in fact, a reminder of the simple fact that horrific racism, poverty, social tumult, and so on, are as common as the humdrum aspects of life in South Dakota. Because it is concerned with life's minutiae, the bulletin's mundane quality initially seems to counterpoint the solemnity and awfulness of the torrid scene that immediately precedes it. However, Aurelia's long drive out of the prairie town and "into the vastness of the hills" while listening to the local news reveals the extent to which the horrifying has (sadly) become routine; the tone of the final scene consequently captures this reality, confronts the reader with the shocking fact that this should be the case, *and*, perhaps most importantly, shows Aurelia getting on with life in the face of adversity and worse.[59]

The realism of the concluding scene is, then, very much in keeping with the style found in all three novellas, where the ordinariness of the café's closure and the students' impending visit only serves to throw the awfulness of earlier stories into starker relief; the reader's incredulity (and even their anger) grows when she considers that instances of murder, swindle and racism occur in the land of the Cosy Cup Café. It is extremely telling that Cook-Lynn chose to abut this unremarkable news with the awful details revealed in the pages immediately preceding the final sentence. Here, the reader follows the 1995 trial of two men who raped and murdered a fourteen-year-old girl from the reservation in 1980. The final chapters of *In the Presence of River Gods* occur during the time of the murder, and the reader shares Aurelia's dismay at the fact that no one is arrested in relation to the girl's disappearance. Cook-Lynn's character also finds it unfathomable that there are "no suspects" when the girl's bullet riddled and badly decomposed body is discovered in the sacred waters of the *Mni Sosa* nine months after her disappearance. These events then culminate in the Epilogue that finds Aurelia attending the court and listening to the evidence of the two defendants. Through a mixture of the protagonist's narration and directly reported testimony from the court, we learn that the men, who were teenage boys when they committed this monstrous crime, had finally chained their victim "to the back of [a] pickup and [...] drag[ged] her down" by the Missouri, where they then shot her five times and dumped her body in the water.[60] Like so many of the stories told in Cook-Lynn's trilogy, this fictional representation of a heinous crime has roots in a real legal case and in historical fact, and many readers will be only too well-aware of the fact that Cook-Lynn recreates a thinly veiled account of the Candace Rough Surface case.[61]

---

59   Ibid., 462.
60   Ibid., 461.
61   See Don Terry, "From '80 Crime, White–Sioux Tension Today," *New York Times* (February 20, 1996) <http://www.nytimes.com/1996/02/20/us/from-80-crime-white-sioux-tension-today.html?pagewanted=all&src=pm> accessed February 2,

The author's decision to do so gives rise to an extremely important set of questions. Above all else, this move bears testimony to Ms. Rough Surface's memory, and gestures towards some degree of justice, if not retribution.[62] With regards to fiction and the process of writing, the inclusion of this and other legal cases serves to emphasize the extent to which Cook-Lynn's fiction exists within the aesthetic mode that is realism. This has two effects. Firstly, as Stripes, Rozelle, Kathleen Danker, and others have argued, *From the River's Edge* and the other books in the trilogy produce certain codes and events that allow the reader to develop a sense of Sioux life today, to begin to understand the reality of tribal experiences in modern America, and to reflect on matters such as the Black Hills case, the Pick Sloan dam, events at Pine Ridge etcetera. In order to create this verisimilitude, the Crow Creek Sioux writer weaves social, cultural, and political facts into the fabric of the fiction itself; as a result, her creative writing often mirrors her academic arguments, just as her scholarship has often considered the role and effect of fiction. For instance, Cook-Lynn's critical charge that the wider world has no meaningful image of the "American Indian intellectual" is echoed by Philip's claim that "Indian life in America isn't like it is for intellectuals in Africa ... Here in Indian Country you just waste away."[63] Similar moments occur throughout the trilogy, with the omniscient narrator describing the American Indian Movement, life on the Crow Creek Reservation, federal Indian policy and the government's assimilationist

---

2012), and "Suspect finally pleads guilty after 16 years" (*Minnesota Daily*, May 8, 1996).

62   It is important to note that even though the men who killed Ms. Rough Surface, Nicholas A. Scherr and James E. Stroh, were charged and convicted, they were tried for manslaughter rather than murder (mainly because Stroh confessed of his own volition and Scherr then agreed to plead guilty to the lesser charge). Furthermore, despite the fact that the men confessed to raping their victim, neither was tried for rape, simply because the time frame for prosecution of that crime had elapsed by the time Stroh approached the police. So, justice was certainly delayed in this case, and it was also diluted somewhat. Nevertheless, the men *were* convicted.

63   Elizabeth Cook-Lynn, "American Indian Intellectualism and the New Indian Story," *American Indian Quarterly* 20.1, special issue: "Writing about (Writing about) American Indians" (Winter 1996), 57; *Aurelia*, 393.

programs, the ridiculous 1960s shamanism of the American countercul-
ture, and so on. Secondly, and more importantly, Cook-Lynn's use of what
could be called an indigenous realist mode of storytelling allows her to
focus on *tribal* realities, and to apply concepts that are central to Sioux
life and beliefs to her writing. That is to say, in the bid to create a "moral
fiction" that speaks to the concerns of her people and has relevance to contemporary Indian perspectives and experiences, Cook-Lynn explores the
"indigenous/tribally specific literary traditions from which the imagination
emerges."[64] Thus, Aurelia, who is a storyteller-character, often reminds the
reader that, for the Sioux, "all accomplishments and events and doings [...]
must contribute in a good way to the communal life given to [the tribe]
by [the ancestors]."[65] Evidently serving as a spokesperson for Cook-Lynn's
vision of how the tribal storyteller should act, and the contribution that
she should make, Aurelia is central to the trilogy's "search for a direct link
to the origin tales of the people" and the author's attempt to portray the
certainty of that link.[66]

Yet, certain commentators have expressed dissatisfaction with the
plainspoken nature of Cook-Lynn's creative work. For instance, the *New
York Times* reviewer Robert Houston described the first novel in the *Aurelia*
trilogy, *From the River's Edge*, as a "heavily flawed" piece of fiction that
made extensive use of "an inappropriate and pedantic narrative voice."[67]
This early review takes exception with the narrator's repeated interventions,
the long passages describing Aurelia's inner consciousness, the author's
attention to historical detail, and the novel's overall shading of the social
and cultural contexts that shape life in South Dakota. Houston's greatest
critique is reserved for the book's directness, its tone and its communication of a particular message, and in many ways, his overall argument meshes
with Catherine Belsey's oft-quoted claim that literary realism "performs

---

64   "American Indian Intellectualism and the New Indian Story," 72.
65   *Aurelia*, 123.
66   Ibid., 49.
67   Robert Houston, "Stealing Cattle and a Way of Life," *New York Times Book Review*
        (September 8, 1991), 35.

[...] the work of ideology" and little else.[68] Disputing the type of claim once made by Irving Howe, who once argued that earlier generations of (American) realists were able to "brilliantly observe how social and individual experience melt into one another so that the deformations of the one soon become the deformations of the other," Belsey, William Solomon, and others have suggested that the realist text is in fact the most restrictive form of the readerly text, and that it forecloses interpretation and limits narrative scope.[69] As George Levine has more recently pointed out, the scholars who took center stage in the 1960s, 1970s, 1980s, and even later were "radically anti-realist," largely because they deemed the "very notion of representing 'reality' in any credible way [...] as [indicative of] reprehensible *naiveté* or simple bad faith."[70] Despite this, Levine and others have argued, strenuously, that realism has a crucial role to play in the modern world. Rachel Bowlby, for one, insists that:

> Realist works can disturb or please or educate us by showing reality as not what we think we know, by showing realities we have never seen or dreamed, or by making speakable realities that might have seemed only idiosyncratic or incommunicable.[71]

"It is time," Bowlby concludes, "for realism to be put back into the critical picture, centre-stage."

Amongst those of us working in the field of Native American Literary Studies—like many of our colleagues working in postcolonial studies—there has been the realization that despite being out of vogue with the theoreticians, realism has never really left the stage.[72] More important,

---

68   Catherine Belsey, *Critical Practice* (London: Routledge, 2002), 67.

69   Irving Howe, *Politics and the Novel* (New York: Columbia University Press, 1992), 162–163. See also William Solomon, "Politics and Rhetoric in the Novel in the 1930s," *American Literature* 68.4 (December 1996), 799–818.

70   George Levine, "Literary Realism Reconsidered: 'The world in its length and breadth,'" in *Adventures in Realism*, ed. Matthew Beaumont (London: Blackwell, 2007), 13.

71   Ibid., xxi.

72   Laura Moss's essay "'The Plague of Normality': Reconfiguring Realism in Postcolonial Theory" offers a comprehensive overview of exactly why "realism not only persists but

however, is Cook-Lynn's relationship to the formal conventions usually associated with the realist mode. On some levels, the *Crow Creek Trilogy* adheres to the basic precepts that define the mode; the reader is presented with an opening enigma in the form of John Tatekeya's missing cattle, the theft of which signifies a loss of particular morals and values in the Dakotah world. That loss, in turn, calls for or necessitates a new hermeneutic code, and subsequent action and events in the trilogy find the reader and Aurelia drawn together in the process of reading the world as it exists in Indian Country. As is so often the case in literature, this hermeneutic code is coupled or paired with the proairetic code, which adds to the narrative tension by implying that other significant events are afoot, and that something else is bound to happen. In *Aurelia*, Cook-Lynn writes:

> The theft of John Tatekeya's cattle occurred just about the time when groups of young American Indian men began to patrol the streets of urban America. Streets like Franklin Avenue in Minneapolis-St Paul, where men in red berets would resist police violence toward "relocated" Indians and participate in a variety of activities which were soon to become the substance of a full-fledged political movement called "Red Power" and "AIM", claiming national and international attention.[73]

The reader has no way of knowing what Aurelia's relationship to, or impression of, the American Indian Movement is at this stage in the narrative, but the reference intentionally establishes a critical nexus between: the narrator's commentary on the dramatic changes that have occurred in Tatekeya's lifetime; an increasing amount of tribal consciousness during the 1960s (the consciousness that Sean Teuton associates with a tribal realist approach in

---

thrives" in certain political and cultural contexts: *Jouvert: A Journal of Postcolonial Studies* 5.1 (Autumn 2000) <social.chass.nesu.edu/ jouvert/v5i1/moss.htm> accessed, February 21, 2012. Moss's essay focuses specifically on postcolonial literature and criticism—areas that Cook-Lynn sees as being separate from the "indigenous theory" that "scholars in Indian studies [*sic*] are now beginning to think more appropriately in terms of" (*A Separate Country: Postcoloniality and American Indian Nations* [Lubbock: Texas Tech University Press, 2012], 3). Nevertheless, her comments on literary realism and its various applications go a long way toward addressing the criticisms levelled by Belsey, Solomon, and others.

73   *Aurelia*, 12.

the post-sixties American Indian novel); the novella's presentment of key themes informing Sioux experiences; and the protagonist's vision of the realities of the world around her.[74]

This nexus is important for two primary reasons. Firstly, Cook-Lynn's deliberate move from the now cattle-less Tatekeya lands to the complex versions of Indianness found in Minneapolis serves to reveal the extent to which the novel has the type, and degree, of constructedness that Roland Barthes associates with the realist text. That is to say, the narrative includes a decidedly controlled and contrived shift from the empty heartlands to the city, and the reader senses that Aurelia will act as the seer, the story-teller who mediates between these two tribal contexts and reveals certain realities both to those in her own community and to non-Dakotah peoples. In this way, the omniscient narrator's ability to reveal her inner thoughts is, like the shift between Tatekeya's world and that of AIM, a reminder of the simple fact that the trilogy is a highly mediated literary form in which Cook-Lynn actively *fabricates* a new sense of Dakotah realism. Cook-Lynn's sagacious protagonist is then the truth-teller in an increasingly disordered, chaotic Sioux world, one in need of renewal and the protection and/or restoration of cultural practices in a contemporary setting. Secondly, and more importantly, the Crow Creek Sioux author subverts traditional realist conventions, most notably by disallowing any definite sense of closure—either at the end of each novella, or at the end of the trilogy as a whole. "Though classicists have always believed in endings," Cook-Lynn writes, "the real Dakotah storytellers like Aurelia did not. You see, she thinks of the story only if it goes on and on into the next story and the next and beyond."[75] This disruption of the codes that customarily apply to literary realism simultaneously reminds the reader of the author's agency and control of the narrative, *and* re-emphasizes the relationship that storytellers such as Mary Louise Defender Wilson—whose Dakotah name is Wagmuhawin—have with their culture, landscape, community, history, and stories. Although the narrator's point may appear to be a simple

74   Teuton, *Red Land, Red Power*, 33.
75   *Aurelia*, 341.

enough one, it is crucial to any understanding of the text. That is to say, the stories that Aurelia refers to are like Wagmuhawin's; continuing and ever-present, they connect past, present, and future, reminding the people that "history is always there—[that] you're standing there dragging all these things behind you."[76] Finally, Cook-Lynn's allusion to the "real Dakotah storytellers," like her rather direct comments on mixedblood authors and critics, is sure to strike a nerve with some readers, many of whom will read the reference to "real" as yet another sign of the Sioux writer's traditionalist essentialism. However, as Womack persuasively argues in *Reasoning Together*, "Cook-Lynn does not claim a purity for the tribal voice that she sees as a real, contemporary, ongoing necessity—only the human right to tell one's story."[77]

Ultimately, these novels are about finding a way to tell that story; they are about exploring the tribal real, which is comprised of both contemporary stories and ancestral stories, and framing both in a reconstituted, reframed literary form. As a means of seeing this development clearly, we can return to the news items that the older Aurelia listens to in 1995, and realize that even though the counterpointing of the horrific details of the murder trial with the soporific intonations of the newsreader seems odd initially, it is an entirely appropriate conclusion for a collection of novellas that are, fundamentally, concerned with injustice on one hand, and the manner in which story "goes on and on into the next story and the next and beyond" on the other.[78] Here, the ten o'clock update can be read as both a sign that the horrors and injustices of the past flow into the present—where the trial of two men who callously murdered an Indian girl isn't even headline news—and, significantly, as a reminder of Aurelia's dogged resistance and resilience. We may well note Aurelia's persistence in her journey, the image of justice finally being imminent in the murder case, and the sense that the bulletin underwrites the extent

---

76 Wagmuhawin, NEA National Heritage Fellow website bio: <http://www.nea.gov/honors/heritage/fellows/fellow.php?id=1999_05&type=bio> accessed February 18, 2012.

77 Craig Womack, "A Single Decade," in *Reasoning Together*, 76.

78 *Aurelia*, 341.

to which the People endure, even despite great loss and suffering. In this latter reading the sense that time and memory operate in a particular manner within the novellas is crystallized, and I would argue that by emphasizing time and memory in this way, Cook-Lynn explores the way in which Dakotah "history" can be "recreated [...] in the context of [...] modern tribal lives."[79]

79 *Anti-Indianism*, xi.

CHAPTER 3

"Indigenous to the Land, an Immigrant to the Culture": Sherman Alexie and the Third Space of Sovereignty

> Twenty years ago, we never knew we'd spend the rest of our lives in the reservation of our minds, never knew we'd stand outside the gates of the Spokane Indian Reservation without a key to let ourselves back inside.[1]
>
> — SHERMAN ALEXIE

In a recent interview with Enrique Cerna, the author Sherman Alexie stated, quite simply: "I've traveled all over the place; I'm published in twenty-two countries; I've been in places where no Spokane Indian has been."[2] Undoubtedly reflecting the self-assurance that is so often associated with the author, Alexie's declaration also establishes an important line of connection between the personal vision of his Spokane/Coeur d'Alene heritage in the first instance, and of his status as a writer in the second. With regard to his tribal heritage, Alexie has professed to be "very aware of my Spokaneness" and has often been at pains to point out that the "tribe heavily influences [his] personality and the ways in which [he sees] the world."[3] Much of that influence emanates not only from his experience of growing

---

1   Sherman Alexie, *First Indian on the Moon* (New York: Hanging Loose Press, 1993), 104.

2   Sherman Alexie, *Conversations at KCTS 9*, directed by Enrique Cerna (Seattle: PBS—KCTS, 2008).

3   Åse Nygren, "A World of Story-Smoke: A Conversation with Sherman Alexie," *MELUS* 30.4, Home: Forged or Forged? (Winter 2005), 155.

up on the reservation in Washington, but also from his relationship with his family. Indeed, Alexie has spoken about his mother, Lillian, who is not only "the drug and alcohol treatment counselor for the tribe," but is also the "youngest fluent speaker of Spokane" and a "powwower and ceremonial person."[4] Meanwhile, in his semi-autobiographical poem "Size Matters," Alexie refers to his maternal grandmother, Etta Adams, as "an epic hero," and explains how the "tribe depended upon/Her magic."[5] Alexie is also keen to underline the extent to which indigenous standpoints have had a bearing on American society, explaining to interviewer Ross Frank "Our culture, our stories, [and] our lives influence American life on a minute by minute basis."

As well as articulating a palpable sense of "Spokaneness," the author has also displayed a tendency to question the values that arise out of the contemporary reservation experience. In particular, Alexie suggests that "the idea of the reservation" can be something of a hindrance to Natives today, largely because it forces tribal communities to exist "firmly within borders."[6] Not only do these borders act as agents of restriction and constraint but, to Alexie's mind, they lead to a form of societal inertia that is itself troubling and disabling on many levels. Indeed, the author has described the Spokane Indian reservation as a "monoculture"—a stagnant, "tribally-controlled small town" where he was pilloried as a result of his eccentricity as a child and young adult.[7] Rather than being a culturally

---

4   Sherman Alexie, interview by Eleanor Wachtel, "Writers and Company," CBC radio (December 26, 2010), podcast online at <http://www.cbc.ca/player/Radio/ Writers +and+Company/2010/ID/1720854498/> accessed February 6, 2012.

5   Sherman Alexie, *Face* (Brooklyn: Hanging Loose Press, 2009), 120. Quite possibly the inspiration for the character Big Mom in *Reservation Blues*, Adams's spirit might also have influenced Alexie's depiction of Etta Joseph, the plain-speaking 118-year-old Spokane elder who blunts the scholarly probing of anthropologist Spenser Cox during the story "Dear John Wayne"—a reading that is, perhaps, both corroborated *and* complicated by the fact that the author's maternal grandfather was "a half-white man named James Cox" ("Sacagawea," *Time*).

6   Nygren, "A World of Story-Smoke," 167.

7   Sherman Alexie, interview by Ross Frank (2001) "Sherman Alexie in Conversation with Ross Frank PhD", <http://www.youtube.com/watch?v=ZWolPAoDk3g>

affirming and politically protected space, the Spokane Indian reservation was, for Alexie, a "static" place, one where children were generally "taught to be suspicious of the outside world [...] thought to be suspicious of white folks, and anything related to white culture."[8] Furthermore, Alexie believes that reservations are, in fact, colonial constructs designed to hold, limit, and ultimately eradicate Native people. In a recent radio interview with CBC's Eleanor Wachtel, the Spokane writer suggested, rather unambiguously, that "reserves were created as rural death camps for Indians," and even went as far as to argue that "the idea of [reservation life] becoming the dominant mode of identity [...] is a way of accepting the definition of people who wanted Indians to disappear."[9] More importantly, perhaps, Alexie's perception of the reservation as an insular and stagnant zone feeds into his judgment of tribal literature today. "Native American literature is provincial" he argues, and, as a result, "every Indian's literary vision extends only as far as they can see."[10]

At first glance it can be difficult, perhaps maddeningly so, to reconcile Sherman Alexie's sense of "Spokaneness" with his personal response to the moribund nature of life in Spokane. He was, Alexie explains, "comfortable with the idea of being an off reservation Indian" at a very young age.[11] Crucially, his decision to leave the reservation school for Reardan High school during his teenage years, his subsequent time at Gonzaga University, and his current residency in Seattle are not, for Alexie at least, signs of an attempt to idiosyncratically (re)define the self in individual terms or to completely remove himself from the tribe. On the contrary, Alexie defines his move away from the reservation in terms of an effort to recover what he calls the "kinetic and nomadic" nature of pre-contact

---

accessed April 22, 2012; Duncan Campbell, "Voice of the New Tribes," *The Guardian* (January 4, 2003), <http://www.guardian.co.uk/books/2003/jan/04/artsfeatures. fiction> accessed April 18, 2012.

8   *Conversations at KCTS 9.*

9   Interview by Eleanor Wachtel (CBS radio).

10 K.E. Semmel, "An Interview with Sherman Alexie," *The Writer's Chronicle* 43.6 (May 2011).

11 Interview by Eleanor Wachtel (CBS radio).

life in the Americas. His keenness to interpret indigenous movement in such innovatory terms has resulted in Alexie describing the decision to "leave the reserve" as "the most revolutionary act possible for a Native."[12] To his mind, then, indigenous peoples can form a more complete identity by doing so, thereby collectively enriching their tribal culture in the long term. Beyond, or perhaps more accurately *alongside*, these personal and cultural concerns are questions of artistry and literary form. Creatively, Alexie professes "to go for a wider lens, have multiple characters, generational, different geographies."[13] According to Alexie the impulse to generate multi-genre, achronological, and multicentered literary works arises out of his "want[ing] to be a moving target" at all times.[14] This aspect of Alexie's work—the writing's near borderless ranging across personal, cultural, and temporal spaces—has caught the eye of countless commentators. Over twenty years ago the poet Alex Kuo made reference to "Sherman Alexie's territory" in his introduction to *The Business of Fancydancing*, which was Alexie's first collection of poetry and prose. More recently, the headline to a *New York Times* article by Eric Konigsberg read "In His Own Literary World, a Native Son without Borders."[15] David L. Moore has identified the potential for exploration that comes with the "territory," and points out that Alexie's "five genres—poetry, short fiction, novel, non-fiction and film—weave through such modern and postmodern questions as psychological and social border crossings."[16] His appraisal follows the direction of several scholars who have felt compelled to write about

12   Ibid.
13   Semmel, "An Interview with Sherman Alexie."
14   David L. Moore, "Sherman Alexie: Irony, Intimacy, and Agency," in *The Cambridge Companion to Native American Literature*, ed. Joy Porter and Kenneth M. Roemer (Cambridge: Cambridge University Press, 2005), 302.
15   Eric Konigsberg, "In His Own Literary World, a Native Son without Borders," *The New York Times* (October 20, 2009), <http://www.nytimes.com/2009/10/21/books/21alexie.html?_r=0> accessed February 17 2012. That title was, to all intents and purposes, a rehash of the headline that appeared above an earlier *New York Times* piece on Alexie; Timothy Egan's 1998 article ran under the caption "An Indian without Reservations" (January 18 1998).
16   Moore, "Sherman Alexie," 297.

the Spokane author. One of those scholars is Daniel Grassian, who was quick to identify Alexie's ability to "expand [...] the boundaries of Native American literature."[17]

Alexie's outspokenness has, of course, attracted some detractors too. Many critics, particularly Native ones, have found his rather unvarnished and outspoken account of reservation life disquieting, to say the least. While finding fault with Alexie's descriptions of the oppressive and stifling nature of tribal communities, these commentators have commented on the conspicuous absence of kinship or tribalism in his writing. For instance, the late Louis Owens complained that, in Alexie's fiction, "there is no family or community center toward which [... the] characters [...] might turn for coherence," while Gloria Bird took exception to what she saw as the author's production of "a pan-Indian, non-specific representation of an Indian community" with "exaggerated 'Indian' qualities" in his novel *Reservation Blues*.[18] Elizabeth Cook-Lynn, meanwhile, has taken issue with Alexie's interest in influences emanating from popular culture and his claim to be the "first practitioner of the Brady Bunch-school of Native American literature."[19] "If this is an accurate description of how native issues are presented and how they are perceived in the mainstream," she writes, then "the American Indian voice" is "less intellectually honest and more irrelevant that at any time in our history."[20] The Crow Creek Sioux scholar may well have been thinking of Alexie when she suggested, a few pages later, that "today's popular Indian Voice [... is] self-centered and self-referential, mixed-blood and tribeless."[21] His brashness and ingenuousness have been criticized on the reservation as well. In 1998 a staff member at the Spokane cultural center told a visiting journalist that it seemed to her

17   Daniel Grassian, *Understanding Sherman Alexie* (Columbia: University of South Carolina Press, 2005), 40.

18   Louis Owens, *Mixedblood Messages: Literature, Film, Family, Place* (Norman: University of Oklahoma Press, 1998), 79; Gloria Bird, "The Exaggeration of Despair in Sherman Alexie's *Reservation Blues*," *Wicazo Sa Review* 11.2 (1995), 51.

19   Kelly Blewster, "Tribal Visions," *Biblio* (March 1999), 29.

20   Elizabeth Cook-Lynn, *Anti-Indianism in Modern America*, 85.

21   Ibid., 88.

that the popular writer "has used the reservation for personal therapy, and in so doing, he's hurt a lot of people."[22] Alexie's, somewhat solipsistic, declaration that he is all "for sovereignty of the self"—made in 2008—would appear to corroborate the claim that his individualism overrides any sense of tribalism that he may have once had.

Yet, for all that, there is something fundamentally arresting about the sovereignty that the author describes. Alexie's particular version of personal autonomy, if considered in the context of his "Spokaneness" and his position as an "off reservation Indian," points to an intricate, many faceted in-between space; an interstitial territory that facilitates various forms of movement, and, most importantly, sanctions the kind of freedom that he longs for. On a basic level, this independence of the self offers something of a solution to the difficulties that Alexie faced when he realized that he "didn't fit in" on the reservation, but "didn't fit into the white world either."[23] On a more complex level, the lacuna or interspace between Native and non-Native territories can be presented as a location where, according to Homi Bhabha, "the intersubjective and collective experiences of nationness, community interest, or cultural value [... might be] negotiated," and where "strategies of representation or empowerment" can at least be interrogated.[24] Crucially, in Alexie's definition this self-determined (personal) state is not cleanly, wholly hybridized, exilic, or cosmopolitan. Instead, the author (like the narratives he creates) claims to range across a number of zones—creative, discursive, historical, and cultural—in order to (re)define Indianness in the twenty-first century. The confluence of images and influences that arises out of this compelling mash-up, which Alexie refers to as a literary "mix-tape," far exceeds the theoretical form of hybridity or cosmopolitanism that, according to Christopher Taylor, "overlook[s] the existence of First Nations as coherent cultural, political,

---

22   Timothy Egan, "An Indian Without Reservations," *New York Times Magazine* (January 18, 1998), 25.
23   Interview by Ross Frank.
24   Homi Bhabha, *Location of Culture*, 2.

and legal bodies."[25] In fact, Alexie has explained how "the social function of art is very important to me," suggesting that writing is "not just for art's sake."[26] By choosing to be off the reservation on one hand, but by remaining palpably aware of the social, political, and economic security of the community in Spokane on the other, Alexie effectively straddles or, more properly, shuttles between what are interlinked but ultimately *discrete* territories. In doing so, he creates an in-between narrative space that allows him to defy the limits surrounding ethnic identity, draws attention to the material conditions of Native people in the United States today, and warrants examination in aesthetic and literary terms.

It possibly goes without saying that the authorial position that Alexie lays claim to is, then, incredibly nuanced; in the first instance, his distance from the reservation allows him to elude the conservatism that he claims to have experienced in his community—what he describes as a "fundamentalism about Indian identity, and what 'Indian' can be"; in the second instance, his strong sense of Spokaneness prevents him from being straightforwardly identified as a cosmopolitan, hybridized writer. Hence, even though Alexie revels in the universal nature of storytelling and is—by his own admission—desperate to "embrace all of the possibilities in the world," he insists that his personal perspective is that of an Indian writer.[27] In this way, his position in American society is informed by his tribalism, just as his tribalism is, in turn, informed by his relationship with both mainstream culture and the political, economic, and social realities of the

25   Christopher Taylor, "North America as Contact Zone: Native American Literary Nationalism and the Cross-Cultural Dilemma," *Studies in American Indian Literatures* 22.3 (Fall 2010), 31.

26   Sherman Alexie, "I Can Only Run the Marathon Sober" (October 30, 2009) <http://bigthink.com/ideas/ 17129> accessed February 26, 2012.

27   *Conversations at KCTS 9*. This point became abundantly clear during his 2001 interview with Ross Frank, in which he précised Salmon Rushdie's theory that "there are two stories: the story of home and the story of leaving home. That's all. That's all that exists in the world. Every novel, every poem, every movie is about that." The indigenous writer's response to this notion was that he, too, was (re)writing these well-worn stories, but that he had "an Indian spin on" them, "and a Spokane Indian spin at that" (interview by Ross Frank).

day. The result is that Alexie's writing can be said to engage with what Sean Teuton has called "the complexities of cultural interaction"—a move made possible by the fact that he locates and surveys interstitial spaces in order to view American Indian and European American identities as something other than "static racial categories."[28]

Correspondingly, Alexie fits into neither the "nationalist," "tribalist," "nativist," nor the "cosmopolitanist" or "hybridist" categories that some commentators have identified.[29] Although this is partly because there is often more common purpose between Native writers and critics than many writers allow, it is also because Alexie's creative writing and his personal conviction evade essentialized tribalism *and* attenuated hybridism in equal measure.[30] So, rather than suggest that the Spokane writer "struggles with a deepening sense of ambivalence about his position as a Spokane/Coeur d'Alene Indian in the United States of America," as Jennifer Gillan does, I would argue that he actually revels in the anomalies and aberrations.[31] In fact, in his 2002 essay "What Sacagawea Means to Me [and Perhaps to You]," the author refers to the "successive generations of social, political and

28   Sean Teuton, *Red Land, Red Power: Grounding Knowledge in the American Indian Novel* (Durham, NC: Duke University Press, 2008), 199.

29   Rob Appleford, "A Response to Sam McKegney's 'Strategies for Ethical Engagement: An Open Letter Concerning Non-Native Scholars of Native Literatures,'" *Studies in American Indian Literatures* 21.3 (Fall 2009), 59 & 60.

30   Weaver, *American Indian Nationalism*, 22. The point that Alexie's position bears resemblance to Native critics who were ostensibly at odds, is borne out by the fact that his notion of being an "off reservation" Indian can be linked to various aspects of the "boundary busting" described by Paula Gunn Allen in her work *Off the Reservation*, and the "postmodern frontier[ism]" that Louis Owens called for. Even though these critics (Gunn Allen and Owens), often held slightly different views regarding tribalism and literary form—and even though Owens criticized Alexie's fiction quite extensively—it is still the case that the Spokane writer's recent interviews, fiction, and poetry are concerned with the construction of similarly nuanced and compound version(s) of Indianness. As John Newton writes, "By the time we get to Sherman Alexie [...] binary discriminations are clearly untenable" (427).

31   Jennifer Gillan, "Reservation Home Movies: Sherman Alexie's Poetry," *American Literature* 68:1, "Write Now: American Literature in the 1980s and 1990s" (March 1996), 105.

artistic mutations" that have taken place in America, and describes these "mutations" as both "beautiful and painful."[32] In this short opinion piece he professes that his country is the consequence of a beguiling, profound, almost beautiful, set of "contradictions," and argues that America "exists, in whole and in part," as a result of them. Alexie's sustained attention to what he sees as a torturous yet compelling form of historical, racial, and cultural transformative flux creates in him a near wonderment at the vast array of knotty, co-mingled, and frequently paradoxical personal and public zones found in contemporary society.[33] A continued fascination with the nature and effect of these interactions has influenced the aesthetic shape of Alexie's writing throughout his literary career. It has also caused him to reflect on the definition of tribal "territory."

This attention to territory has, I would suggest, inspired him to create literary forms that might well correspond with some of the political sites and activities that have recently been outlined by Kevin Bruyneel. Bruyneel, logically and quite fairly, contends that tribes "must be able to express sovereignty beyond narrow, restrictive boundaries."[34] He also points out the means by which indigenous communities and activists are doing so today. Before delving into specific examples of tribal autonomy, the critic identifies certain suppositions concerning Native presence and agency, one of which runs as follows: "if the tribe is 'part of the United States,' it is not sovereign, but if it is to be sovereign, it cannot be part of and thus make demands on the United States."[35] As well as echoing what Jana Sequoya Magdaleno once called "the paradoxical injunction entailed by the figure of the American Indian (that is, if Indian, then not contemporary; hence, if contemporary, then not Indian)," this supposition is, Bruyneel suggests, a

---

32   *Time* (July 8, 2002) <http://www.time.com/time/magazine/article/0,9171,1002814, 00.html> accessed February 24 2012.

33   Ibid.

34   Kevin Bruyneel, *The Third Space of Sovereignty: The Postcolonial Politics of US– Indigenous Relations* (Minneapolis: University of Minnesota Press, 2007), xv.

35   Ibid., xiv.

fine example of what Bill Ashcroft has described as the "imperial binary."[36] In response to that binary, Bruyneel explains, many indigenous activists "work across American spatial and temporal boundaries, demanding rights and resources from the liberal democratic settler-state while also challenging the imposition of colonial rule on their lives."[37]

Alexie's writing operates in a similar manner and to similar ends. By examining specific geographic, cultural, and personal sites, and by doing so through a sustained consideration of historical context and interactions, the Spokane writer fabricates a beguiling representation of territory and time. His work considers a broad range of borders and boundaries, which include, but are not limited to: the tribal, the political, the individual, the economic, the generational, the physical, and the intercultural. This itinerant aesthetic allows Alexie to locate, test, and very often *exceed*, rigidly defined versions of Indianness and/or cosmopolitanism. His ability to connect place and time is readily apparent in his earliest collections of poetry and prose and in his most recent work. His first collection of poetry and prose features countless images of movement and space, most notably in pieces such as "Traveling," "Distances," "House Fires," "Reservation Love Song," and "The Reservation Cab Driver." Subsequent collections exhibited a similar interest, with *First Indian on the Moon* (1993) including pieces such as "Reservation Drive-In," "Vision: From the Drum's Interior," "On the Amtrak from Boston to New York City," and "Rediscovering America."

36   Jane Sequoya Magdaleno, "How (!) is an Indian? A Contest of Stories, Round 2," in *Postcolonial Theory and the United States: Race, Ethnicity, and Literature*, ed. Amritjit Singh and Peter Schmidt (Jackson: University of Mississippi Press, 2000), 284; Bill Ashcroft, *Post-Colonial Transformation* (London: Routledge, 2001), 35.

37   Bruyneel, *The Third Space of Sovereignty*, xvii. It should be noted that even though Bruyneel's version of a "third space" builds on Bhabha's definition of hybridity, it is far more politically and materially involved. Importantly, his account of political activists' movement across historical and geographical space accentuates both these spaces as vital sites of resistance. In this way Bruyneel attends to the concern that "the *notion* of hybridity [...] tends to collapse both the temporal and spatial specificities of resistance": Gerry Smyth, "The Politics of Hybridity: Some Problems with Crossing the Border," in *Comparing Post-Colonial Literatures: Dislocations*, ed. Patricia Murray and Ashok Bery (London: Macmillan, 2000), 52 (emphasis added).

Meanwhile, in *Old Shirts & New Skins* (1993), the collection published by the American Indian Studies Centre at the University of California, Los Angeles, we find poems such as "Architecture," "Archaeology," "Postcards to Columbus," "Spokane, 1976," and "The Last Indian Bar in Spokane." This direct engagement with journeys, crossovers, and interchange has kept apace in his most recent publications. *Face* (2009), his book of poetry and short prose, features pieces titled "Dangerous Astronomy," "The Fight or Flight Response," "Mystery Train," and "When Asked What I Think About Indian Reservations, I Remember a Deer Story," while poems and short stories such as "Go, Ghost, Go," "Breaking and Entering," "On Airplanes," "Fearful Symmetry," and "Food Chain" can be found in his Pen Faulkner Award winning *War Dances* (2009). Indeed, the concerns evident in pieces such as "Traveling" and "Father coming Home" in his first book, *The Business of Fancydancing*, recur in "The Father and Son Road Show" in *Face* and "Catechism" in *War Dances*. Through his attention to points of contact and exchange that take place on (and between) the Spokane Indian reservation and the wider world, Alexie's poetry and prose assumes many of the qualities seen in the political dealings that Bruyneel refers to in his book. That is to say, the writing itself could be said to "reclaim or remark [...] boundaries, whether in the name of the tribal, intertribal, or a general indigenous identity."[38] In the examination that follows I wish to concentrate on the material, historical, and cultural borders visible in a selection of Sherman Alexie's poetry and prose (primarily work featured in *The Business of Fancydancing* [1992], *Old Shirts & New Skins* [1993], *First Indian on the Moon* [1993], *Face* [2009] and *War Dances* [2009]). Specifically, I would like to consider the ways in which the writer creates metaphors and symbols that detail patterns of passage and transition, often by imagining the body as a corporeal site of mutation, memory, and movement, and by drawing attention to the transmutations—and the sometimes revitalizing conflicts—found in twenty-first-century America.

38   Ibid., xix.

Alexie's lyric poem "The Lost Colony of Roanoke, 1587," one of a number of pieces that he has published online, scans as follows: "On the telly,/The British man wonders,/'Why did the Roanoke settlers disappear?/And what tore them asunder?'/I must protest./Or confess./The settlers are not gone. They're here./In my belly."[39] In eight short lines—just thirty-three words—the poet invokes a complex set of seemingly divergent images: colonial history alongside present-day technology; official inquiry alongside familiar rejoinder; indigenous resistance alongside concession and recognition; the putatively "vanished" settler alongside a palpable physical presence. The poem is a striking example of the swiftness that Alexie brings to bear in his effort to bring historical narratives into contact with contemporary concerns. This is largely because this poem condenses and collapses centuries-old contact and conflict into short lyric form. Thematically speaking, the piece delivers huge cultural and historical questions in a radically undersized form. Even if it is comical, this historical abridgement offers an intensity of movement and kinesis that is very much in keeping with Alexie's overall aesthetic. Through the deployment of a number of strong enjambments the poem moves from a potentially vacuous contemporary scene ("On the telly,") through to a purportedly objective zone in which transatlantic contact can be examined. In the second half of the poem, lines four through eight, run-on lines are replaced by a number of end-stopped lines which introduce the reader to the first-person narrator's response(s) to colonial exchange. The first of these end stopped lines, the grammatical unit "I must protest.," simultaneously challenges the presenter's sense of pastness—both in terms of colonial America as a discrete, separate entity, and the disappearance of the settlers—and, more importantly, articulates Native resistance and defiance. What follows is a beautiful moment of

39   Sherman Alexie, "The Lost Colony of Roanoke, 1587," <http://www.guernicamag. com/poetry/2911/ sherman_alexie_lost_colony_of_roanoke_1587_8 _1_11/> (August 2011) accessed January 17 2012. My colleague Rowland Hughes reminds me that it is worth noting that Alexie chose to publish this poem in an online magazine that shares a title with Pablo Picasso's iconic anti-war mural *Guernica*—a move that may, in itself, be interpreted as a commentary on international aggression and imperialism.

parallelism, in which the speaker's ground for "protest" is, on one hand, aligned with the stark reality that the "settlers are not gone"—they are, instead, very much "here" in Alexie's America. On the other hand, the brief line "Or confess" is allied with the snapper "In my belly." Thus, "They're here."—which can be initially read as the end of the grammatical unit— could be said to introduce the punch line; a punch line that, mind you, arises out of the gravely serious reality of wars between the settlers and the indigene. Finally, the proximate placement of "protest" and "confess" suggests, on some level, that the narrator regards the relationship between the colonizers and the colonized with a degree of ambivalence; in one line the poem insinuates that reparation has never been made. In the next, it points to historical horrors that must not be perpetuated or repeated. Finally, the piece seems to laugh at its own gravity.

Collectively, the theme, style, and effect of "The Lost Colony of Roanoke, 1587" are typical of Alexie's aesthetic. The writing vocalizes difference while also playing with, and undercutting, the assumptions that often accompany the recognition of difference. Through this artistic practice the author brings specific geographic and cultural spaces into contact with one another, before relentlessly working across those spaces in order to highlight variations and modifications. This technique is a fine example of what Dean Rader describes as "the lyric poem as a mode of defiance."[40] Rader's perceptive and imaginative study of Alexie's poetry in his new work *Engaged Resistance* exhibits a profound interest in the idea of "resistance in motion," and he cites Eric Gary Anderson's attentiveness to "the metaphor of migration [as a means] to explore regional and cultural examples of resistance and displacement" as being a great influence on his work.[41] Both of these approaches to the literature are greatly valuable, and have, in some way, shaped my particular interest in Alexie's metaphors of space, distance, and travel. Beyond the question of genre, which is Rader's primary concern, and beyond Gary Anderson's focus on migration, there

---

40   Dean Rader, *Engaged Resistance: American Indian Art, Literature, and Film from Alcatraz to the NMAI* (Austin: University of Texas Press, 2011), 114.

41   Ibid., 150.

is, however, the matter of boundaries: personal, social, political, economic, generational, and temporal. It is Alexie's response to, and interest in, borders and the act of shuttling back and forth across them that I wish to consider above all else.

"I spend my days following tangents toward metaphors. It's strange and lovely work."[42]

The first section of *The Business of Fancydancing* is titled "Distances"—a name that does, in many ways, identify the theme that has become a constant within Alexie's writing. The first piece in this section, a prose work titled "Traveling," opens with the lines "My eyes were closed tight in the reservation November night and the three in the morning highway was the longest in tribal history."[43] The internal rhyme between the words "tight" and "night" emphasizes the sense of being cloaked in two forms of darkness; the darkness of sleep and the darkness of the "reservation November night." Similarly, there is an apparent scansion at play within the line, through which Alexie possibly divides the opening sentence into personal and public spaces (the five closed syllables of "my eyes were closed tight" giving way to the complexity of ten syllables of "in the reservation November night"). The "and" at the end of the first sentence links these spaces to a "morning highway" that is described as "the longest in tribal history." Again, the two syllable words "morning" and "highway" lend a sense of balance to the first half of the sentence; a balance which is then possibly disrupted or complicated in the closing words "the longest in tribal history." Not alone do these two opening lines bring the personal pronoun "my" into contact with the communal "reservation," but they also create a clever form of time/space compression that associates the image of the

---

42   Tweet from @sherman_alexie (January 16, 2012).
43   *The Business of Fancydancing*, 13.

present-day road with the historical experiences of the tribe. The density of these lines allows Alexie to suggest, and to traverse, what David L. Moore calls the "psychological and social border crossings" that are very much a part of contemporary Native American experiences.[44]

The decidedly poetic lines that introduce the story "Traveling" are followed by a process of narratological mapping which sees the first-person narrator introduce a number of familial, spatial, and (inter)cultural spaces. The reader quickly learns that the speaker's father is "driving a blue van filled with short Spokane Indians," and that this small troupe is returning from the "Kamiah All-Indian Six-Feet-and-Under Basketball Tournament."[45] In this context the title is doubly significant since it identifies the act of moving off the reservation, *and* possibly refers to traveling as an act of violation; in basketball parlance the ball carrier is penalized and loses possession if they move more than a step and a half without bouncing the ball. After he has described the space inside the blue van, and explained the connections between the inhabitants, Alexie's protagonist goes on to list a number of small towns stretching from Idaho to Spokane: "Orofino, Lapawai, Lewiston, Rosalia, Spangle."[46] This necklace of towns running along Routes 12 and 195 are markers, both in terms of the distance covered and proximity to the reservation. Arrestingly, these roads are state roads, rather than interstate roads, and mention of them suggests a localism or insularity that is very much in keeping with the darkness alluded to in the opening lines. It is just as important to note, however, that the trip in the blue van *does* take the team and their coaches across state lines; the first three towns mentioned are in Idaho. Possibly reminding the informed reader of the fact that Spokane people once inhabited tribal lands in what is now known as the Idaho panhandle, the van's trajectory takes it and its passengers seamlessly across state lines that go unseen and unannounced. What the narrator does notice, and comments on, as he passes through these "small towns" are "all the Indians in the bars drinking their culture or

44   Moore, "Sherman Alexie," 297.
45   *The Business of Fancydancing*, 13.
46   Ibid.

boarded in their houses so much in love with cable television." Once again, there is a natural scansion with the sentences, and this would appear to give rise to various meanings. The phrase "all the Indians," coming after "all the small towns," gives the impression of there being a principally cohesive or collective group identity, and it has the effect of seeming to gather the people together. However, it soon turns out that the speaker is referring to two different cohorts—those in the bars or those in their homes. Not only is there a vacuity about their respective pastimes, drinking and watching television, but Alexie's Indians are, in the first instance, divided between themselves and, in the second instance, hemmed in. They are "boarded up," having become passive consumers in a way that divides rather than unites them. This perception of division is reinforced by the narrator who quotes an "old Indian man from Worley" who once said: "Every highway in the world crosses some reservation, cuts it in half."

Significantly, the blue van, which is traveling on the highway itself, straddles between and passes the houses and bars; rather than crossing over or bisecting, it travels along the dividing line, crossing borders and boundaries as it moves through the dark night. The vehicle itself becomes a liminal site, and Alexie's characters agents of movement. There is also a sense of community amongst the passengers, whom the narrator refers to as "the other Skins," and this possibly counterpoises the anonymity caused by the boards that hide "all the Indians" who the speaker imagines as being burrowed in bars and semi-dark sitting rooms. In fact, the change of register—from the conversational "Indians" to argot "Skins"—offers a moment of differentiation or demarcation between the groups. Furthermore, even though it is the case that most of the van's occupants remain nameless for the duration of the story, these "short Spokane Indians" do have common cause since they have, presumably, been representing their reservation at the basketball tournament. In a move that reinforces this point, the young narrator, whose name is possibly Arnold Victor, breaks two pieces of dried bread and passes "it around to the other Skins" in what could be read as an act of communion and solidarity. Finally, there are extremely close links between many of the passengers; two of the coach's sons are on the team, and the assistant coach, Willie Boyd, is a life-long friend and relative from the reservation. The two adults josh the young Victor boy and make jokes about his self-professed hunger as they drive along, and before long the whole team has woken from their light sleep. Up to the end of the first section of the story, the action is relatively unremarkable, and the most remarkable element of the story is the wonderfully poetic and prescient voice of the adolescent storyteller.

As they near home the "talking stories and laughter" are brought to an abrupt halt, however, and a State Trooper suddenly detains what the narrator describes as "the blue van filled with Spokane Indians."[47] Confronted with the face of officialdom, the young narrator turns once again to the idea of his tribe's history. "The Trooper walked up to my father on the driver's side cool and sure," he says, "like he was ordering a hamburger and fries or making a treaty."[48] In this moment, the government agent, protector of the road and enforcer of rules (and limitations), is casually but emphatically tied to the military and political figures that once carved up the American West. The slightly paradoxical suggestion that the Trooper approaches the car with the degree of airiness that he might assume if he were purchasing junk food (itself associated with American cultural imperialism) *or* requisitioning indigenous lands, establishes a dissonant line of association that is both disarming and unsettling. A subtle, and possibly sarcastic, undercurrent adds further complexity to the scene, in that the Spokane never signed a treaty with the American government.[49] With this knowledge to hand, the reader just might pause to consider the balance of power between the Trooper and the occupants of the blue van; on some level, the van is an autonomous space, and the passengers are, ultimately, "kinetic and nomadic." A sense of agency or control is perhaps communicated by the

---

47 *The Business of Fancydancing*, 13.

48 Ibid.

49 In 1855 the Yakima, Nez Perce, Blackfoot, and other tribes signed treaties with the treaty party led by Governor Isaac Stevens as it toured through present day Idaho, Montana, and Oregon. People from the lower Spokane band were busy harvesting salmon during the summer months, and they refused to meet Stevens in June, July, and August—the months when several of the treaties were signed. A subsequent treaty council in December 1855 failed, and, as a result, the Spokane tribal reservation was created by executive order in 1881.

fact that Mr. Victor is the first to speak: "Excuse me, officer, what's the problem?"[50] Punctuated as it is, the father's question could, perhaps, be said to lay a sarcastic or slightly mordant emphasis on the designation "officer." The first comma suggests a pause that frames the title, thereby presenting it as an afterthought or an addendum to the question posed. The adversarial tone continues as the Trooper begins his line of questioning, and accuses the van's driver of weaving across the road, possibly as a result of drinking earlier in the evening. The official's title is used once again in response to this interrogation, and from the passenger seat Willie Boyd chances his luck by making a joke about the empty cooler sitting on the floor of the vehicle. Indeed, the humor continues as the Trooper inspects the rear of the van: "We all going to jail, enit" an anonymous voice says, to which another unidentified passenger responds "only if being Indian is illegal." The first speaker says that "being Indian has been illegal in Washington since 1972," which just happens to be the year he was born.[51]

As well as displacing the tension arising out of the unfolding episode, the repartee is an important enunciation of sorts; it revisits the legality of tribal presence, contemporizes the image of the Indian who has unlawfully ventured off the reservation, and even signals a degree of indigenous resistance. On this level, the exchange may remind readers of the issues debated in Supreme Court cases such as *Idaho versus Coeur d'Alene* (1997). In that case the tribe "filed [... a] federal court action against the State of Idaho, various state agencies, and numerous state officials in their individual capacities" and "sought, *inter alia*, a declaratory judgment establishing its entitlement to the exclusive use and occupancy and the right to quiet enjoyment of the submerged lands" of Lake Coeur d'Alene (No. 94–1474). In a close-run 5–4 decision, which was authored by Justice Anthony Kennedy, the Court ruled that the tribe's suit against Idaho and the state's officials could not proceed in federal court, simply because each of the states enjoys Eleventh Amendment immunity in suits that are filed by Indian tribes. If read within this context, Mr. Victor's defiance may seem to imitate this

---

50   *The Business of Fancydancing*, 14.
51   Ibid.

challenge to authority as personified in the State Trooper. This defiance continues when he refuses to get out of the van on the first time of asking, and insists "'I didn't do shit.'"[52] Sadly, Mr. Victor's stand is short-lived, and before long the narrator's father is being forcibly brought on a cultural tour of American history. Coerced into singing *The Star-Spangled Banner*, the coach is faced with a number of bizarre, seemingly random questions that the Trooper seeks very specific answers to. It becomes apparent that the answers he insists on are culturally informed and often ignore verifiable truths. For instance, the Trooper ignores historical fact and insists that it is Babe Ruth who holds the record for the most home runs during a single season of Major League baseball. Accordingly, Roger Maris, the Cleveland Indians' right-fielder, who broke Ruth's record in 1961, is once again maligned and overlooked.[53] Similarly, the state agent insists that the Americans invented Velcro, that Frank Sinatra is the "greatest entertainer of all time," that cream cheese is far preferable to lox (dried salmon) on a bagel. The *coup de grâce* comes when he asks the "suspect" if he is "now or" ever has "been a member of the Communist Party."[54] Here the overeating, overconfident Ruth is allied with American consumerism and capitalism, and any deviation from homogeneity, any break in the master narrative, is rejected as unpalatable, if not intolerable. In this way, Alexie's imagination pits the underdog against the governmental agent and his party line—a move that possibly associates Mr. Victor with the author's own father; a man who loved conspiracy theories, regardless of whether they came from

---

52 Ibid.
53 Maris's *New York Times* obituary described him as "the man with the asterisk in the record books: *Hit 61 home runs in 1961 in a 162-game season," and explains that the asterisk was "inserted into the record books by Ford C. Frick, the commissioner of baseball, who apparently reflected the traditionalist view of many fans that the Olympian feats of Babe Ruth must be defended against long seasons, short fences and newly arrived sluggers" (*New York Times*, December 15, 1985) <http://www.nytimes.com/learning/general/onthisday/ bday/ 0910. html> accessed January 24, 2012.
54 *The Business of Fancydancing*, 14.

the political left or right.[55] Although many of the questions might be considered trivial and petty, the answers that are solicited, and the manner in which they are solicited, can be read as a disconcerting commentary on the cultural status quo in America. Moreover, the officer's continued hounding of the driver reflects forms of official abuse arising out of white hegemony. The preference for one answer over the other may appear arbitrary and possibly even inconsequential as a result, but there is an important balance of power and a prevailing form of cultural colonialism being played out on the roadside. Hence, even though there is something mildly comedic about the State Trooper's preference for a whiter-than-white cream cheese over the salmon that was once the staple diet of the Spokane people, it is still the case that this moment amounts to a personal tragedy and a gross humiliation for Arnold's father and the team. Worse still, it is a continuation of historical affliction during the long the journey that the people have made on the tribal highway. By the end of the story "all the Indians [... are] silent" as they cross the broad roads "leading home to the Spokane Indian Reservation."[56] The final insult arrives when the van runs out of gas and stops "dark in the endless night."[57] The adults sit in the front as the young basketball players try to push the van towards home. Before long the narrator's brother succumbs to the grimness and the futility of the situation: "'I'm so damned tired,' he said, stopping pushing, stood still."[58] There, on the pitch black reservation road, hope seems too far off in the distance to spot. Yet, for all that, there might just be something affirmative about the final sentence, in which the younger brother puts his "shoulder to the cold metal and wait[s] for something to change." Although surely not marking an epiphany of any sort, the younger boy's stance doesn't just place him in the direction of the reservation or on the longest highway in what has become a difficult tribal history. On the contrary, it sees him facing the

---

55   Maya Jaggi, "All Rage and Heart," an interview with Sherman Alexie, *The Guardian* (May 3, 2008) <http://www.guardian.co.uk/books/2008/may/03/featuresreviews. guardianreview13> accessed March 2, 2012.
56   *The Business of Fancydancing*, 14.
57   Ibid., 15.
58   Ibid.

future, poised to move again, waiting for something to change; willing for change to come about. This concluding scene could, on some level, be said to present the reader with an image that is as much about resilience as it is resignation, as much about stamina as it is about frailty.

In *The Third Space of Sovereignty*, mentioned above, Bruyneel asks: "How has the United States as a people and a government—as a nation and a state—imposed temporal and spatial boundaries on indigenous people, for what purpose, and with what consequences?"[59] In the scene described above, the exchange between the father figure and the Trooper is a fictionalized account of cultural and political boundary making. The van's progress on the long, hushed highway is halted by the highway patrolman, and the pattern of movement is abruptly disrupted. Any degree of objectivity that might inform the historical record is similarly dispensed with, and moments in contemporary history (moments that Mr. Victor would have lived through) are shaped and framed by the policeman's rather skewed ideological vision. Here, the indigenous basketball players are treated as anachronistic interlopers before being subjected to a line of questioning that constructs a particularized version of recent historical events. As a result, both the highway and the storied past are sites governed by specific margins and restrictions. The impositions are glaringly evident. As well as generating a sense of pathos, however, it's crucial to recognize the other effect of the story's ending; the young narrator is waiting for a change—a change that, if enacted, would signal the dissolution of colonial domination and restrictive boundary making. Thus, it is possible to say that Alexie's writing has, from the very beginning, sought to draw attention to and "reclaim or remark [...] boundaries."[60]

Indeed, *The Business of Fancydancing* is littered with images of place, distance, and movement. The randomly cited "EDWALL, WASHINGTON—186,000 miles" in "Distances," the voice of the first-person speaker in "Native Hero" who states, baldy, "I can never call the reservation home," the "bus station at the beginning of everything else" and

59   Bruyneel, *The Third Space of Sovereignty*, xix.
60   Ibid.

the "rest stop miles from anywhere red or white, or anything somewhere in between" (both of which feature in the short prose piece "Lottery"), are but a few examples of the author's sustained engagement with spatial constructs. That attention is continued in "Love Hard," where the near confessional speaker tells the listener "In my father/I'll find the hard edges of the earth/where I was raised, dust," and "Indian Boy Love Song (#2)" in which he pleads "Indian women, forgive me./I grew up distant/and always afraid."[61] Importantly enough, images relating to place and distance are central to the prose piece "Translated from the American" and the poem "Transient" as well. In these instances, a striking, and arresting, interplay between spaces, the body, self, tribe, time, and even non-Native culture becomes apparent. The shifts and nuances in the prose piece center on images of interchange, crossover, and (unsurprisingly, given its title) translation. Another van features in this short tale. Unlike the vehicle that carries the basketball team in the opening story, this van isn't crossing state lines. Instead, it takes senior citizens "from powwow to powwow."[62] The passengers and main protagonists are intergenerational, and we learn in the opening three lines that there are three generations present: a mother called Agnes, an unnamed son or daughter, and Joseph, Agnes's grandson. Tensions are running high in the van, which is heading west for The Spokane Tribal Celebration. The main bone of contention appears to be the fact that the unnamed narrator has married a Caucasian and, according to Agnes, left the tribe in order to attend college and "be with the Catholics."[63] Further complications lie in the fact that her offspring cannot speak Salish and her grandson is half white. Both issues only serve to rub salt into the wounds. Significantly enough, the little boy becomes a site of contention between the two older passengers, and the grandparent comments on his looks as the van travels along: "'He still has blue eyes,' [Agnes] said [...]. 'When are they going to change?' she asked."[64] The narrator describes this ongoing line of

61   *The Business of Fancydancing*, 31 & 55.
62   Ibid., 20.
63   Ibid., 21.
64   Ibid., 20.

interrogation as "the only solid question between" them, and refers to it as "the last point after which we both refused the exact." Agnes then describes an unsettling dream that she has, in which she has to cut off Joseph's leg as a result of sudden, exponential growth which results in the boy's body nightmarishly blocking her exit from his bedroom. After recounting the dream she touches her grandson's leg and whispers something in Salish. This simple act angers the unnamed narrator, who insists that she says whatever she is saying in English. When she refuses, the first-person voice says simply: "I began to count mile markers, made mental lists of everything I really needed: a new pair of shoes, a winter coat for the baby, a ticket for a Greyhound traveling back or ahead five hundred years."[65] The first of three references to the bus in this collection, the Greyhound often symbolizes a form of distance and travel that is both geographical and chronological.[66] By tying the "mile markers" to a time before the historical experience of colonial settlement (five hundred years "back") and to the vision of an indigenous future (five hundred years "ahead"), Alexie creates a literary image that appears to simultaneously collapse and expand distance and time; the present is a friable moment that shapes and is shaped by tribal history, continuance *and* change.

It becomes readily apparent that Agnes's entrenched attitude concerning race and her unforgiving traditionalism arise out of a limiting essentialism that potentially alienates her from own children. Yet, it is still the case that the three generations are traveling from one powwow to the next, meeting relatives, gathering "gifts from a thousand cousins" that are "buried in the trunk" of the van.[67] Despite the near total breakdown in communication, and despite the lead protagonist's journey through college, a mixed-race marriage, and life off the reservation, there is, then, an overarching sense of connection and connectedness. That connectedness has, on one level, to do with the deep-rooted bonds that exist behind—and sometimes within—every family's site of discord and hostility; it charts

65   Ibid.
66   Ibid., 20, 32, 60.
67   Ibid., 20.

the embroiled nature of the commonplace mini-tragedies that afflict so many parent and child relationships. On another level, that connectedness arises from a palpable sense of Spokaneness; the unnamed narrator professes to only "half-believing" the power of the Salish name that his mother has given to the child they called Joseph. And even though s/he says that Agnes holds "Joseph tightly against her chest, despite me," the little boy is an interlocutor of sorts; not only does his DNA connect indigenous and Caucasian experiences, but his grandmother's love for him clearly challenges, even supersedes, her essentialized views. Crucially, two key lines are revealed in the final sections of the story. In the first of these the narrator says that "In some small, ordinary way, Indians are still nomadic, always halfway."[68] With a wonderful combination of melancholia, prescience, and pragmatism the speaker presents the journey from the reservation to college to powwow neither as a moment of cosmopolitan, hybridist frontierism, nor as a redemptive return to Spokane values and a landscape tradition.[69] Instead, there is a beautiful logicality and regularity about this trip, which literally brings the protagonists from one reservation town to the next, but which, figuratively speaking, sees them journeying from the reservation to a world where Catholic education, foreign languages, and racial intermarriage are commonplace, and back again. This natural movement is familiar to many readers, culturally specific to the context of the narrative, and, on some level, a political act too. In the first instance, the slightly predictable back and forth argument between a mother and child is likely to be recognizable by a universal readership. It is partly for this reason that Ian Jack, once an editor at *Granta*, is so fond of Alexie's work. "Fiction, if it's any good," Jack writes, "should persuade you of individual and inner lives." Alexie, he continues, is capable of creating characters that are "as complex and odd as everyone else."[70] In the second instance, it's very

68   Ibid., 21.
69   Alexie refers to the landscape tradition in the poem "Spokane Tribal Celebration, September 1987" later on in the collection. There the first-person narrator says "I/ know the only time Indian men/get close to the earth anymore is when Indian men/ pass out and hit the ground." (74).
70   Quoted in Campbell, "Voice of the New Tribes."

much in keeping with a pattern that Thomas King outlines, whereby "a lot of Indians who go off the reserve, who come back to the reserve, who work, who go off the reserve again, who keep going back and forth, and they manage."[71] Furthermore, by pitting the unnamed narrator's wider perspective against Agnes' conservative tribal values, Alexie rehearses the discourse surrounding the fact that "there are a lot of Indian people who buy into that concept that if they leave the reserve they'll never get back"—a conception that King says "just isn't true." Third, although it may not always be easy for Alexie's young protagonists—or King's—to move "back and forth across the institutional and discursive boundaries of settler states," they do so of their own volition and to their own satisfaction.[72] Finally, and perhaps most importantly, this shifting or ranging across borders in no way erodes or abrades what Alexie calls his Spokaneness. When asked by an Indian deputy at the gates to the powwow grounds whether they have "alcohol or drugs in the car," Alexie's nameless narrator replies "We don't have anything except us."[73] This fleeting response underlines the primacy of family, a reliance on the tribal network, and, above all else, a powerful sense of "us."

It is important to note that Alexie compiles a range of voices and experiences in *The Business of Fancydancing*. Although the personal "I" of the poem "Transient" or the "me" of "Father Coming Home" is present throughout the collection, there are distinct moments when an omniscient third-person narrator rises to prominence. Thus, the book offers something that resembles a plurality of perspectives. Yet, regardless of whether the voice addressing the reader is the semi-confessional "I" or that of an unspecified and depersonalized narrator, it is still the case that a particularly effecting set of images, themes, and metaphors occur time and again. Opening with the lines "I would remember you/as the beautiful stranger I saw/only once, on the Greyhound/ shuttling past me at 2 a.m./in the

71   Quoted in Jace Weaver, *That the People Might Live: Native American Literatures and Native American Community* (New York: Oxford University Press, 1997), 150.

72   Bruyneel, *The Third Space of Sovereignty*, 20.

73   *Business of Fancydancing*, 21.

city where I chose to live," the unrhymed poem "Transient" ends with the image of the narrator's demented state and his/her suicide: "You led me to the window that could take in/the whole landscape or the fine edge .../We had come together/to call this space arched in our backs home."[74] Notably, the themes that are central here—traveling, the passing of time, forms of tragedy, and space (particularly geographical and corporeal space)—are evident in the poem "Evolution." Told from an all-knowing, all-seeing point of view, this piece features Buffalo Bill, who "opens a pawn shop on the reservation/right across the border from the liquor store/and [...] stays open 24 hours a day, 7 days a week."[75] Along with their jewelry, televisions, and the other material possessions that they "have to offer," the Indians eventually pawn their "hands [... and] their skeletons." Finally, "when the last Indian has pawned everything/but his heart, Buffalo Bill takes that for twenty bucks," closes the pawn shop and opens "THE MUSEUM OF NATIVE AMERICAN CULTURES."[76] In "Missing" the third-person narrator tells of "A crazy woman from some/reservation" who "finds Crazy Horse [...] fancydancing in the eyes and ears and mouths of Indian boys" who have "government checks every hour punched into their hearts."[77] Flanking Alexie's playfulness with general tropes of Indianness—in the form of "the last Indian" and a ghostly Crazy Horse—is a definite sense of the body as a locus of personal and cultural expression. Alexie's figuring of physicality exceeds, and interrogates, the traditional image of the Indian body as stable object; instead he places the body on historical and spatial borderlines, thereby employing blood, heart, and corporeal materiality as affecting literary symbols for historical suffering and contemporary survivance on both an individual and collective level.

Nowhere is this more obvious than the poem "Giving Blood," which begins with the lines "I need money for the taxi cab ride home to the reservation and/I need a taxi/because all the Indians left this city last night while

74   Ibid., 32–33.
75   Ibid., 48.
76   Ibid.
77   Ibid., 71.

I was/sleeping/and forgot to tell me."[78] A vampirish economic bargaining sees the poem's narrator, "Mr Crazy Horse," craving the "twenty bucks" that the blood bank pays per pint. Reliant on selling himself, quite literally, the poem's narrator describes an extensive, but rather idiosyncratic, screening process that involves him answering questions about having "enough heart." This culminates in the feeding of data into the bank's computer system, and the nurse's confirmation that "we've already taken too much of your blood/and you won't be eligible/to donate for another generation or two."[79] The economic imperative that forces this Indian man into a dire situation resonates with countless other images in the collection— not least the lines in "The Business of Fancydancing" that read "Money/ is a tool, putty to fill all the empty/spaces, a ladder so we can reach/for more .../It's business, a fancydance to fill where it's empty."[80] As is so often the case in Alexie's poetry, enjambment is used to lay particular emphasis on certain abstractions here: currency is underlined and emphasized in the first instance, and is then associated with the emptiness—literal want and hunger—that is often found in reservation spaces. Parity of esteem in financial terms might, therefore, fill the void, the economic black hole, that is present in so many of the pieces in this collection. But, like so many of Alexie's early protagonists, Crazy Horse is broke. Worse still, after being classified and measured, this contemporary Crazy Horse meets a fate similar to that experienced by an earlier generation of tribal peoples (indeed, the fact that he cites June 25, 1876, as his birthday places him within a particular historical context—even if it distances this Crazy Horse from the historical figure born sometime between 1840 and 1845). Unmoored and physically assailed, he is faced with a pseudo-scientific rationale that further diminishes his worth. The leeching of his life's blood is crucial to this erosion of power and importance.

The attention to blood, time, and distance continues through to the final story. Dealing with the same father and son who feature in the opening

---

78 Ibid., 78.
79 Ibid.
80 Ibid., 69.

story, "Gravity" features the homecoming of Junior, one of the Victor
boys. Back from a journey that he reckons has taken more than four years,
Junior is unable to tell, precisely, how long he has been gone. While looking at the dashboard clock he decides that "there must be a new language
for measuring time."[81] He also taps "the odometer, hoping for a vision of
all the miles." In his father's company Junior remembers, and hears, several
stories, and revels in being home. Minor changes have occurred—his father
has glaucoma; the house now has a microwave. These developments are
presented as part of the going on of life; regular, everyday changes that are
folded into the daily routine. Junior's father, referring to the microwave,
jokes knowingly "just a little bit of assimilation, enit?"[82] Significantly, the
second paragraph of "Gravity" reads:

> Every Indian has the blood of tribal memory circling his heart. The Indian, no matter
> how far he travels away, must come back, repeating, joining the reverse exodus. There
> are no exemptions, no time to pull off the highway for food, gas, lodging.[83]

Although blood is a recurring metaphor throughout *The Business of
Fancydancing*, this reference to "the blood of tribal memory" is particularly
explicit, calling to mind not only N. Scott Momaday's phrase "memory in
the blood," but also the positive and negative connotations associated with
this biological concept. In his examination of the tropic value of "blood
memory," Chadwick Allen points out that even though it is the case the
phrase "names both the process and the product of situating oneself within
a particular American Indian family's or nation's 'racial memory,'" it could,
if read "out of context," "distressingly echo[...] Nazi racialist beliefs."[84]
Reading the significance of the biological metaphor a little differently,
Stuart Christie has pointed out that "blood is a doubled figure within
the colonial imaginary" insofar as "it confers the power of an indigenous

---

81   Ibid., 80.
82   Ibid., 83.
83   Ibid., 80.
84   Chadwick Allen, *Blood Narrative: Indigenous Identity in American Indian and Maori
      Literary and Activist Texts* (Durham, NC: Duke University Press, 2002), 98 & 95.

people and its proprietary traditions [...] alongside the potential menace of alienation apart from those same traditions."[85] In Alexie's writing blood is a complex metaphor that speaks to virtually all of these complexities, and "blood memory," in particular, axiomatically refers to a form of cultural memory that often arises out of a historical experience of pain. On this level, blood memory underlines the reality that, to Alexie's mind, "there is no way of knowing" exactly "what an American Indian identity is" anymore, "except perhaps through [indigenous peoples'] pain."[86] As a result, Indians are "always wandering."[87] The gravitational pull that brings Junior back to the reservation arises from a certain sense of the peripatetic, of the author's idea of Spokaneness *and* travel, Indianness *and* universalism, the act of being at home *and* of being away. This detail is underlined when the father produces a scrapbook that purports to tell of his son's journey. Rather than particularize his son's travels in any real way, the book contains newspaper clippings relating to a broad-spectrum of local and national events. One photograph recalls the time "the Seattle high school teachers went on strike"—a happening that is recorded on the basis that Junior "must have read about" it. As it happens, the younger Victor "lived a couple of blocks from a school" and did pass some picketers. The conceit here is that the book isn't the "complete illustrated history of Chief Victor, Junior," as the father jokes it might be, but is, instead, a storybook that frames the Seattle that the Indian passes through. It is, as Junior notes, a book of "possibilities."[88] What follows is a firestorm of remembrances and recollections, amidst which Junior thinks to himself "everything the same by halves, missing only my definition, my naming. Absence is a powerful name, a powerful magic I feel in all the empty spaces in the house where I have not been in so long."[89]

85   Stuart Christie, *Plural Sovereignties and Contemporary Indigenous Literature* (New York: Palgrave Macmillan, 2009), 39.

86   Nygren, "Conversation with Sherman Alexie," 157.

87   Ibid.

88   *The Business of Fancydancing*, 81.

89   Ibid., 82.

It is hardly surprising, then, that Alexie continues his examination
of wandering, heritage, corporeal manifestations, and spatial figurations
in his recent collection of poetry and prose, *Face*. Even less so, when we
consider the fact that he referred to "blood memory" just four short years
before this book appeared in print. Indeed, poems, prose, and mixed-genre
pieces such as "The Father and Son Road Show," "Vilify," "Face," "The Blood
Sonnets," "Scarlet," "Gentrification," and "Ten Thousand Fathers" deal with
these themes and tendencies. By the same token, during the promotional
tours that followed in the wake of *Face* and his subsequent work *War
Dances*, Alexie continued to describe his experience in terms of a journey
that has taken him from the Spokane Indian reservation to "places where
no Spokane Indian has been" and back again. In March 2011 the author
described his well-documented move from the reservation high school to
a new school in Reardan as follows: "It was only 22 miles, geographically.
But I might as well have been Lewis and Clark for the journey it took."[90]
Nine days prior to making that comment Alexie described his journey to
Reardan to an audience at Western Connecticut State University. "When
I walked across the street that was my Atlantic Ocean," Alexie told Enrique
Cerna, "and that school was my Ellis Island. I am an immigrant, and I am
also indigenous."[91] There is, to my mind, a distinct line of continuation
between the biographical reckonings of *The Business of Fancy Dancing* and
the writer's recent works. Hence, even though Jennifer K. Ladino's point
that Alexie has "moved away from dealing strictly with tribal issues" is well
taken, I find it difficult to corroborate her contention that the author's later
work marks both a "geographical shift in Alexie's literary career—away
from reservation life and into the urban sphere" and "an ideological shift, a
turning point in Alexie's own beliefs concerning tribalism."[92] This is partly

90   Sarah T. Williams, "Man of Many Tribes," *Star Tribune* (March 23, 2011) <http://
      www.startribune.com/entertainment/books/11435616.html> accessed March 28
      2012.

91   The author also told Enrique Cerna that Reardan "might as well have been Manhattan"
      (*KCTS 9*).

92   "'A Limited Range of Motion?' Multiculturalism, 'Human Questions,' and Urban
      Indian Identity in Sherman Alexie's *Ten Little Indians*," *Studies in American Indian
      Literatures* 21.3 (Fall 2009), 38.

because I believe that the author is reacting to the *"negative parts* of tribal thinking" rather than tribalism *in toto*.[93] Likewise, I find Åse Nygren's point that the reservation is almost entirely "a geographical space of borders and confinement" in Alexie's earlier work, but has, in more recent times, been recast purely as "a mental and emotional territory," slightly troubling.[94] Alexie was exploring the expressive freedom that accrued from imagining himself to be "in a reservation of [... the] mind" long before he published *Toughest Indian* (he started doing so in 1989). The Spokane/Coeur d'Alene author has *always* sought to cross boundaries, to confound expectations, and to realize a form of personal and aesthetic sovereignty that is informed or underpinned by what he calls his Indianness. In other words, it is important to remember that when Alexie suggests that "the most revolutionary act possible for a Native is to leave the reserve, to pursue your life, to be kinetic, to pursue your identity off the reservation," the "identity" he refers to is still an Indian one. To do otherwise might also elide the material realities of the reservation and conceal the author's personal investment in the tribe; even though Alexie suggests that he might have "betrayed" his tribe, he continues to visit the reservation "every month" and continues to be "very aware" of his Spokaneness.[95] Moreover, even though Alexie has escaped what he sees as being a certain strain of fundamentalist dogma on the

93 During his 2003 conversation with Duncan Campbell, the author described how it had been his desire to marry a Native American woman, thereby paraphrasing the lines from the collection of poetry *One Stick Song*, in which he writes: "I made a very conscious decision to marry an Indian woman, who made a very conscious decision to marry me. Our hope: to give birth to and raise Indian children who love themselves. That is the most revolutionary act" (17). When Campbell raises the question of whether or not Alexie and his wife, Diane, expect their two boys to follow suit Alexie answers: "Of course, we would prefer it. But the only thing I can be assured of is that they will probably partner with people who like books," before adding, "Maybe that's the new tribe."

94 Nygren writes: "While in Alexie's early fiction, the reservation is a geographical space of borders and confinement, in his more recent fiction, *The Toughest Indian in the World* (2000) and *Ten Little Indians* (2003), the reservation changes its ontology and becomes a mental and emotional territory" (150–151).

95 Interview by Ross Frank; Nygren, "A World of Story-Smoke".

Spokane Indian reservation (a dogma that he rebelled against from a very early age) his writing is still deeply informed by his Spokaneness; indeed, Alexie's tribal heritage continues to be a crucial element in his scrutiny of the interface between American and Indian culture. Consequently, Alexie's most recent work continues his erstwhile interrogation of American borders, albeit from a broader, more autonomous perspective. For this reason, even though Nygren and Ladino rightly point out that Alexie is, by his own admission, "no longer a reservation Indian" and has "worked hard since [9/11] to shed *the negative parts of tribal thinking*," we must be wary of suggesting that his writing, or his personal circumstance, exhibits a tidy, linear, one-directional trajectory that runs from reservation to urban, tribal fundamentalism to "polyculturalism," or "from angry protests to evocations of love and empathy."[96] In fact, I would argue that *Face* exhibits a very similar concern with sites of inquiry and exploration, mutation and tension, and that this is made possible by Alexie's stunning ability to bring reservation and urban spaces into contact in his poetry and prose.

"War Stories," a cross-genre piece that features in the opening section of *Face* and shares a title with Part 1 of the book, deals with the perplexed nature of contemporary life in exactly this way. In terms of form, the piece is divided into two poetic sections—the second of which is presented as a series of footnotes to the first—and three paragraphs in prose, which are effectively footnotes to the second of the two poetic sections. This structure or, more properly, contrivance, allows Alexie to present the reader with a succession of complexities and clarifications that are both ironic on some level, and underline the complexity of history, cultural presence, legal definition, and storytelling in the present moment. Comprised of six stanzas written largely in terza rima form (there is some variation), the interrelated poems deal with violence, perspective, insight, and grief. Alexie's trademark deployment of enjambment, through which he often blindsides

96   Jennifer K. Ladino, "'A Limited Range of Motion?' Multiculturalism, 'Human Questions,' and Urban Indian Identity in Sherman Alexie's *Ten Little Indians*," *Studies in American Indian Literatures* 21.3 (Fall 2009), 38; Sarah T. Williams, "Man of Many Tribes" (emphasis added); Nygren, "A World of Story-Smoke", 151.

the reader, is used to serve up some deliciously shocking moments. For instance the rather unremarkable deed described in the opening line, in which the narrator claims to have "an uncle who punched a man's eye," is revealed to have been rather more appalling than it first appears when one reads the second sentence and discovers that the blow knocked the man's eye "Straight out of his skull."[97] That same sentence also carries some sense of retribution, and possibly further horror, since the narrator explains "My uncle died."[98] But once again, the enjambed structure provides a snapper, since the third line relates the fact that the uncle died "Young," rather than as a result of the fight. And so it goes. Crucially, the linearity of the narrative/story that the poem tells may or may not be immediately disrupted by the placement of a footnote at the end of the second sentence. At this point, a slightly more curious, or possibly more discerning reader, might scan the tercet note and read the narrator's confession that the aggressor "wasn't really my uncle. I lied." By offering an alternate third line to the first poem's opening stanza, the poet comments on veracity and truth while simultaneously closing off the rhyming scheme. The reader, meanwhile, has a hand in forming this alternate tercet through an independent, and interactive, readerly act. This, in turn, raises questions about interpretation and perspective; how we choose to regard things is consequently under scrutiny. Do we, as reader, decide to read the remaining stanzas of the second poem at this point, thereby cutting to the heart of the story? Or do we return to the first poem in the knowledge that the uncle is a fictitious character, but that the "one-eyed man" may (or may not) have been on the receiving end of the "real" cousin's punch? Either way, any precepts or presumptions that the reader may have been following or may have held are likely to have been upset at this point.

This interruption or disruption of the poem's inner narrative comments on the way in which we see things or make discoveries. Accordingly, the interpolation offered by the presence of footnotes ties in with the overall theme of "War Stories": point of view. The eighty-five year old

97   *Face*, 18.
98   Ibid.

man who is minus one eyeball explains to the narrator how the trauma
of his loss, and his monocular state thereafter, paradoxically offered him
a greater depth of understanding, a depth of interior vision: "Before your
uncle's punch, I was closed and cruel,/But now I see more with one eye
than two./I had to lose some sense to get sense."[99] The old man's wisdom,
which arises out of his newfound understanding of the futility of conflict
and, subsequently, a greater sense of compassion and understanding, is
emblematized in "the beauty of grief" mentioned in the final lines of this
first poem. The fact that the half-blind victim would "sing/An honor
song" for the speaker's uncle were it not for the fact that he "got no voice"
serves to reinforce the notion of a beautiful grief. And were it not for the
information offered by way of footnotes, this first six stanza poem might
end with this single, thought-provoking image of struggle and maturation. The full work, which is both poems and the prose piece, discloses
information that spurs further thought and consideration however. In
the first instance, footnote "1" reveals the identity of the one-eyed man;
the narrator's cousin explains that "There was a war on the rez/In those
days./ It was always self-defense/When any rez boys maimed any white
men.ª" Suddenly, the fight and its aftermath is seen from a number of
different angles: the original fracas was interracial; the main protagonists still live on the reservation where the tension existed; respect for
the honor song, newfound perspective, and an appreciation for grief is
cross-cultural. Intriguingly, note "a"—which follows on from the passage
of direct speech attributed to the speaker's cousin—sets out the basics of
State of Washington Law 9A.16.050. Thus, if one takes the opportunity to
read each footnote in succession, thereby breaking (or perhaps following)
the natural order of the poem/prose, then the fundamentalist, militant
attitude of the "rez boys" becomes associable with conservative American
values that prioritize the right to bear arms. At this point, the narrator,
rather ironically, poses the question: "So, in defending his Indian-ness,
was my cousin practicing a form of self-defense?" Before venturing an
opinion, the unnamed first-person narrator mentions the "innumerable

99   Ibid., 18.

beatings [that his cousin has] given to white and Indian guys alike."[100] After emphasizing the fact that the cousin doesn't always discriminate when choosing his targets, the speaker rationalizes that "violent men will always find logical and rational and emotional and compelling ways to justify their violence."[101] Another meeting point between Indian valor and war making on one hand and militarization and brutality on the other is established in footnote "2," which consists of two stanzas in the second poem that deal with issues arising in the first poem. Describing the honor song, the speaker explains:

> We Indians love to sing songs about death;
> We celebrate war's length and depth and breadth;
> We sing more about the life that comes next
>
> Than the one we live now. And we proudly
> Carry the flag of this brutal country
> And never fret about that irony.[b]

By honing in on both the cultural specificity of the honor song and the somewhat incongruous image of Indians fighting under the United States flag—sometimes at the behest of the military-industrial complex—Alexie revels, once again, in the "contradictions [...] the successive generations of social, political and artistic mutations that can be so beautiful and painful."[102] The poem swirls around various locations, offering commentary on local conflicts and international wars in a voice that ranges from the sardonic to the acquiescent. Alexie's position allows him to appreciate various perspectives, and "War Stories," like so many of his poems, searches out alternate viewpoints. For instance, in footnote "b" the poet refers to the "war veterans' dance" that is held at every powwow that takes place in the "rez arena" of a "Holiday Inn conference room," and forthrightly states "I understand why we do that. I respect their service and sacrifice."[103] He then

---

100   Ibid., 19.
101   Ibid.
102   "What Sacagawea Means to Me (and Perhaps to You)." Online.
103   *Face*, 20.

constructs another image, one in which the powwower starts "an honor dance for those Indian men (and women) who refused to go to war," for, in the words of the imaginary emcee, "all those Indians who have never picked up a gun."[104]

Alexie's dramatizations of his position as that of "the genocided Indian who is also the dream-filled refugee," a poet who is "indigenous to the land but an immigrant into the culture," places him, more or less, in the position of the exile.[105] The late Edward Said believed that, whereas the majority of "people are principally aware of one culture, one setting, one home," the exile is "aware of at least two" spaces. That awareness, Said continues, creates a "plurality of vision [that] gives rise to an awareness of simultaneous dimensions, an awareness that [...] is contrapuntal."[106] Meshing quite easily with the author's recent point that "Native American life is bipolar [... to] be colonized is to be bipolar," the doubling that Alexie imagines is libratory rather than divisive, a site of enunciation rather than of splitting.[107] Hence, even though Alexie admits that he feels compelled to despise America and its troubling incongruities—"as a Native American, I want to hate this country and its contradictions"—he displays a wonderful ability to perceive, and interpret, what the Irish poet John Montague calls "the many voices, agreeable and disturbing, which haunt [the] land."[108] Significantly, in his compelling study of Montague's poetry, the Irish American scholar and poet Daniel Tobin argues that his subject possesses a "migratory mind," and, as a result, his poetry:

---

104 Ibid.
105 Ibid., 27.
106 Edward Said, *Reflections on Exile and Other Essays* (Cambridge, MA: Harvard University Press, 2000), 186.
107 Paul Steinmetz, "Sherman Alexie shakes up university crowd" (March 22, 2011) <http://blog.ctnews.com/steinmetz/2011/03/22/sherman-alexie-shakes-up-university-crowd> accessed March 26, 2012.
108 John Montague, "The Unpartitioned Intellect," in *Irish Writers and Society at Large*, ed. Masaru Sekine, Irish Literary Studies 22 (Totowa, NJ: Barnes and Noble, 1985), 167.

unites order and chaos, identity and difference, the history of his own province and the metaphysics of the universe, within a single reality that can be expressed only as a *coincidentia oppositorum*, a communion of opposites.[109]

Alexie's writing arises out of a similar ability to construct a *coincidentia oppositorum*; his kineticism simultaneously brings him into contact with the energizing elements of a globalized world and creates a sense of exile or "sadness" that he says Native Americans "celebrate." The piece "Vilify," and the footnotes to it, exemplify this pattern. There the first-person narrator satirically analyses the political, cultural, and, to some extent, spatial dynamic created by the epic sculpture of four American presidents on the face of Mount Rushmore. The first of the five tercets quickly lampoons the heroic grandeur of the site by opening with the lines "I've never been to Mount Rushmore. It's just too silly" and continuing "even now, as I write this, I'm thinking/About the T-shirt that has four presidential faces on the front and four bare asses/on the back."[110] The first and second lines of the poem become the refrain that is repeated alternatively throughout the poem, thereby reinforcing the idea that the sculpture is a ludicrous and absurd gesture, while the vision of the "four bare asses" of America's "fathers" chimes with pop-cultural parody of the nation's heroic past. The rough treatment that is meted out to sixteen of the United States' forty-three presidents (all of whom had, according to the speaker, "a heart chewed by rats") is tempered somewhat by the first line of the second tercet: "Don't get me wrong. I love my country."[111] In much the same way, a form of rhetorical opposition is fabricated when the levity offered by the thoughts of "four bare asses" and the gossipy reference to "JFK's whoring and drinking" is contrasted by the darkness of the final tercet. There the poet plaintively asks: "Answer me this: After the slaughterhouse goes out of business,[12] how long/will it go on stinking/Of red death and white desire? Should we just

---

109 Daniel Tobin, *Awake in America: On Irish American Poetry* (Notre Dame, IN: Notre Dame University Press, 2011), 117 & 130.

110 *Face*, 29.

111 Ibid.

cover the/presidents' faces with gas masks?"[112] The antithetical images offered within the poem are perhaps best understood in light of the first footnote to "Vilify." Here Alexie explains that even though the villanelle has, more often than not, been employed as a means to "express the painful and powerful repetitions of grief" he has, in fact, "tried to write a grief-filled villanelle that is also funny."[113] Used in this way humor becomes, in Alexie's own words, "a temporary visa" that not only allows him access to audiences that indigenous writers might not otherwise reach, but also permits the poet to map out—and the reader to explore—the complex territory(-ies) that tribal and non-tribal communities inhabit in contemporary America. The poem's consideration of these complexities is furthered not only in Alexie's footnoted reference to "Native Americans [who] are notoriously and ironically patriotic" to America, but also his discussion of the "gorgeous and grotesque" character of America's presidents, and his musings on the fact that a former CIA agent who was involved in the assassination of Robert Kennedy might have been half Apache.

Above all else, the poem "Vilify" (along with its footnotes) reminds us of the body politic; in corporealizing the nation's history Alexie refers not only to the presidents' heads and asses, but also the physical and moral weaknesses that drove them to blood-spattered duels, slave-holding, extramarital affairs, and, of course, genocide of the nation's indigenous peoples. Crucially, the mutations and (re)formations that appear in this, and several other poems, are posed as anxieties that exist within the very DNA of modern America. Significantly, certain aspects of these bodily sites, or, more specifically, Alexie's personalized narrative approach to these sites, might remind the reader of Gerald Vizenor's identification of a "tension within the blood."[114] Although Vizenor is referring to the figure of the Métis in particular, and is therefore more concerned with mixedbloodedness than Alexie, his image of an individual who is "both white and tribal,

112   Ibid., 30.
113   Ibid.
114   Quoted in Jace Weaver, *Other Words: American Indian Literature, Law, and Culture* (Norman: University of Oklahoma Press, 2001), 36.

an uncertain creator in an urban metaphor based on a creation myth that preceded him in two world views and oral traditions" could be an exposition of several of Alexie's characters, and perhaps even the author himself. Significantly, even though certain scholars, most notably James Ruppert, have stressed the mediatory aspect of functioning in two contexts, the tribal and the non-tribal, and have suggested that Native writers function in two contexts, others have pointed out difficulties with seeing bicultural residency in simple, untroubled terms. For instance, Jace Weaver has reminded readers that indigenous writers often find themselves in an "unstable location," a place where they are "at once liminal and littoral to two ways of being and knowing."[115] While Weaver's sense of being adrift or unmoored may not, at first glance, appear to interconnect with Alexie's vision of himself as an artist who consciously adopts a kinetic style, it is, nevertheless, very much in keeping with the Spokane author's description of "being an Indian writer or artist of any form these days."[116] In the twenty-first-century United States, Native writers are, Alexie explains, "always working in two very mutually exclusive roles, as an Indian writer and a writer," and there are "a lot of conflicts" created by the friction between these two roles.[117] Crucially, Alexie *mobilizes* those conflicts, forcing the reader to accompany him back and forth across cultural, historical, geographic, and imaginative spaces; to look on as the author works back and forth against the grain. In this way, his rezoning of creative and racial territories coheres with a form of hybridism that Weaver describes as a moment of "subversion," one in which "the Indian reader becomes," by times, "the insider, privileged, empowered," while "the *métropole* is pushed to the periphery."[118] In the poem "Introduction to Native American Literature" Alexie refers to indigenous and non-indigenous spaces in order to make exactly this point. The opening line "Somewhere in America a television explodes" establishes a national frame of reference before giving way to allusions to "the reservation landfill,"

---

115 Ibid.
116 Interview by Ross Frank.
117 Ibid.
118 Weaver, *Other Words*, 37.

"anonymous corner bars," and a "city [that] runs over itself" by the free-
way.[119] Most importantly, the narrator (presumably Alexie himself) states,
for the record, "Because you have seen the color of my bare skin/does not
mean that you have memorized the shape of my ribcage." And when the
reader comes to "ask forgiveness," Alexie writes, Native American literature
will give them "a 10% discount."[120] He counterpoints indigenous grief with
well-intentioned—but ineffective—liberal guilt. Subsequently, the reader
is exiled, unforgiven, and made to feel isolated and exteriorized. In this way,
the "*métropole* is pushed to the periphery, made liminal ... in the same way
that a non-Native town may exist on the border of a reservation."[121] In this
moment the author materializes individual and collective experiences, and
does so by referring to a "body" of fiction and the creative and readerly
sites in which the literature resides.

    Anthony Purdy argues that the body is often seen as "a primary site
of ideological inscription," which, in literature and criticism, is used to "1)
decentre or disrupt the mind/body hierarchy; 2) to ground criticism in
the local, the historical and the concrete; and 3) to enable the production
of discursive resistances or transgressions that strategically *re*-figure the
body."[122] Whether it is in the memory of a boy "pissing/From the top" of
a wheat silo, a girlfriend whose "breasts and belly—/Are just as golden/As
the summer wheat," or of being "the rez Hamlet who missed/His father so
much that he bled red ghosts," Alexie exhibits a profound interest in the
physical inscriptions that Purdy refers to. Often, as in the poem "Wheat,"
he links personal and physical space. There, the poet's reminiscences about
one childhood friend relieving himself and his own early sexual encounters
are followed by the memory of sprinting "into [...] barbed wire" during an
attempt to get away from the local cops, but escaping "Bloody but mostly
unhurt."[123] By mapping out experiences on the body, Alexie establishes a

119 *Face*, 4.
120 Ibid.
121 Weaver, *Other Words*, 37.
122 Anthony Purdy, *Literature and the Body*, ed. Anthony Purdy (Amsterdam: Rodopi,
     1992), 5.
123 *Face*, 44.

palpable sense of what Purdy calls "the local, the historical and the concrete." Providing something of a bridge between the hazy memories of childhood and the poem's conclusion—in which Alexie claims that it was by roaming in the neighbors' wheat fields "step by step, row by row" that he "learned how to escape"—the image of the "bloody" boy "Concealed/In that wheat field" complicates the earlier reverie. More importantly, it forms a bridge to the final section of the poem, in which a level of searing introspection undercuts the poet's earliest, almost quixotic, recollections even further. "As a child, I was surrounded/By wheat fields. Isolated,/I often felt small and rhymeless."[124] Whilst it's not quite a transgression, there is something of a refiguring of the indigenous body in the poem's final line; perhaps tilting against the notion of an indigenous landscape tradition and/or a sense of belonging, the poet learns how to "escape." Yet, for all of the talk of moving on, and moving out, this poem is rooted in Spokane, and, as a result, it is emblematic of Alexie's constant creative choice to return to that space. It is also reflective of the author's conviction that "there are two stories: the story of home and the story of leaving home. That's all. That's all that exists in the world. Every novel, every poem, every movie is about that."[125] After paraphrasing Salman Rushdie's point that home is the basis for all narratives, Alexie added: "I just have an Indian spin on that and a Spokane Indian spin at that."[126] His words point, once again, to a particular vision of the local and the universal; Spokane and "places where no Spokane Indian has been." I would suggest, then, that Sherman Alexie has a deep sense of the writer's residency in the contemporary world, and quite possibly shares the view once articulated by Flannery O'Connor:

> When we talk about the writer's country we are liable to forget that no matter what particular country it is, it is inside as well as outside him [...]. To know oneself is to know one's region. It is also to know the world, and it is also, paradoxically, a form

124 Ibid, 45.
125 Interview by Ross Frank.
126 Ibid.

of exile from that world. The writer's value is lost, both to himself and to his country, as soon as he ceases to see that country as a part of himself.[127]

What we see in *Face*, then, is a continuation of the concerns found in Alexie's earliest work; namely, a concern with the Spokane Indian reservation and the act of leaving the Spokane Indian reservation. Universal themes and tales of distant places orbit around this specific axis, even as the author's vision of the wider world often allows him to reinterpret the reservation. In "March Madness" Alexie offers another take on the villanelle, and attempts to explore the epic tragedy associated with sporting endeavor. In his treatment of UCLA's legendary 2006 NCAA basketball tournament win over their rivals Gonzaga, the poet ends the first, third, and seventh tercets with the word "haunted," and the second, fourth, and sixth tercets with "wanted." Initially capturing the unpredictable and exhilarating nature of a single elimination tournament that often brings out almost superhuman effort from the college players, Alexie recalls the infamous moment when J.P. Batista narrowly missed an opportunity to win the game in the dying seconds: "When Batista missed the shot, I wanted/To punch God."[128] The theological (and often comical) rumination that the poet indulges in during the first six tercets comes to an abrupt end in the seventh tercet however, when the poem moves from despair about sport to an altogether more affecting form of desolation. "I'm haunted," Alexie writes, "By missed shots and missing fathers."[129] In this moment the "Shakespearean comedy/And tragedy of the NCAA" is personalized and particularized in the image of the father's absence. Harking back to the basketball scene between Junior and his father in *The Business of Fancydancing*, "March Madness" has an almost confessional tone, through which Alexie remembers his father and, by proxy, remembers his childhood on the reservation. Once again, he corporealizes those memories. In the first of seven two-line stanzas that bring the poem to its rhythmic conclusion, Alexie writes: "My father, my

127   Flannery O'Connor, *Mystery and Manners: Occasional Prose* (New York: Farrar, Straus, & Giroux, 1969), 35.
128   *Face*, 137.
129   Ibid., 138.

drum, you were the all-star/Of hopeless and blood and orphan and scar." The next stanza reads: "My father, my drum, you were the all-star/Of hook shot, and broken tooth and wrecked cars."[130] While the references to blood, teeth and scars undoubtedly materializes the poet's personal relationship with his father—and does so in a rather explicit fashion—it also gestures towards the "alcoholism, self-destructive behaviour, poverty ... and the breach between generations" that Penny Petrone believes to be the "real problems in the lives and tragedies of Indians today."[131]

The image of the body as a physical space upon which cultural and political experiences are mapped out, as a kinetic entity, and as a site of inherited borders and genetic exchange in contemporary America is prevalent throughout *Face*. "Scarlet," a poem that hinges on the "torrential" acne of a young, otherwise pretty, female barista, questions the nature of loveliness at the outset. Although "Whatever potential/She has for beauty has been obscured/by ... open wounds which resemble burns," the woman has striking turquoise eyes and an "alto voice/[that] belongs onstage or in the studio."[132] Alexie dismantles the barrier between himself and the anonymous cafe worker, whose race or origins are unknown, by declaring "This scarred woman forces me to remember/That my skin was nearly as pocked and razed."[133] Even though the young poet "didn't live in a first-world city," which the barista does, he locates common ground, insofar as he recognizes that she too is "uninsured and untreated."[134] Of far greater importance, however, is the fact that he sees her "use a fingernail to attack" her own skin, and realizes that the young woman—like the poet—"digs and digs at what wounds her."[135] "Estranged from the tribe that offers protection,/What happens to the soul that hates its reflection," Alexie asks in the final moment, thereby locating a line of connection between urban exiles even while he differentiates between the site of origins and emphasizes the realities of his Spokane

130 Ibid.
131 Quoted in Weaver, *Other Words*, 41.
132 *Face*, 63.
133 Ibid.
134 Ibid., 64.
135 Ibid.

childhood. A specific pain leads to a common malaise. In "Song Son Blue,"
a poem that may remind the reader of Langston Hughes's themes as well
as his bebop rhyming scheme, Alexie links his recently "shorn hair" to the
death of his father—again returning to motifs concerning the body, individual interiority, and the haunting that arises out of his relationship with
his father. In this piece, which directly follows "Scarlet," the expectations,
and discourtesy, of certain members of Alexie's non-Native readership are
ridiculed, and the author takes direct issue with "the casual racism" of the
"rude assholes" who find his short haircut to be "'so corporate.'"[136] As well
as pointing out his readers' failure to recognize that, for many tribes, the
cutting of one's hair is a sign of mourning, Alexie takes the opportunity to
use a punchy, almost rap-style lyric to forcefully demonstrate the "sacred
despair" that the physical change signifies.[137] Once again he accentuates
the friction that occurs when cultures and basic cultural differences are
brought into contact, and does so by paradoxically cursing *and* absolving
those "few fans who somehow dare/To ask [...] about [his] shorn hair."[138]

    "The Blood Sonnets" and "Tuxedo with Eagle Feathers" continue
this interrogation of personal and social spaces, and are, perhaps, two of
the more arresting poems in the collection. In the first of the "The Blood
Sonnets" the author makes yet another reference to the absent father; the
figure about whom one character in *The Toughest Indian in the World* says:
"I lifted my father and carried him across every border."[139] Thus, the father
who "would leave,/drinking,/for weeks" that is mentioned by the young
Alexie in *The Business of Fancydancing*, is every bit as preoccupying for
the forty-something author. Opening with the lines "When my father left
me (and my mother/And siblings), to binge-drink for days and weeks,/I
always wept myself into nosebleeds," "The Blood Sonnets" is a poem about
"absence" and loss; the author recalls a "Drunk daddy [... who] hit the

136   Ibid., 65.
137   *American Indian Religious Traditions: An Encyclopaedia*, ed. Suzanne J. Crawford
     and Dennis F. Kelley (Santa Barbara, CA: AB-CLIO, 2005).
138   *Face*, 65.
139   Sherman Alexie, *The Toughest Indian in the World* (New York: Grove/Atlantic, 2001),
     238.

road" and a son who missed him "so much that he bled red ghosts."[140] In the closing lines of the second sonnet, the poet acknowledges the fact that he is "separated/By my gender," from his friend Ellen, but claims, in the rhyming couplet, to have been created "By my mother's blood, so I am, by birth,/A part of all women's blood and mirth."[141] Once again working with metaphors for partition and federation, distinction and connection, Alexie finds in the "mother's blood" a source of union that facilitates empathy and understanding. Intriguingly, he also revisits, once again, the wheat fields where he brought his first love, and describes the loss of his virginity. This event was, the poet recalls, marked by a particularly frantic, angst ridden moment when he ejaculated and realized that his "sperm was racing toward her egg."[142] In a typical moment of comi-tragedy, Alexie describes the girl's attempts to arrest the progress of the sperm who have been unbound and are now uncontrollable: "She pushed me away with her hands and legs,/Basketball-muscled, then climbed out the door,/And jumped up and down in the muddy snow/In a Chaplinesque attempt to abort/What we had not conceived./I drove her home."[143] This journey into the Spokane wheat-fields, and adolescent rite of passage, is also marked in blood; the narrator explaining that the young girl's parents "ignored the bloodstains" that had formed on their daughter's grey pants by the time she returned home. In the final sonnet images of earth and blood are dramatically tied to the anguish associated with the absent father. "With six shovels, my six cousins bury/My father's coffin in gravel and mud," Alexie writes, "Then hug my grief-smacked mother (now married/To dirt) and leave her coat covered with blood."[144] The poignant portrayal of the mother as a woman who is given to the earth is especially striking, as is the notion that she is marked by the familial blood that comes from her nephews' "blistered hands." Rather than compose a scene of funereal silence, eternal rest, or stoic forbearance, Alexie focuses on "grief, obscene/And malodorous, sticky to the touch."

140　Ibid., 48.
141　*Face*, 49.
142　Ibid., 50.
143　Ibid.
144　Ibid.

On many levels, the hard reality of his father's passing, which signals an end to a long life of alcoholism, diabetes, and personal strife, is by far the worst in a long line of deaths and moments of grief on the Spokane reservation. A reminder not only of his sister's funeral following her death in a house fire—a funeral that he writes about in *The Absolute True Diary of a Part-Time Indian*—the ritual surrounding the father's burial is a physical battle, one that takes place amidst mud and blood: "This is grief, one shovel punch/To my teeth, one punch to my mother's neck [...]. Grief, you killer, riddler, giver of tests."[145] Finally, there is an entreaty to the almost personified figure that is Grief, when the poet asks, plaintively, "If we lie with our father in the mud,/Will you make us a gift out of his blood?"

Images of land and death as elements that shape both personal and cultural experiences and perspectives is continued in "Tuxedo with Eagle Feathers," in which Alexie writes: "I've been to dozens of funerals and wakes;/I've poured dirt into 100 graves."[146] In this "hybrid sonnet sequence," which mixes poetry and prose, the poet once again exhibits his dual concern with Spokane and Seattle, family and self, tribalism and individualism, heartache and hopefulness, comedy and tragedy. In the opening lines Alexie recalls a powwow that he attended "six years ago, or maybe [...] eight or ten" in Spokane, Washington.[147] Over the course of the gentle introduction he mentions several constituents of bucolic tribal gatherings— "fry bread," "dancers," his "mother and aunts" telling "highly sacred dirty jokes." The reverie is shattered when the poet encounters "The man who, as a boy, bullied [him]—/Who screamed, 'You ain't no fucking better/than the rest of us Skins!'"[148] Delivered in a punchy four line stanza that counterpoints the restful atmosphere created by the prose introduction, the lines of poetry inject a sense of urgency and perhaps even menace. Yet, there is a certain pathos evident in the following lines, and it quickly becomes evident that the childhood bully has succumbed to the wretched life of

145 Ibid.
146 Ibid., 80.
147 Ibid., 79.
148 Ibid.

the alcoholic; not merely a faceless, stock figure—the drunken reduced to selling eagle feathers in the powwow grounds. On the contrary, this man is one of Alexie's own, a tribal member who has lost his way; his alcoholism and the social toll of that illness is particularized and qualified in a way that exceeds the earlier representations of Indian drunkenness that the Spokane author has been criticized for. As well as establishing a rounded, albeit slightly tarnished, sense of the powwow, the interaction between the two men also sets the scene for a crucial consideration of tribal politics and culture. Out of "pity" Alexie buys the feathers, pondering on the fact that he is "the rich and famous writer" while the other man is, quite simply, "a drunk." Yet, it is not just his status as a writer of world renown that distinguishes his fate from that of his one-time tormentor. Indeed, "there have been plenty of rich and famous drunk writers." Instead, it is his sobriety that separates him from his "drunken childhood and [...] drunken profession." Significantly, he goes on to suggest "my sobriety gives me sovereignty," and explains that even though "most Indians use 'sovereignty' to refer to the collective and tribal desire for political, cultural, and economic independence," he is using it to mean "The individual Indian artist's basic right to be an eccentric bastard.'"[149] In direct and excoriating prose Alexie specifies his intention to brandish his version of sovereignty as a weapon to "attack Elizabeth Cook-Lynn, the Sioux Indian writer and scholar who":

> Has written, with venomous wit,
> That Skins shouldn't write autobiography.
> She believes that "tribal sovereignty"
> Should be our ethos. But I call that bullshit!
>
> My tribe tried to murder me—[150]

According to Alexie, indigenous sovereignty "is never about culture," but is, instead, always about economic sovereignty.[151] "Native American

---

149 Ibid.
150 Ibid., 80.
151 Joshua Nelson, "'Humor Is My Green Card': A Conversation with Sherman Alexie", *World Literature Today* (July–August 2010), 41.

sovereignty," he explains, "is expressed in terms of casinos, cigarettes, fireworks [... and] the worst parts of capitalism." Worse still, he continues,
a particular strain of "anti-intellectualism on Indian reservations, inside
Indian communities" usually results in leaders of multi-million-dollar
tribal corporations going "out into the business world without high school
diplomas."[152] In essence, Alexie draws a line of continuance between the
social and cultural problems faced by the tribes and what he calls the
"ugly fundamentalism" associated with Cook-Lynn's rigid and prescriptive version of tribal sovereignty.[153] His solution to these interconnected
problems—fundamentalism and poverty—is education and "economic
advancement."[154] "If you study what separates me,/The survivor, from the
dead and car-wrecked,/Then you'll learn that my literacy/saved my ass," he
writes in "Tuxedo with Eagle Feathers," before declaring "I wasn't saved by
the separation of cultures; I was *reborn* inside the collision of cultures."[155]

Having spent the first two sections of the poem examining life on the
Spokane Indian reservation (both the positives and the negatives), he then
expends considerable time and energy considering the work of Dorothy
Grant, the First Nations fashion designer whose luxurious clothing company aims "to share the richness of the Haida culture, to create a vehicle
for transformation, pride and self-awareness, and to employ First Nations
people."[156] In a subtle but notable inversion of images that appear earlier
on in the sonnet, Alexie refers to tribal emblems and how they are used:
"O, Dorothy Grant, who blends traditional Haida symbol and imagery
with twenty-first-century fashion. O, Dorothy Grant, who makes tuxedos with gorgeous eagle ravens flying up the lapels."[157] By juxtaposing the
bully's rather abysmal prostituting of the eagle feather at the powwow with
Grant's empowered, and empowering, reformulation of ancient signs, Alexie
underscores not only the rewards associable with this kind of profitable

152   Ibid.
153   *Face*, 80.
154   Nelson, "'Humor Is My Green Card'," 41.
155   *Face*, 80.
156   www.dorothygrant.com.
157   *Face*, 80.

innovation, but he also celebrates the continuance of indigenous culture through original and imaginative practices. Furthermore, there may well be something of a bridge created by the description of the "beautiful young women shaking their jingles" in the opening lines of this piece, and Alexie's account of Grant's chic clothing lines later on in the poem. Taken together, these images offset—even outweigh—the grimmer aspects of reservation life, and suggest a wider set of opportunities to Native readers. Importantly, Alexie's account of meeting Grant in a "Target parking lot in Albuquerque," where she meets him so that he can try one of her tuxedos on for size, relates a shared sense of humor and cultural understanding; as it happens "Dorothy Grant's gorgeous clothes did not fit," a fact that results in author and fashion designer swapping jokes about the appearance of indigenous men, and about the realities of tribal life. "'Looks like you've had a little too much commodity cheese,' Dorothy said and laughed."[158] The Spokane author then explains to the readers that he's "built like a chicken"—a "big shouldered man with a belly and thin legs." Grant's quick witted response is that her clothes are designed with Indian men in mind and are, therefore, "all sized for giant human chickens."[159] As well as demonstrating a form of black humor (possibly even survivor's humor given that Alexie refers to himself as "The survivor" earlier in the poem), and revealing a shared understanding between these two contemporary Indian artists, the scene speaks about cultural, geographical, and historical borders. The hybridized sonnet form that Alexie is inspired to write as a result of having held Grant's finely tailored suit in his hands, is, he writes, "An indigenous celebration of colonialism or maybe a colonial celebration of the indigenous."[160] In this, rather paradoxical, vision of indigenous art, Alexie proposes a poetic salute not to the processes that resulted in the genocide of tribal peoples, but rather the contemporary Indian's ability to mobilize creative and inventive responses to the current situation; to take experiences of life, both on and off the reservation, and quite literally refashion them in a way that makes

158   *Face*, 81.
159   Ibid.
160   Ibid.

sense to, and inspires, other indigenous peoples, while also assuring Native peoples' place in the modern world. Here, the cultural specificity of the "highly sacred dirty jokes" told by the poet's aunts or the Haida influence behind Grant's fashion lines are neither threatened nor devalued by broader American culture. As Alexie then writes:

> This sonnet, like my reservation, keeps
> Its secrets hidden behind boundaries
> That are simple and legal at first read
> (Fourteen lines that rhyme, two rivers that meet,
>
> Poem and water joined at one confluence).[161]

As well as acknowledging necessary "boundaries" and "legal" rights, Alexie is keen to note that "colonialism's influence/Is fluid and solid, measurable/ And mad," and insists upon the artist's right to cross borders, examine convergences, and avail of every opportunity find new forms of expression.[162] It is this insistence that seems to elicit the Spokane writer's considerable frustration at what he perceives as Cook-Lynn's overly prescriptive vision of "tribal sovereignty."

Sherman Alexie's claim that he fled the reservation in "a '56 Chevy" ("the indigenous version of the *Mayflower*") in order to escape "religious persecution" is, perhaps, a little dramatic.[163] Indeed, given that the opening lines of "Tuxedo with Eagle Feathers," like countless other poems and stories, portray a definite affection for home and a continued relationship with the Spokane Indian reservation, it may even be possible to interpret the author's tale of "persecution" as emanating from what he himself describes as his "binary, pathological, lying nature."[164] Whatever the case may be, his writing has always been shaped by a profound interest in the borders and crossings associated both with life *on* the reservation and the acts of *leaving* and *returning* to the reservation. The "aboriginal chance" that his wife

161   Ibid., 81.
162   Ibid., 82.
163   Nelson, "'Humor Is My Green Card,'" 42.
164   Ibid, 43.

Diane gives their sons by bringing them to a powwow in Spokane—an event that Alexie himself can't face, largely because of painful memories of the "powwow bullies who made [him] cry"—is no less important to the author than his ambition to spare his children the pain often associated with reservation life.[165] In fact, he has spoken of "ending the cycle" whereby Indian children often grow up in homes with alcoholically dysfunctional parents. What we find then, in Alexie's work, is not a rejection of tribal values *per se*, but an interrogation of the terms and territories that define indigenous identity in the contemporary moment. Over the space of a long and illustrious writing career he has knowingly oscillated between spaces, genres, and stances, and in doing so has constructed an aesthetic that aims "to express sovereignty beyond narrow, restrictive boundaries."[166] Alexie's preoccupation with roots and routes, which is reflected in wonderfully affectionate and poignant lines such as "I lifted my father and carried him across every border," is a central part of his ongoing, dynamic treatment of the tribe's relationship to place, family, and the modern world.[167] That pattern of movement, that shuttling across imaginative zones that evoke various different times and spaces, is the leitmotif in Alexie's writing. It is hardly any wonder, then, that he should conclude "Tuxedo with Eagle Feathers" with an unambiguous, unrepentant line that reads "I claim all of it; hunger is my crime."[168]

165 *Face*, 83; *Conversations at KCTS* 9.
166 Bruyneel, *The Third Space of Sovereignty*, xv.
167 *The Toughest Indian in the World*, 238.
168 *Face*, 82.

CHAPTER 4

"All the Talk and All the Silence": Literary Aesthetics and Cultural Boundaries in David Treuer's *Little*

> [...] art exists that one may recover the sensation of life; it exists to make one feel things, to make the stone *stony*.[1]
>
> — VICTOR SHKLOVSKY

> [...] stories are what [Native Americans] *do*, as much as what we *are*. Stories expand or narrow our imaginative possibilities. Physical freedom won't matter if we can't imagine ourselves free as well.[2]
>
> — DANIEL HEATH JUSTICE

As noted in the Introduction, critical discourse within the field of Native American Literary Studies has recently sought to interrogate the interface between cultural knowledge and artistic expression in the novel form. In a brief but comprehensive contribution to this discussion, James H. Cox, co-editor of the influential journal *Studies in American Indian Literature*, has drawn considerable attention to an ongoing deliberation between critics favoring "tribally specific literary critical practice" on one hand, and those advocating "aesthetic or formalist [...] analyses of Native literatures" on the other.[3] This "battle of the bookworms," as Scott Lyons drolly describes

1   Victor Shklovsky, "Art as Technique," *Russian Formalist Criticism: Four Essays*, ed. Lee T. Lemon and Marion J. Reis (Lincoln: University of Nebraska Press, 1965), 12.

2   Daniel Heath Justice, *Our Fire Survives the Storm: A Cherokee Literary History* (Minneapolis: University of Minnesota Press, 2006), 206.

3   James H. Cox, "The Past, Present, and Possible Futures of American Indian Literary Studies," *Studies in American Indian Literatures* 20.1 (Summer 2008), 104.

it, has most often been viewed in terms of a critical split between those who champion tribally informed readings of the fiction and those who advocate more literary and formal interpretations.[4] The rationale behind including Ojibwe novelist and critic David Treuer amongst the formalists is the main concern of this chapter. I will assess Treuer's debut novel *Little* (1995) not only in terms of the New Critical edict laid down in his critical collection, *Native American Fiction: A User's Manual* (2006), but also in terms of the decisive and occasionally discordant conversation about indigenous fiction now underway. During the course of this examination, I will question the efficacy of separating Native American writers and critics into two distinct groups—the aestheticians and the materialists—and suggest that there is in fact a great deal of synergy between the domains of art and culture. Before doing so, however, it is perhaps worth succinctly outlining the debate as it currently stands.

Broadly speaking, the tribal nationalists or literary separatists—most notably, Jace Weaver, Craig Womack, Robert Allen Warrior, and Elizabeth Cook-Lynn—are on one side of the discussion. These scholars share an unambiguous commitment to a hermeneutics based on fiction's ability to reflect the intellectual, imaginative, and political sovereignty of the Native American tribes. In *American Indian Literary Nationalism* (2006), Weaver identifies the "explication of specific Native values, readings, and knowledges" within the fiction as his ultimate goal.[5] Cook-Lynn, meanwhile, insists that "there is no more interesting possibility [for Native American

---

4   Scott Richard Lyons, "Rhetorical Sovereignty: What Do American Indians Want from Writing?," *College Composition and Communication* 51.3 (2000), 447–468.

5   Jace Weaver, "Splitting the Earth: First Utterances and Pluralist Separatism," in *American Indian Literary Nationalism*, ed. Jace Weaver, Craig S. Womack, and Robert Warrior (Albuquerque: University of New Mexico Press, 2006), 6. Prior to the publication of this jointly edited work, Warrior's *Tribal Secrets: Recovering American Indian Intellectual Traditions* (Minneapolis: University of Minnesota Press, 1995), Weaver's *That the People Might Live: Native American Literatures and Native American Community* (New York: Oxford University Press, 1997), and his later work *Other Words: American Indian Literature, Law, and Culture* (Norman: University of Oklahoma Press, 2001), along with Womack's *Red on Red: Native American Literary Separatism* (Minneapolis: University of Minnesota Press, 1999)

literature ...] than the possibility that nation-centered theories of fiction may assist in the articulation of an ethic that would defend the authenticity of the native/tribal voice."[6] These approaches underline the extent to which Native communities are politically and culturally defined; the extent to which tribal peoples are, as LeAnne Howe writes, "people of specific landscapes" who tell "specific stories [...] about emergence from a specific place."[7]

Several scholars have resisted this approach. Kenneth Lincoln, for one, believes that an interpretative methodology that prioritizes indigenous ways of knowing (as laid down by the nationalists) threatens literary studies. In a particularly excoriating review of Womack's *Red on Red: Native American Literary Separatism* (1999), he describes the suggestion that we judge Native American literatures "by their own criteria, in their own terms" as a form of essentialist "xenophobia." He concludes that Natives and non-Natives are "not separate" but are, instead, "all in this together."[8] Lincoln's line of reasoning seems to follow Arnold Krupat's earlier argument that "Native American written literature [...] is an *intercultural* practice" and that "essentialized categories like Native/non-Native [are] an obstacle to

---

mapped the critical landscape with regard to indigenous autonomy, independence, and separatism.

6   Elizabeth Cook-Lynn, *Anti-Indianism in Modern America: A Voice from Tatekeya's Earth* (Champaign: University of Illinois Press, 2001), 42.

7   LeAnne Howe, "Blind Bread and the Business of Theory Making, By Embarrassed Grief," in *Reasoning Together: The Native Critics Collective*, ed. Craig S. Womack, Daniel Heath Justice, and Christopher B. Teuton (Norman: University of Oklahoma Press, 2008), 333.

8   Kenneth Lincoln, "Red Stick Lit Crit," review of Craig S. Womack's *Red on Red: Native American Literary Separatism*, *Indian Country Today* 26.44. It should be noted, however, that Lincoln was one of the first non-Native scholars to suggest that Native American literatures were deserving of sustained and intelligent scholarly attention and his book *Native American Renaissance* used "an interdisciplinary methodology based on anthropological, ethnographical, and historical sources" in order to examine the complex literary and cultural aspects of tribal fiction (Teuton, *Reasoning Together*, 201).

real critical work."⁹ That reading of hybridization seems, in turn, to have influenced Elvira Pulitano's hypothesis that "a 'pure' or 'authentic' form of Native discourse [...] based on a Native perspective, is simply not possible since Native American narratives are by their very nature heteroglot and hybridized."¹⁰ As well as querying the usefulness of tribal separatism in this way, some scholars working within American literary studies have expressed doubts about the notion that literature can have material consequences. Frederick Luis Aldama believes that scholars of tribal literatures often make "the misstep of confusing the fictions they analyze with the real historical, political, and judicial acts that inform the real world *hors texte*," and he wants critics to "ask themselves if it is true that the narrative fictions they analyze have the power to mobilize and organize Native people's aspirations and struggles in the world and how they can effect such transformation."¹¹

Despite the considerable critical heat produced by this debate, yet another group of commentators has come to regard the stark divide between aestheticians and culturists as something of a distraction. In response to

---

9   Arnold Krupat, *The Turn to the Native: Studies in Criticism and Culture* (Lincoln: University of Nebraska Press, 1996), 21 & 9 (emphasis added). Krupat has revised his opinion somewhat over the past decade and has recently argued that "[c]riticism of Native American literatures [...] proceeds from one or other of [a number of] critical perspectives," that include "nationalist, indigenist, and cosmopolitan." He continues to prioritize "cosmopolitan" readings, however, especially what he refers to as "cross-cultural translation" (*Red Matters*, 1, x).

10   Elvira Pulitano, *Toward a Native American Critical Theory* (Lincoln: University of Nebraska Press, 2003), 13. In truth, there is nothing particularly innovative about these claims; in 1987 Duane Niatum stated his opinion "that there is not a Native American aesthetic that we can recognize as having separate principles from the standards of artists from Western European and American cultures" (554).

11   Aldama, review of *Red Matters: Native American Studies* by Arnold Krupat and *Grave Concerns, Trickster Turns: The Novels of Louis Owens* by Chris LaLonde, *American Literature* 75.3 (2003), 665. I should note that Aldama isn't suggesting that fiction is necessarily apolitical. Indeed, he is at pains to point out that "the power of a novel by Sherman Alexie or Louis Owens [possibly] lies in its ability to open the reader's eyes to the brutalities of colonialism." Rather, his aim is to draw attention to the gap between the literary and the real world.

what he describes as "an apparent fissioning" between the "constructivists" and the "materialists," Stuart Christie finds agreement in the relationship between the "autonomy of linguistic signs" and "the autonomy of actual indigenous peoples, places, and the material worlds they inhabit."[12] Christie's critical approach is shaped by his conviction that everyone involved in the project of reading tribal fiction "must share a common commitment to ensuring present-day and future indigenous sovereignty."[13] Similarly, Robert Dale Parker, pursuing a different critical agenda than the tribal nationalists, argues, persuasively enough, that "Indian writing stands out [...] not only for its differences from other writing, its profound differences of cultural reference and understanding, but also because so much of it is as good as the best other writing."[14] Interestingly, this assertion does not prevent non-Natives from commenting on the cultural differences and tribal specificities of Native American literature. On the contrary, it gives the discerning reader credit for appreciating indigenous difference. Many tribal nationalists agree with this sentiment. Weaver has outlined his vision of a "pluralist separatism," insisting that tribal intellectuals "want non-Natives to read, engage, and study Native literature."[15] His only caveat is that scholars conducting research in the field must "do so with some respect and a sense of responsibility to Native communit[ies]."

12 *Plural Sovereignties and Contemporary Indigenous Literature* (New York: Palgrave Macmillan, 2009), 4.

13 Stuart Christie, *Plural Sovereignties*, 5. Christie, like Matthew D. Herman, seems to suggest that the majority of critics once prioritized either constructivist or materialist positions. While I agree that such a divide has occurred, I think it is important to note that, more often than not, it has been non-Native scholars who have found it necessary to differentiate between cosmopolitan and nationalist/indigenist positions. As regards tribal positions, however, Jace Weaver has been quick to point out that "there is more that unites [Native critics ...] than divides [them]" (*American Indian Literary Nationalism*, 22).

14 Robert Dale Parker, *The Invention of Native American Literature* (Ithaca, NY: Cornell University Press, 2003), 8. Parker explains that his "motives for studying Indian literature are aesthetic and literary."

15 *American Indian Literary Separatism*, 11.

Any sense of agreement that may have begun to seep into the field was, to some extent, problematized by the publication of *Native American Fiction* however. Not alone does Treuer advocate something akin to a New Critical approach to Native literatures, arguing that "the study of Native American fiction should be the study of style," but in his bid to "expose the sentiments that drive the desire for culture [...] in the novels and in their interpretation," he goes so far as to suggest that "there is no such thing as Native American literature—at least, no such thing as Native American novels anyway."[16] In the wake of this statement, Matthew Herman has drawn the conclusion that the "ideological axis" of *Native American Fiction* is a "formalist-aestheticist one," while Cox has identified Treuer as one of the main proponents behind the bid to privilege literary aesthetics over tribal culture.[17]

---

16   David Treuer, *Native American Fiction*, 198.

17   Matthew Herman, *Politics and Aesthetics in Contemporary Native American Literature: Across Every Border* (New York: Routledge, 2009), 44; Cox, "The Past, Present, and Possible Futures of American Indian Literary Studies," 104. Although Treuer may, as David Milofsky suggests, have expected "to draw some criticism," he might not have realized how much criticism his essays would receive (*Denver Post*). Matthew L.M. Fletcher, a member of the Ojibwe tribe and director of the Indigenous Law and Policy Center at Michigan State University, describes Treuer's books as an act of "cultural suicide": Matthew L.M. Fletcher, "*Native American Fiction* Tough on Indian Culture," *Indian Country Today* (August 3 2007) <http://works.bepress. com/cgi/viewcontent,cgi?article=1021&context=matthew_fletcher>. In a slightly glib, but nevertheless cutting, retort to *Native American Fiction*'s reading of his novel *Reservation Blues* (1995) Sherman Alexie has commented that his erstwhile friend has written "a book to show off for white folks," and that "Indian[s are] giggling at him" for having done so ("The World's Toughest Indian: Sherman Alexie: Author, Screenwriter, Trash-talker," interview by Jon Lurie, *Rake Magazine* [May 29, 2007] <http://archives.secrets ofthecity.com/magazine/reporting/straight-talk/ world-s-toughest-indian>). More seriously, perhaps, Krupat has focused on the various flaws evident in Treuer's research, and points out that the Ojibwe writer rather incongruously denies the existence of Native American fiction before offering a "user's manual" for this "nonexistent" genre. This, Krupat argues, is akin to "an atheist offering a user's manual to God!": "Culturalism and its Discontents," 135.

When read within the context of the arguments put forward by Lincoln, Pulitano, and others, Treuer's critical maneuvers—although lamentable in the eyes of many scholars—are not entirely shocking. Truth be told, he is possibly applying interpretative paradigms that were established by African American literary scholars such as Henry Louis Gates Jr. a full two decades ago. Treuer's dissatisfaction with the tendency of cultural questions to outweigh matters of style and artistry within the study of indigenous literature bears more than a passing resemblance to Gates's earlier anxiety that "black literature [had come] to be seen as a cultural artifact [...] a document that bore witness to the political and emotional tendencies of the Negro victim."[18] Yet, the claims made in *Native American Fiction* appear astonishing when we consider the author's engagement with his Ojibwe heritage. Specifically, one might be forgiven for assuming that a writer who is compiling, along with his brother Anton, "the first (and only) practical Ojibwe language grammar," would be interested in understanding how tribal languages and values might be reflected in the novel.[19]

Our level of expectation might intensify once we learn that in 2007 Treuer was awarded a Guggenheim Fellowship to write *Rez Life: An Indian's Journey Through Reservation Life* (2012), a non-fiction book about Leech Lake, and is now using his skill as a writer to discuss Ojibwe presences and experiences. It is difficult, then, to reconcile Treuer's intolerance of cultural readings with his dedication to Ojibwe life and traditions in Leech Lake. More significantly, perhaps, *Native American Fiction*'s methodology appears to be a little one-dimensional when the complex nature of recent scholarship in the field is taken into account. And while it is certainly the case that scholars of American literature are currently reassessing formalist

18   Henry Louis Gates, Jr., *Figures in Black: Words, Signs, and the "Racial" Self* (Oxford: Oxford University Press, 1987), 29–30. As Kenneth W. Warren pointed out at the time, "Gates feels that the literariness of black literature has never been fully acknowledged": "Delimiting America: The Legacy of Du Bois," *American Literary History* 1.1 (Spring 1989), 177. Treuer, like Gates, calls for a greater attention to the intricateness and deftness of fiction by minority writers.

19   "A Language too Beautiful to Lose," *Los Angeles Times* (February 3 2008) <http://articles.latimes.com/2008 /feb/03/books/bk-treuer3> accessed November 12 2010.

models of interpretation, Treuer's collection nevertheless strikes one as anachronistic. In particular, his methodology appears—as he himself feared it might—to be a "dangerous turning back of the clock" to a time when academic norms were used to discuss the universal beauty of fiction.[20] More remarkable than either of these particulars, however, is the extraordinary discord that seems to exist between Treuer's critical perspective in *Native American Fiction* and the themes and images we encounter in his debut novel *Little* (1995).[21] Garnering strong reviews and commendations for its unrelenting examination of reservation life in northern Minnesota, the book mobilizes what Karsten Fitz describes as "cultural memory," and it has been read as a narrative act of "'re-membering' [that] serves as a connection to the tribal past, a rootedness in the land and a belonging to a tribal community."[22] On this level *Little* might seem to be the very thing that Treuer claims doesn't exist: Native American literature.

So how are we to understand this discrepancy? Might it be the result of an ideological *volte face* on Treuer's part? Or might it be more appropriate to consider the critical direction of *Native American Fiction* as an act of reasoned disingenuity, a counterpoise designed to bring the interstices between culture and style into stark relief?[23] Perhaps it is the case that

---

20   *Native American Fiction*, 3. The recent "New Formalism, Aesthetics, and American Literary Studies" panel at the Northeast Modern Language Association conference is an indication of this recent interest in New Formalism.

21   Treuer has written two other novels, *The Hiawatha* (1999) and *The Translation of Dr Apelles* (2006). The latter was published the same year as *Native American Fiction*, and could, therefore, seem to be more relevant to any comparative analysis of Treuer's fiction and his recent scholarly output. However, I'm of the opinion that the critical energies evident in *Native American Fiction*—a collection in preparation from the late 1990s—are more fully realized in *Little* than they are in his subsequent work.

22   Review of *Little*, by David Treuer. *American Indian Culture and Research Journal* 22.1–2 (1998), 274.

23   Treuer's firm conviction that Native American fiction "is, by virtue of its simply being in English [...] inextricably in conversation with, American English literature" seems to rule this out however. This is largely because it places him amongst a group of writers who, Womack believes, are "more interested in reconciling Native literature to the American mainstream than they are in reconciling Native literature to tribal

Fitz, in searching for the cultural significance of the novel, underplayed the ways in which *Little* assembles various aesthetic conventions? Or maybe reviewers have failed to tackle the difficult question of how, *exactly*, *Little* is an Ojibwe novel? Finally, we might ask whether any apparent friction between *Native American Fiction* and *Little* reflects the circumstances facing indigenous fictionists and scholars today. That is to say, could Treuer, by publishing both books, be confronting not only his ambition to write from a particular background, but also the need to protect his tribe's cultural privacy while consolidating his position as a critically acclaimed and internationally known author?

In response to these rather perplexing and involved questions, I would like to examine *Little*'s intervention in the debate surrounding "tribally specific literary critical practice" and "aesthetic or formalist [...] analyses of Native literatures." I do so by offering a textual analysis of the novel in light of *Native American Fiction*'s rationale—a move that seems entirely appropriate where the goal is to reach a deeper understanding of Treuer's opinion regarding the task facing tribal novelists and the state of Native American Literary Studies today. My motivation originates in Treuer's suggestion that his creative writing is styled not only to "subvert stereotypes in order to gain the type of artistic freedom guaranteed non-Native writers by virtue of their whiteness," but also to permit his characters to "shield themselves from the kinds of scrutiny people are used to bringing to bear on Native American fiction."[24] As such, I wish to consider the possibility that *Little* allows the author to explore the relationship between the "autonomy of linguistic signs" and "the autonomy of actual indigenous peoples, places, and the material worlds they inhabit" that Christie has described.

The novel gestures toward such issues as individual and collective silence, trauma, and cultural memory, while its complex literary metaphors comment on globalization, Native American sovereignty, and the dynamic

---

America and seeking tribal literary autonomy": Padraig Kirwan, "Language and Signs: An Interview with Ojibwe Novelist David Treuer," *Journal of American Studies* 43.1 (2009), 103; Womack, *Red on Red*, 130).

24   Kirwan, "Language and Signs," 104 & 110.

relationship between Native American fiction and American literary studies. It could even be argued that *Little* deliberately stages the debate surrounding aesthetics and culture, so that the book's subject matter, structure,
and style express Treuer's concern with the question of "how novels act."[25]
Rather than describing *Native American Fiction* as a "decidedly unexpected
turn" in the wake of the Ojibwe writer's "astonishing first novel," we would
do better to use a close textual analysis of *Little* to expose the need for a
"distinction between reading books *as* culture and seeing books as capable
of *suggesting* culture."[26] *Little* does indeed reveal the inextricable linkage
between culture and literature, but in doing so, the novel also calls upon
the reader to ask how Native cultures and languages inform works of tribal
fiction. The novel consequently compliments Sean Teuton's insistence that
"our readings of culture and books should provide cogent explanations that
refer accurately to the real *and* literary lives of American Indians."[27] By
the same token, the novel establishes a connection between the "literary
lives of American Indians" and American literary studies by calling attention to Native American literature's engagement with universal literary
precepts. The analyses that follow explore the novel's apparent contestation
of the belief that tribal literatures can be read in terms of a stark "either/
or" dichotomy: Native American fiction or American fiction, artistically
ornate or culturally effective, fixedly tribal or fluidly intercultural. I will
be interested in whether Treuer, in refusing to come down on either side,
attempts to locate a compromise between real world contexts and literary
freedom.

25   *Native American Fiction*, 6.
26   John D. Kalb, review of *Native American Fiction: A User's Manual* and *The Translation
      of Dr Apelles: A Love Story*, by David Treuer, in *Studies in American Indian Literatures*
      20.2 (Summer 2008), 113; *Native American Fiction*, 6. Kalb's theory deals with the
      matter a little too tidily to my mind—not only because there seems to be a line of
      continuance between both books' interest in literary aesthetics, but because it is
      difficult to believe that two works by the same author could be so polemically poised.
27   Sean Teuton, "Writing American Indian Politics" in *Reasoning Together: The Native
      Critics Collection*, ed. Craig S. Womack, Daniel Heath Justice, and Christopher B.
      Teuton (Norman: University of Oklahoma Press, 2008), 117 (emphasis added).

"Empty Spaces, Gaping Holes"

Set primarily in 1980, the novel is comprised of the personal narratives and stories of the residents of a northern Minnesota reservation called Poverty. Elegiac and oftentimes ponderous, the book is framed by Donovan's recollection of the events that follow Little's untimely drowning in the town's water tower. Treuer has suggested that his first novel "is about how stories are told, how we never get it in one sitting, but piece it together."[28] Various narrators present the reader with a number of complex storylines that span several decades. The dramatic action concerns the entangled lives of three children—Donovan, Little, and Jackie—as well as the adult narrators, a good number of whom are interrelated in some way. Included amongst the reservation's population are Duke and Ellis, their one-time lover Jeannette, and her daughter Celia (Little's mother), as well as Celia's boyfriend Stan. Stan mistakenly believes that he is Little's father, when in fact Celia became pregnant as the result of a vicious rape by Father Gundesohn, an Anglo-American parish priest assigned to the reservation. The priest's successor, the aptly named young "disciple" Paul who hails from St. Paul, Minnesota, completes the central cast of characters. Donovan, who has been rescued from a snowstorm by Duke and Ellis, is Little's childhood friend and the principal narrator of events. Much of our insight into life on the reservation comes about as a result of his reportage, even though Jeannette, Duke, Ellis, and others all act as storytellers at different points in the novel.

Neither a spectral presence nor a fully involved member of the community, the eponymous character Little is, as one reviewer has it, an "ever-present absence."[29] "Little slips in and out, either at the lake, at Poverty with Duke and Ellis, or somewhere with Donovan and my Jackie," Violet

---

28   David Treuer, interview, *"Little* Doesn't Wear Feathers," <http:www.pioneerplanet. com/columnists/ docs/GROSSMAN/docs/009265.htm> accessed March 6 2008.

29   Sima Rabinowitz, review of *Little,* by David Treuer, *Hungry Mind Review* (August 14 2001).

explains, and "he flits around, his hands, his word."[30] Even in death he remains elusive, and in the novel's opening scene Donovan recalls how, after Little's drowning, the family "didn't even have the body, not even his clothes, his hair, no memories of anything he ever said. Nothing but his one word, 'You.'"[31] A selective mute, the boy is "deformed, not retarded," Donovan explains, and his only real physical disability lies in the fact that his fingers are joined together and his hands resemble claws.[32] Although "he didn't speak," this most certainly wasn't because "he couldn't."[33] On the contrary, Little "*chose* not to tell what he knew" and used "his one word, 'You,'" regardless of context, mood, or motivation.[34]

Following Donovan's initial description of Little's muteness, Jeannette explains that her grandson "refuses to speak about his past"—a refusal that is described as a "wisdom [which] those of us who lived through the old times [...] learned long ago."[35] Thus, it is at a very early stage in the novel that a linguistic fissure becomes the leitmotif around which the novel's many narratives are arranged. Indeed, striking descriptions of silence occur time and again in Treuer's novel. Duke explains that Ellis, the second of the twins, "got his [name] because of his silence, the way he sat still."[36] At one point Violet describes the circumstances surrounding Little's conception as an "impossible secret" before explaining directly to the narratee that she "could keep [... her] own secrets, not save everyone else's."[37] At the very end of the book, Donovan realizes that countless stories had been "kept apart and down" prior to Little's drowning.[38] In narratological terms, these extended silences and physical absences create an opening very similar to the "textual [...] hole" that Rita Ferrari finds in Louise Erdrich's *Love*

---

30   *Little*, 181.
31   Ibid., 4.
32   Ibid., 221.
33   Ibid., 6.
34   Ibid., 6 & 4.
35   Ibid., 46.
36   Ibid., 55.
37   Ibid., 181 & 186.
38   Ibid., 246.

Medicine and *Tracks*, and Little's "ever-present absence" seems to be very much in keeping with the "paradoxical presence and absence" that Erdrich establishes in those polyvocal and multiply-narrated novels.[39] Since Nancy J. Peterson and others have argued that the "absent presence" in *Tracks* displaces the "historical narrative" that ordinarily frames, and regulates, discourse concerning tribal peoples, it has to be significant that the pattern of disarticulation or aesthetic dissemblance in *Little* has a very similar effect: the novel's description of "the deficiencies of right, the diminishing borders, even the history" of the American Midwest challenges the very notion of a master narrative.[40] This questioning of cultural, historical, and geographical positioning continues in Treuer's depiction both of the Euro-American settlers' bid to smooth "over the spaces that to them appeared as silences" and of the "absences of memory" that plague Donovan's father.

Importantly enough, the "pas tout" found in *Little* is comparable to the aesthetic strategies deployed by other ethnic writers—not least the "crack in language and space" that Richard Hardack finds in Toni Morrison's *Jazz*.[41] For this reason Treuer's fiction could be said to express an interest in the form of imaginative autonomy that Morrison describes as "freeing up language from its sinister, frequently lazy, almost always predictable employment of racially informed and determined chains."[42] It is fair to say, then, that the expressive hide and seek found in *Little* can be read in terms of both the Derridean influence in Morrison's work and the poststructuralist "play of absence and presence" that Ferrari finds in Erdrich's novels.[43] What

39   Rita Ferrari, "'Where the Maps Stopped': The Aesthetics of Borders in Louise Erdrich's *Love Medicine* and *Tracks*," *Style* 33.1 (1999), 146 & 144.

40   *Little*, 12.

41   "'A Music Seeking Its Words': Double-Timing and Double-Consciousness in Toni Morrison's Jazz," *Callaloo* 18.2 (1995), 451.

42   Toni Morrison, *Playing in the Dark: Whiteness and the Literary Imagination* (Cambridge, MA: Harvard University Press, 1992), xi. This idea gains considerable currency when one considers that the young writer began writing *Little* while under the African American writer's tutelage at Princeton.

43   See Philip Page's "Traces of Derrida in Toni Morrison's *Jazz*," *African American Review* 29.1 (Spring 1995), 55–66, for a detailed analysis of a Derridian influence in Morrison's fiction.

is important about this connection in terms of *Native American Fiction*'s caution to be "careful about how we use, and [...] interpret, literary devices" is Treuer's use of narratological silences to deter what Duane Niatum calls a "conventional and prescriptive response" to Native American literature. In doing so, he encourages the "free play between reader and writer" that Niatum endorses.[44]

There are other important ways in which the novel's aesthetic shape and form express Treuer's bid to achieve the "artistic freedom guaranteed non-Native writers" and thereby "construct narratives unchained from the projects of historicizing."[45] One of the most notable of these is Little's single utterance "You." "You!" appears on several occasions throughout the book, and at one point toward the end of the novel this single word is placed dead center on the page.[46] This word becomes, in Treuer's words, "a bullet that Little shoots at everyone and shoots out of the book."[47] Little addresses his utterance both intratextually, at a plot level, toward those living in Poverty, *and* extratextually towards the reader. If viewed as a metafictional tactic, "You!" reminds us of our role in construing meaning within Native American literature, and might even be said to disclose what Treuer describes in *Native American Fiction* as "the responsibility vested in the reader to interpret" broadly.[48] This approach calls to mind Jonathan Culler's view of theory as "a constellation: a series of juxtaposed clusters of changing elements that resist reduction to a common denominator, essential core, or generative first principle."[49] Accordingly, I would argue,

---

44   Duane Niatum, "On Stereotypes," in *Recovering the Word: Essays on Native American Literature*, ed. Brian Swann and Arnold Krupat (Berkeley: University of California Press, 1987), 554.

45   Kirwan, "Language and Signs," 76; *Native American Fiction*, 184.

46   "You" features on pages 4, 7, 95, 208, 219 and 233.

47   Kirwan, "Language and Signs," 115.

48   *Native American Fiction*, 99.

49   In making this assertion I am drawing on Eugene O'Brien's summary of Culler's critical work: "The Question of Theory," review of Jonathan Culler, *Literary Theory: A Very Short Introduction* in *Other Voices: the (e)Journal of Cultural Criticism* 2.2 (March 2002). Christopher B. Teuton has also made reference to Culler, most recently in his efforts to examine the role that theory can play within Native American Literary

"You!" asks the "real reader" to consider the implied reader's response to the indigenous novel.

The repeated use of this pronoun speaks to what David Stirrup describes as Treuer's concern with the "self-reflexivity of *reading* Native American literatures," by which he means the tendency to read certain themes, images, and characterizations as signs of "Indianness."[50] Furthermore, it might not be too great a stretch to see Little's moments of narration, such as they are, as a response to our expectation that Native fiction include "stock characters, whose job it is to 'set the record straight' or to 'truth-tell' about cultural issues."[51] Because the child simply refuses to speak at all, "You!" can be interpreted as an aesthetic riposte to the non-Native readership who, according to Jace Weaver, "remain most interested in those indigenes who provide them with an entrée into Native culture [... or] appear to offer initiation into a hidden world of tribal wisdom."[52] The stark interruption raises questions concerning the role of the narrator (and the implied author) within Native American fiction. One final discursive function of the child's expressive parsimony is, by corollary, to underline the Native author's right to withhold certain narratives. That is to say, Little's refusal to say anything more than "You!" dissembles what Treuer regards as the norm whereby tribal writers feel compelled to "create [...] narratives that bleed out our rich cultural specificities into the world, translated and trammeled."[53] Yet, even though Treuer is eager to re-evaluate the means by which Native American literature can engage its cultural context, his fiction suggests that the issues facing the Ojibwe people do not *always* translate into literary

---

Studies. Importantly, Teuton argues that "a reference to the social existence and obligations of theory" is "glaringly absent" from Cullers's definition of theory: "Theorizing American Indian Literature: Applying Oral Concepts to Written Traditions" in *Reasoning Together*, 209. In response, he suggests that we add another characteristic of theory to the list: "Theory arises out of the dialectical relationship among artists, art, critics and Native communities."

50   David Stirrup, "Life after Death in Poverty: David Treuer's *Little*," *American Indian Quarterly* 29.3–4 (Summer–Fall 2005), 667.

51   Kirwan, "Language and Signs," 105.

52   *American Indian Literary Nationalism*, 2.

53   *Native American Fiction*, 182.

issues. At least some of the silences in *Little* gesture toward a privileged space in which the community privately considers forms of cultural and linguistic continuance.[54] It is not only a question of the indigenous writer retelling tribal stories in a new literary or cultural context, but also one of creating an engaging literature that would force us to consider the means by which ethnicity is actually formed within Native communities, in contrast to the way it is understood by a general readership.

While these aesthetic strategies provide Treuer with the means to challenge critical assumptions concerning Native American fiction, they are not specifically informed by Ojibwe culture. On the contrary, the narrative structure and symbolism of *Little* appear, on the face of it, to reflect Treuer's preference for style over culture. His artistry seems, as Stirrup notes, to "close down" a cultural reading, allowing the novelist to slip free of a "heavy cultural burden."[55] For this reason alone the book seems far removed from the "nation-centered theories of fiction" that Cook-Lynn and other nationalists are calling for. This form of distancing might well be intentional, not least because the "expectations that authors must be accountable spokespersons for their ethnic groups can," as Gates reminds

54   While this image is not strictly in keeping with the idea of an endlessly readable text or, by corollary, a "readable" culture, it nevertheless seems to be the case that there are aspects of his tribal and spiritual life that Treuer would rather not discuss in his creative or critical writing. This has, in part, led Scott Lyons to suggest that Treuer is "a culture cop," and "is involved [...] with the old essentialist project of protecting traditional culture from the threats of incorporation, exploitation and change": *X-marks: Native Signatures of Assent* (Minneapolis: University of Minnesota Press, 2010), 103. Lyons disagrees with Treuer's stance on cultural information, largely because he believes that tribal cultures "are constantly changing, adapting and evolving as time goes by" (104). He also charges that *Native American Fiction*'s central argument that "Native American fiction doesn't exist" in the way that critics often believe it does, essentially "tells us nothing about what the literature is [...] trying to do" (106). Lyons may be entirely correct in this last point, but I would suggest that *Little* is, in fact, a better example of "what the literature is [...] trying to do." We might, therefore, find that Native American writing is being defined in action rather than via academic or critical debate. Tribal culture will, presumably, define itself by similar, internal, processes.

55   *Native American Fiction*, 146.

us, be "well nigh be unbearable for an 'ethnic' author."[56] Sanford Pinsker recalls how Philip Roth once "found himself heckled by a Yeshiva University student who sharply questioned his credentials as a legitimately 'Jewish' writer" because Roth's characters "seem cut off from the well-springs of Jewish identity."[57] Nor is this a solely American concern. James Joyce's writ-

---

56 Henry Louis Gates Jr., "'Ethnic and Minority' Studies," in *Introduction to Scholarship in Modern Languages and Literatures*, ed. Joseph Gibaldi, 2nd edn (New York: Modern Language Association, 1992), 294. In a thoughtful and meditative essay titled "The End(s) of African-American Studies" Kenneth W. Warren examines the question of African American scholars' moral or social obligations. He points out that although the expectation that the black intellectual bears a social responsibility is perhaps unfair (a point that Gates makes when he refers to the "burden of representation") it is nevertheless the case that Gates himself "*does* [believe that he has] a responsibility, which he is fulfilling nicely through African-American studies, which is presumed to serve the group interests of black people" (640). Warren goes on to state that "the scholar's business 'is not the salvation "business"' but [is] rather something else," and quotes Hortense Spillers in doing so (652). John Michael also offers a discussion of the moral imperatives that may or may not inform African American scholarship in his work *Anxious Intellects: Academic Professionals, Public Intellectuals, and Enlightenment Values* (Durham, NC: Duke University Press, 2000). He considers both the role of Gates and Cornel West as "black public intellectual[s]" and the social and political interventions made by American intellectuals such as Stanley Fish, Todd Gitlin, Michael Beacute, and Allan Bloom. I would argue that Treuer is, to some extent, an "anxious intellectual" as defined by Michael; eager to secure artistic and critical freedom, but nevertheless aware—often painfully so—of the "real-world" context in which the Ojibwe language, traditions, and community are under assault from many angles.

57 "The Tortoise and the Hare: Or, Philip Roth, Cynthia Ozick, and the Vagaries of Fiction Writing," *Virginia Quarterly Review* 81 (2005), 215 & 216. Intriguingly, Pinsker's essay compares the work of Roth to that of Cynthia Ozik, a writer steeped in a Jewish American heritage—a position that "meant [she was committed to] religious study and observance, community affiliation and work on behalf of Israel," but was also "an acolyte of high modernism," a person, in her own words "besotted with the religion of Literature" (216 & 217). Pinsker explains that the "intertwining strands of Jewish thought and modernist literature" were "as much a curse as a blessing" for Ozick, largely because "she set one tradition against the other" throughout her early years as a writer (ibid.). Ozick's preferred way of surmounting this tension in later years has, he claims, been to clearly distinguish between her religious identity and

ing shows that "in Ireland, the problem of being a writer was" not simply "a
linguistic problem" but, as Seamus Deane points out, "a political problem"
as well.[58] Because Joyce "distrusted all enthusiasm" and looked upon the
"possibility of maintaining one's integrity as an artist while being involved
with a community's enterprise [...] with skepticism," many commentators
argue that he held a "detached ambivalence" toward Irish nationalism.[59]

---

her creative one. "Ozick now insists that she is a writer. Period. No adjectives need
apply"; her Jewishness "is quite another matter" (219). I would suggest that Treuer,
like Ozick, has, in a very similar manner, figured his Ojibwe heritage in terms of his
position as a literary artist, before ultimately deciding to treat these two aspects of
his identity as discrete entities. In this way, his fiction and his critical essays are, to his
mind, separate from his Indianness on many levels. Yet, as Pinsker and Ozick have
noted, there is an almost inevitable interplay between heritage and authorship, and,
as a result, writers often find themselves operating in the space where "the artist" and
"the community member" meet—even if only in regard to specific sets of themes,
tropes, and so on. Perhaps *Native American Fiction*'s greatest claim, as a result, is its
insinuation that we need to come to a closer understanding of the complexities that
regulate the relationship between Indianness and literariness.

58   Seamus Deane, "Joyce the Irishman," *The Cambridge Companion to James Joyce*, edited
     by Derek Attridge (Cambridge: Cambridge University Press, 2004), 31.
59   Padraic Colum, "With James Joyce in Ireland," *New York Times* (June 11, 1922)
     <http://www.nytimes.com/books/00/01/09/specials/joyce-colum.html> accessed
     November 11, 2010; Deane, "Joyce the Irishman," 31; Emer Nolan, *James Joyce and
     Nationalism* (London: Routledge, 1995), 130. It is of no little significance to the
     current discussion that several Irish scholars have sought to reassess Joyce's feelings
     about the complex nature of the nationalist cause. Nolan, for instance, attempts to
     "make sense of Joyce's attitude towards Irish nationalism," and describes "what his
     critics see as detached ambivalence" as "a painful deadlock" for the writer. Joyce's
     "writings about Ireland may not provide a coherent critique of either colonised or
     colonialist," she continues, "but the very ambiguities and hesitations testify to the
     uncertain, divided consciousness of the colonial subject"—a consciousness that Joyce
     "is unable to articulate in its full complexity outside his fiction" (*James Joyce and
     Nationalism*, 130). In many ways, Treuer's *Little* exhibits some aspects of this "painful
     deadlock"; the book pushes away from the typical representation of Indianness, but
     Treuer continues to work with, and write about, communities and characters from
     his Minnesota homelands. Moreover, in doing so he would appear to be concerned
     with *both* his own artistic vision *and* a fuller expression of the complexities that
     inform literary discourse in relation to Ojibwe experiences today. It might also be

In light of recent conversations within Native American Literary Studies, Treuer's writing might exhibit a similar detachment toward local versions of tribal autonomy.

What is the relationship between the novelist's apparent indifference to political and social contexts, on one hand, and his signs of narrative "ambivalence" on the other? Just as Joyce Ann Joyce railed against the fashion of poststructuralist approaches to African American studies during the 1980s, so Native American scholars distrust literary techniques associated with the decentering and destabilizing impulses of deconstruction and postmodernism.[60] Sean Teuton has been quick to pose the problem for tribal writers: "If we, like postmodernists, deconstruct the Indian," he writes, then "how are we [...] to present a reliable construction of tribal peoples, either for US society or for ourselves?"[61] In this regard Little's continual "flit[ting] around" and his propensity to "slip in and out"— although perhaps liberating for the child himself—fail to express a tribal presence. Given that "political commitment becomes more difficult where meaning is endlessly deferred and contradicted," as Linden Peach points

---

interesting to some readers to note that Scott W. Klein's essay "Nathan Zuckerman as Irish Jew: James Joyce, National Difference, and Roth's *The Counterlife*," *Philip Roth Studies* 4.2 (Fall 2008), 153–169, points out that Roth and Joyce each meditate on questions of ethnic determinacy and national identification. *Little*, I would suggest, flirts with a similar set of questions. Moreover, Treuer has created a novel with universal significance and, in so doing, seems to have heeded Joyce's point that "the particular is contained in the universal": Laurent Milesi, "Introduction: Language(s) with a Difference," in *James Joyce and the Difference of Language*, ed. Laurent Milesi (Cambridge: Cambridge University Press, 2003), 4.

60 See Sharon P. Holland, "The Revolution, 'In Theory,'" review of *Negrophobia and Reasonable Racism: The Hidden Costs of Being Black in America* by Jody David Armour, *Blackness and Value: Seeing Double* by Lindon Barrett, and *Race Men* by Hazel V. Carby, *American Literary History* 12.1–2 (Spring/Summer 2000), 327–336.

61 Sean Teuton, "Placing the Ancestors: Postmodernism, 'Realism,' and American Indian Identity in James Welch's *Winter in the Blood*," *American Indian Quarterly* 25 (2001), 629. In a similar vein, Womack states simply in *Red on Red*, his critical study published in 1999, that it "is way too premature for Native scholars to deconstruct history when we haven't yet constructed it" (3).

out, one cannot equate the imaginative freedom *Little* suggests with the political aims of Weaver and others.

Yet Treuer's novel appears to pre-empt this criticism in that it makes Little's flurrying around problematic within the space of the narrative itself. Donovan's account of how the family is haunted by the fact they "didn't even have [Little's] body" continues the problem of the boy's flapping, an ephemerality both beguiling and frustrating on many levels.[62] His absent presence appears to be a less than perfect solution to the various material concerns facing Poverty's community. In a chapter titled "Wisconsin November 1968," this lack is presented as a difficulty and restriction once again. Here Donovan and his father are described as leaving an "almost empty" apartment devoid of "family heirlooms."[63] The older man, unmoored by his own mother's wavering account of who his father might have been, is described as having only "absences of memory" to hold onto as he drives toward the reservation. He is a man who has "nothing to know."[64] Driving through slush that makes it impossible to follow the "yellow lines in the middle of the road," the father is profoundly troubled by a deficiency of knowledge that will, in turn, trouble Donovan—whom he abandons in a snowdrift. When Donovan is eventually found by Duke and Ellis, the little boy appears, through the "bubbled and waved" frozen windscreen, to be a "jumble of rags" in a car that has the appearance of being "underwater."[65] This lack of definition creates a precariousness that threatens to drown out tribal voices.

What becomes increasingly evident in *Little* is that Treuer is not so much concerned with "the endless flux of becoming" that one finds in Morrison's characterizations, nor with the "narrative technique" that Erdrich uses to "dissolve [...] the boundaries between the seen and unseen, fact and fiction, memory and event."[66] To the contrary, Treuer's novel

---

62   *Little*, 4.
63   Ibid., 18.
64   Ibid., 20.
65   Ibid., 35.
66   Rita Ferrari, "'Where the Maps Stopped': The Aesthetics of Borders in Louise Erdrich's *Love Medicine* and *Tracks*," *Style* 33.1 (1999), 146.

rigorously interrogates the boundaries between literary form and tribal presence, pointing out fiction's limits and capabilities. Accordingly, rather than simply corroborate Stirrup's contention that the book engages in a "teasing of disclosure and refusal" by "invit[ing] a cultural reading" on some occasions and "clos[ing] down such invitations" on others, the readings that follow will assume that the novel launches a directive against cultural readings *in toto* and does so in a manner that has artistic, cultural, and political relevance for Native novelists, Ojibwe people, and a global readership.[67]

"All the Talk and All the Silence"

The most obvious way that Treuer's novel might be said to have such relevance is its contemplation of the relationship between narrative form and cultural trauma. In *Little*, images of sorrow, silence, and repressed memory can, it might be argued, amount to a fictional commentary on the condition that Lawrence W. Gross calls "Post Apocalypse Stress Syndrome" (PASS).[68] A malady amongst indigenous communities in America, Gross attributes PASS to extreme historical trauma and claims it can "be thought of as post-traumatic stress disorder (PTSD) raised to the level of an entire culture."[69] It often results in "despair and dysfunction" within the community—a parallel that is crucial to any reading of Treuer's *Little*.[70] Indeed, "dysfunction" of this type is evident in many of the relationships in the novel. Duke and Ellis' account of how they were torn away from the reservation,

---

67 Stirrup's written essay does a remarkably good job of revealing various tensions within Treuer's novel, and I concur with many of his readings of the book. My task here, however, is to search for some other possibilities; specifically, those which deal with sovereignty and territory in an Ojibwe context.

68 "The Comic Vision of Anishinaabe Culture and Religion," *American Indian Quarterly* 26.3 (Summer 2002), 450.

69 Ibid.

70 Ibid., 451.

"didn't see Jeannette or our lake for thirty years," or even "know that she
had burned the cabin after we left," bears witness to the sense of dispossession that Little's grandmother poignantly describes as "being peeled
back from the land the way the skin of smoking fish curls over to expose
what is soft and white, what can be flaked away by the wind, by even the
softest, weakest hands."[71] In this regard, Fitz's suggestion that the book is
primarily about "coming to terms with personal and communal memories"
seems entirely apt, as does Daniel Drew Turner's characterization of the
novel as "reflective and evocative."[72] Treuer's declaration that the novel is
"a funeral song"—in which he sought to explore a form of cultural and
personal melancholia—adds further authority to these interpretations.[73]
How, we must now consider, does the community deal with this "despair
and dysfunction"?

Particular forms of silence, secrecy, and absence serve as coping mecha-
nisms that allow the community to exist as a cohesive whole despite the
traumas of the past. Jeannette describes her memory of an unspoken past
as "the secret of what carried me home to Poverty." Duke similarly explains
to Donovan that "it don't matter who [Little's father] was [...]. Just like
it don't matter who left you by the road."[74] The need to "care of your ma"
is more important. Although Celia says she "wanted to tell [Stan] that it
wasn't him" who had gotten her pregnant with Little, she withholds the
truth in order to hold on to some form of family cohesion.[75] In this way
Little explores what Amy Novak has described as the "narrative methods
available to a culture to tell of and work through trauma."[76] By representing the "kind of privacy and secrecy" through which "the members of that

71   *Little*, 31 & 51.
72   Karsten Fitz, review of *Little*, by David Treuer, *American Indian Culture and Research
      Journal* 22.1–2 (1998), 271–275.
73   Kirwan, "Language and Signs," 110.
74   *Little*, 69 & 5.
75   Ibid., 135.
76   Amy Novak, "'A Marred Testament': Cultural Trauma and Narrative in Danticat's *The
      Farming of Bones*," *Arizona Quarterly* 62.4 (2006), 98 & 94. Novak's essay examines
      Edwidge Danticat's *The Farming of Bones* (1998), a novel about Haiti.

community communicate with one another," Treuer suggests that the community surmounts instances of historical fracture and shared turmoil.[77]

The expressive parsimony of *Little* also echoes Lyotard's claim that survivors of cultural trauma "do not speak […] because they cannot speak, or because they avail themselves of the possibility of not speaking."[78] Under these conditions, Little's muteness and the concealment practiced by several of the book's narrators resist what Treuer describes as a hermeneutic convention whereby the Native writer is "the informant" and "the world"—that is to say, the global readership—"is the ethnographer."[79] For this reason, we might do well to remember what Dori Laub, in reference to the Holocaust, calls the "vicissitudes of listening."[80] In order for any revisionist historical understanding to come about, Laub contends, we must both "know 'the lay of the land'—the landmarks, the undercurrents, and the pitfalls" within the story and demonstrate our willingness to respect the tellers silences.[81] If we pay close attention to "how novels act," we see that Treuer challenges us, as readers, to heed its various forms of narrative omission.

Aesthetically speaking, these "textual holes" are designed to reiterate W.H. New's point that "no one who does not listen learns to hear."[82] Paula Gunn Allen similarly admonishes scholars working within the field of Native American Literary Studies to respect the form of "privacy and modesty" found within tribal communities.[83] By conscientious acts of listenership, readers can move towards an understanding of the community's trauma while recognizing its right to silence. The result, as Cathy Caruth explains,

77 Kirwan, "Language and Signs," 108.

78 Jean François Lyotard, *The Differend: Phrases in Dispute*, trans. Georges Van Den Abbeele (Manchester: Manchester University Press, 1988), 10.

79 Kirwan, "Language and Signs," 114.

80 Dori Laub, "Bearing Witness or the Vicissitudes of Listening," in *The Holocaust: Theoretical Readings*, ed. Neil Levi and Michael Rothberg (Edinburgh: Edinburgh University Press, 2003), 221.

81 Ibid., 222.

82 W.H. New, "Learning to Listen," in *Native Writers and Canadian Writing*, ed. W.H. New (Vancouver: University of British Columbia Press, 1990), 5.

83 Paula Gunn Allen, "Special Problems in Teaching Leslie Marmon Silko's *Ceremony*," *American Indian Quarterly* 14 (1990), 380.

is a "link between cultures: not as a simple understanding of the pasts of others but rather [as an] ability to listen through the departures we have all taken from ourselves."[84] The arrangement of stories in *Little*, whereby a series of narrators reveals interconnected pieces of information in a slow and often incomplete manner, comments on the "paradoxical process of remembering and forgetting in the narration of individual and cultural trauma," as various narrators point out a loss of their expressive abilities.[85] On this level, Treuer can be said to "urge [...] readers to consider silence and to embrace the unsettling of what they might like to be authoritative."[86]

The novel presents the reader with a fictional space in which the characters retain the unassailable right to shield themselves from scrutiny while *"beginning to emerge and speak again."*[87] Indeed, one might wonder if *Little*, like *Native American Fiction*, is an attempt to reflect "the inherent right and ability of [tribal] peoples to determine their own communicative needs and desires [...] and to decide for themselves the goals, modes, styles, and languages of public discourse."[88] Or does the loss of voice mean the loss of

84   Cathy Caruth, "Trauma and Experience," in *The Holocaust: Theoretical Readings*, ed. Neil Levi and Michael Rothberg (Edinburgh: Edinburgh University Press, 2003), 197. Given that Treuer's father, Robert, fled Vienna in 1938 after his parents had "been declared Jewish [...] and dispossessed," it might be worth considering the extent to which Donovan, Little, and Jackie exhibit many of the symptoms shown by the children of Holocaust Survivors. Treuer's father discusses his experiences on Minnesota public radio, and that program can be accessed at: http:// minnesota. publicradio.org/display/web/2007/ 01/22/midday1/. See also: http://people.mnhs. org/authors/biog_detail.cfm?PersonID=Treu325. Little seems to carry what Caruth calls "an impossible history within" himself, in that he is a "symptom of a history" which the other residents on the reservation are wholly cognizant of but "cannot entirely possess" for much of the novel (*Little*, 194). The community's response to his muteness is to form another conspiracy of silence: "[e]ven though we never talked about it," Violet recalls in her account of life on the reservation, "I think that Celia tries to hide him" (*Little*, 181).

85   Novak, "'A Marred Testament'," 93.

86   Ibid., 95.

87   *Little*, 13.

88   Scott Lyons, "Rhetorical Sovereignty: What Do American Indians Want from Writing?," *College Composition and Communication* 51.3 (February 2000), 449.

the power of articulation within Native American literature and everyday life?[89] While impenetrable silence prevents the reader from categorizing Treuer's novel as a work of Native American fiction, it may also keep the author from producing fiction of tribal significance. *Little*, however, appears to provide something of a metafictional commentary on this very issue. Rather than ensuring personal or communal freedom, the secrecy that surrounds the boy's conception, lifetime, and his stifled self-expression actually disrupts continuity and kinship within the community. On several occasions the playful ambiguity created by the boy's muteness becomes a disturbing form of introversion that threatens to crack open the small child and his extended family. In these moments, a stunted, "deformed" version of tribal voice prevents the forms of expression required for community.

"Words Struggling to Break the Surface"

The novel provides a striking metaphor for this disabling verbal retention when "Little's intestines [get] stopped up," so that he "screamed with" pain. Donovan thought Little was going to die because he "couldn't open up and it was torturing him."[90] The failure to "open up" is, to some extent, a somati-

---

89   As long ago as 1997, Greg Sarris noted the importance of the fact that writers such as Louise Erdrich were "dealing with the drinking and funkiness we all know from everyday life," and how "new Indian writing is a reflection of these authors' complex lives, growing up walking a cultural tightrope, on the one hand hearing echoes of old tribal stories and on the other hand immersed in MTV" (Dinitia Smith, "Heroes Now Tend to Be More Hard Edged, Urban and Pop Orientated," *New York Times* (April 21, 1997) <http://www.nytimes.com/ 1997/04/21/books/heroes-now-tend-to-be-more-hard-edged-urban-and-pop-oriented.html?ref=dinitia_smith>. Weaver cites a similar use of language used by Womack in response to a question about the "future of Native American literature" as being crucial to our understanding of the fiction, When asked what that future would consist of, Womack summarily stated "More and funkier." (*American Indian Nationalism*, 74).

90   *Little*, 101.

zation through which the psychic wound materializes. Here, "open[ing] up" would provide both psychological and physical relief. This scene associates narrative possibility with physical well-being in that Little's constipation dramatizes the festering that occurs when secrets are held for too long, a threat not only to *his* well-being but to that of the community as well. Upset by Little's sudden illness, Donovan is perplexed by the homonymic relationship between "track" and "tract," and misunderstands the type of "motion" required for a cure:

> I had been confused at what was going on in the first place. I asked and they said it was his "track." I thought they said "Tract," that his tract wouldn't move, and that meant us. They said they needed the Tract to move, and confusing Little's bowels with our group of houses I tried to help the best I could by packing all of my stuff into garbage bags, which I set by the front door.[91]

Donovan mistakes Little's need for physical release with a need for geographical relocation. In this instance the "free play" in language causes a moment of confusing misdirection, which can do little to relieve the situation.[92]

The boundaries between aesthetic freedom and cultural respectability come under scrutiny again following Little's constipation. Little is out fishing with the other children from the reservation. In a moment of absolute lucidity, Little suddenly leaps and attempts to catch, by hand, a fish he has spotted in the river. Once in the stream, Little sinks to "the bottom of the river" with "his legs and arms wrapped around" the "northern pike."[93] Clinging to the fish for all he is worth, the boy is dragged further under-

---

91   *Little*, 101.
92   Interestingly, the allusion possibly calls to mind (and inverts) Roberson's contention that "Native American novels are structurally 'incentric, centripetal, converging, contracting'": Susan L. Roberson, "Translocations and Transformations: Identity in N. Scott Momaday's *The Ancient Child*," *American Indian Quarterly* 22.1/2 (1998), 32. Rather than being "healed" by the prototypical homecoming to the reservation, Treuer's characters must follow other routes, and for Little, Donovan, Jeannette, and others, the homecoming is not a sufficient panacea to their concerns.
93   *Little*, 112–113.

water and is at risk of drowning even though the stream is "no more than seven feet" deep.[94] In a desperate bid to save his friend, Donovan fills his pockets with stones to keep from being carried off by a current "stronger than" he is and jumps in the river. Their struggle ends on the riverbed after Donovan succeeds in wrenching Little free of the pike.[95]

On the one hand, we can see Little's dive into the water as a sheer expression of freedom. We can also see the scene, on the other hand, as another instance of the complex relationship between fiction and culture. The terror of Little's disappearance in the river links the pike to water Manitou, or Micipijiu, who "lived in any body of water [that the Ojibwe] embarked upon and posed a real threat" to the community.[96] In response to this possibility, Stirrup suggests that Little might be attempting "to make himself one with the water," in which case his immersion would indicate an "agreement of union with the water spirits."[97] In light of Treuer's explanation that "one of the things [he] was trying to do in *Little* was see what happens when the characters' spirituality is *not* evoked," there seems to another possibility.[98] Rather than establishing Little's connection with Ojibwe tradition, the fact that he is perilously "weighted" on the river's floor could indicate immobility, or stasis. That image might, in turn, comment on the "cultural burden" that tribal fictionists and literatures often bear. When Little and Donovan finally emerge from the river, the narrator bluntly proclaims "the fish was dead." This disquieting image of loss makes the point that Native writers may well "kill the literature" if they "aren't careful about how [they] use, and how [they] interpret, literary devices

94 Ibid., 113.
95 Ibid., 112 & 113.
96 Victoria Brehm, "The Metamorphoses of an Ojibwa *Manido*," *American Literature* 68 (1996), 679.
97 Stirrup, "Life after Death in Poverty," 662.
98 Dinitia Smith, "Heroes Now Tend to Be More Hard Edged, Urban, and Pop Orientated," *New York Times* (April 21 1997) <http://www.nytimes.com/1997/04/21/books/heroes-nowtend-to-be-more-hard-edged-urban-and-pop-oriented.html>.

and cultural forms."⁹⁹ Thus the pike seems to support both sides of the critical argument, serving either as a tribal touchstone or as a sign at play in a field of signifiers.

Then there's the fact that many aspects of this incident repeat features of Fleur Pillager's third drowning at the end of Erdrich's earlier novel *Tracks* (1989): Fleur "bent over, picked some stones up, and dropped them into her pockets [...] searched the smooth rocks piled around her, rejecting some and keeping others [...] and then walked into the water."¹⁰⁰ Erdrich's narrator establishes a relationship between Fleur and the "lake man" in Matchimanito, and glosses the experience as her attempt to come to a spiritual accord. Thus, where one author uses cultural information to invite a "bicultural reading that deconstructs the essentialist assumptions of both Native and Western readers," the other challenges those same assumptions by "shield[ing]" cultural information from the reader's gaze and emphasizing the dangers of literature and culture being treated as interchangeable.¹⁰¹ In *Little*, the water acts as a space in which there are no borders. This lack of boundaries would remind us of the intercultural "salad-bowl" that supposedly results from multiculturalism (Lyons). From this perspective, the river is indicative of a Native American Literary Studies in which Native and non-Native voices are intermingled—a space in which, Lincoln insists, "We're not separate. We're all in this together." Indeed, because the novel is set in northern Minnesota, the river may well be American literature's most symbolic waterway, the Mississippi, thereby reminding us that Treuer's book is part of a broader, intercultural literary milieu.

---

99   *Native American Fiction*, 200. It should also be noted that in making this point in *Native American Fiction* Treuer would appear to be reiterating the late Louis Owens's warning that traditional beliefs "irreplaceable ... [to] specific Indian cultures" risk becoming mere "signifiers" of Indianness and might be drained of life when dragged out of context and paraded within the fictional form (*Mixedblood Messages*, 12).

100 Louise Erdrich, *Tracks* (New York: Flamingo, 1994), 211–212.

101 Mark Shackleton, "'June Walked over It like Water and Came Home': Cross-Cultural Symbolism in Louise Erdrich's *Love Medicine* and *Tracks*," in *Transatlantic Voices: Interpretations of Native North American Literatures*, ed. Elvira Pulitano (Lincoln: University of Nebraska Press, 2007), 203.

In the second instance, the "rocks, flat round, small, large" that Donovan loads into his pockets continue the examination of cultural meaning, not least because they are reminiscent of the "black pebble" Roland Barthes proposes as the very figure of the empty signifier. The endless possibilities for meaning implied by the black pebble would stand in contrast to the "burden" of the culturally symbolic pike. Indicating instability rather than freedom, flux is no less problematic than being weighted down. Although Donovan's buoyancy is the very antithesis of Little's dead weight, it is no less problematic. There is something frenzied about the second boy's unanchored state. Where Little "didn't seem to have any problem with staying down" (possibly because he is anchored to the tribal sign), Donovan is assaulted by the river "banging into [his] ears, jetting up [his] nose."[102] He is in danger of drowning, not because he is fastened to the river's floor, but because he is very nearly swept up in its current. It is not until Donovan grabs hold of Little and, by way of Little, the pike, that he regains stability.[103]

Donovan's weightlessness recalls earlier passages in which he comes close to being drowned—either by the drifting snow that surrounds his father's "sinking" car or the "absences of memory" that his father bequeathed to him. Before abandoning the young Donovan on the reservation, his father tells himself: "his son was a weight that would hold him under the water. His son would be the one who held his hand as the snow drifted into his mouth while he drowned."[104] Thus it seems likely that Donovan's moments of instability underscore the fact that he has neither ancestral stories nor memories to hold on to. Where Little's experience suggests that including tribal stories in the novel form can be highly problematic, Donovan's part in the same scene also reminds us that those same stories are nevertheless precious to tribal communities who are secure in their

---

102 *Little*, 113.

103 In keeping with the scene's suggestion of excesses (cultural burden on one hand and narratological transience on the other) Little's heaviness almost proves to be too much for Donovan. "Little's weight stopped me short," he explains, and his friend's deformed body is "plastered" so tightly to him that he "couldn't move" (*Little*, 114).

104 *Little*, 19.

traditions. On this level, the river's pulsating current might be aligned with the challenges presently confronting indigenous communities—namely, global exchanges that threaten to wash away native voices and traditions.[105] In other words, in response to the "liquidizing forces of postmodernity and recent waves of globalization" that now concern many scholars, Treuer reiterates his conviction that "difference matters."[106]

I would argue, therefore, that the "crucial [...] distinction between reading books *as* culture and seeing books as capable of *suggesting* culture" that is outlined in *Native American Fiction* is, to some extent, foreshadowed by the artistry of this scene in *Little*. This is because Treuer differentiates between contemporary fiction and Ojibwe culture, separating each into discrete, but vital, constituencies.[107] Finally, because the episode illustrates the fraught relationship between Little's immovability and Donovan's floundering, it can also be read as something of a plea for a restorative balance and a sense of steadiness. Composure of this nature is germane both to the Native American writer's endeavor to find a means by which to reflect tribal concerns without revealing cultural details, and to the listening skill required of non-Native readers who conduct research with "respect and a sense of responsibility" to indigenous communities. By "touching, filling, completing everything with holes in it," Little's death "two hundred feet off the ground" produces a sense of stability absent for much of the novel.[108]

---

105   Treuer has written about his anxiety that the loss of the Ojibwe language in a world populated by "Starbucks and GameStop and Wal-Mart and the Home Depot" will effectively mean that his people "lose our sense of ourselves and our culture" ("A Language too Beautiful to Lose").

106   *B/ordering Space*, ed. Henk Van Houtum, Olivier Kramsch, and Wolfgang Zierhofer (London: Ashgate, 2005), 2; Lyons, "Battle of the Bookworms," *Indian Country Today* (August 10, 2007).

107   *Native American Fiction*, 6.

108   *Little*, 231. Little's plunge might also remind readers of Paul de Man's concept of "falling"—the poststructuralist's method for describing the slippage that occurs as one signifier gives way to another in an endless chain of signification (1971). Indefinable, illimitable in life, his fall is the natural culmination of a short life spent "slip[ping] in and out." Specifically, Little's passing creates a certain sense of what de Man describes as *unreadability*; his death (whether suicide or death by misadventure) causes a

"We Had Been Let In"

It seems completely fitting that the water associated with Little's conception, "dam-break" menace, and death, be replaced with a less totalizing form of the same element—a gentle rain. His passing allows the traumatic past to be absorbed, figuratively speaking, into a more manageable circulatory system within the reservation's boundaries:

> The June after Little's drowning broke over us in a way we will always remember [...]. Those wisps of air current were enough only to lift a few hairs, enough only to make us pull closer to one another; me to Jackie, Violet to Lyle, who had finally come back. This is what the nighttime rains brought us, so we knew it was for us. Finally.[109]

The novel ends with a description of "millions" of "fertilized fish eggs" that, in combination with the summer showers, restore natural order in the wake of the traumas and dispersals that penetrate the narrative. Donovan's retrospective narration suggests but does *not* reveal the restorative stories told in the wake of Little's fall. This is possibly Treuer's way of saying that the "cultural forms" with which he is concerned cannot be "pulled from the contexts and languages that give them meaning."[110] At the same time, however, the signs of rebirth and renewal indicate an expressive freedom that the story lacks until the very end.[111] Germinating in the cultural and geographical space of the reservation's fishery, these flourishing eggs suggest both the propagation of narratives and the potential for Native American fiction to give birth to countless stories. "Soon there would be more and more," Donovan explains, "too many to count, too many to know."[112] The novel ends with an assertion that "American Indians are in the process

---

proliferation of meaning, a polysemy, that has profound significance. The child remains unfathomable to the end.

109   *Little*, 245.
110   *Native American Fiction*, 199.
111   *Little*, 248.
112   Ibid. Although slightly conventional, the novel's conclusion brings into stark relief the community's newfound ability to share its own story(s), and the ending presents

of building new worlds"—worlds that "are true to [Native] history but cognizant of present realities."[113]

Let us now reconsider Treuer's prioritization of New Critical aesthetics in light of Little's death by drowning. Informed by the practical criticism of T.S. Eliot and F.R. Leavis, *Native American Fiction* urges us to focus on the timeless qualities of the American Indian novel, its promulgation of humane ideals, and the successful marriage of content and form. This approach does not necessarily require us to read indigenous fiction in terms of Anglo-American precepts, however. Instead, Treuer's novel challenges the very critical precepts that would encourage a lay readership to read for the indexes of Indianness. He argues that Native art, in this case fiction, can refresh the way that we see the tribal world.[114] Rather than imply that "we must read *either* for culture *or* for language," as Krupat accuses him of doing, Treuer implores the reader to reconsider the connection between the two and so come to a fuller appreciation of the Native authors' right to "make larger the worlds of [their] prose through significant linguistic and cultural detail."[115] Such a reassessment is undoubtedly underway within Native American Literary Studies, and Treuer's fiction reminds us that "listening [to], engaging [with], debating, and criticizing" literature's notional and theoretical effect "will have a dramatic influence on where our field goes from here."[116]

---

the reader with the sense that Donovan and the family are about to embark on a private journey in which they will explore broader narratological spaces.

113   Lawrence Gross, "The Comic Vision of Anishinaabe Culture and Religion," *American Indian Quarterly* 26.3 (Summer 2002), 449.

114   This is a necessary move because, as Daniel Heath Justice points out in his essay "Seeing (and Reading) Red," there has been something of a "tokenization" or "privileging" of certain Native writers and themes within Native American Literary Studies. In some cases this effectively "reinforce[s] the overculture's assertion that Indians are generally alike": Devon Abbott Mihesuah and Angela Cavender Wilson, *Indigenizing the Academy: Transforming and Empowering Communities* (Lincoln: University of Nebraska Press, 2004), 105.

115   *Native American Fiction*, 202.

116   Cox, "The Past, Present, and Possible Futures of American Indian Literary Studies," 110.

Ultimately, Treuer's displays of aesthetic freedom challenge "overdetermined ways of speaking about" tribal literature and experiences. In his fiction, as in *Native American Fiction*, the Ojibwe author finds possibilities for inventiveness within narrative itself that enable him to move beyond the extant interpretative zones and imagery that the mass market has prepared us to deal with. By experimenting with recent theoretical perspectives, Treuer draws attention to the cultural freedom available in tribal writing. By supplanting traditional responses to Native American literature, *Little* begins to work through and manage historical trauma while narrating continuity with the tribal past. The novel's silences and revelations demonstrate that the "First Nations' practices of self-determination and politico-philosophical thought have remained in continuous, autonomously defined existence, even if hidden from Euro-American view."[117] The novel withholds certain stories, I am suggesting, both in order to reference the horrors of colonization and representation *and* to prepare the ground for a newly imagined, liberatory form of Native American fiction writing.

---

117 Ulrike Wiethaus, *Foundations of First People's Sovereignty: History, Education, and Culture* (New York: Peter Lang, 2008), 2.

CHAPTER 5

Portrait of the Artist: Authority, Autonomy, and Authorship in Louise Erdrich's *Shadow Tag*

Reviewers of Louise Erdrich's novel *Shadow Tag* (2010) have been somewhat divided in their understanding of the creative and personal energies that shaped the novel. *Washington Post* staff writer Ron Charles is keen to separate *Shadow Tag*'s fictional representation of marital discord and domestic abuse from the biographical detail surrounding Erdrich's relationship with the late Michael Dorris in his analysis of the novel, in which Erdrich's protagonist, Irene America, writes a work of diary fiction (the red diary) while keeping a purportedly non-fictional diary (the blue journal). "*Shadow Tag* is no roman à clef, no act of spousal revenge," Charles insists, before rejecting outright the idea that Erdrich's grim tale is informed by events in the author's own life.[1] To his mind, neither the novel's account of a successful creative and personal union that enters freefall and ends in a bitter divorce, nor its affecting account of suicide, can be linked to real-life events; events that include the dissolution of the Erdrich–Dorris marriage in 1996 and the Dartmouth professor's suicide in 1997, following the loss of the woman described in the popular press as "his muse, writing partner, and mother of his daughters."[2] On the contrary, Charles argues, the novel

---

1   "Love in the Time of Bitterness," review of Louise Erdrich's *Shadow Tag*, *Washington Post* (February 3 2010) <http://articles.washingtonpost.com/2010-02-03/news/36852962_1_shadow-tag-louise-erdrich-irene> accessed April 26, 2012.

2   Michelle Green, "The Final Chapter: Facing Divorce and Sex-Abuse Allegations, Author Michael Dorris Takes His Own Life," *People Magazine* (April 28, 1997) <http://www.people.com/people/archive/article /0,,20121946,00.html> accessed May 2 2012.

actually "says far more about the universal tragedy of spoiled love than it reveals about [Louise Erdrich's] private life."

On the face of it, Leah Hager Cohen appears to concur with this assessment. In a review titled "Cruel Love" she suggests that critical references to the marriage between these literary titans, the divorce, allegations of child abuse against Dorris, and his subsequent death, might appear "prurient" if not entirely "loathsome."[3] There are many critics who would agree with this initial assessment. Despite sharing some of Charles's reticence, however, Hager Cohen is by no means as reserved when it comes to commingling the contextual, the personal, and the fictional. We might, she counsels, "miss something if we approach this book *simply* as fiction." Accordingly, the reviewer unpacks the Native American themes dealt with in *Shadow Tag*, and reminds readers of the sociopolitical contexts that this work of tribal fiction exists within. In that way, she draws attention to the fact that Irene America is an Ojibwe woman who is writing a doctoral thesis on George Catlin and his nineteenth-century portraits of America's indigenous peoples. She also notes that Irene has abandoned an earlier study on the Métis rebel Louis Riel. Other important allusions to tribal concerns are glossed in her review. Amongst these is the fact that Irene's husband Gil, who is "the wrong fractions of Klamath and Cree and landless Montana Chippewa" and is consequently not an enrolled member of any tribe, is nevertheless known as the "Native Edward Hopper" in the American art world.[4]

Hager Cohen's analysis stretches far beyond the thematic however, and although she allows that it is usually "a fool's errand to parse fact from fiction," she asks her reader to consider the fact that Erdrich has been in a marriage that bears uncanny resemblance to that of her protagonist. Indeed, Hager Cohen reasons, by reconstituting so many of the "facts" of her life in this fictional account of a failed relationship, Erdrich appears to have "seeded her narrative with [...] an imperative to do so." As a result, she

3   "Cruel Love," *New York Times* (February 5, 2010) <http://www.nytimes. com/2010/02/07/books/review/ Cohen-t.html?pagewanted =all&_r=0> accessed April 20, 2012.
4   *Shadow Tag*, 13 & 8.

chooses to sketch a comprehensive picture of the once "iconic" marriage between Erdrich and Dorris during the course of the review, and, in complete contrast to Charles's approach, the *New York Times* reviewer suggests that Erdrich's troubled protagonists are fictional analogues for Erdrich and her late ex-husband. Ultimately, she argues that a comparative analysis between the author's private history and her fictional work is not only necessary but is also sanctioned on some level. To be fair to her, there does seem to be some motivation for arguing that Erdrich's experiences have shaped her role as storyteller since 1997. The author has publicly noted the need to refer to those tragic events, and has spoken about her former husband's illness and suicide, albeit briefly. As such, the remarkable forbearance and strength she has shown in maintaining a composed silence throughout the tabloid press's dissection of her personal life, has been coupled with the author's reasoned understanding that she lives in the public eye on one level, and her realization that her story may help others on another. It was in that spirit, and in that context, that Erdrich addressed a crowd in Dartmouth just a few months after Dorris's death and explained: "no one who loves a suicide will ever be intact again. We are left holding the curve of the question mark, above the dark period of that decision."[5] Significantly enough, it was during that speech that Erdrich made reference to "Nurse Louise [who] took care of the weaker, frightened, uncertain, impulsive, sorrowing Louise who had, once upon a time, immersed herself in her fictions." For early readers of *Shadow Tag*, Hager Cohen amongst them, it was hardly difficult to see the relationship between the "Nurse Louise, [the] realist" and the half-sister Louise whom Irene America discovers midway through the novel. This heretofore unknown blood sister keeps the family together in the months after Irene and Gil's untimely deaths, and turns her attention to saving the children who have lived through the storms of the turbulent, all-consuming marriage.

---

5   Louise Erdrich (Class of 1976), Convocation Speech at Dartmouth College, September 23 1997 <www.dartmouth.edu/~dcare/pdfs/Erdrich_Address.pdf> accessed May 3 2012.

Despite the relative merits of Charles and Hager Cohen's analyses, both accounts give rise to some troubling questions. In the first instance, even though Charles certainly appears to offer something of an antidote to the more pass-remarkable and invasive analyses that might plague Erdrich's novel, the contention that the book is, above all, a "beautiful and urgent" account of a "*universal* tragedy" might actually serve to draw a veil across broader contextual issues that the novel might be said to comment on (emphasis added). To my mind, a rush toward the "universal" possibly does more than orientate the reader away from the "prurient"; it very nearly elides *Shadow Tag*'s consideration of the dense and difficult issues being worked out within tribal communities today, and insufficiently attends to the reality of indigenous sovereignty.[6] This is regrettable, given the various forms of aesthetic and cultural sovereignty that seem to be suggested by the book's storyline, themes, and symbolism. In fact, reading this novel simply as an engrossing but clear-cut account of a widely experienced, common malaise is something of a missed opportunity. In the second instance, while many readers will surely be interested in fiction's ability to comment on extratextual concerns, and will therefore be motivated to search out and interpret *Shadow Tag*'s culturally specific concerns and readings, few scholars are likely to follow Hager Cohen's lead in reading the book as a thinly fictionalized account of Erdrich's biographical "back pages." This is partly because any attempt to read the fictional through the biographical, to lay one palimpsestically on top of the other, comes dangerously close to revisiting the tabloid press's interest in, and treatment of, events in Erdrich's private life. Moreover, the majority of critics working within the field of Native American Literary Studies are *au fait* with the sensitivities

---

6   To be fair, there is only so much that a book reviewer can do in eight hundred words, and Charles does pay attention to some of the novel's contextual issues, especially when he argues that Erdrich takes "a peculiar relationship [... and frames] it as a classic feminist theme and a queasy re-enactment of the exploitation of American Indians." Hence, I am not quibbling with any perceived lack of depth in Charles's pithy and extremely insightful review. What I am questioning, however, is the extent to which he focuses on, and amplifies, the universal and general above the tribal and specific.

surrounding the scholarly impulse to "read into" or "know" more about the lives of indigenous authors, the risk that scholarly inquiry might appear as a problematic echo of ethnographical and anthropological encroachments into Native lives and spaces, and the problems with treating literary fiction as tribal myth or tribal reality. Finally, and perhaps most obviously, the apparent similarities between *Shadow Tag*'s fictionalized storyline and the author's life notwithstanding, the two are not the one and the same. In fact, I would argue that Erdrich reconstitutes and rehashes media accounts of her private life—rumors and half-truths—in order to take control of the story, to problematize fixed notions about story and truth, and, at the same time, to debunk the myth surrounding her own supposedly "iconic marriage." Thus, the complex, interleaved narratives found in *Shadow Tag* possibly emphasize the Ojibwe author's right to maintain her privacy in her personal life more often than they reveal salacious details or beseech a biographical reading. Accordingly, rather than presenting the reader with "glaring similarities" between her own life and that of her protagonist, and providing the reader with an "imperative" to read deeply into her back pages, Erdrich's apparent directive *for* interpretation possibly serves to remind the reader of the perils of interpreting Native American fiction as verbatim.[7] In truth, it may even be because of readers' earlier attempts to find fact in that fiction that Erdrich decided to rename the character Louise after the hardcover edition had been reviewed.[8]

7   This is the very opposite of the directive against interpretation found in the "Notice" at the opening of Mark Twain's *The Adventures of Huckleberry Finn*. According to Sacvan Bercovitch that directive is delivered in deadpan, so even though it seems to push the reader *away* from "moral" and "motive," it paradoxically suggests that the novel actually "requires [a certain type of contextual] interpretation": "Deadpan Huck: Or, What's Funny about Interpretation," *The Kenyon Review* 24.3/4 (Summer 2002), 98.

8   In subsequent editions this character is known as May, thereby undoing the significance that Hager Cohen places on the fact that Irene's half-sister is the author's namesake. I might not have noticed this fact, had it not been for a lively and immensely enjoyable dinnertime conversation with Gwen Westerman and LeAnne Howe at NALS in 2011 (Gwen had written about the American version and together we pieced together the facts surrounding this change of name). I am also indebted to

Hence, neither Charles's faith in the universalism of art, nor Hager Cohen's particular brand of sleuthing, seem to reveal the extent to which Erdrich's book is a richly layered work that is informed by a host of aesthetic, cultural, and personal concerns. The question, then, is how, *exactly*, does this quasi-metafictional text work across the series of doubled spaces that are signposted in its title, and how does Erdrich mobilize these spaces in order to interrogate, or comment on, the fictionist's role within various, often overlapping, communities: that is, the literary community, the tribal community, the American community, and the international community of artists? In answering this question it might be wise to take James Cihlar's logic that *Shadow Tag* comments "on the reality that famous authors must maintain public images, even as they strive to protect individual privacy" and stretch it a little further; namely by considering the possibility that the book comments not just on Erdrich's position as a famous writer who has been mistreated by the tabloid press, but that it also comments on her position as an Ojibwe writer, and on the position of the Native American artist and of indigenous communities in general.[9] After all, this is a novel that features a painter who is recognized as a famous Native American artist, his historian wife, and the next generation of Ojibwe scribes. In that context, *Shadow Tag* is not just about the troubles that Louise Erdrich has encountered in her lifetime, or even about the press's treatment of it (though these things almost certainly did inform the novel). Instead, this book is, to a large degree, about the unique treatment meted out to tribal writers, who must deal with the expectation that their literary work is, fundamentally, about truth telling. In this way, the novel presents the reader with the fine balance between testimony and various twists and turns (radical changes in narrative perspective and so on), which appear to be in keeping with

Erdrich's editor at HarperCollins in the United States, Terry Karten, for clarifying the circumstances surrounding this change. In June 2012 Ms. Karten confirmed: "In the original hardcover edition of *Shadow Tag* published [in the United States], Irene's half-sister was named Louise. The author decided to change that character's name to May, and we made the correction in our first paperback printing of the novel." (private correspondence via email).

9   "*Shadow Tag*" (review), *Prairie Schooner* 85.1 (Spring 2011), 174.

Erdrich's oft-noted engagement with the "fluidity of identity that has come to epitomize so much postmodern self-conception," and her construction of any number of structural, temporal, or story-bound "ambiguities."[10] So, as with David Treuer's *Little*, *Shadow Tag* is often about the unknowable, the unrepresentable, the undefined nature of language and story. Here is a story that invites an engagement with Native American experiences and concerns on one hand, but offers the reader little by way of definite answers or assured knowledge on the other; here is a story that often refuses access to the heart of the matter. Crucially, and almost paradoxically, it is also about creating the fullest *version* of the story possible; even though the book's multiple viewpoints, perspectives, and insights, fail to provide one "true," definitive story, they do provide us with a sense of continuance and acuity. The version of events that the reader becomes privy to comes from within Irene America's family; the various redactions, amendments, additions et cetera that are made to the story that is finally told are chosen by her daughter Riel, who is suddenly revealed as the third-person narrator at the end of the book.[11] Autonomous, uncensored (except by her own judgments), and free to work outside of standard literary conventions, primarily because she is a student in creative writing, Riel has taken control of the narrative, owned it, protected it. Her narrative, which incorporates a gamut of issues including shattered love, alcoholism, indigenous lifeways, tribal artistry, and so on, is entirely her own.

Crucially, Riel owns the silences too. If the complex relationship between author/implied author/narrator tells us anything in this instance, it is that we, the readers, are in thrall of someone else's story, and that the teller's position is key. Thus, in response to both Charles's eagerness to focus purely on the "universal" aspects of the novel, and Hager Cohen's unabashed inquisitiveness about the author's life, the goal of this chapter is to consider *Shadow Tag*'s interrogation of narrative positions, Erdrich's

---

10 Rita Ferrari, "'Where the Maps Stopped': The Aesthetics of Borders in Louise Erdrich's *Love Medicine* and *Tracks*," *Style* (Spring 1999), 146–147; Karla Sanders, "A Healthy Balance: Religion, Identity, and Community in Louise Erdrich's *Love Medicine*," *MELUS* 23.2 (Summer 1998), 142.

11 *Shadow Tag*, 251.

balancing of aesthetic and cultural concerns, the representation of Native peoples, the treatment and understanding of indigenous writers and presences, and the question of "truth" in art and in literature. In short, I wish to examine the author's dexterous interweaving of the tribal *and* the universal, what are cultural specificities and what are generally experienced. I do so primarily because *Shadow Tag* forcefully and urgently confronts key questions surrounding narrative perspective, critical interpretation, authorial autonomy, and self-determination within literary studies today.

Portrait of a Marriage

A taut and, in many ways terse, account of a steadily unraveling marriage, Erdrich's novel deals not only with the failure of a relationship, but with the flailing responses of the parties involved. Married for "nearly fifteen years," Irene and Gil have been partners in an ardent relationship that is described in terms of a symbiotic—almost consuming—energy and a perilous proximity. We learn that Gil has never "painted anyone who could project emotion through her flesh with such urgency," and it seems that Irene's "offhand self-confidence about her body" has fed not only the art work itself, but also a lifestyle that the wider public envies.[12] The setting for their affluent, "sexy marriage" is a house on Mount Curve Avenue (which, according to the American Institute of Architects, is home to some of "the most splendid mansions" in Minneapolis's wealthy Lowry Hill neighborhood), and their family life appears, at least on the surface, to be quite perfect.[13] Their children—a "shy six year old" called Stoney, "raffish" daughter Riel, and Florian, who is a budding math genius—attend private schools, and the casual onlooker could be forgiven for presuming that the

---

12   *Shadow Tag*, 32 & 8.
13   Larry Millet, *AIA Guide to the Twin Cities* (Minneapolis: Minnesota Historical Society Press, 2007), 16.

household revels in the pseudo-intellectual, bohemian existence cultivated by Irene and Gil. Yet, as the book opens it is abundantly clear that Irene is facing a crisis and is now questioning it all. Indeed, Erdrich's character has come to realize that, as far as her marriage was concerned, "there were bad omens from the beginning."[14] Over time, it has slowly dawned on Irene that Gil's portraits are inspired by both the desire to pay homage to her beauty *and* the desire to frame and control her life. So, even though his portraiture is, rather poetically, described as "an act of fascinated love" at one point, Irene has come to the realization that instead of being "the same kind of person" as her husband, she is "just food."[15] What disturbs her most, Irene realizes, is not simply that her husband "wished to possess" her, but that she made the mistake of allowing him to believe that he could do so.[16] For his part, Gil's all-too literal interpretation of the marital vows to "have" and to "hold" have driven him to seek out his wife's diary in a bid to plumb her inner thoughts, and to follow her inner narrative.

Of course, that prying has not gone undetected, and Irene has sensed that something is amiss. Unnerved, and maddened, by the realization that she may have suspected, and obviated, Gil's actions on an almost unconscious level for some time now, she notes, "I realize that I didn't include many truths in my red diary. And I hid it."[17] This deepening sense of shadowing causes Irene to seek out a safer "private room," one in which she can record—and form—her thoughts in an entirely uncensored and unencumbered manner. Crucially, Irene decides to keep two diaries, thereafter using one as a weapon of resistance and one as a source of both personal comfort and evidence of her motivations. Over a number of months she packs the "faux diary," the original red one, with an intentionally misleading and excoriating commentary on her marriage and the charade that it has become.[18] Stored in its usual hiding place in the filing cabinet, the red diary offers a partly fictionalized version of events, and is designed to fool

14   *Shadow Tag*, 18.
15   Ibid., 36 & 90.
16   Ibid., 18.
17   Ibid., 17.
18   Charles, "Love in the Time of Bitterness."

Gil into thinking that he has penetrated Irene's thoughts on those occasions
when he fails to honor her right to privacy and chooses to "enter [...] his
wife's basement office" unannounced and uninvited.[19] However, her insights
are often little more than fabrications or untruths or statements directed
at her husband. Most notable, perhaps, are the fictitious and spiteful tales
that recount invented love affairs and which state, unambiguously, that
Gil isn't the children's father.[20] Toward the end of the novel, Irene even
utilizes the red diary to implore her husband to set her free: "*Please let
me go* she scrawled on the next blank page."[21] The second diary, the blue
notebook that is kept under lock and key in the bank vault in uptown
Minneapolis, is something of an emotional and intellectual escape route
from Gil's loathsome spying. It contains Irene's unedited (and putatively
ingenuous) account of the marriage's final days, her thoughts on its dissolution, and her observations on her plight and that of her children. Thus, the
blue journal obviously stands in stark contrast to the ruinous and morbid
fictions found in the red diary.

Charles's point that this novel should be placed alongside great
works of literature that deal with universal themes and concerns is well
taken. The novel has a mercurial quality about it, and Erdrich manages
to conjoin heartbreaking sadness with a sense of gothic foreboding, a
thriller's pace, and allusions to an abundance of philosophical, scientific,
and aesthetic reference points. On a similar note, Cihlar astutely notes
that "the notion of split selves recorded in color-coded journals is a sly
nod to [both ...] *The Golden Notebook* by Doris Lessing" and "the deliberate deceptiveness" of Anaïs Nin's journals.[22] Other important literary
referents abound. *Shadow Tag* also revisits, on some level, several of the
literary techniques and themes found in Graham Greene's *The End of the
Affair*. Both works involve marital disharmony, ill-fated attraction, and,
ultimately, death. Even more significantly, a woman's diary is central to

19   *Shadow Tag*, 5.
20   Ibid., 27, 29, 152, 153, 183.
21   Ibid., 198.
22   Cihlar, "*Shadow Tag*" (review), 174.

the plot in each; Greene's jealous protagonist, Maurice Bendrix, is certain that he can rekindle the love that his former lover, Sarah Miles, once had for him, and he goes as far as to hire a detective, tasked with the job of searching out Sarah's diary, reading it, and reporting back. It is via this prying that Bendrix, like Gil, hopes to track someone else's inner thoughts and change her course. Neil Jordan's cinematic adaptation concretizes the sense of antipathy and attraction that permeates Greene's novel, and it is difficult not to compare Ralph Fiennes's declaratory opening line—"this is a diary of hate"—with Irene's clipped and emphatic pronouncement: "I have two diaries now."[23] As a professional writer, albeit a blocked one, Irene appears to share Bendrix's notion that all scribes, even historians, "arbitrarily" choose "that moment of experience from which to look back or from which to look ahead."[24] That is to say, her announcement "I have two diaries *now*" seems to attest to the fact that she has chosen her "moment of experience"; it also attunes the reader to the likelihood that there have been, or will be, narrative switchbacks, detours, and contradictions. It could even be argued that this line prepares the reader for a form of literary fraudulence, while also underlining the moment when Erdrich's protagonist begins to look ahead, to anticipate the future. By keeping two diaries, two "records" of events, Erdrich's character readily problematizes the notion of the "truth," and draws attention to the ways in which the past can either be whitewashed or go unrecorded altogether. This possibility is concretized later on in the novel, when Irene reasons, "To have meaning, history must consist of both occurrence and narrative."[25]

23 The contextual circumstances surrounding the novels are analogous too, insofar as many critics and readers speculated—and continue to speculate—about the extent to which the more salacious details included in Greene's novel were autobiographically informed. This is quite simply because Greene left his wife Vivien in 1948, and did so in order to embark on tumultuous affair with an American woman, Catherine Walston. Walston refused to marry the author and, as William Cash recalled at the time of Greene's death in 2011, Bendrix's lot could be read as a surreptitious retelling of the author's inner turmoil: *New Statesman* (April 27, 2011).

24 Graham Greene, *The End of the Affair* (London: Vintage, 2004), 1.

25 *Shadow Tag*, 105.

This point strikes Erdrich's protagonist as she considers the affair that she had (or may not have had—the reader can't be sure) with an old friend, Germaine, whom Gil suspects is involved in the mystery surrounding his wife's faithfulness. "If she never told," Irene continues, "if the two of them never talked about it, there was no narrative."[26] This amounts to a challenge to the notion of history itself; without the story, there is no event, no history to be recorded or known. This philosophical quandary within the heart of the novel raises huge questions relating to theories of truth, structuralism, poststructuralism, the "lie of fiction," and so on. Indeed, the reflexive, tautological structure of Erdrich's questions forces us to face epistemic questions about narrative and event, perspective and position, truth and subterfuge. The limits of writing and interpretation are tested here, and Erdrich, like Greene before her, appears to engage with the unending possibilities and explorations made possible by language. The densely packed psychological spaces that Erdrich creates, her presentment of the torsions, commitments, and unmooring that love can trigger, and the near effortless way in which she gestures toward over five hundred years of colonial history, all demonstrate, quite clearly, why the author has been a Pulitzer Prize finalist. There are countless avenues for further literary analysis to be found amongst the array of brightly woven threads that *Shadow Tag* dangles before the reader, whether it is Florian's precociousness in math, Stoney's birth amidst the traumatic events of September 11, 2001, or the renaissance portraits that Gil loves so dearly.

To my mind, one of the more striking universal themes explored is that of women's rights in the modern world. Despite being affluent, cultured, and highly intelligent, Irene America finds herself being controlled and abused by an extremely domineering husband. It is surely significant, then, that Irene's need to find a vaulted writing space carries at least an echo of Virginia Woolf's oft-cited view that "a woman must have money and a room of her own if she is to write."[27] Erdrich's initial references to Irene's "private room" and "private little closets" establish a vein of rich

---

26   Ibid.
27   Virginia Woolf, *A Room of One's Own* (Orlando: First Harvest, 1989), 4.

allusions that presage the feminist theme that runs throughout.[28] In the first instance, the reader is reminded of the manner in which Woolf railed against the constraints that prevented women from writing, and her struggle with a controlling male presence whose standards very nearly destroyed her artistic abilities—in Woolf's case this power was exerted by her father, Leslie Stephen. After Stephen's death, Woolf noted in her diary: "His life would have entirely ended mine. What would have happened? No writing, no books."[29] The British writer's vision of the limits that restricted women artists, and the subsequent sublimation, or worse, death, of creative and personal energies finds an important corollary in Erdrich's novel. In that regard, it is also important to note that Woolf's diaries, essays, and public lectures often raised complex intertwined questions concerning issues of authorial freedom and women's liberty.

However, it also appears to be the case that Erdrich is making other allusions too, and possibly moving beyond, or even problematizing, a feminist narrative that straightforwardly links her, as a woman writer, to Woolf—a writer from a different time, place, and class. The density of these allusions, and the manner in which they are made, possibly undermines Charles's claims about the novel's utter universalism, and Hager Cohen's intrusive line of analysis. In the first instance, it seems to be particularly significant that Erdrich should conflate the three spaces that Woolf availed of: the novel itself, the diary, and the room of one's own. Although the act of revealing Irene's thoughts through the publication of her personal diary may appear to collapse the barriers between the narrator-author and her audience, this device actually *intensifies* the idea of autonomy and privacy (all the more so if one intends to read Irene as a proxy for Erdrich herself). That is to say, even though Erdrich's use of the diary frame cultivates a sense of immediacy that invites the reader to empathize with Irene's plight (primarily because the protagonist shares the "facts" of her marriage with the reader), the reader cannot escape the

28 *Shadow Tag*, 4.
29 Elaine Showalter, "Killing the Angel in the House: The Autonomy of Women Writers," *Antioch Review* 50.1/2 (Winter/Spring 1992), 208.

reality that both of Irene's diaries (the blue diary and the red journal alike), are, like the character Irene, fictional. Moreover, the reader soon learns that Irene's diaries are not only narrative vehicles of Erdrich's devising, but are fictional and duplicitous in-and-of themselves. When coupled with the conceit that Riel has, in turn, edited those diaries and has written the story that we now read, it becomes obvious that *Shadow Tag* is, in fact, a reminder of exactly how little we know about Irene's story (and therefore Erdrich's). This gives rise to a certain set of questions: Which of Irene America's diaries are the more imaginative? Where does the story begin and (real) life end?[30] Instead of reassuring the reader that the ensuing tale is provided by a reliable, trustworthy narrator, or that the diary, as the literature of record, offers a prescribed zone in which a discernible, construable, or unwavering story resides, the first-person narration at the beginning of *Shadow Tag* actually serves to highlight the elusive nature of narrative itself; it underlines vagaries in memory and recollection. Thus, as well as referring to the reflexive nature of narration, which is invariably modified or stranded with various layers of intentionality, the opening statement, "I have two diaries now," might also confront the amorphous, unknowable nature of narrative in a world where stories—perhaps even rumors—seem unending and develop exponentially.

In the second instance, as well as underlining the financial and personal imperative by having her protagonist writing in a solitary space, Erdrich also seems to point to America's colonial history and the indigene's place in the nation state by having Irene write her "true" story amidst Minneapolis's stockpiled wealth and valuables. Hence, it would seem that as an Ojibwe woman writer, Erdrich is interested in a broader set of autonomies—versions of selfhood that cannot be easily or clearly mapped onto the imperatives of what Mridula Nath Chakraborty, after Robyn

30   Not only does the novel's conclusion force us to radically reassess or query both the fictionality of the blue journal's contents and the version of events that we are privy to, but, through the description of Gil and Irene's deaths, it vividly ties the end of the story to the end of life. More will be written on the significance of this below.

Wiegman, describes as the "Eurocentric teleological narrative of a 'unified female subject' [that is itself] a 'fictional landscape.'"[31] It would appear that *Shadow Tag*'s author is not interested in writing from *one* discrete space, be it as a member of the Turtle Mountain band of the Ojibwe, as a woman, or as a universal artist. Instead, Erdrich insists on her right to produce fiction from all of those spaces, and plots the resulting work on something akin to a Venn diagram. So, even though her project is certainly about feminist agency and what Woolf described as the strength to "tell the truth about my own experiences as a body," it is also about the Ojibwe author's right to withhold and safeguard that truth as she sees fit—regardless of whether it relates to Ojibwe ways of knowing or the author's relationship with her family and the ancestors.[32] As I will show below, this project is also about commingling various forms of complexly and richly imagined sovereignties together; personal and communal, gendered and tribal, aesthetic and political. My goal, then, is to examine the novel's complex engagement with both universal *and* Ojibwe concerns, and its commentary on the role of the author.

Life/Writing

Erdrich's decision to produce a work of diary fiction is crucial to this investigation. Woolf once referred to the diary as "a capacious hold-all." Rachel Langford and Russell West have referred to diary writing as "an uncertain genre" that is:

---

31 Mridula Nath Chakraborty, "Wa(i)ving It All Away: Producing Subject and Knowledge in Feminisms of Colours," in *Third Wave Feminism: A Critical Exploration*, ed. Stacy Gillis, Gillian Howie, and Rebecca Munford (London: Palgrave Macmillan, 2011), 102.

32 Showalter, "Killing the Angel in the House," 207.

uneasily balanced between literary and historical writing, between the spontaneity of reportage and reflectiveness of the crafted text, between selfhood and events, between subjectivity and objectivity, between the private and the public, [that] constantly disturbs attempts to summarize its characteristics within formalized boundaries.[33]

As such, the genre facilitates a consideration of layered narrative structures, and is ideally placed to interrogate the imbricated, often thorny, structure of narrative itself. Erdrich deploys the diary's "special relationship to privacy, intimacy, and secrecy" in a number of ways, using it to examine various subject positions, and to interrogate understandings of memory.[34] Diaries that surface in the wake of a particular event can be interpreted as artifacts created by the interplay between historical event on one hand, and a series of discrete, distinct, responses to, or memories of, those same events on the other. Written in installments that, more often than not, signal date and time quite clearly, the diary becomes a narrative space in which the recent—but sometimes distant—past can be recalled, cataloged and evaluated. As a result, the act of diary writing and the end product, the diary itself, can potentially disrupt the binary construct that pits "traditional history," one true version of events, against an absolute and dissolute form of postmodern fragmentation. This opportunity to recount "personal experience in [a] historical and social context" facilitates a deeper understanding of "'the intimate theater of history.'" Hence, we might do well to note the extent to which *Shadow Tag*'s overall engagement with acts of narration, historical representations, and mnemonic structures *per se* potentially revives the study of diary form within literary studies, but also has resonance for a international audience who may be interested in the diary's contribution to various aspects of the social, political, and cultural discourse. The themes in this book are, as Charles's points out, certainly broad; as well as working with themes and issues that humanities scholars work through collectively, *Shadow Tag* also reconsiders notions of ethnography and truth telling within a tribal literature. I will return to

33   Irina Paperno, "What Can Be Done with Diaries?," *Russian Review* 63.4 (October 2004), 561.
34   Ibid., 562.

this question of cultural specificity and Ojibwe contexts below. Suffice to say, for now, that the nested, overlapping structure of Erdrich's narrative presents the reader with four levels of narration: there is the novel itself, which the reader approaches as the work of Louise Erdrich; there are the two diaries featured within the novel; finally, there is Riel's *paratextual* "editor's note" that simultaneously gives shape and perspective to the other narratives, *and* explodes the notion that *Shadow Tag* straightforwardly reveals a story of a doomed marriage or Irene's attempt to deal with it. As a result, this particular history of the Americas is open to interpretation on many levels, and the framing of the narrative will be of widespread interest, especially amongst scholars interested in genre, the interweave between "truth" and aesthetics, feminism, narrative theory, and so on. It will also attract considerable attention from those interested in poststructuralism, postmodernism, and postcolonialism.

Indeed, even though it is almost twenty years since Nancy Peterson published her brilliant essay on the "crisis" caused by "the impossibility of writing traditional history in a postmodern, postrepresentational era," the novel's structure shows that Erdrich continues to be interested in what Peterson defines as "the debate about whether historical narratives can be objective representations or are (merely) subjective constructions of a researcher's and a culture's ideologies."[35] Erdrich's use of the diary as a narrative device therefore seems perfectly apt if one reads *Shadow Tag* as a response to the "crisis" of history and representation. Fundamentally, Irene's diaries cause a rupture; the various texts found in *Shadow Tag* interpenetrate, and the signs found in one infinitely refer back to those found in the other. That opening line, "I have two diaries now," appears to underline the extent to which meaning is constantly deferred, and meshes with Derrida's concept of constant transfer. Produced in the absence of a listener, the text creates a gap between writer and reader. That gap produces, in turn, a degree of uncertainty that places meaning beyond our reach. Diary writing consequently produces the very *trace* that the French philosopher spoke of;

35 Nancy J. Peterson, "History, Postmodernism, and Louise Erdrich's *Tracks*," *PMLA*, 109:5 (October 1994), 982.

the text actively deconstructs the gap between the fictional and the real, the private and public. Revealing a "presence-absence" (one that is associable with the philosopher's concept of *différance* and "arche-writing") the diary, as text, initiates a process of infinite referral and mediation rather than being a source of meaning or truth.[36] It is possibly for this reason that Dorrit Cohn argues that a "diarist's past history normally emerges in the order it presents itself to his [or her] memory: fragmented and allusive, rather than continuous and explicit."[37] Ania Loomba calls this the "slippage between words or signs and their meaning."[38]

Erdrich plays with that sense of slippage, absence, trace, fragmentation, and *difference* throughout *Shadow Tag*. While I do not have time to consider the novel's gestures towards questions of trauma and loss in a post-9/11 context, I would point out that Irene's diaries produce a powerful sense of "presence-absence" by placing the words of a dead woman full center on the page. These are the diaries of the dead; a contrivance that ties in with the possibility that the diary represents "a lasting trace of one's being—an effective defense against annihilation."[39] Speaking from beyond the grave, Irene, like Treuer's character Little, embodies a haunting or spectral form of free play. Lost amidst the echoic narratives created by this improvisation, the reader (who is simultaneously Irene's reader, Riel's reader, *and* Erdrich's reader) is placed at the center of a reflexive, self-referential loop from the very beginning. In this way, the diary appears to accommodate, even initiate, the type of decentering suggested by the poststructuralists. For instance, at one point the seemingly unobtrusive, heterodiegetic third-person narrator sees a crucial scene from Irene's perspective and presents the affair between the protagonist and Germaine as a *fait accompli*, reporting:

---

36   Jacques Derrida, *Of Grammatology*, trans. Gayatri Chakravorty Spivak (Baltimore, MD: Johns Hopkins University Press, 1997), 71.
37   Dorrit Cohn, *Transparent Minds: Narrative Modes for Presenting Consciousness in Fiction* (Princeton, NJ: Princeton University Press, 1978), 209.
38   Ania Loomba, *Colonialism/Postcolonialism* (London: Routledge, 2005), 36.
39   Paperno, "What Can Be Done with Diaries?," 563.

> After making love, they'd been shaken by their comfort with each other [...]. He wanted to continue, to see Irene again. But it was immediately clear to her that they should return to their own difficult lives and pretend that nothing had happened.[40]

Just twenty pages later the same narrator slips into Gil's mind and notes his growing conviction that Irene "hadn't fallen for Germaine's dark skin and his enrolment number."[41] Despite the unmediated style and "real time" delivery of this information—both of which appear to attest to its veracity—the so-called "facts" of the affair are unknown to us. Moreover, the whole question is called into doubt or even contradicted by the yarns that Irene spins in her Red Diary. "There was no affair," she writes there at one point, later adding "I am faithful to Gil for obvious reasons."[42] Yet, soon after, Irene writes about various, probably fictional, infidelities and calls the children's paternity into question.[43] It is through this constant shifting and uncertainty within *Shadow Tag*'s various narratives that the allusion of truth versus fiction is deconstructed; the reader is left with nothing other than the trace produced by the gap between fidelity and infidelity, history and representation. The reader is also left with the abiding sense that writing could easily amount to an act of infinite referral when Riel admits that she has narrated the story in full; at this point the reader realizes that the reportage of the post-coital scene was based on her re-imagining of it:

> I have put it all together, both of her diaries. The Red Diary. The Blue Notebook. Her notes on Catlin. My memory charts. I have also filled in certain events and connections. Sometimes, it has helped me to talk to May. Other times, I imagined that I was my mother. Or my father. I have written about them in many ways [...].[44]

It could also be argued that Riel's creative writing project is the trace of Irene's diaries, which are the trace of a marriage, which, as I will discuss below, is possibly a trace of certain aspects of American history and culture.

40 *Shadow Tag*, 104.
41 Ibid., 124.
42 *Shadow Tag*, 100 & 121.
43 Ibid., 152 & 183.
44 Ibid., 251.

And on it goes—the trace, of a trace, of a trace. At one point the narrator imagines Irene thinking to herself that: "Her name was now a cipher joined to simulacra."[45] Other approximations of poststructuralist thought appear in *Shadow Tag*, and to some extent, Irene's reflexive and knowing commentary, and her double-diary, display an awareness of what Michel Foucault once called the possibility for "multiple, shifting and even self-contradictory identities."[46]

Interestingly, this idea of "shifting and even self-contradictory identities" and Foucault's meditations on surveillance, selfhood, knowledge, and power may also inform an analysis of the symbolism and imagery associated with painting and aesthetics throughout *Shadow Tag*. Foucault's theories might also help us to unpack some of the book's more troubling images, especially those arising out of family scenes in the home, Irene's constant posing, the couple's disastrous visits to family therapy, and the narrators' references to confused paternity. For example, it would appear that Irene finds herself under the type of confinement that Foucault deals with in *The History of Madness* (1961). In dealing with the incarceration and surveillance of those who were deemed "unreasonable," *The History of Madness* outlines the institutionalization of those who were considered to be demented, the unemployed, deviant mothers, and so on. Noticeably, Gil believes that Irene slots into at least two of these categories, and his position at the center of the house, which is consolidated by his position as main earner and artist in residence, possibly figures him as the warden in a structure that more closely resembles a Panopticon than it does a happy family home. Other

---

45   Ibid., 39.
46   Elizabeth Eckermann, "Foucault, Embodiment and Gender Subjectivities: The Case of Voluntary Self-Starvation," in *Foucault, Health and Medicine* (London: Routledge, 1997), 153. Importantly, during the 1980s scholars such as Teresa de Lauretis began to focus on the question of subjectivity and feminism, and (like Nancy Peterson) sought ways in which feminism could negotiate poststructuralist anxieties about subjectivity and identity, thereby remaining useful in the face of various levels of social constraint and repression. (Theresa de Lauretis. "Feminist studies/Critical studies: Issues, terms and contexts," in *Feminist Studies/Critical Studies*, ed. Teresa de Lauretis [Bloomington: Indiana University Press, 1986], 9).

types of unsettling surveillance occur within the Minneapolis home. At one point, the children's faces are "remote and watchful."[47] Elsewhere, in another of the novel's disturbing sequences, Irene awakens from a deep sleep to "feel someone watching her" and is not surprised to find Riel at her bedside: "Riel was staring calmly at Irene. Irene stared back at her. The weight of her daughter's gaze was unbearable."[48] The act of looking and objectification is further extended during this scene when Irene, having left Riel to her own bed, finds Florian "facing into the glare" of his computer screen. Initially interpreting her son's embarrassed reaction to her sudden presence as a sign that he is furtively viewing Internet pornography, Irene is shocked to see that Florian is actually viewing some of the more graphic and "ugly" portraits of her that Gil has done. The obvious correlation between one set of explicit images and another, between high art and sordid porn, is concretized by the son's reaction to his mother's apparent prostitution of her body and her victimization. Florian rails at the representation of Irene that he finds in many of the paintings, telling her: "You should have made him quit. You should have exerted some control."[49] The scene ends with another form of gazing, with the teenager "staring at his mother" contemptuously before detachedly asking, "Why don't you just have another drink and go to bed?"[50] Prior to this, during the "three nights [that] Irene kept herself sober," Irene and the children had paused outside the house and "watched their father through the window. They looked at him fondly, as if he were an animal in the zoo."[51]

These disturbing instances of surveillance within the family have segued from, and meshed with, the couple's original relationship as artist and muse; as well as "reading [Irene's diary] in order to discover whether"

---

47 *Shadow Tag*, 139.
48 Ibid., 195.
49 Ibid., 197.
50 Ibid.
51 Ibid., 169. The use of the attributive adjective "their" before the noun "father" is interesting here. Irene is one of the onlookers and, despite the fact that the phrasing suggests otherwise, Gil is clearly not her father. The sentence could be read as an error on Riel's part and seen as a moment when her voice, her perspective intrudes.

or not she is faithful, Gil uses his portraiture to "keep her in focus," or objectify her further. One might say that Irene has fallen victim to Gil's near "limitless authority" and his "old master techniques" not only in the artistic sphere, and is subsequently under near constant surveillance both in the downstairs "living quarters" and in the loft studio. Indeed, Gil's misogynistic tendencies—as well as his tendency to subject others to psychological torment—are encapsulated in the paintings that have been produced during his career:

> She had allowed him to paint her on all fours, looking beaten once, another time snarling like a dog and bleeding, menstruating. In other paintings she was a goddess, breasts tipped with golden fire. Or a creature from the Eden of this continent, covered with moss and leaves. He'd done a series of landscapes, huge canvases vast with light, swimming Albert Bierstadt or Hudson School replicas, in which she appeared raped, dismembered, dying of smallpox in graphic medical detail. She appeared under sheaves of radiance, or emerging from the clay of rough ravines.[52]

From November 2 to December 16 2007—the period when Gil is engrossed in what will be his last painting of Irene—his gaze intensifies, and the artist realizes that it is his wife's "elusiveness" that allows him to objectify her in a manner that he feels is especially arresting, emotionally fiercer than anything he has ever painted before.[53] In one extremely disquieting scene that takes place during this time, he surveys his sleeping wife, who has drunkenly drifted off mid-pose. After a while, the narrator informs us, Gil "walked over to [Irene ...], and gently teased her knees apart [...]. [He] stepped back, adjusted his lights to shine starkly between her legs. Her face was thrown into shadow."[54] The relationship in *Shadow Tag*, wherein a largely docile Irene is met with Gil's misogynistic and often violent behavior, certainly appears to reflect the abusive and disquieting aspect of the gaze. Erdrich's characterization of Gil and her decision to present him as a painter, a practitioner in the field of the visual arts, allows her to consider not only the economics of the relationship that her characters are in, but

52   *Shadow Tag*, 30.
53   Ibid., 81.
54   Ibid., 160.

also the place that, according to Susan Rubin Suleiman, "the female body has occupied [...] in the Western cultural imagination."[55] Suleiman argues that the "poetry, mythology, religious doctrine, medical [...] psychoanalytical treatises, and prose narrative" of the West all exhibit a fascination with the body, and that woman's body in particular inspires "fear and loathing" as well as "attraction." "Beautiful but unclean, alluring but dangerous" she writes, the "woman's body [...] has appeared mysterious, duplicitous—a source of pleasure and nurturance, but also of destruction and evil."[56]

Like a contemporary René Magritte, Gil works on a near-pornographic image, and sees the painting created as being a fundamental part of his identity as an artist. In the process, he engages in what Susan Gubar, in her discussion of pornography and art, describes as "predictable, programmatic sadism [...] that eroticizes domination with tragic consequences."[57] The consequence of that sadism, Gubar explains, is the "transformation from image to act and act to image, [through which] we become imprisoned in a world of mirrors that teaches us to see women as the willing, the desirous, and deserving slaves of punitive masters."[58] Erdrich's image of her protagonist, supine—watched and wanted but also seen as an abjection of sorts, her face in shadow—is both a reference to the title and an echo of an earlier section of the novel, in which the narrator suggests that by remaining "still, in one position or another," Irene had allowed her husband to produce a "double," a "reflection" that he now "owned." In short, Gil "had stepped on her shadow."[59] In the final event, the scene implies a certain desirous revulsion on Gil's part, and it is not difficult to see that this old master is both "usurping female subjectivity and experience" through his work, but may also be projecting his fears about identity and prowess—sexual and

55 Susan Rubin Suleiman, *The Female Body in Western Culture: Contemporary Perspectives* (Cambridge, MA: Harvard University Press, 1986), 1.
56 Ibid.
57 Susan Gubar, *For Adult Users Only: The Dilemma of Violent Pornography*, ed. Susan Gubar and Joan Hoff (Bloomington: Indiana University Press, 1989), 55.
58 Ibid.
59 *Shadow Tag*, 39.

artistic—onto the visual frame that he constructs around his wife's body.[60] Of course Gil is never compared to Magritte, or other famous painters of women's genitalia, including Gustave Courbet or Marcel Duchamp. He is, instead, the "Native Edward Hopper," a man who famously placed a mirror on the wall of his studio, just next to his easel, in order to watch his wife in the studio behind his. As well as copper fastening the reader's sense that Gil's solipsism is absolute and all consuming, Erdrich's comparison might also initiate reconsideration of collectivist or collaborative art projects. This is simply because Hopper's relationship with his wife and muse, Josephine Nivison Hopper, bears almost uncanny resemblance to the marriage between Erdrich's protagonists. Indeed, Gail Levin points out that Jo "performed every dramatic *mise en scène* that he recorded in paint," and describes her as Hopper's "only model."[61] While there is nothing exceptional about a husband painting his wife—a point that Gil makes quite early on in the novel—there is nevertheless a crucial energy or synergy created by some collaborations between husband and wife. Like Gil, who relies on Irene to create the pose necessary to create wonderful art, Hopper was deeply indebted to his wife. For that reason, Gaby Wood has argued that Hopper would never have produced his beguiling series of "shadow-faced, round contoured ciphers" without Jo's presence or their shared fantasies.[62] It is also interesting to note that during the course of their marriage and working relationship the Hoppers staged and recorded ever more elaborate poses, and fabricated overstated, often disturbing, fantasies concerning the female body and about specific female characters, including secretaries, strippers, usherettes, and nudes. In this context, the comparison that Erdrich makes between her artist and his historical predecessor seems to be especially rich and portentous, all the more so when one considers that

60   Susanne Kappeler, quoted in *For Adult Users Only*, ed. Gubar and Hoff, 57.
61   Amy K. Levin, *Gender Sexuality and Museums: A Routledge Reader* (Oxford: Routledge, 2010), 94.
62   Gabby Wood, "Man and Muse," *The Observer* (April 25, 2004).

the worst of the omens that Irene noted was Gil's wish to possess her.[63] Yet, she also consented to that: "I loved you and let you think you could."[64]

Mirror, Mirror

If "men act and women appear," John Berger once famously argued, then the effect is that woman "turns herself into an object—and most particularly an object of vision: a sight."[65] It is surely no great shock, then, to discover that Irene has learned to keep herself under surveillance—both through her diary writing and through her consideration of the portraits that she has appeared in. In essence, she has learned to live under Gil's gaze and play her part in his engagement with portraiture's "tradition of social role-playing and masquerade."[66] In street argot, Irene has come to "watch herself." Driven to distraction by her abusive, controlling husband, she is reduced to scrutinizing her actions and motivations. Increasingly conscious of her drinking, she makes notes and resolutions: "Three days is a long time, she wrote [...]. Long enough. I have proved that I do not need to drink."[67] Her next action is, predictably enough, to pour herself a drink. Very possibly a reaction to the crisis within her home life then, drinking is both a means of exerting or reinstating some level of "influence" over her own body while also enacting an obliterating form of self-abuse.[68] Not unlike the anorexic, who starves herself in order to control the body and reinvent

---

63   *Shadow Tag*, 18.

64   Ibid.

65   John Berger, *Ways of Seeing* (London: BBC/Penguin, 1972), 47.

66   Shearer West, *Portraiture* (Oxford: Oxford University Press, 2004), 205.

67   *Shadow Tag*, 171.

68   On another level, Irene's addiction might also be interpreted as a way of ceding control; Irene could be said to remove herself from, or negate, the structures and rules associated with the middle-class urban household. She is, quite simply, "out of it" for much of the time.

herself as master of her own destiny, Irene recasts this imbibing as a form of self-control. Other, more distressing attempts at corporeal autonomy, which then runs dangerously close to self-harm, are examined within the novel's closing stages. Perhaps the most affecting of these is a scene in which the narrator explains that Irene, who has been raped by Gil just moments before, "walk[s] into the bathroom, lock[s] the door, and [takes] off her clothes."[69] "Alone in hot steam, in the bathtub," Erdrich's much-maligned protagonist begins to masturbate, and after a while, we are told, she "came so many times she got a cramp in her hand and started laughing."[70] This scene suggests, on one level, that the excessive and extreme masturbatory act produces a type of precarious pleasure that is akin to Irene's destructive drinking. On another level, however, this reaction to Gil's attack, namely the proximity between trauma and pleasure, suggests a degree of masochism on her part, and may even call testimony relating to the rape into question. In fact, the narrator reports—however accurately—that Irene tells her half-sister, Louise/May, that the sexual exchange between husband and wife may not have been rape: "it wasn't exactly, I ..."[71]

The extent to which Irene objectifies her own body and sees herself in terms of the iconography of the art world seems to be key here. In the bath, Irene recreates herself as the sensuous, "indolent" female muses that appear in works such as Pierre Bonnard's *Nude in the Bath* (1936), thereby enabling Gil to yearn for both his own wife and the incarnation of Bonnard's Marthe de Méligny that he finds "shimmering and dreaming in the bath."[72] In much the same way, Irene's diary writing and her willingness to feature in Gil's paintings can be read as a form of self-objectification, one that can lead to harmful forms of self-discipline and even self-loathing. This becomes evident when Irene reviews the catalog from Gil's gallery in Santa Fe and reflects on both the attractiveness and the menace that is evident in the paintings:

69   *Shadow Tag*, 221.
70   Ibid.
71   Ibid., 225.
72   Ibid., 215.

> The new images were a mixture. Some were starkly sexual, stirringly tender. Others were such cruel portrayals that her eyes smarted and her cheeks burned as if she'd been slapped. She has a gloating, cavernous, hungry beauty in some. In others she was a guileful thing, greedy, or possessed of a devious sweetness that she found hateful.[73]

Here Erdrich's protagonist fixes her eyes on her own body and feels an intense dislike for an image that has been created while she was effectively watching herself through Gil's eyes, as muse. The act of diary writing seems to be in keeping with this watchfulness, and the need to catalog her thoughts and actions seems driven by a certain amount of self-awareness and self-loathing. "I was no victim," she allows at one point, "I was passive. I was vain."[74] Even more disturbingly, Riel begins to imitate her mother's actions, albeit unconsciously. At one point we learn that in order to prepare for the apocalypse that she believes is impending, Riel "struck herself with a ruler. She slapped her own face. She stood in painful positions, held her breath underwater in the bathtub, pulled her hair, and raised bruises on her legs."[75] Although her motivations are certainly very different, Riel reacts to what she sees as internal weaknesses, and mimics the self-flagellation of her mother (and that of Pauline Puyat in Erdrich's *Tracks* and *Last Report of the Miracles at Little No Horse*).

There is more than self-loathing going on here, however, and it is important to note that Irene's poses and her diaries are complex performative gestures that may well reflect more than low self-esteem. For instance, while this emotional impulse can certainly be read as a tragic moment of self-blame or thought of as the self-interrogation of a woman who has fallen victim to crushing domestic abuse, it could also be read as a confession of sorts. They could also be read as acts of resistance, as I will argue below. In terms of concession or admission, it is important to note that Erdrich's protagonist recognizes her own frailties, and she notes that even though Gil has certainly "broken the rules," she herself has "broken other

---

73   Ibid., 31.
74   Ibid., 184.
75   Ibid., 118.

rules."[76] She also cultivates inscrutability and quite intentionally, perhaps even spitefully, refuses to communicate with those who are attracted to her, including her husband. We learn, by way of the third-person narration, that "Irene liked to think of herself as alluring in her silence," and almost imagines herself as part ingénue, part femme fatale.[77] She plays on the aura of detachment that she cultivates, knowing that the "power she owned lay in her feigned indifference."[78] While casting herself as enigmatic and unknowable, she poses for her enthralled husband, and purposely maintains a distance that, in his words, drives him almost to despair.[79] So, even though Irene America is certainly a product of a misogynistic society on one level, Erdrich's protagonist is most certainly aware of the fact that she is, to some extent, implicit in her husband's gaze.

This also seems to link Jo Hopper and Irene America, and a comparison of both women reveals a very complex form of shadowing. Associated not only by the manner in which the fictional Irene shadows the real Jo, or by the manner in which each woman becomes a shadow of their husband's making, the two are also linked by the fact that each played a complicated game of shadow tag through their relationship with fantasy and fiction. On one hand, Jo, who was a painter, and Irene, who is a professional researcher, find their own ambitions being slowly sublimated as they pour their energy into their husbands' work. Jo's account of "time passing, passing, drop by drop of one's life blood–hair graying, fashions changing, an entirely new slant on art rampant and 25 years of my life gone," as well as her conviction that Hopper's likenesses of the "poor dead birds that run into [the lighthouses at Cape Elizabeth] on a dark night" must be symbols for her own experience, bear almost uncanny resemblance to Irene's figuring of herself as a "dead woman."[80] Both women are painfully aware of ceding control, but are unable, or unwilling, to do anything about it. On the other hand, they almost seem to masochistically relish the treatment that they

76   Ibid., 47.
77   Ibid., 20.
78   Ibid., 21.
79   Ibid., 11.
80   Wood, "Man and Muse."

received. "'I'm so excited,' Jo wrote in 1959, 'He has me stretched out in back with not a stitch on—playing dead.'"[81] Erdrich even reconstitutes the ironic manner in which the toxicity and the intensity of Hopper's favorite paint, "lead white," became a metaphor for his marriage by having Gil buy "extra lead white [... and build] up a stash in his studio closet."[82] Likewise, it is hardly coincidental that Jo Hopper produced a series of diaries that bore witness to terrible fights, instances of "mutual domestic violence," her husband's almost crushing ego, and his selfishness when it came to sex. Not unlike the red diary and blue notebook, Jo's diaries provide some context to the complex and almost unfathomable story of a marriage, and reveal the extent to which the marriage was, according to Barbara Novak, one of the Hoppers' closest friends, "really a folie à deux."[83]

That sense of madness or crazed love might also help us to understand the degree of intent, and possibly even viciousness, that we find in Irene's diaries; in sexual terms she has "ceased to care what I show of my greed. Even cruelty ..." and, most importantly, states that she finds this "thrilling."[84] The narrator's description of a certain degree of prepossession in this instance is corroborated by Irene's "testimony" in the blue journal: "You have painted me for nearly fifteen years," she writes, before stating, rather unambiguously and bitterly, "In that time, I have had secrets."[85] There is, then, a sense of gratification that Irene cultivates from her detachment and physical manipulation of Gil. Effusive, extroverted, and dangerously passionate in her writing, Irene is despondent, bitter, and world-weary at home: "*I am gone, this is over, the end is clear*" she thinks to herself, despite ultimately conceding "where there are children involved [... one is] always forced to suppress an absolute awareness of finality."[86] In using the blue diary as a

---

81 Ibid.
82 John D. Morse, "Oral History interview with Edward Hopper," (June 17, 1959), Archives of American Art <http://www.aaa.si.edu/collections/interviews/oral-history-interview-edward-hopper-11844> accessed May 2, 2012; *Shadow Tag*, 82.
83 Wood, "Man and Muse."
84 *Shadow Tag*, 49.
85 Ibid., 17.
86 Ibid., 49.

site in which she can discretely store a particular set of emotions, Irene also appears to embrace a dark, near-noirish sense of death and intrigue. She also gestures toward a form of emotional (if not physical) necrophilia or vampirism—an allusion that ties in with Gil's artistry and representation of his wife described above. The diaries contain a line of commentary that possibly reveals the fact that Irene has seen the house as a mausoleum of sorts for some time now. She thinks of herself, alternately, as a living doll forced to exist within the confines of an oppressive relationship and a stifling family environment, and as a mummified version of her former self. "I wonder how you can make love to me," she writes in her blue notebook, "I am a dead woman whose reflexes alone can be activated."[87]

Of course, this fatalism, when coupled with her alcoholism, actively increases the reader's sense that Irene's narration is unreliable, and her judgment clouded. With regard to her drinking, Erdrich's diarist often moves to hide this fact, and acknowledges that she has taken "too much wine" on a few rare occasions in her diary. Most references to a distinct problem come from the other characters, however, and it becomes evident that she has been drinking heavily while writing the diaries.[88] Perhaps the most poignant, and pathetic, of the references to Irene's disease is Stoney's innocent inclusion of a wine glass in an everyday portrait of his mother, a painting that is supposed to present her in habitué.[89] For that reason, and in light of certain actions she has taken during the course of the narrative, the reader is forced to question not only how reliable she is as a narrator, but also how reliable she is as a mother. In truth, Irene's disclosure that the "worst things *we've* done have involved the children" implicates her in some of the more tawdry events that have occurred in the Mount Curve home.[90] As a result of these uncertainties, and in light of the complex, destructive, symbiosis that exists between Erdrich's characters, we cannot always be sure who is watching, or chasing, who.

87 Quoted in Leah Hager Cohen, "Cruel Love."
88 *Shadow Tag*, 162, 86, 168, 171, 197, & 223.
89 Ibid., 53.
90 Ibid., 47.

Like some skewed version of Oscar Wilde's *The Picture of Dorian Gray* (1890), in which both the portrayed *and* the portraitist are reliant on one another for their very existence, Irene and Gil accept the moral and personal hazard that their destructive symbiosis necessitates. By then, death does seem to be the only means of shattering the image of their failed marriage or the iconography that surrounds the art and Irene's role as muse; iconography that they have become enslaved to. Even Gil's near absence at Stoney's birth on September 11 2001, seems to be in keeping with his swapping of the mediated "unreal" or "too real" (which is how Don DeLillo described 9/11) for the actual or the real: "They'd had to fetch him from riveting [news] commentary for the actual birth" the narrator explains.[91] The effect

---

91 *Shadow Tag*, 51. As well as glossing Baudrillard's notion that modern life is "spectralized [...] the event filtered by the medium—the dissolution of TV into life, the dissolution of life into TV," this scene possibly comments on what Catherine Morley calls "the literary [and artistic] preoccupation with the visual image and the seeming impossibility of realism in the wake of the September 11th terrorist attacks": Baudrillard, *Simulations* (Cambridge, MA: MIT Press, 1983), 55; Catherine Morley, "Plotting against America: 9/11 and the Spectacle of Terror in Contemporary American Fiction," *Gramma/Γράμμα: Journal of Theory and Criticism* 16 (2008), 293. *Shadow Tag*'s 9/11 theme, while certainly too complicated to flesh out in this chapter, and the novel's references to Native American history and the colonization of the Americas, does, I would argue, pose some very difficult and significant questions to those currently examining "9/11" fiction. It does so by meshing moments of historical spectacle (Catlin's shows for instance) and tribal suffering in their homeland, with recent conversations about patriotism, Americanism, and the threat from outside. This is an important point when we consider the work of scholars such as Michael Rothberg, who has considered why, exactly, post-9/11 fiction suffers from "a failure of the imagination." Rothberg argues: "Gray's diagnosis of failure is, in my opinion, largely correct for the earliest fictional responses to America's recent 'trauma.' His alternative—a 'deterritorialized' grappling with otherness—is, I will argue, both necessary and not entirely sufficient. While Gray's model for the kind of deterritorialization of the novel he would like to see in the wake of 9/11 derives from recent immigrant fictions that open up and hybridize American culture, I call for a supplementary form of deterritorialization. In addition to Gray's model of critical multiculturalism, we need a fiction of international relations and extraterritorial citizenship. If Gray's account tends toward the centripetal—an account of the world's movement toward America—I propose a complementary centrifugal mapping that charts the

is that Gil and Irene are paradoxically caught between static definitions and constant reflexivity, both of which limit their communication with each other, with their art and scholarship, and with their communities. This unendurable tension is illustrated by the fact that Gil lectures Irene on the meaning of kitsch and cultures' need "to be self-referential [...]. [To] have mirrors" on one hand, while following his personal quest "to get at the truth" in his art on the other.[92] Of course, his vision/version of "truth" is also somewhat undermined by the fact that much of the portraiture he produces is staged, if not contrived.

By distilling their marriage down to a series of repeated images and practices, Erdrich's characters effectively shrink their world—a diminution that is metaphorically suggested through the novel's repeated references to the Schwarzschild radius—and trap each other in certain poses before ultimately giving themselves over to the black hole that is their shared psychosis and their double-suicide (tortured artist, cuckolded husband, muse, sexually voracious wife, and so on). For that reason, they are fixed and static; Gil may have "abandoned her and painted other subjects" for a time, but he is ultimately bound to Irene as his muse, and has sought his own reflection in her presence since they first met. Similarly, Irene seems irresistibly drawn to him; despite the fact that the divorce papers were issued and Gil entered treatment in December 2007, he is back living in the house by Memorial Day. And, even though she warns him that there isn't "going to be any sex. That's over," her resolve seems to crumble slightly with her clarification that "It will be years before I let you sleep with me. Or paint

---

outward movement of American power. The most difficult thing for citizens of the US empire to grasp is not the internal difference of their motley multiculture, but the prosthetic reach of that empire into other worlds." ("A Failure of the Imagination: Diagnosing the Post-9/11 Novel: A Response to Richard Gray," *American Literary History* 21.1 [2009], 153). If space allowed, I would very much like to consider the ramifications that Rothberg's proposition has for indigenous writers, who are keen to engage with images of otherness, territorialization, and America's particular (if not peculiar) version of multiculturalism.

92   *Shadow Tag*, 95 & 12.

me."[93] So, these characters are bound to one another, constrained by their life choices and attractions. Even in his final moments, while drowning in the lake, Gil "seemed to stay in one place no matter how hard he kicked."[94] True to form, Irene follows the habit of half a lifetime and jumps in after her floundering husband—possibly in a bid to save him, but perhaps in order to join him in death and therefore end her suffering.

If Irene's diary keeping can be read in Foucauldian terms, then the figuration her body in *Shadow Tag* might also be said to register her subjectivity through the "arts of existence." Foucault argued "that the self is not given to us [... and hence] we have to create ourselves as a work of art."[95] Irene America appears to create herself in this fashion, and Erdrich's character is acutely attuned to the authority of her body and power inherent in her near-collaborative role in the making of art that bankrolls the household. The unnamed narrator recalls how she "never complained of cold or hunger, pain or boredom," and had "the patience and avidity of an artist."[96] There is also a performative aspect and studied quality about the "air of neglect" that she adopts, and the manner in which she wears "her hair coarsely tangled [or] painstakingly applied unfashionable shades of makeup" when socializing with Gil.[97] The narrator also believes that Irene is capable of conveying complex emotions by modeling for Gil, and that her bearing carries messages unbeknownst to the painter. In recounting the marriage's "final scene," Riel notes that such "a moment might be captured on film [...]. Or in a painting" and imagines Irene addressing Gil with the words: "You have captured it in my portraits without knowing what you've caught, I think."[98] It also appears to be the case that Irene projects her body as a location that can withhold, confound, contradict, or enable. Although it is important to remember that Riel creates Irene's

---

93 Ibid., 239, 241, 242.
94 Ibid., 244.
95 *Michel Foucault: Beyond Structuralism and Hermeneutics*, ed. Hubert L. Dreyfus and Paul Rainbow (Chicago, IL: University of Chicago Press, 1983), 237.
96 *Shadow Tag*, 32.
97 *Shadow Tag*, 20.
98 Ibid., 49.

narrative, she does, nevertheless, feel compelled to imagine her mother allowing secrets to "rest like dragonflies on the surface of [her] body." The first-person narrator underlines the extent to which her body can contain secrets: "Once you even painted an elaborate, transparent, veined wing on my inner thigh and I thought—he sees!"[99] Therefore, even though Irene appears to sit dutifully for the portraitist who seeks to control her life, her role in the artistry signals something other than straightforward acquiescence or compliance. In fact, her posing affords her a certain agency, not only because Gil is dependent upon her, but also because it provides her with the opportunity to create an alter ego—a self that defies or exceeds the boundaries and restrictions that afflict her personal life. In sum, there is the distinct possibility that the protagonist's life modeling is far more effective, nuanced, and, perhaps most importantly, self-aware than it might first seem. In this context, Erdrich's framing of Irene's masturbatory act in the bath can be read as a subversion or complex remediation of earlier art forms. Thus, rather than associating her character with the objectified gaze, Erdrich possibly presents the reader with an empowering form of what Luce Irigaray describes as autoeroticism, or an extended form of self-embrace that banishes any sense of a lack that might be emblematized by Irene's not holding a paintbrush.

If one were to continue mining the anti-Freudian seam, then Irene's diary writing could be seen as something of an antidote to the talking cure, or to the therapy that is doing so little for herself and Gil. Writing becomes her way of tackling both the image of the hysterical, irrational woman and the "double" that she has released into the world via the paintings. Hence, Irene might also be said to watch herself through the diaries in a useful and formative way—a move made possible by the fact that the diary has "high potential for self-reflexivity."[100] It is through the diaries that the character positions herself as the real author, and she records a particularly rounded version of the story that is then passed on to, and ultimately mediated by, Riel. This move safeguards the family's story even if it does

---

99   Ibid., 17.
100 Paperno, "What Can Be Done with Diaries?," 564.

not save the family, effectively allowing mother, then daughter, to control the narrative. Moreover, Irene clearly demarcates one account of events in the "vaulted" blue journal—a status or position that might suggest that it has a higher value. A "truer" reflection of events or a covert coda to its red companion, this journal is a textual arbiter that will contextualize Irene's actions and explain her motivations—a fact made clear by the mother's instruction that Riel be given the key to the bank vault once she turns twenty-one. Hence, even though the homonymic relationship between "red" and "read" compounds the difference between the "private" blue diary and its "public" twin, it is still the case that even the private journal will be laid open in time, and it therefore "externalizes and objectifies the inner, socializes and historicizes the intimate, essentially working as the archive of the intimate."[101] In this way, Irene deploys the "aesthetic value and function" of the diary to her own ends; inspecting her own motives for staying with Gil, standing sentinel over the children, and watching for ways in which she can exert her own power and personal sovereignty. She does so in spite of the fact that the "two diar[y]" model can lead to what Elisabeth Mermann-Jozwiak calls the "split-self" or perhaps what Hélène Cixous regards as "the uncanny stranger on display."[102]

Although quasi-confessional, the tone of Irene's opening line, "I have two diaries now," is ultimately assertive, and suggests that she has begun not just a process of self-scrutiny, but also a form of rebellious self-control." As such, it may be an example of what Foucault calls a "good management of the body [... which] include[s] a setting down in writing carried out by the subject."[103] With that, the double-entry method of diary writing allows Irene to produce two discrete spaces: the red diary is a subversive space through which she can "manipulate" and "even hurt" her husband,

---

101   Ibid., 572.

102   Elizabeth Mermann-Jozwiak, "Re-membering the Body: Body Politics in Toni Morrison's *The Bluest Eye*," *Literature Interpretation Theory* 12.2 (2001), 191; Hélène Cixous, "The Laugh of the Medusa," trans. Keith Cohen and Paula Cohen, in *The New French Feminisms*, ed. Elaine Marks and Isabelle de Courtivron (Amherst: University of Massachusetts Press, 1980), 250.

103   *The Use of Pleasure*, trans. Robert Hurley (London: Vintage Books, 1990), 115.

Gil. The blue journal accommodates personal reflection, thereby allowing
the protagonist an opportunity to articulate, interrogate, and, if necessary,
justify, her actions. It is easy, then, to see how Erdrich's deft mobilization
of the diary form results in a narrative structure that is, as Ron Charles'
argues, perfectly positioned to initiate a consideration of representation,
power, objectification, and interpretation in the broadest of universal terms.
However, even though this exploration of literary and critical references is
certainly warranted, and worthwhile, we might do well to remember that
Shadow Tag presents us with the story of a contemporary Native American
family, whose concerns and motivations are, in many ways, distinct from
those universally found elsewhere. While Gil may be "the wrong fractions of
Klamath and Cree and landless Montana Chippewa" and (like his wife) "an
Indian with no relatives," his artwork, his relationships, and the countless
discussions or thoughts that he has during the course of the narrative, do
reflect the complex milieu in which Native issues are debated and worked
through. As well as being about "the exploitation of American Indians,"
colonization, and representation, this novel reflects on indigenous aesthetics and the various forms of autonomy that the tribes have a right to:
political, cultural, literary, artistic, and spiritual autonomy.[104] Furthermore,
it also reflects on the indigenous writer's entitlement to withhold certain
forms, and certain pieces of information, in general, and Erdrich's preroga-
tive in particular. In short, we must consider the fact that despite having
lost her way somewhat, Irene has been raised Ojibwe by Winnie Jane, "a
homeschooler, an AIM activist, a ceremonialist, a keeper of journals, and
gravely thoughtful."[105] As well as finding Louise/May, venturing back to
powwows, and thinking of her mother with increased regularity, Irene
follows paths of study that play a vital role in spawning Riel's interest in
her Ojibwe ancestry. There is, then, more to the novel than its disclosure
of intimate, personal details about life on Mount Curve Avenue—a name
that suggests that this story is anything but straightforward.

104 Charles, "Love in the Time of Bitterness."
105 *Shadow Tag*, 92.

Postindian Shadows

Before turning to the ways in which the novel deals with questions of Ojibwe narrative and sovereignty, it is certainly necessary to examine the book's extensive references to colonial exchanges, the historical mistreatment of tribal peoples, and contemporary indigeneity in modern America. Perhaps the first thing that is striking in this context is Irene America's name, which ties her to the colonizers' bid to label and define the country and its people:

> The explorer Amerigo Vespucci had signed the first map of the eastern coast and thereby accidentally named two continents and, much later, an ancestor of Irene's. America.[106]

Insult is added to injury when "guns, liquor, god, and government" become the new "source of American Indian surnames that once were so intensely personal."[107] Like David Treuer's character Ellis, who is named after Ellis Island simply because he stands there, saying nothing, Irene America is accidentally misnamed, and the misnomer becomes a painful reminder of the extent to which the Indian was, according to Anishinaabe scholar Gerald Vizenor, "an occidental invention."[108] There are coded references to the disinheritance that accompanies the colonial, and later the capitalistic, process. In a moment of trademark laconicism, Erdrich refers to Gil's paintings in a rather loaded fashion, noting that Irene "did not have an *America*. They'd always had to sell them immediately."[109] For his part, Gil wishes that "he'd kept some of the earliest, the best portraits. They were

---

106 Ibid., 39.

107 Ibid.

108 David Treuer, *Little* (London: Granta, 1997), 55; Vizenor, *Manifest Manners: Narratives on Postindian Survivance* (Lincoln: University of Nebraska Press), 11. Treuer writes: "The English speaking loggers *without any foothold or clues to his personality*, called him the same name as the island they first set foot on, the first place of dry America that they had seen."

109 *Shadow Tag*, 132.

selling for more."[110] As well as glossing his rapacious commodification of his wife's image, and, by proxy, that of her people, Gil's lament offers a pointed commentary on the economics of colonization, which usually decrees that the earliest exchanges reap the maximum rewards and riches.

There are other ways in which the shifting and, by times, near paradoxical significances that are encoded in the act of naming surface in the narrative. For instance, the discovery that Irene has drowned long before we read her (present tense) statement, "I have two diaries now," is another way in which Erdrich plays with a Vizenorian sense of the "absence of the real" (the "absence of the real" being the critic's way of saying that stereotypes and representations have, to some extent, replaced surviving Indians). In the first instance, the "real" Irene, the woman we believed we were following across the pages of *Shadow Tag*, has only created a literary space that is devoid of real sentiment or honesty. Second, the book ends with the revelation that the central protagonist has been absent all along; as mentioned above, Riel has refashioned her diaries and framed them within a highly mediated narrative form. Of course, the disclosure that comes in the final pages of the novel is foreshadowed throughout—Irene's spirit has been captured and her individualism has been displaced long before she drowns saving Gil. The reader is constantly reminded of this fact via the paintings—the other *America*s—that have now taken her place, reducing her name (and her character, her identity) to the status of "cipher," or nonentity. Various forms of mirroring occur throughout the novel, and several of these represent this displacement quite clearly.

Firstly, because portraiture encapsulates the "idea of mimesis, or likeness," it can be tied to the act of mirroring on a fundamental level.[111] With that, according to the narrator, Gil's self-indulgence as an artist is initially supported by Irene's vanity (both of which are intrinsically linked to the image of the mirror), and both parties see a distorted but attractive version of themselves reflected in the other's gaze. The collaboration that results from this relationship gives rise to countless *America*s, portraits that not

---

110   Ibid., 8.
111   West, *Portraiture*, 12.

only mirror Irene, but, in time, form part of a complex string of associations; the *America*s mirror each other, they are a signifier of Irene's reflection of her husband's wishes, they produce a false likeness of the model (Irene), and of her iconic marriage. In due course, the circumstances of that failing marriage/collaboration also give rise to another form of mirroring, in that the red diary is a reflection—albeit a twisted, garish funhouse image—of the blue notebook. Another searing image that captures this doubling and reflection is an "extraordinary rape scene from [a staged version of the film] *Rashoman*" which the narrator refers to. The narrator recalls how a "mirror lay on the ground," and a "man fell brutally upon the mirror and fucked his own image" while the "victim watched him from the shadows."[112] The shallowness and viciousness of this assault prefigures the description of Gil's attack on Irene. This seems to bear out Susan Griffin's point that there occurs a "transformation from image to act and act to image" which causes both the parties in the gaze to "become imprisoned in a world of mirrors."[113]

The absence of the real threatens Irene on many levels, and taking after Baudrillard (who once argued that "simulation threatens the difference between 'true' and 'false,' between 'real' and 'imaginary'") Erdrich's character uses the term simulacra in a negative sense.[114] Although she feistily fights the aesthetic mimicry that is Gil's portraiture with her own particular form of narrative dissemblance, her heart is never really in it. Like the system that produces empty signs or simulations that have no value, meaning, or connection to the "real"—the condition known as simulacrum—Irene's personal and professional relationship with Gil produces an empty life for her, and is quite literally soul destroying: "A soul could be captured through a shadow. It was in the Ojibwe language. Waabaamoojichaagwaan—the word for mirror also can refer to shadow and to the soul."[115] Even her death could be interpreted as a fatalistic suicide of sorts, since following Gil into the lake seems to be the only way in which she can escape the restrictions of

---

112   *Shadow Tag*, 184.
113   Quoted in *For Adult Users Only*, ed. Gubar and Hoff, 55.
114   *Simulations*, 5.
115   *Shadow Tag*, 40.

the hollow life that has been carved out for her. This rather fatalistic view of the way in which her identity has been nullified or tied to simulacra almost certainly coheres with the Platonic notion that "the simulacrum is more than just a useless image, it is [also] a deviation and perversion of imitation itself—a false likeness."[116] All of this, including Gil's readiness to admit that "the problem of painting [is that] it's all reference [... All] kitsch," might bring us back to the philosophical roots of simulacra and Plato's decision to banish the "painter [...] from his republic" because of "his deep mistrust of 'the imitator,' who, 'being the creator of the phantom, knows nothing of reality.'"[117] Evidently delighting in, and electrified by, a particular form of aesthetic vampirism or necrophilia, Gil readily acknowledges that the art created in his eyrie produces a "phantom," a figure that "glided eerily in and out of the chiaroscuro of street lamps."[118] As noted above, Irene is, by her own admission, a "dead woman" and "food," descriptions that accentuate several contemporary artists' fascination with the phantasmal and voracious. In response to his wife's accusation that he's turning her into a kitsch icon, he goes as far as to state, simply, "No Irene, I'm painting death," and shortly afterwards the narrator explains that Gil felt obliged "to conceal the painting he was having trouble with" because the "picture was disturbing [...]. Irene looked dead."[119] Instead of being appalled by this outcome, which darkly foreshadows Irene's untimely death and might unnerve a loving husband, Gil instantly recognizes that the unsettling image of death "made the painting interesting, too."[120] He is even pleased with the spectral or haunting quality that the painting has taken on, not least because this will give it a particular value in the circulatory system of value created by the postmodern art scene. Though this turn of events is hardly surprising, given that Gil "had been mourning a death without knowing exactly who had died or how it had come about," it is still extraordinarily unsettling

116   Michael Camille, "Simulacrum," in *Critical Terms for Art History*, ed. Robert S. Nelson and Richard Shiff (Chicago, IL: University of Chicago Press, 1996), 31–32.
117   *Shadow Tag*, 94; Plato, *Republic*, quoted in Camille, "Simulacrum," 32.
118   *Shadow Tag*, 122.
119   Ibid., 98.
120   Ibid.

that Gil imagines himself to be capturing "the truth" in his paintings.[121] If that is the case, then his *America* series, however subversive and knowing they might aim to be, ultimately perpetuate the economics of exchange that have culminated with the death of the Native. Now fixated with death—a fixation that arises, ostensibly, from the death of his marriage and by extension the death of his muse—his paintings organically, if not intentionally, follow the arc found in Thomas Cole's The Voyage of Life. "Gil had given his entire attention to her youth first, but after that he devotedly painted the effect of experience on flesh"; when Irene's postpartum "breasts, hot with fever as her milk came in," he painted them too. These paintings call to mind the "Western fantasy of primitive origins" found in such works as Jan van der Straet's engraving titled *America*. That plate, which is part of a series of engravings titled *Nova Reperta*, portrays Vespucci "the female figure of America [... from] her languorous state" and carries the text "Americus rediscovers America."[122] Gil's interest in the way that Irene's "body [...] drew back into itself and toughened" as the children grew, possibly consolidates the link between Irene's body, the colonial history of the American West, and, interestingly enough, American exceptionalism and narratives of endurance and strength.[123] Of course, in the postmodern moment in which Gil creates his art, death has become the defining moment, the final destination. Yet, it is also the case that Gil believes that the Americas might yet prove to be his salvation, if not in terms of helping him to cipher his wife's inner narrative—he has turned to the diaries in order to feed that particular hunger—then at least in terms of his standing as an artist. In a moment tinged with Gil's trademark neediness and narcissism, he concedes the proximity of his artistry to Catlin's, noting that the earlier painter "happened to hit the moment [...]. One year his subjects were alive, the next year they were dead."[124]

121 Ibid., 10 & 12.
122 Michael Gaudio, *Engraving the Savage* (Minneapolis: University of Minnesota Press, 2008), xiv.
123 *Shadow Tag*, 12.
124 Ibid., 123.

It is hardly any wonder that, as a result, Irene shares the emotions of the Sioux medicine men that "predicted dire consequences for those whose souls [Catlin] captured on canvas."[125] Or that like Vizenor, who troubles over the static representation of tribal peoples, she worries about the likelihood that the proliferation and widespread of countless Americas—*America 1. America 2. America 3. America 4.*—will have a detrimental effect on her emotional and spiritual wellbeing. Cognizant of the fact that her husband's paintings have laid her body and her soul bare to the world, Irene ruminates on the effect and style of Catlin's work. Just as she knows that Catlin's paintings "stole their subjects and, for the rest of the world, *became more real*, until it seemed they were the only things left," Irene realizes that the *America*s, or rather their creator, has stolen her identity and given rise to an iconic image long since fixed in the public mind.[126] Just as importantly, her experiences show her that the colonial process is ongoing, since they allow her to see "patterns" and between past and present. Like Howe's historian character, Auda Billy, Irene states clearly, "I notice patterns. Symmetry is very powerful to me."[127] And, as in *Shell Shaker*, the patterns of colonization are often marked out in terms of the woman's body. "By remaining still, in one position or another, for her husband, she had released a double into the world. It was impossible, now, to withdraw that reflection. Gil owned it. He had stepped on her shadow."[128] Trapped between a disabling stasis and a vexatious indeterminacy, Irene realizes that Gil's art plays with notions of indelible permanence, through the recreation of historical poses, even as it unsettles those same master narratives. According to the narrator, she tells him "you're making kitsch out of me'" even though she simply wants their marriage to "be authentic. Real."[129]

125   Bruce Watson, "George Catlin's Obsession," *Smithsonian* (December 2002) <http://www.smithsonianmag.com/arts-culture/catlin.html?c=y&page=3> accessed May 4 2012.

126   *Shadow Tag*, 173 & 141 (emphasis added).

127   Ibid., 173.

128   Ibid., 39.

129   Ibid., 95.

Significantly, the wonderfully layered texture of Erdrich's novel allows the reader to think of Irene's experience both in terms of contemporary Native American subjectivity and the historical experiences of the ancestors who once posed for Edward Curtis and, more specifically, George Catlin. Irene's doctoral research into the life and work of the latter, when placed alongside her sitting for Gil, invites a consideration of the extent to which Catlin's portraits of tribal peoples in the nineteenth century were exploitative and created a fixed, static representation of the Indian—a representation that Vizenor believes is still existent and seeks to deconstruct. When we consider Gil's solipsism, we might easily be reminded of Catlin's art and life. The late W. Richard West, a citizen of the Cheyenne and Arapaho Nation of Oklahoma and a Peace Chief of the Southern Cheyenne, once explained that "a native person is challenged [...] not to feel on some level a profound resentment toward Catlin," largely because his "obsession with depicting Indians has an extremely invasive undertone."[130] "There's no question," West added, "he was exploiting Indians and the West as a commodity." It is not difficult, in this light, to see how Gil's artistry has a similarly invasive undertone since it is based on the manipulation of his wife, her image, and, of course, her body. While part of Gil's project may be to disrupt, rather than perpetuate, the peddling of Indian wares, he ends up selling another set of images instead of critiquing historical representations of the Native. Indeed, one of the more frightening aspects of the book is the manner in which this exploitation is physicalized through Erdrich's conjoining of images of the painter at work and the subsequent rape of his wife. As well as euphemistically entering "his wife's basement office" in order to violate her privacy, we find him "bent over, and add[ing] a few terse strokes" to one of the portraits near the very beginning.[131]

Yet, despite the often thorny and problematic ways in which their relationship and their actions are figured, there are grounds to read Irene, Riel, and perhaps even Gil, as what Vizenor describes as "postindian warriors." Vizenor explains that "the postindian is a literary figure" and "a producer

---

130 Quoted in Watson.
131 *Shadow Tag*, 5.

of texts," one that engages in a "type of literary production [that] is a form of conflict, requiring courage and skill" in order to engage in acts of resistance and to guarantee Native survivance.[132] To be sure, there are certainly elements of the mother and daughter's character that suggest that they are, above all, story makers. By the same token, a great amount of emotional and storytelling dexterity is evident in the written accounts that they put together; the wonderful *coup de grâce* that Riel delivers with her admission of omniscience, and Irene's ability to make Gil believe that "she was trying to communicate with him through metaphors," suggest as much. I would also add that Vizenor's claims that "the postindian arises from the earlier inventions of the tribes, only to contravene the absence of the real with theatrical performances," and "the postindian is the absence of the invention, and the end of representation in literature" have relevance to any extended reading of *Shadow Tag*'s imagery.[133]

It is significant that despite Irene's cynicism about the act of naming, her moniker *does* powerfully underline her connection to the American landscape and the American nation. Erdrich concretizes this fact at specific points in the story: "Remember this, the announcer cried out when the drum stopped, this is your land, this is all Indian land!"[134] The act of misnaming, and the repercussions that follow, might also go some way toward explaining her desire "to be a historian" searching out patterns and "symmetry."[135] On this level, Irene's name points to the historical relationship between the Ojibwe people and the federal government of the United States of America, and possibly even ties in with a point that Erdrich made during an interview with Bill Moyers, when she stated:

> The American flag comes out first at every powwow. There's an incredible relationship that is felt—there is—a heart to heart feeling about the government that we are nation to nation with you. *It's a sense of equality. That you will recognize us, that*

132 *Manifest Manners*, 4.
133 Ibid., 5 & 11.
134 *Shadow Tag*, 128.
135 Ibid., 173.

we did not vanish as you thought. That we survived. We exist ... We have our language. We have your words in our language. We have your constitution in our language.[136]

By highlighting the depth of the connection and the discreteness of indigenous and federal spaces simultaneously, Irene America's name suggests a form of postindian presence that has the effect of contextualizing, and repositioning, the reader's sense of the nation's full history; that is to say, the history that gives proper attention to pre-contact and contemporary presences alike.

For that reason, and because the diaries gloss the "intimate theater of history," it is also necessary to remember that Irene's surname links the personal to the national rather explicitly. The diarist's awareness of indigenous peoples' historical experiences and contemporary presences, her understanding of her own position within the body politic, her encounters with the non-Native audience who view her husband's paintings, and several of the actions that she is forced into during the course of the marriage, connect her to the history of America. In mobilizing the position of the diary as a means to tease out the notion of subjectivity and the record of events, Erdrich resituates the author in time and place. What *Shadow Tag* offers, then, is a specific, often interiorized—but not an entirely individual—history of America: this is the story of an Ojibwe woman, Irene America, her homeland, and Native American experiences. Accordingly, Erdrich appears to be profoundly interested in examining the ways in which certain discrete, sovereign spaces and autonomies overlap and inform one another.[137] At the

136 Bill Moyers, "Interview with Louise Erdrich," PBS (April 9, 2010) <http://www.pbs.org/moyers/journal/ 04092010/watch2.html> accessed April 26 2012 (emphasis added).

137 Indeed, it seems important that the author has spoken about the classification of her writing as Ojibwe and American, explaining, "I'm very proud as an enrolled member of the Turtle Mountain Band to be able to say that I'm doing something and that I'm writing books [...]. [B]ut again, in other venues if I get to be 'quintessentially American' what's wrong with that? Woman, mother, writer [...] people just have to use labels": "Writers on a New England Stage: Louise Erdrich" (May 16 2008) <http://www.nhpr.org/post/writers-new-england-stage-louise-erdrich>. It is also of the greatest significance that she is acutely aware of the need for a great deal of cultural

same time, she also examines the extent to which "truthful records" must be
interrogated, if not treated with skepticism, and there seems to be a line of
connection between the inscrutable nature of personal relationships and the
impenetrability of the historical narrative throughout *Shadow Tag*. A case
in point is the truth contained in the objective, "real" historical text that
Irene reads—Columbus's diary. Canny readers will know only too well that
this text is a transcription of the original diary put together by Bartolomé
de las Casas, and therefore is not entirely faithful to Columbus's original
expression, vision, or interpretation. As a good student of literature, the
principle narrator, Riel, should also be aware of Camus's reckoning that
"fiction is the lie through which we tell the truth." Within this context,
the narrator's relationship to the story in *Shadow Tag* is, in many ways, a
reflection of Erdrich's ongoing interest in fiction's ability to include several
complex narratives that "slid[e] from one thread to another across time
and place" and to allow protagonists to "tell their own stories and those of
other family members."[138] *Shadow Tag* also recalls other aspects of Erdrich's
oeuvre, by times appearing to "weave [... the] audience into the fabric of
[an] extended family," while on other occasions seeming to "place [...] the
reader in a paradoxically dual stance, simultaneously at the fringe of the
story yet at the very center of the process."[139]

specificity, noting "there's so many wonderful writers who are coming up: Sherman
Alexie, Eric Gansworth, Kim Blaeser, Leslie Silko, wonderful writers, Linda Hogan,
who are beginning to write stories not of Native America but of their particular tribes.
Their tribes. Their tribal ways, voices, language. It's all a whole different world. My
background on my mother's side is as different from Dakota or an Abenaki person
or a Narraganset or a Wampanoaag person as a person from China is from a person
from France. These are such different lifeways in their origins" (ibid.; emphasis
added).

138   Shelley Reid, "The Stories We Tell: Louise Erdrich's Identity Narratives," *MELUS*
25.3/4, "Revising Traditions Double Issue" (Autumn–Winter 2000), 76.

139   Ibid. See also: Kathleen M. Sands, "Louise Erdrich's Love Medicine," *Studies in
American Indian Literatures* 9.1 (1985), 12–24; E. Reid, "The Stories We Tell," 65–86;
Karah Stokes, "What About the Sweetheart? The 'Different Shape' of Anishinabe
Two Sisters Stories in Louise Erdrich's *Love Medicine* and *Tales of Burning Love*,"
MELUS 24.2 (Summer 1999), 89–105.

Gil's art, like Irene's diaries and her doctoral dissertation, also seems to mesh with the notion of complicated, sometimes irreverent, but possibly fuller takes on American history. Like Catlin, who departed from contemporary norms by humanizing Natives at the very time when the federal government sought to "dehumanize [them] in an effort to deal with them politically," Gil chooses an aesthetic that rows against popular convention. By painting Irene with the "American flag stuck up [her] ass" he disrupts the stereotype of the Indian princess in a profoundly disturbing way; in this vision Irene is penetrated by the patriotic emblem that fuelled American imperialism and expansion on one hand, and she is made to appear in a stark and shocking pose that simultaneously subverts and explodes the earlier aesthetic tropes. By having Irene "appear under sheaves of radiance, or emerging from the clay of rough ravines," Gil consciously challenges and interrupts the image of the indigene as "Edenic innocent, uncivilizable savage, noble savage, infantilized adult."[140] Revisiting and reconstituting the work of Bierstadt, Cole, and others, he creates pieces that, to his own mind, confront the viewer with "problems of exploitation, the indigenous body, the devouring momentum of history," thereby creating an aesthetic that simultaneously recenters the Native, disrupts the expansionist rhetoric of Manifest Destiny, and disassembles extant modes of representation.[141] Subsequently, Gil's art could easily have great political meaning and relevance, largely because of its postindian take on romanticized images of plains warriors and Indian princesses. His art is consequently reminiscent of *Self-Portrait* by Cherokee artist Jimmie Durham in 1987, a large relief sculpture based on the artist's body and covered in flayed skin that records Durham's experience as a Native, or James Luna's oft-cited *The Artifact Piece*, for which he "placed himself in an exhibition case," the Americas comment on the repression, objectification, representation, and museumification of Native peoples.[142] Gil's art could even be said to be an

---

140 Jimmie Durham and Jean Fisher, "The Ground has been Covered," *Art Form* (Summer 1988), 101.

141 *Shadow Tag*, 11.

142 See: Janet C. Berlo and Ruth B. Phillips, *Native North American Art* (Oxford: Oxford University Press, 1998).

attempt at generating "the rich social critique" produced in the portraits of Minnesota Chippewa artist David Bradley. Throughout his work Bradley repeatedly uses "certain symbols which you could call popular cultural iconography like the 'American Gothic,' 'Mona Lisa,' 'Whistlers Mother' [...] as archetypical images everyone can relate to [... and then fits] archetypical things, clichés in amongst" them in order to comment on sociopolitical issues facing tribal communities today.[143]

Yet, there are some significant difficulties with reading Gil's work in this way. Most notably these concern the work's exploitative nature, questions surrounding reception, Gil's position as an artist, and the repetitive use of certain images. With regard to the matter of reception, we learn that the explicit, prurient imagery found in the portraits causes Irene to feel "that her presence was embarrassing to other Indians, especially older people."[144] Moreover, she realizes that art dealers and visitors to galleries as well as buyers will have "seen her utterly exposed, through Gil's eyes" via the portraits.[145] The reader learns, by way of Riel's reworking of note cards left by her mother, that Irene even finds a depressing parallel between the performing bears who once appeared in Catlin's traveling American show in London and her own situation:

> [Those] bears died of the disgust of being constantly looked at. The more Irene thought about this, the more such a death made sense. It seemed reasonable. It seemed that people had forgotten what a terrible thing it was to be looked at, and then she began to imagine that in giving away her image, to be looked at and looked at, she was somehow killing herself of disgust.[146]

It is certainly tempting to suggest that Gil's aesthetic is self-indulgent rather than socially or culturally informed. The Native audience's reaction to the pieces possibly arises out of the fact that "he had used [Irene's] humiliation"

---

143   David Bradley, "March 1989 Interview by Dorothee Peiper-Riegraf" <www.peiper-riegraf-collection.com> accessed May 16 2012. Gil has painted the *Mona Lisa* on one of his beloved doors, and did of course use Irene as a model for this painting.

144   *Shadow Tag*, 90.

145   Ibid.

146   Ibid., 171.

to his own ends.[147] Like Fritz Scholder—the quarter Luiseno painter who produced grisly, expressionistic portraits of Natives throughout the 1970s and 1980s, including *American Portrait No. 46* and *Indian No. 1*—Gil's work is controversial and often hated by Indians. In fact, it seems that Scholder is an important analog for Gil, since the former's work also sought to challenge, and possibly destroy, conventional portraiture of the Native American. To some minds, Scholder's twisted, dystopian paintings of the Indian, which included images of skeletal figures draped in the American flag and so on, appeared to address:

> head-on uncomfortable truths about the lives of contemporary Indians. Alcoholism, poverty, historical and contemporary injustice—[his] images presented the issues in a bold, direct style that offered no easy solutions.[148]

This interpretation, which appears in the catalog for a retrospective on Scholder held by the National Museum for the American Indian in Washington DC in 2008 chimes with one critic's suggestion that Gil's *Americas* portray "the iconic suffering a people."[149] Interestingly, in much the same way as the fictional Gil deems this reading to be "chokingly reductive," Scholder insisted that art is apolitical and that painting is, above all, "a renaissance activity."[150] This fact is underscored by a certain amount of symmetry (to use Irene's term) between Gil and Scholder's thinking about the role of the artist and their position in the art world. Just as Scholder believed that he had been "mislabeled an Indian artist because [he] had done a series on the American Indian," and denied the categorization throughout his career, Gil feels it necessary to make "the big leap" from being identified as a Native painter to being described simply, or, to his mind, *purely*,

---

147 *Shadow Tag*, 36.
148 "Fritz Scholder: Indian/not Indian," exhibition brochure (Washington DC: National Museum of the American Indian, 2008).
149 *Shadow Tag*, 36.
150 "Fritz Scholder," Academy of Achievement interview (July 29 1996) <http://www.achievement.org/ autodoc/page/sch1int-1.> accessed May 9 2012.

as an artist.[151] Ironically enough, Gil's proclivity for "truth," his attempts at masterful technique, and his tenuous link to any tribal community all serve to demonstrate why, exactly, his aesthetic might have limited relevance to sociopolitical discourse about sovereignty or survivance amongst the tribes: it is of interest only to "non-Indian people in the art world."[152]

This distinction might cause us to revisit the question of universal themes, tribal concerns, and personal biography. With regard to the first two issues there, and to be fair to reviewers who have written about the novel for the mainstream press, reviews thus far have acknowledged the range and originality of Erdrich's novel. They have also alluded to the narrative's stranding together of a series of subjects that generally affect all readers alongside those affecting indigenous peoples exclusively. Ron Charles notes the author's ability to bring these issues into contact in the space of the novel. Hager Cohen draws attention to *Shadow Tag*'s uniqueness, at least in terms of Erdrich's oeuvre, and argues that this book is "unlike any other Louise Erdrich novel." The reviewer quickly clarifies her point

151   This refusal to be categorized as an Indian or an Indian artist "made him a controversial figure for many other Native artists, who felt that he was denying the source of his own commercial success," and that his "personal decisions sometimes smacked of opportunism" (NMAI). It is interesting that Erdrich doesn't refer to the controversial Scholder. Artist-in-residence at Dartmouth College in 1973—during the author's second year as an undergraduate there—his legacy, and his biography, seems to have informed Erdrich's characterization of Gil and her commentary on the cultural and political context that his art is created in. Indeed, it seems fair to suggest that the author's decision to mention "Rauschenberg ... And George Morrison" while omitting reference to Scholder, is a means to spur a little digging on the reader's part and suggest the range of aesthetic practices and the degrees of cultural and tribal identification that exist. While Rauschenberg was a quarter Dutch, quarter Swedish, quarter German and quarter Cherokee painter who never met his Cherokee grandmother, Morrison was, according to Gerald Vizenor "a Native modernist painter, and his inspiration was both innate, Native by sentiments of natural reason and memory, and learned by art history, museums, and galleries": "George Morrison: Anishinaabe Expressionist Artist," *American Indian Quarterly* 30.3–4 (Summer/Fall 2006), 647. It might also be interesting that Erdrich chooses to mention Rauschenberg and Morrison; neither painter caused the kind of controversy or division that Scholder did.

152   *Shadow Tag*, 90.

however, adding, "That isn't to say it's devoid of the Native American themes that permeate her many previous books." In this regard, it is obvious that Erdrich has produced, rather adroitly, a book that works on several levels, and may catch the eye of both the mainstream audience and more specialist readers, especially those eager to explore Ojibwe fiction. It also allows the author to satisfy her want to "to be as true as [she] can for Native readers but [...] also [...] true to the writing" as well.[153] It seems that there is more to it than that, however, and I find it difficult to believe that there isn't something else lurking in the shadows, something behind the book's direct—usually disturbing, but sometimes gauche—commentary on marital discord, American history and Indianness in modern America. What could it be? Well, it is possibly the writer's engagement with the very notion of authorship, the classification of literature as "Native American," and, most importantly, the autonomy and sovereignty of the tribal author and of tribal communities. It is also possibly Louise Erdrich's engagement with the notion of postindian identity.

Not as concerned with new historicity, or with revising narrative forms in order to undermine the masternarrative yet stabilize language and story in the wake of poststructural play, *Shadow Tag* presents the reader with a series of provocative clichés and truisms—quite literally *portraits* of the Indian— before forcefully and dramatically disassembling the literary framework that holds these together. In short, it turns out that Riel's character has successfully and deftly managed to manipulate the reader, and has performed her mother's story and that of the family in general. Accordingly, her final divulgence is very much in keeping with the performative aspect of postindian authorship, and it not only introduces us to a distinctly Vizenorian "universe where the meaning of words and concepts is highly mobile," but also demonstrates and enacts the tribal author's control over the story.[154]

---

153 Lynn Neary, "From Erdrich, A Page Turner With Deceit At Heart" (February 7 2010) <http://www.npr.org/ templates/story/story.php?storyId=123420779> accessed May 3 2012.

154 David J. Carlson, "Trickster Hermeneutics and the Postindian Reader: Gerald Vizenor's Constitutional Praxis," *Studies in American Indian Literatures* 23.4 (2011), 17.

Hence, even though the possibility of postindian presence is well glossed during the course of the novel, albeit somewhat problematically in Gil's art, Irene's scholarship, and Riel's adoption of old Indian ways, it is Riel's final statement that finally shatters the idea of linear realism. Crucially, it may also shatter some readers' hopes of finding verisimilitude or "real" Ojibwe stories within the text—a possibility that seems key when considered not only in the context of Hager Cohen's claim that *Shadow Tag* has a trace of the autobiographical about it, but also recent conversations about aesthetic sovereignty and the sociopolitical function of art and literature. Since the accounts of life in the Mount Curve home have been highly mediated, edited, censored, or possibly even misremembered, the reader is made palpably aware of the effect that an author's presence (both implied and real) has upon the story. In that moment, we are reminded of both Riel's subjectivity and Erdrich's arch-mastery.

The allusion to *Rashomon*, a 1950s Japanese movie directed by Akira Kurosawa, possibly tips us off to, or prepares us for, this eventuality. Set in twelfth-century Japan and featuring "a sexual encounter that may be rape, and a death that is either murder or suicide," the film provides four different versions of a chance meeting between a bandit, a samurai, and the samurai's wife. At the trial that follows the samurai's death during the encounter in the woods, it becomes evident that "the bandit, the samurai's wife, the samurai (who, having died, testifies through a spirit medium), and a passing woodcutter" have all seen things quite differently. Kurosawa offers the viewer camera shots that seem to support each of the witnesses' testimony.[155] Erdrich's encoded reference to *Rashomon* has two extremely significant effects. Firstly, it rouses interest in an ongoing debate between the "*positivist* approach [that] maintains that a true explanation [...] can be found or tested by scientific standards" on one hand, and the "*interpretivist* approach [which] does not seek an objective truth so much as to unravel

---

155   Karl G. Heider, "The Rashomon Effect: When Ethnographers Disagree," *American Anthropologist* 90.1 (1988), 74.

patterns of subjective understanding" on the other.[156] Broadly speaking, this underlines the author's continued interest in new historicism, narratological point of view, revisionism, and so on. More specifically, and perhaps more importantly, the jolt that is delivered at the end of *Shadow Tag* could easily be designed to remind the reader that we actually know very little, and that we are at the mercy of the autonomous author. To push that point a little further in a way that is relevant, Erdrich's point would seem to be that irrespective of the countless rumors, allegations, and tall-tales that have been peddled about her private life and her relationship with the late Michael Dorris, we the public know very little. This is as it should be. That point, which has specific salience to this author's work, can, in turn, be broadened out once again when we consider that Ojibwe lifeways, like tribal criticism, are firmly in the hands of Anishinaabe communities and indigenous scholars.

Secondly, the fact that the *Rashomon* effect is introduced, and manipulated, during the course of the novel might cause us to ruminate on the possibility that in the production of all art there is an arch-master—an artist, director, or author who produces and controls the form while manipulating the audience. Hence, even though Kurosawa's movie (like the short stories it is based on and like Erdrich's novel) poses difficult questions *about* multiple perspectives, it seems to arise out of a single vision—the director's own. In one sense, Erdrich's allusion to Kurosawa's film could be a timely reminder that, aesthetically speaking, a single Ojibwe writer is in control of the various perspectives that the audience is made privy to. Yet, and following on from that point, the reference to multiple perspectives can also serve to remind us that the artist, especially the artist working within a tribal context, can cultivate a vision that is informed and shaped by the collective consciousness that writers like Howe call tribalography. For that reason, we must note the crucial distinction between Gil's art and Riel's novel writing. A wide range of perspectives influences the younger artist's creative writing

---

156   Wendy D. Roth and Jal D. Mehta, "The Rashomon Effect: Combining Positivist and Interpretivist Approaches in the Analysis of Contested Events," *Sociological Methods Research* 31.2 (November 2002), 132.

project: tribal voices, literary influences, contemporary events, and so on. The tragic mistake that Gil and Irene make, by comparison, is failing to see beyond the images reflected in either the portraits or the portraitist—a fact clearly echoed in Irene's visceral response to the small innovative theater's introduction of a mirror to the sexual encounter in *Rashomon*. Hence, whereas Riel's writing attempts to keep—and to proffer—a great amount of perspective, and is often informed by conversations with Louise/May (which are not directly transcribed), Gil espouses a Deleuzian system in which "the viewer [the artist, his muse] and [...] manipulation become more important than any underlying ideas."[157] Consequently, it is not so much the fact that Gil's lineage comes from the wrong fractions of unrecognized tribes, or that he earns a living by addressing themes that concern the wider Native American population that becomes stifling; it is instead the fact that he exhibits none of his daughter's collectivist spirit, her appreciation of tribal ways, or her relaxed approach to her chosen medium. Whereas Gil wants to find "truth" in his art and even works toward a final, lasting statement—an artistic legacy that he wants to sign with his own blood— Riel, like Irene it must be said, sees the stories as being part of an evolving process. In that respect, the spirit that she produces her art in resonates with Rebecca Belmore's *Mawu-che-hitoowin: A Gathering of People for any Purpose* (1992), a large installation that comprised of several empty chairs, each of which had headphones attached, through which the viewer/listener could hear the voices of Anishinaabe women from Canada recounting their own experiences and life stories. The structure and style of Erdrich's novel plays a crucial part in communicating that sense of continuance and development, particularly her creative use of diary writing. As Irina Paperno explains: "The diary is best not read as a book with a beginning and end, but as a process."[158]

---

157   Devin Sandoz, "simulation / simulacrum" <http://lucian.uchicago.edu/blogs/ mediatheory/keywords/ simulation-simulacrum> accessed May 14 2012.
158   Paperno, "What Can Be Done with Diaries?," 573.

Life/Writing 2

In many ways, *Shadow Tag*'s symbolism and imagery, its organization of narrative(s), and its near metafictional production and reception of Native American fiction is a commentary on Ojibwe presence and autonomy in modern America. Although a Baudrillardian sense of simulacra as sites of diffusion, diffraction, and dissolution holds sway for much of the novel—mainly through Erdrich's attention to the debilitating forms of mirroring—the novel successfully marries a profound literariness with specific tribal concerns. Riel's dramatic announcement at the very end of the novel reveals that she has stitched the oral and the graphic together—her conversations with Louise/May, her mother's diaries, and her intuition. Although not specifically concerned with cultural knowledge in the first instance, her mode of storytelling mingles living memory with recorded narrative, and does so in a way that celebrates the tradition of Ojibwe storytelling even though she is a novice. Crucially, Riel's project begins when she has found a place within the extended family; Oberfach delivers the key to Irene's bank vault when Riel reaches twenty-one and is living with her "sisters [...] brothers [...] cousins [and] aunts."[159] Just as interesting, perhaps, is the fact that Riel explains that the lawyer "did a lot to shield us in those years following our parents' death," and says, "we just call him Ober."[160] The pet name of the man who holds the key to Irene's journals is the same as that given to Ernst Oberholtzer, the traveler and book-collector who made his home amongst the Ojibwe during the first quarter of the twentieth century. The island inhabited by Ober (the historical figure), Mallard, is home to more than eleven thousand books, and Erdrich has carefully noted "the ongoing hospitality that the board of the Oberholtzer Foundation has shown toward Ojibwe people, Ojibwe writers and language teachers, storytellers."[161] This

---

159 *Shadow Tag*, 249.
160 Ibid.
161 Louise Erdrich, *Books and Islands in Ojibwe Country* (Washington DC: National Geographic Society, 2003), 125.

act of naming says something about the fictional worlds, shared narratives and discrete cultural spaces as a result. The intricate narrative that she weaves together thereafter bears not only close relation to the Latin *fictio*, which often designated serious forms of play or postulation, but also indigenous narrative's contravention of what Christopher B. Teuton has called "the ephemeral nature of orality and the static nature of graphic forms."[162] The circumstances surrounding Riel's authorship and her discovery of a new family also have profound resonance when we consider the significance of the notebooks themselves, and their role in guarding and disseminating knowledge. Specifically, it is difficult not to be reminded of the customary recording of Anishinaabe knowledge (*gikendaasowin*) "in personal notebooks or on scrolls made of *wiigwaas* (birch bark)" when considering both *Shadow Tag*'s structure and Erdrich's interest in the traditional uses of birch bark.[163] Read within this context, the diaries in *Shadow Tag* could be taken as a way for Riel to connect with information that she has not previously known, to learn from her mother's words. The circumstances surrounding the diaries and the pattern that emerges from Riel's reworking of several stories cohere with LeAnne Howe's sense of a tribalography. Riel's pronouncement "I have put it all together [...]. The Red Diary. The Blue Notebook. Her notes on Catlin. My memory charts. I have also filled in certain events and connections. Sometimes, it has helped me to talk to May. Other times, I imagined that I was my mother. Or my father. I have written about them in many ways" seems to "pull all of the elements together" in the way that Howe believes necessary.[164] Importantly enough, Riel's actions are in keeping with Jill Doerfler's succinct and rich description of

---

162 Christopher B. Teuton, *Deep Waters: The Textual Continuum in American Indian Literature* (Lincoln: University of Nebraska Press, 2010), 31.

163 Wendy Djinn Geniusz, *Our Knowledge is Not Primitive: Decolonizing Botanical Anishinaabe Teachings* (Syracuse, NY: Syracuse University Press, 2009), 80. I should note that Geniusz refutes the notion that Anishinaabe scrolls are examples of primitive mnemonics, but in her *Books and Islands in Ojibwe Country* Erdrich does use the phrase "mnemonic scrolls" (*National Geographic*, 11). It seems safe to say that both writers have a very similar sense of the scrolls' power and significance nevertheless.

164 *Shadow Tag*, 251.

Anishinaabe tribalography as a narrative that is "not completely fiction or history but a story that draws on the past, present, and future."[165] An echo of this sense of guardianship and instruction, albeit not necessarily of the passing of cultural knowledge, that accompanies the act of tribalography can be found in Riel's acknowledgment to her parents: "Thank you parents, you left me with your marriage, my material, the stuff of my life."[166] There is no small sense of healing and ceremony within *Shadow Tag*.

It is also worth noting that elders such as "Keewaydinoquay [an Anishinaabe medicine woman and ethno botanist] had at least two bound notebooks in which she kept gikendaasowin," and that the people she instructed in Anishinaabe ways, people such as Mary Geniusz, "only saw the portions of the notebook that Keewaydinoquay wanted her to see."[167] Hence, that *gikendaasowin* should be conspicuously absent from the manuscript produced by Erdrich's omniscient narrator is itself significant in many ways. Firstly, Riel is at the start of a journey. Describing the day that her parents drowned, she writes: "I remember the three of us kids, the dogs with us, standing on the pavement of the broad warm highway that circled the island. And now as I remember it, I see it was midday, the sun right over us that day, and the pavement was hot on our feet [...] and it felt good."[168] Accordingly, it could be the case that it is the act of inheriting the story, even a non-Ojibwe story, that is important, and that Riel must learn the value of protecting stories before she can begin to recover tribal stories and deepen her knowledge of Ojibwe lifeways and spiritualism. Hence, even though Irene's diaries may be culturally void, at least in terms of the *types* of stories they tell, they can still suggest why tribal peoples must find "a way to connect with what [they] don't know, or are missing, and might learn

---

165 Jill Doerfler, "An Anishinaabe Tribalography: Investigating and Interweaving Conceptions of Identity during the 1910s on the White Earth Reservation," *American Indian Quarterly* 33.3 (2009), 295.

166 *Shadow Tag*, 251.

167 Geniusz, *Our Knowledge is Not Primitive*, 81.

168 *Shadow Tag*, 253.

as a result."[169] Second, it is important to note that the diaries are mediated and edited by Riel, which makes her a gatekeeper of sorts. As readers, we have no way of knowing what, exactly, Irene's diaries comment on, and we are not to know whether Riel has chosen to retain much of the information found therein (indeed, the diaries make up just a fraction of *Shadow Tag*, a novel that runs to 253 pages in its paperback format). Given that Irene was once a "very promising scholar" and published "brilliant" essays that are likely to have had material consequence within the academy and tribal communities, we must consider the possibility that her journals are likely to include information that is either personal to family, or culturally sensitive and tribally informed/specific. Or both.

Although an errant, very nearly erstwhile, student of history, Irene began her graduate career by studying the "mental state" of the Métis rebel Louis Riel.[170] Erdrich's profound interest in what she calls "the murky and mysterious" parts of the Louis Riel story is well known, and the author recently praised graphic novelist Chester Brown for creating a text that focuses on the "historical complexity of Riel's actions" as well as his "mental state [and] his fatal sense of fair play when fighting a ruthless enemy."[171] Of itself, her references to Riel gestures toward a profound interest in the interstitial connection between personal and national, private and public, and, finally, notions of truth and story in historical terms. Relevant to any reading of *Shadow Tag*, surely, is the fact that Riel kept a diary during his

---

169 Greg Sarris, *Keeping Slug Woman Alive: A Holistic Approach to American Indian Texts* (Los Angeles: University of California Press, 1993), 57.

170 Leader of the failed Red River Rebellion, Riel had a particular fervor for two things: his Catholic fate and Métis nationalism. Neither spared him from incarceration in the St-Jean-de-Dieu and Beauport asylums from 1876 to 1878, or from being tried, and hung, for high treason following a second failed rebellion during the winter of 1884–1885. Fans of Erdrich's earlier novel *The Plague of Doves* (2009) might also recall that book's treatment of Riel's life, and its description of the ways in which the nationalist leader continued to be a part of indigenous lives long after his death.

171 Louise Erdrich, review of "Louis Riel, A Comic Strip Biography" by Chester Brown, *The Circle: Native American News and Arts* (February 8 2009) <http://thecirclenews. org/index. php? option=com_content&task =view&id=68&Itemid=50> accessed May 15 2012.

time in prison and was a prolific letter writer. It is significant, then, that Erdrich's ill-fated, abused, and maligned protagonist should turn to the act of diary writing as a means of mounting a defense, finding expression, and launching a search for independence. Accordingly, Louis Riel's struggle for sovereignty is revisited not just through Irene's doctoral work, but through her diary writing as well, thereby drawing together historical research and a more germane, personal, and effective form of recordkeeping. Her research on "the depressed Métis patriot" has long since been abandoned however, and the focus of Irene's recent doctoral study is Catlin—the painter who once described himself as the Native's historian. She is also reading "the diary of Christopher Columbus, the one he kept on his first voyage," as mentioned above.[172] As well as reminding us that it would be dangerous, even reckless, to believe that the thin slivers of text provided from the blue and red journals reflect the whole, the layering of stories in *Shadow Tag* underlines the imprudence of believing that fiction provides a "full story" or complete knowledge. As we know, readers—especially non-Native ones—often like to believe that they know virtually everything about a tribal culture once they have read one book.

The studied lack of *gikendaasowin* works in a third way then. It reminds us both of the "non-Native researcher's inability to interpret these records without the help of Anishinaabe consultants," while simultaneously underlining the tribal speaker's right to privacy, to storied autonomy.[173] Fourthly, and finally, this point regarding privacy and the forms of sovereignty highlighted in the (non)telling of certain stories can surely be related to Erdrich's position as an internationally famous writer whose work, and life, garners a huge amount of attention. To my mind, the ambiguities and the uncertainties found in *Shadow Tag* serve to remind us of the conventions of authorship and artistry; it is about fiction rather than the author. Erdrich plays with the idea of truth and fiction, novel and diary, and does so in a way that reminds us of the slipperiness of storytelling more than anything else. In this novel, as in other works by the Ojibwe author, we are more

172 *Shadow Tag*, 22.
173 Geniusz, *Our Knowledge is Not Primitive*, 95.

often confronted with the empty space rather than the definite article. Thus, if *Shadow Tag* has a message to offer us about Erdrich's life, it is probably this: we know little or nothing about the real life of the "real" author.[174] What *Shadow Tag* offers is a long deliberation on the means by which indigenous artists produce, and negotiate, narrative spaces that can accommodate discretion and expression in equal measure.

Hence, if the goal is to understand Erdrich's interweaving of the literary and the tribal, it might be no harm to return to the Derridean notion of trace and absence, but this time consider Teuton's extremely useful interpretation of Derrida's "notion of context dependency."[175] Teuton argues that "Native American forms of signification actively engage presence and absence through two interdependent and reciprocal modes of communication, the oral and the graphic"—an interpretation that places Erdrich's play with concepts of trace or *différance* on a slightly different footing than that imagined by Nancy Peterson. Peterson shortens Derrida's point (she writes "there is nothing beyond the text"; Spivak's original translation reads "There is nothing outside of the text"), which might change the meaning somewhat; rather than emphasizing the manner in which the world is *itself* a text, this translation possibly suggests that the real world has no significance *for the text*.[176] This question of how we interpret there being "no outside-text" is especially important to Teuton's reading, since he mobilizes the phrase in support of the argument that Native "texts" have *always* had the type of textual complexity that Derrida was interested in, and are, therefore, exactly the type of narrative that spurred the philosopher's interest in the dynamism created by a consideration of life as text, text as life. As such, "Native American signification [...] avoid[s] the pitfalls that both oral and graphic modes of communication are prone to in isolation."[177] This reading becomes especially relevant when we remember that Erdrich has striven

---

174   Not unlike Irene's affair with Gil, there is no (hi)story of the final days of Erdrich and Dorris's marriage; the family have chosen not to speak publicly about this terrible time in their lives.

175   *Deep Waters*, 30.

176   Literally, "there is no outside-text"; *il n'y a pas de hors-texte.*

177   Teuton, "Theorizing American Indian Literature," 31.

to draw a line of connection between traditional forms and contemporary writing, even taking the time to remind us that: "Ojibwe people were great writers from way back and synthesized the oral and written tradition by keeping mnemonic scrolls of inscribed birchbark. The first paper, the first books."[178] In that context, I would suggest that *Shadow Tag* illustrates, fulsomely, why it might be useful to explore indigenous narrators' relationship to the "chain of differential references."[179] Language may hold no truth *per se*, but it does have specific origins.

In this way, *Shadow Tag* decisively engages in what David Carlson calls "the act of asserting autonomy and having that autonomy acknowledged by others."[180] Whereas Gil is keen to push away from Native contexts, both artistically and personally, Irene believes that her mother would have protected her from his domination and feels the lack of family support quite keenly. Her diary(s), and the narrative lines that it/they construct and follow, are part of a crucial attempt to explore her roots, her identity, and the factors that shape her life. I would argue that the quasi-confessional line, "I have put it all together," which finally unveils Riel as the master of ceremonies and stories, offers the firmest indication that it does so. Named after a proud Métis rebel, Riel explores the possibility of meshing the oral and the graphic, and subsequently produces a form of fiction that makes use of mnemonic charts, overheard conversations, diaries, and historical research. That fact alone is hugely significant. Despite the naivety, albeit an endearing naivety, about Riel's earliest attempts to explore her identity "as an Indian, American Indian, a Native person" or her decision to "work on her old-time Indian abilities," the conclusion of the novel sees her very much at home amongst her relations. In that context, Ojibwe heritage is neither exotic nor overlooked, but simply *is*. In her own words, she "realizes that the old-time Indians are us, still going to sundances, ceremonies, talking in the old language and even using the old skills if we feel like it,

---

178   *Books and Islands*, 10–11.

179   Jacques Derrida, *Of Grammatology*, trans. Gayatri Chakravorty Spivak (Baltimore, MD: Johns Hopkins University Press, 1997), 158.

180   Carlson, "Trickster Hermeneutics and the Postindian Reader," 17.

not making a big deal."[181] That realization marks an important point of departure, since Riel has, to all intents and purposes, recovered a sense of identity that challenges certain representations of tribal peoples. In moving from her immersion in Catlin's letters and his accounts of tribal life during her teenage years, through to the steady, assured confidence we see in the closing pages of the novel, this character achieves a powerful mastery not just of story, but of life as well. The measured and deliberate tones of the last pieces of narration also reflect a nuanced and sophisticated understanding of the diversity of indigenous experiences—both good and bad. Florian and Stoney have chosen very different paths to their sister. Florian, a reformed addict, has begun his second stint in rehab. Stoney, meanwhile, is Stoney by name and stony by nature: "He doesn't often talk to me or Florian," Riel explains, and "He didn't like living with a big family."[182] Compositely these descriptions reiterate a truism which Gil ponders early on in the novel: "real Indians are so complex and various that they frustrate classification." Importantly, these young adults are modern day Indian survivors who deal with several forms of cultural trauma, and who carve out an existence in a complex, often terrifying new world order. Beneath Riel's creative and fantastic vision of "possible scenarios of the future," which include "sudden panic, a bomb launched toward Minneapolis, an asteroid targeted to hit the Walker Center, a 100 percent fatal pandemic virus" and several other ghoulish prospects, there is an unmistakable resolve and resilience. Erdrich's Indians, like everyone else in post-9/11, and then recession-struck, America, are just getting by.

181 *Shadow Tag*, 59, 62, and 248–249. The fact that Riel has been taught very little about Ojibwe lifeways and has "decided she would not be just a Native person, an American Indian, an Ojibwe or a Dakota or a Cree, but a person of example" is interesting, insofar as it comments on the lack of instruction that Irene or Gil have given her about her tribal identity *per se* (*Shadow Tag*, 62).

182 *Shadow Tag*, 248.

Reality Through Art

In his Nobel Lecture, delivered in 2005, the late Harold Pinter recalled an earlier paean that he made regarding the "exploration of reality through art," in which he had argued, "There are no hard distinctions between what is real and what is unreal, nor between what is true and what is false. A thing is not necessarily either true or false; it can be both true and false." Pinter went on to state, for the record, "as a writer I stand by [these assertions] but as a citizen I cannot."[183] I would argue that *Shadow Tag* is a long meditation on the "exploration of reality through art," and that Erdrich's novel ponders both the autonomy and the citizenship of the tribal artist. On one hand, the various contradictions, revelations, and perspectives incorporated into the narrative serve to disclose the elusive nature of truth in art. These aesthetic maneuvers give the lie to the notion that *Shadow Tag*, or other works of Native fiction, are *necessarily* biographical, revelatory, or realistic. Broadly speaking, this move points up the danger of believing that the narrative or the visual image has the power to capture the essence of a tribe. That, in turn, might remind us of the tribe's autonomous right to self-definition and to privacy. Hence, if *Shadow Tag* has any biographical relevance (and I would certainly allow that it does), it is because Erdrich's investigation of the way that "truths challenge each other, recoil from each other, reflect each other, ignore each other, tease each other, are blind to each other" is a rejoinder to *New York Magazine*'s investigative search for the "truth" after Michael Dorris's suicide.[184] Erdrich examines moments of mirroring and simulation that are concomitantly postmodern and near gothic (through their concern with types of doubling: doubled narratives, doubled images, double selves); disassembles master narratives and gives the lie to narratives of representation by offering a counterpo(i)se; and, most importantly, reminds non-tribal readers that the cultural stories and

---

183 "Art, Truth & Politics" <http://www.nobelprize.org/nobel_prizes/literature/laureates/2005/pinter-lecture-e.html> accessed May 2 2012.

184 Ibid.

traditions that often inform the novel and lie in its shadows are not always on show in the fiction itself, and are not for widespread dissemination. In essence, the doubling, the fissures, the uncertainties, and the various moments of ambiguity and confusion found in *Shadow Tag* might serve to remind us that we ought to interpret indigenous literatures with a certain degree of hesitancy.

That is not to say that Irene's sense of citizenship, stifled as it has been, or Riel's communitivism (to borrow Weaver's useful term) are not predicated on both women's appreciation of the tangible and the mate-rial—family, ancestry, shared knowledge. On the contrary, both mother and daughter are fully aware of the effect that the atomization of individuals and small family units has upon their lives. At one point, Irene tells Gil that her mother, Winnie Jane, would not have let him "fuck me up like this" if she were still alive.[185] That absence very possibly leads to Irene's death. By comparison, the new realities that open up to Riel after her mother's death, when she becomes part of a far wider network of family and community, are key elements of her survivorship. There are truths here that underpin and gird up the author's existence. At the same time, as writers, as artists, Irene and Riel explore the complex intersection of what Pinter calls the real and unreal. By breaking free of the shackles of representation (represented in Riel's move away from one-dimensional representations of old-time Indian and toward Ojibwe lifeways), and by successfully meshing the citizen's sense of the real and the artist's vision of the elusive truth together, Riel finally engages what Vizenor describes as the "traces of tribal survivance, trickster discourse and the remanence of intransitive shadows."[186] That success comes in the wake of her parent's death, and with it their excessive engagement with rootless simulacra and static representation.

If we consider the possibility that the "traces of tribal survivance" are found in *both* the "postmodern shadows [that] counter paracolonial histo-ries, dickered testimonies, simulations ... the banal essence of consumerism,

185   *Shadow Tag*, 34.
186   Gerald Vizenor, "The Ruins of Representation: Shadow Survivance and the Literature of Dominance," *American Indian Quarterly* 17.1 (Winter 1993), 7.

[*and* in] trickster pronouns, transformations, and the shimmers of tribal consciousness [...] heard in literature," then we might realize the full significance of Erdrich's title.[187] Irene may have fallen silent, but the diaries remobilize her shadow, freeing it from the gaze and the static pose that is quite literally captured in the representations that are the Americas; she lives on in Riel's story, and the shadow that was once caught or tagged has finally floated free. However, this is not purely a postmodern gesture—far from it—and the novel contains countless "transformations, and the shimmers of tribal consciousness." This fact is made explicit by the narrator's reminder that, in the Ojibwe language, "Waabaamoojichaagwaan—the word for mirror also can refer to shadow and to the soul: your soul is visible and can be seen."[188] What is most arresting then, is that the plot, structure, and symbolism of *Shadow Tag* gesture toward a palpable sense of what lies beneath, what is left unrevealed. This novel contains many of the energies and impulses found in works such as Greene's *The End of the Affair*, which opens with Bendrix's statement, "A story has no beginning or end." It even echoes Ernest Hemingway's rejected ending for *A Farewell to Arms*: "It is not fair to start a new story at the end of an old one, but that is the way it happens. There is no end except death and birth is only the beginning."[189] In the final instance, however, *Shadow Tag*'s structure and style possibly brings us back to Nanapush's advice at the very end of *Tracks*. There, at a moment when many readers will still be searching for the hermeneutic code that might crack open the text, Erdrich's wily old narrator tells us that: "it comes up different every time, and has no ending, no beginning. They get the middle wrong too."[190]

187   Ibid.
188   *Shadow Tag*, 39.
189   *The Sunday Times* (July 8, 2012).
190   *Shadow Tag*, 8.

CHAPTER 6

Choctalking: The Realities of Fiction in LeAnne Howe's *Shell Shaker*

> Every map is a political map and tells a story—that we are alive everywhere across this nation.[1]
>
> — JAUNE QUICK-TO-SEE-SMITH

It seems entirely fitting that Jaune Quick-to-See-Smith's collage *War shirt 1992* should adorn the cover of LeAnne Howe's *Shell Shaker* (2002). Presented on canvas, Smith's mixed media collage consists of "cut and pasted newspaper headlines and archival material, over which she splashes paint and marks the raw outline of American Indian images and icons."[2] The piece represents a complex meeting point in which a number of elements come into contact: the ocular and the narratological, the historical and the contemporary, the tribally specific (the image of the war shirt) and pop-culture pastiche (advertisements for "Chief Sleepy Eye Brand" and so on). The various constitutive pieces that the collage consists of could be said to be intertwined or imbricated, an aesthetic that, in the eyes of some commentators, could be taken as a sign of hybridization or syncretism. Yet, one could argue, just as easily, that the piece creates a disjunction or disconnection between the image of a culturally significant, sacred garment on one hand, and putative, stereotypical representations of indigenous identity and presence on the other. Thus, in collating a compendium of

---

1   Jaune Quick-to-See-Smith, *Postmodern Messenger, Exhibition Catalogue* (2004).
2   Benjamin Genocchio, "Art Review: A Horse Trader's Daughter, With Visions of Injustice," *New York Times* (November 12 2006).

diverse, entangled, and knotted cultural artifacts, stories, and historical resonances, *War shirt 1992* presents the viewer with an unsettling, engaging, and potentially disruptive aesthetic form. In this instance, the artist creates a form of interplay that forces us to reassess key elements of the collage itself, especially the relationship between the spiritual garment on one hand and the manufactured image on the other. The aesthetic dissonance is provocative, suggestive, and seductive. "Smith's paintings want to be looked at," Dean Rader suggests, "They want to communicate. They invite us into their uneasy home."[3] In fact, Rader believes that Jaune Quick-to-See-Smith creates a "narrative landscape" and, in so doing, "asks us to bear in mind the materials, methods and methodologies of colonization, indigenous histories and identity."

And so it is with Howe's *Shell Shaker*. This enlivening, eclectic, and often hectic novel brings together a plethora of stories concerning the historical and contemporary experiences of the Choctaw nation. Various geographical, spiritual, familial, and narratological spaces are revealed or plotted during the course of Howe's novel, and, as a consequence, images that relate to the act of mapping, the basis of narrative or storytelling, and the subject of community and place become recurring motifs throughout. Concerned with the ways in which Choctaw lifeways have been mapped out across time, Howe appears to be especially concerned with various forms of travel, exchange, contact, and consumption in both pre-contact and post-contact America. Rather than compartmentalizing past and present-day experiences into discrete, autonomous spaces, *Shell Shaker's* storyline follows a wild and lawless (but never confused) narrative structure that provides the reader with a powerful sense of the connectedness that informs and shapes events in the Choctaw world. Accordingly, Howe focuses on moments of exchange and trade between the tribes and, latterly, between the tribes and the colonizers, and the narrative pays considerable attention to transactions that occur in a number of key locations: narrative site, bodily sites, spiritual sites, national and international sites, and

3   Dean Rader, *Engaged Resistance: American Indian Art, Literature, and Film from Alcatraz to the NMAI* (Austin: University of Texas Press, 2011), 52.

so on. As such, the book examines and reflects on the tribe's relationship to place, to the spirit world, to cosmological forces, to the American continent, and to the world. A crucial aspect of this exploration of Choctaw presence is the interrogation of movement within, and between, key sites inhabited by indigenous peoples, and the novel deals with the question of sovereignty and self-determination across a number of contested, and often overlapping, spaces.

The goal of this chapter, then, is to consider the manner in which *Shell Shaker* reflects the web of being that orders the Choctaw world, and reflects on the various forms of tribal sovereignty arising from the relationships formed within that web. By engaging with Howe's multi-layered, multi-pointed canvas, I hope to suggest that the novel reflects the complexity of the Choctaw worldview, underlines continued indigenous presence, interrogates the meeting point between indigenous peoples and colonial "path-finders," differentiates between confirmatory and detrimental forms of exchange and communication (in both pre-contact and post-contact times) and, above all, proves not only that "speech acts create the world around us," but also that indigenous writers shape the world through their fiction.[4] Specifically, I hope to demonstrate how, exactly, the web of contiguous, interrelated stories that Howe creates—that rich "rhetorical space"—maps out moments of cross-cultural contact, colonial movement, consumption, and (inter)national trade, thereby underlining the extent to which colonization is reliant not only upon particular forms of commerce and exploitation, but also trade, tyranny, and movement within a given territory.

4   Kirstin Squint, "Choctawan Aesthetics, Spirituality, and Gender Relations: An Interview with LeAnne Howe," *MELUS* 35.3 (Fall 2010), 219.

The Broad Sweep, the Big Canvas

Nathaniel West once declared that he was primarily, indeed *solely*, concerned with his particularized vision as a writer and tended therefore to "forget the broad sweep, the big canvas, the shot-gun adjectives, the important people, the significant ideas."[5] Conversely, LeAnne Howe's literary aesthetic seems to be marked by an unmistakable desire to construct a narrative that captures, as fully as possible, the "broad sweep." Truth be told, Howe has a very specific sense of the method by which she creates fiction. "When I'm in the writing zone," the Choctaw novelist explains, "there are dozens of people standing around my computer screen watching what I type."[6] Amongst those assembled, she reveals, are her "grandmothers [...] mothers, uncles, aunts, ancestors [...] children, and [...] characters," as well as a retinue of "Indian writers" including "N. Scott Momaday, Leslie Silko [...] Simon Ortiz [...] Craig Womack, Joy Harjo [...] Jean O'Brien and Vine Deloria, Jr."[7] The effect is that her writing creates or gives rise to what Rader has wisely described as a "collative theory," in which stories, influences, experiences, and perspectives proliferate and intermingle.[8] Howe has described this art of storytelling as "tribalography," and argues that this approach or style allows her to produce a form of multi-genre literature that responds to, and arises out of, the "Native propensity for bringing things together, for making consensus, and for symbiotically connecting one thing to another."[9] By facilitating the production of a clear and distinct "rhetorical space," as

5   Sacvan Bercovitch, *Nathanael West: Novels and Other Writings* (New York: Library of America, 1997), 793.

6   LeAnne Howe, "Blind Bread and the Business of Theory Making, As Told by LeAnne Howe," *Reasoning Together: The Native Critics Collective*, ed. Craig S. Womack, Daniel Heath Justice, and Christopher B. Teuton (Norman: University of Oklahoma Press, 2008), 333.

7   Ibid.

8   *Engaged Resistance*. Prologue & 65.

9   LeAnne Howe, "My Mothers, My Uncles, Myself," in *Here First: Autobiographical Essays by Native American Writers*, ed. Arnold Krupat and Brian Swann (New York: Modern Library, 2000), 212–228; *Reasoning Together*, 330.

Howe would have it, tribalography is both the sign and the expression of aesthetic, political, and cultural sovereignty.[10] Within that space Howe manages, in her own words:

> to pull the passages of my life, and the lives of my mothers, my mothers' mothers, my uncles, the greater community of *chafachúka* ("family") and *iksa* ("clan"), together to form the basis for critique, interpretation; a moment in the raw world.[11]

What becomes readily apparent, then, is that the creative space that Howe's writing takes shape in is itself shaped by stories, events, and experiences that have a definite materiality or actuality about them. Crucially, this concretization speaks of, and to, the manner in which Choctaw peoples have always been, and continue to be, a part of the "raw world" around us. Tribalography reiterates, reinforces, and, by times, recovers tribal voices in order to demarcate contemporary indigenous spaces and to reveal the extent to which those spaces are in contact and communication with everwider circles of being. Howe's Okla Humma Indians are long-distance travelers. Obviously enough, this style of writing often even exceeds the boundary lines that contemporary authors are conventionally expected to stay within, and the author creates a sense of storytelling that dynamically and inclusively strands personal, familial, and tribal stories into a collective narrative form. This sense of literary production challenges the notion that the author is a subjective, individualized entity and underlines, in the fullest possible way, the complexities of the cultural situations that tribal literatures are produced in. In fact, Howe's description of the authorial process places her fiction at the other end of the spectrum from the "'autotelic' or 'autonomous' literary text"; that is to say, she places her fiction within the cultural, social, and political context that, according to Donald E. Pease, the New Critics believed literary texts must be "utterly separate from."[12]

---

10 LeAnne Howe, "Tribalography: The Power of Native Stories," *Journal of Dramatic Theory and Criticism* 14 (1999), 118.
11 "My Mothers, My Uncles, Myself," 214.
12 Donald E. Pease, "Author," in *Critical Terms for Literary Study*, ed. Frank Lentricchia and Thomas McLaughlin (Chicago, IL: University of Chicago Press, 1995), 111.

A collage of stories and images therefore influences tribalography, and Howe professes herself to be proud of "consciously using the terms story, fiction, history, and play, interchangeably" and to be "from a culture that views these things as an integrated whole rather than individual parts."[13]

Consequently, it should come as no great surprise to learn that the writer describes *Shell Shaker* as a collage of the various narratives (both Native and non-Native) that inform Choctaw culture today. According to Howe:

> *Shell Shaker* is a tribalography. I used some oral stories from my birth mother. I found documents in the historic record; I used stories of Choctaws who were gourd dancers, and stories of women who shook shells, and stories of dancers who covered themselves in white powder before they danced. I also used stories about the women who made sashes from porcupine skins.[14]

The author's description of the manner in which she distinctively blends "oral stories from [... her] birth mother" and "documents in the historic record" is something of an explication of the interplay found in *Shell Shaker*—a narrative that swings back and forth between the eighteenth and twentieth centuries, and ranges across various distinct discursive and linguistic territories.[15] Ostensibly concerned with the mystery surrounding the assassinations of two historically distant, but morally aligned, Choctaw leaders—Red Shoes in 1747 and Redford McAlester in 1991—the plot focuses primarily on the community's response to the greed and mendacity that precipitates their untimely deaths. A sense of doubling, continuation, or even uncanny repetition is first created by the chronological framework and is then echoed, and sustained, through the geographical scope of the novel. That is to say, although the majority of action unfolds either in the Choctaw tribal homelands east of the Mississippi or in Durant, Oklahoma, the wider plot (and it is *very* wide) involves historical and contemporary events which take place in a number of geographically distant sites. These

13   "Tribalography," 118.
14   Howe, "Blind Bread and the Business of Theory Making," 336.
15   Ibid.

sites include New Orleans, Fort Worth (Texas), Santa Monica, Ireland, and London. Indeed, even the "local" terrain has many histories, many stories, many names; the savvy reader will be conscious of the fact that Oklahoma was known as the Twin Territories prior to statehood, and Howe subsequently makes much out of her ancestors' ability to shuttle between different spaces. This preference for overlapping intertwined chronological and spatial settings means that, more often than not, Howe's Choctaw characters exceed the boundaries that fictional Indians are usually expected to stay within. By the same token, as the novel's third-person narrator is keen to point out, the tribe has been responsible for shaping Okla Humma from the very beginning: Durant was founded by Dixon DuRant, a "Choctaw-Frenchman."[16] Imbrications and connections become something of a leitmotif throughout Howe's work as she strives, in common parlance, to "see the whole board."

The historical narrative, which is set in and around the Louisiana region, opens with the words of Shakbatina, a peacemaking shell shaker who intends to become a blood sacrifice by standing "in for [… her] daughter, Anoleta, who has been wrongly accused of the murder of a Chickasaw woman from the Red Fox village."[17] Married to Red Shoes, who was once known by the tribe as "*Imataha Chitto*, the greatest giver," Anoleta is not only charged with murdering his Chickasaw wife, but, more importantly, is aware of Red Shoe's duplicitous dealings with different clans amongst the Choctaws, Conchatys, and Chickasaws and with the "*Filanchi okla* and the *Inkilish okla*"—the French and English colonizers. Indeed, at one point she admonishes him with the assertion: "All you have ever proven is that you fight in the pay of anyone who gives muskets."[18] Red Shoes counters her claim with his argument that the Choctaw "can rid ourselves of both the *Filanchi okla* and the *Inkilish okla*" if the "warriors have enough muskets and powder." His plans run aground, however, when it becomes obvious that his complex agreements will lead the tribe into war and conflict. Not

16   *Shell Shaker*, 59.
17   Ibid., 4.
18   *Shell Shaker*, 81 & 128.

only is Red Shoes eventually shunned by the various clans, but he is assassinated by Haya, Anoleta's younger sister and therefore a descendant of Grandmother, the first peacemaker.

Red McAlester, the leader of the Choctaw Nation in 1991, is a spiritual, if not a literal (re)incarnation of Red Shoes. A latter day chicaner and swindler, his manifold, labyrinthine associations with both the Mafia and Irish Republican Army also lead to ruin and death. Although warned by his lover Auda Billy (a Choctaw historian turned assistant tribal chief) that it is imprudent to involve the D'Amato family or the IRA in the affairs of the casino owned by the tribe, McAlester fails to see danger accruing from his actions. "Let me worry about that, honey," he tells Auda, before adding: "I'm not going to lose control of the tribe."[19] Various forms of self-indulgence and covetousness increasingly drive McAlester, and he is a hostage to hubris, just as Red Shoes once was. He too comes to an inglorious end. In the wake of an early morning gunshot in the Choctaw Nation headquarters, the chief is discovered "leaning back in his chair, his boxer shorts and suit pants down around his ankles [...]. [B]lue-black hair and bloody bone splattered on the wall behind him ... his cheeks ... blotted with the imprint of red lips."[20] The question, of course, is who, exactly, left this "imprint" on McAlester's lifeless body.

Just as Anoleta was held accountable for a mysterious murder at the beginning of the first narrative in Howe's novel, Auda, the daughter of Susan Billy and the eldest of three sisters, becomes the main suspect in the second assassination tale. Although this is partly because Auda is personally and professionally involved with McAlester, the fact that the sheriff finds her in the chief's office when they finally arrive on the scene seems to seal her fate.[21] There is, however, another catalyst that seems to exert an extremely powerful influence on Auda and those around her; the women in the Billy clan are direct descendants of Shakbatina and Anoleta. It subsequently becomes evident that Howe goes to great lengths to outline countless correlations

19   Ibid., 26.
20   Ibid., 27 & 28.
21   Ibid., 27.

between chronologically distinct or distant narratives, thereby exploring the extent to which spiritual and communal experiences are analogous, if not cyclic. Since the plotline focuses on the connection between historical and contemporary events in this way, it is essential, as Patrice Hollrah notes, that the reader takes stock of the fact that "descendants through the females of the historical family have counterparts in the contemporary family" and thereby "understand the importance of ancestors" in Howe's book.[22] Subsequently, Susan Billy's claim "I killed Chief Redford McAlester. It was my gun and I shot him in the head [...] *Osano abi bolle li tok*" dramatically revisits the type of conviction shown by Shakbatina when she states, "I will tear myself from the arms of my family and stand in for my first daughter."[23] Correspondingly, just as the affection that the historical figures Haya and Neshoba have for their sister Anoleta is replicated in contemporary times by Adair and Tema's concern for Auda, the advice of the uncle figures Nitakechi and Isaac Billy is crucial to the outcomes realized in 1738 and 1991 respectively. Thus, instead of merely representing its author's artistic vision, *Shell Shaker* is a reflection on tribal perspectives and the Choctaw sense of the time and space continuum. For that reason, it is necessary to consider the literary and critical implications arising from Howe's decision to adopt what might be considered as a narratological version of the collage aesthetic that Quick-to-See-Smith champions.

And, even though this methodological approach creates what Louis Owens once called a "matrix of incredible *heteroglossia* and linguistic torsions ... [in] an intensely political situation," Howe's characters are not light-heartedly or playfully "slipping between the seams, embodying contradictions, and contradancing across every boundary."[24] On the contrary, the majority of her protagonists are keenly aware of their relationship to the specific cultural, political, and spatial boundaries that designate various

22   Patrice Hollrah, "Decolonizing the Choctaws: Teaching LeAnne Howe's *Shell Shaker*," *American Indian Quarterly* 28.1–2 (2004), 78.

23   *Shell Shaker*, 29, 4.

24   Louis Owens, *Other Destinies: Understanding the American Indian Novel* (Norman: University of Oklahoma Press, 1992), 15; *Mixedblood Messages: Literature, Film, Family, Place* (Norman: University of Oklahoma Press, 1998), 41.

responsibilities and positions within the tribal community. Moreover, those who do "slip [...] between the seams," namely Red Shoes and McAlester, are hardly celebrations of cross-culturalization or hybridization. Accordingly, although Howe constructs a narratological collage and avails of a "multi-directional and multi-genre discursive mode" that is, stylistically speaking, quite similar to the storytelling found in Owens's fiction, her concern is not truly with the prioritization of "hybridized" or "mixedblood" positions.[25] By the same token, even though *Shell Shaker* reformulates tropes, images, structures, and modes of discourse that have become standardized, thereby making use of what Bakhtin called "social dialects, characteristic group behaviour, professional jargons, generic languages, languages of generations and age groups," the novel is not strictly concerned with cultural "mediation" or what James Ruppert describes as the "dialogic relationship between Native and non-Native discourse fields [in order to] to disrupt the easy engagement of the dominant literary discourse."[26]

Rather than celebrating Bakhtinian heteroglossia—namely, the contestation of voices *"within* a language"—I would argue that Howe seems more interested in polyglossia, that is, the contestation *between* languages. In other words, rather than focussing on what Bakhtin refers to as the novel's position on the "border between the completed, dominant literary language and the *extraliterary languages* that know heteroglossia," Howe deploys the concept of tribalography in order to broaden our notion of the dialectic that takes place within the Native American novel. And, rather than expressly creating what James Ruppert defines as the "mediational

25   Elvira Pulitano, "Crossreading Texts, Crossreading Identity: Hybridity, Diaspora and Tranculturation in Louis Owens' *Mixedblood Messages*," in *Louis Owens: Literary Reflections on His Life* and *Work*, ed. Jacquelyn Kilpatrick (Norman: University of Oklahoma Press, 2004), 80–81.

26   James Ruppert, "Mediation and Multiple Narrative in Contemporary Native American Fiction," *Texas Studies in Literature and Language* 28 (1986), x. To be fair to Ruppert he is quick to point out that "contemporary Native American novelists do *more* than create representations of bicultural experience," and is keen to emphasize the genre's ability to enable various forms of "cultural survival" and continuance (x, emphasis added).

text," thereby creating a narratological zone that primarily aims to link Choctaw and non-Choctaw discursive spaces, Howe is interested in mapping out a narrative space that allows her characters to add "experience and knowledge to [... *their*] belief system."[27] During her account of tribal lifeways, Howe explains that the majority of her characters (including the Cherokee Embarrassed Grief and *Shell Shaker*'s Redford McAlester, Tema Billy, and Adair Billy) have "traveled widely, traded information, adopted new tools, and then returned home with new ideas that are both dynamic and destructive."[28] Embarrassed Grief has, the reader is informed, engaged Bakhtin's concept of language and conflict, "swallowed deconstructionism" and Derrida's challenge to the text's "essential" message, *and* become au fait with Foucault's "archaeology of knowledge."[29] Crucially, she has done so *not* in a bid to achieve a form of reconciliation with mainstream America, nor to define herself as being between two cultures. On the contrary, Howe's character ultimately mobilizes, and modifies, theories in order to reach a fuller, and richer, sense of personal and communal story as well as a deeper understanding of the tribe's place in a complex world order. Through this interest in what she calls the "international and intertribal" Howe scrutinizes not only "the nature of tribal interactions" from a Choctaw perspective, but also the development of a Choctaw voice that has relevance in the modern world.[30] And, importantly enough, it is a voice capable of reaching those who speak other languages.

The myriad "interactions" on view in Howe's work bring me, somewhat circuitously, back to the aesthetic figurations of Jaune Quick-to-See-Smith.

27   Ruppert, "Mediation and Multiple Narrative in Contemporary Native American Fiction," 13; Howe, "Blind Bread and the Business of Theory Making," 331.

28   Howe, "Blind Bread and the Business of Theory Making," 330.

29   Ibid., 332. During a recent interview with Kirstin Squint, Howe voiced the opinion that: "speech acts create the world around us. And those are primary, foundational. We can look at verbs and verb tenses, especially in Choctaw, as a way of moving the mountain through the act of speaking." This, too, sounds very much like Foucault's *Archeology of Knowledge*, in which he suggests that discourse "creates a world," "generates knowledge and truth," "says something about those who speak it," and, perhaps, brings about "social, cultural, and political power."

30   Ibid., 330.

Although the collage method deployed by the artist in her painting *War Shirt 1992* unquestionably meshes with Howe's vision of a literary, oral, and theoretical "tribalography," it seems that another of Quick-to-See-Smith's paintings, *State Names I* (2000), offers something of a visual metaphor for the style and structure of *Shell Shaker*. One of a series of paintings in which she represents the map of America, *State Names I* dramatically redraws the continent. In the first instance, Quick-to-See-Smith includes only the state names which are derivations of Native American words or tribes' names (for instance Mississippi, which comes from Ojibwa *mshi-* "big," *ziibi* "river," Arkansas, which comes the Algonquin word *akansa*, and Tennessee from the Iroquoian name *ta'nasi*, are included, but the majority of state names are omitted). Second, by incorporating states and territories that are outside the United States, for instance Quebec and Chihuahua, Quick-to-See-Smith dissembles international borders. The deconstruction of geopolitical boundaries is sustained by the artist's decision to dribble paint from top to bottom across the length of the entire painting, the effect of which is to disrupt and collapse the linearity ordinarily associated with America's national and state borders. Crucially, that disruption of post-contact, political constructs is met with a sense of cultural continuance that is graphically marked out via an act of naming that elaborately, lucidly, and literally maps out the continent's various etymological and historical roots. This, according to Quick-to-See-Smith, is a "political map" that bears witness to tribal continuance and presence; "I think of my work as an inhabited landscape," the artist explains, before concluding that, for her, this space is "never static or empty."

The rhetorical space that Howe creates in *Shell Shaker* is a similarly "inhabited landscape," since the novel deals with the relationship between place and language, naming and mapping, historical "records" and orality, alongside various processes of geopolitical and cultural boundary making and boundary crossing. Indeed, the imagery and plot of the novel puts me in mind of Lisa Brooks's description of the etymology of *awikhigan*, the word for book in the Abenaki language; "the root word *awigha-* denotes 'to draw,' 'to write,' 'to map,'" Brooks explains, and "*Awikhigan* is a tool for image making, for writing, for transmitting an image or idea from one mind to another, over waterways, over time."[31] Brooks concludes that the:

> book is an activity in which we participate, an instrument, and a map. It is a map of writers and texts, as well as a process of mapping the historical space they inhabit. It is a mapping of how Native people [...] used writing as an instrument to reclaim lands and reconstruct communities, but also a mapping of the *instrumental* activity of writing, its role in the rememberment of a fragmented world.[32]

Although the tribal contexts are obviously very different, this particular contextualization of how the Abenaki language reveals the book's capacity to perform "process[es] of mapping" finds an important analog in the Choctaw tradition. There, the root word *Ikbi* "may mean to make—or one who makes, a maker or creator." For instance "*Holisso ikbi* may mean to make, print or publish a book," or it can refer to "the author of a book, a printer, and an editor." With that, "*Chokka ikbi* may mean either to build a house or a carpenter. *Nan ikbi* is either to make things or a manufacturer [...]. [And] *Hina ikbi* (or *Hinikbi*) is to make or open up a road, path or furrow—or a road maker, a plowman, and a pioneer."[33] In the examination of *Shell Shaker* that follows, I will argue that Howe is, above all else, a maker or creator; a creator who writes fiction, edits historical documents, and revisits Choctaw language and story in order to open a path and, as Brooks would have it, to "draw [...] write [and] map" tribal experiences.

"There was once a road, an ancient trade route that began in the east" Shakbatina tells her listener on the very first page of *Shell Shaker*.[34] "Like the wind gathering, receding, returning," the road "went through hundreds of towns until it reached the middle of the square grounds" in the town where

---

31　Lisa Brooks, *The Common Pot: The Recovery of Native Space in the Northeast* (Minneapolis: University of Minnesota Press, 2008), xxi & xxii.

32　Ibid., xxii.

33　"Choctaw Language," Choctaw Nation of Oklahoma website <http://www.choctawnation. com/culture-heritage/choctaw-traditions/choctaw-language> accessed June 2 2012.

34　*Shell Shaker*, 1.

Grandmother and her husband Tuscalusa lived.[35] Although it is originally a corridor of exchange and therefore emblematic of intertribal co-operation and communication, this passageway carries other possibilities and threats: "Down this road came a terrible story."[36] The story in question is the one that tells of Hispano de Soto's arrival amongst Shakbatina's ancestors. That event is greeted by Tuscalusa's plan to "lure the *Osano* [bloodsucker] away" and the "extraordinary" shell shaking dance that Grandmother begins on the day of "*Itilauichi*, the Autumnal Equinox."[37] Not alone does this first-person narration provide the history and context of the events that unfold across the space of Howe's novel, but it also reveals the manner in which various forms of mapping and plotting shape the intertwined narratives that *Shell Shaker* allows the reader to access. In effect, Shakbatina's vivid account discloses the importance of path-finding: she is recounting an ancestral story that directly links her to Grandmother and Tuscalusa, thereby mapping a sense of continuance through time and place; her description also makes reference to commerce and a necessary form of boundary crossing while, at the same time, invoking the image of incursion or colonization by "foreigners"; Grandmother's pioneering dance links her to the Equinox, thereby making known the connection between the Choctaw, the spirit world, and a celestial map; after Tuscalusa's death Grandmother and her sisters become a "flock of strange birds" busily "crisscrossing the *Ahepatanichi*, the river that caused all life to rise up"—when their wings fall off these birds finally land and establish new Choctaw homelands, thereby mapping out the "seven original Choctaw towns."[38] Shakbatina, a direct descendent of the Grandmother of Birds, knows full well the dangers associated with traveling across boundaries since she is about to give her life in order to save Anoleta, the daughter sent to the Red Fox village as "an emissary" from the Choctaw people. Although Anoleta has been sent in good spirit, she has not been magnanimously received—on the contrary, the spiteful

35   Ibid., 1–2.
36   Ibid., 2.
37   Ibid.
38   *Shell Shaker*, 4.

Chickasaw woman mentioned above accuses her of "stealing the affections of her husband," who is, of course, Red Shoes.[39] Yet, the imminent revenge killing of Shakbatina does not mark the end of her journey; her body will be left open to the elements during the bone-picking ceremony and therefore scattered to the winds. Afterwards her "possessions will be divided among [... her] daughters" and her "essence," Shakbatina explains, "will be mingled with theirs. As it should be."[40]

Various geographical, spiritual, familial, and narratological spaces are revealed or plotted during the course of Howe's novel and, as a consequence, the act of path-finding becomes something of a recurring motif. For instance, Shakbatina's concern with "routes"—paths that lead to intertribal (and intercultural) connection, spiritual journeys, the ancestor's presence in the here and now—is palpably present in the contemporary storyline. Here the events that unfold in Durant on Sunday, September 1991, the day of the Autumnal Equinox, are introduced by a third-person narrator who immediately underlines a profound sense of placement. According to this speaker, Auda Billy "sits on the side of her twin bed in the small upstairs bedroom of the house where she was born," a house that "is as warm as wool and people with aunts and uncles, rabbits, ghosts of rabbits, and other relatives."[41] Abundantly populated and built during the nineteenth century, the house itself is in Old Durant, a place that "stopped narrating to the Choctaws after the whites took over the town in 1907." The year 1907 was, of course, the year in which the old territorial lines that demarcated the Twin Territories were redrawn, crossed out, or erased in order to make way for the new Oklahoma state. More importantly, perhaps, it was also the year that "the spirits moved away, shed their skin that bound land and people together." If the links between Shakbatina's discourse on the presence of relatives, the thornier effects of intercultural contact, and the bonds that connect tribe and place weren't already explicit, the modern-day narrator goes on to explain that outside Auda's house the spirits have

---

39   Ibid., 5.
40   Ibid., 6.
41   Ibid., 17.

"returned, pulling stars down from the sky, causing a fifty-mile prairie fire" running from "the Mineral Bayou Bridge in Durant to the outskirts of Hugo, Oklahoma." The fire, we are told, has left "the land along Highway 70 [...] seared black like a piece of burnt toast."[42] The Autumnal Equinox (in 1738 and in 1991) is, then, a day when journeys and stories begin. Howe interrogates the link between specific dates, places, and narratives, plotting each of them on the complicated map that connects the ancestors to the Billy's, the spiritual to corporeal, lands east of the Mississippi to Oklahoma, past to present, and the Choctaw to the Irish and the Italians. Reaching a deeper understanding of *Shell Shaker* is, then, a matter of coming to terms with how, exactly, these contiguous yet intertwined spaces on the "language map" are superbly knotted and dynamic. Howe's interest in path-finding and interconnectedness is reflected in Joy Porter's suggestion that the novel "is at pains [...] to connect stories about the impact of colonialism across generations and across geographical divides."[43] It is also evident in Jane P. Hafen's claim that *Shell Shaker* is a story about "generations of Choctaw peoples who persevere with ritual gestures of 'life everlasting.'"[44] In short, it is a case of following Howe's characters across a storied landscape that maps far more than geography alone.

Yet, it is a powerful sense of geography and placement that gives the novel its structure and design. Indeed, the characters' understanding of place—both local and distant—regulates the encounters and actions that frame the novel's most affecting images of warfare and reconciliation, trade and theft, love and loss. Geographical proximity and contact is crucial from the outset; Shakbatina's account of the growing tensions between the Yanàbi townspeople and the Alibamu Conchatys is immediately followed by Auda's recollection of McAlester's plans to conduct nefarious transactions with a plenipotentiary for the Irish Republican Army. Recalling the historical

42   Ibid.
43   Joy Porter, "'Primitive' Discourse: Aspects of Contemporary North American Indian Representations of the Irish and of Contemporary Irish Representations of North American Indians," *American Studies* 49:3/4 (Fall/Winter 2008), 78.
44   P. Jane Hafen, review of *Shell Shaker* by LeAnne Howe, *MultiCultural Review* 11.2 (June 2002), quoted in Hollrah, 73.

fact that "the old chiefs donated seven hundred dollars to the starving Irish in 1847" McAlester is keen to capitalize on both the prior association between the Choctaw and Ireland, *and* the Irish public's romanticized view of tribal peoples. As he, rather comically, says to Carl Tonica, the tribe's finance manager: "Carl, put a wet towel on your head. The more tribal we appear, the more the Irish love us. The more the Irish love us, the more we're able to move our money in and out of their banks."[45] McAlester also intends to send Auda along with the delegation, not least because she is "one beautiful woman in a traditional Choctaw dress."[46] While the Chief's calculated bid to "reenact the Great Irish Potato Famine of 1847" and the "Trail of Tears" in order to secure "international photo-ops" is entirely cynical, other characters have a far less selfish interest in the diverse types of propinquity created by national and international movement. For these characters, most particularly the women of the Billy clan, it is a case of scrutinizing these relationships in order to understand them rather than benefit from them. It soon becomes evident that Adair Billy, for instance, has an acute interest in the life and times of Jean Baptiste Le Moyne, Sieur de Bienville, the explorer who began exploring the Mississippi river in 1699 and later founded New Orleans. Something of an amateur historian, she "sometimes takes the six-minute walk from her office on Poydras Street," where she works as a financial securities broker, and heads to the French Quarter. There she imagines an earlier time in the city's history, one when the streets were "full of beggars and traders. The homeless of Europe."[47] As a result of Adair's appreciation of Bienville's involvement in "the shifting power struggles [that] influenced [... the] birth" of New Orleans— the only place that she can "imagine living" and a site where "so much Choctaw history occurred"—she develops a finely honed sense of the relationship

---

45 *Shell Shaker*, 24. Howe could never have imagined the corruption that would be revealed in the wake of the Irish banking crisis, nor could she have foreseen the heartache that would be caused by the fallout from said corruption. Yet, *Shell Shaker* was notably prescient in its representation with crooked leaders of newly formed nations—Choctaw and Irish alike.

46 Ibid.

47 *Shell Shaker*, 41.

between the tribes on one hand and foreigners on the other, be it the French, the Spanish, or the immigrants who subsequently came "from all over the world."[48] In one nicely observed moment she sees Bienville's colonial house in her mind's eye and imagines it as "a hotel really"—an image which suggests, quite clearly, the sheer volume of visitors who passed through a space that was, in effect, built "to entertain Choctaws." Howe goes on to explain that it "was a calculated move on [... Bienville's] part" to host the tribe "for several weeks every March" and suggests, by way of the free indirect discourse found in this chapter, that the tribe willingly traded "their muscle for French commodities."[49]

The spatial movement that often accompanies (or even denotes) various forms of intertribal and intercultural transactions is, then, a constant throughout the book. Adair, like McAlester, recognizes the way in which her being in New Orleans reveals the links between the historical past and contemporary life, and even reminds herself that, by working as a broker in "Bienville's town," "she's following a tradition established by her ancestors." "After all," Adair thinks, "Indians were the first commodities traders of the New World."[50] And of course she *is* following in the footsteps of the ancestors. Shakbatina, for instance, had once been responsible for "cultivating special healing plants and mining salt," which she traded "up and down the river for all sorts of things."[51] At the outset Red Shoes, the child of a Chickasaw mother and "a Choctaw warrior from the Western District town of Couechitto" was tattooed with the "inter-tribal sign of friendship" and became, in the words of Divine Sarah "a messenger for both tribes [...] a postman."[52] Shakbatina's decision to barter her life in exchange for that of her daughter Anoleta is, of course, replicated by Susan Billy two and a half centuries later, when she faces Auda's accusers and utters the words: "'I killed Chief Redford McAlester. It was my gun and I shot him in the head.'"[53]

---

48   Ibid.
49   Ibid., 42.
50   Ibid.
51   Ibid., 100.
52   Ibid., 71.
53   Ibid., 28.

With regard to broader, international occasions of exchange and dynamism, Tema, Auda's sister, explains to Aunt Delores that "sometimes foreign ideas are closer to Choctaw ways than you think" and links Sufism, the system of belief put forward by Islamic mystics, to the tribe's beliefs. Her contact with this form of Islamic mysticism arises out of her playing the role of the hoopoe bird in a stage adaptation of *The Conference of Birds*, the epic poem by Persian poet Farid ud-Din Attar. By putting her in a position to make an enlivening, pluralist connection between the Choctaw sense of the collective and the Sufi's belief that everything is connected, Tema's professional role as an actor carries several connotations associable with travel and trade. In the first instance, she is a natural successor to those described by Gore Battiste as the "generation of Oklahoma Indians who became trick riders, screenwriters, Hollywood actors, newspaper reporters, dancers on Broadway, and famous poets"; in essence, the ones who proved that Indians "could still be tribal people, and make it in the white world."[54] Secondly, within the allegorical structure of *The Conference of Birds*, the hoopoe is the mediator and leader, the avian character who explains or translates the doctrine to the other birds, initiates the journey, describes to them the seven valleys of the Way (a structure that echoes the Choctaw reverence for the seven villages established by Grandmother of Birds and her sisters), and, perhaps most importantly, tells the stories which emphasize the spiritual value of, in Tema's words, "destroying the self, and [...] experiencing overwhelming love for the collective."[55] Not alone does the assumption of this role reinforce Tema's Choctaw beliefs, but it also reminds us of the centrality of the messenger within many cultures (the hoopoe was also an intermediary between Solomon and the Queen of Sheba), and, perhaps on a slightly more mundane level, the simple fact that migratory passages are natural to many species, but usually culminate in a return home.[56]

---

54 Ibid., 112.
55 Ibid., 152.
56 Sadly, the "Birds of Britain" website rather stereotypically, and facilely, compares the plumage of the hoopoe to ceremonial costumes worn by tribal peoples, and reports that the bird's "remarkable black and white tipped crest, when elevated like

Significantly enough, it is to her aunts Delores and Dovie that Tema is speaking to when she outlines her newfound understanding. Although "not blood relations" to the Billy sisters—Auda explains that they are, in fact, "Indian-way aunts"—the Love Sisters spent the earlier part of their lives traveling and acting. In 1924 they started working on the world-famous 101 Ranch owned by the Miller Brothers; afterwards they "toured the country in *The 101 Real Wild West and Great Far East Combined*" (Howe invents the title of this wild west show, but the inspiration for the name is two shows that really took place in the 1930s; namely the 101 Ranch Show and the Pawnee Bill Far East Show). According to Battiste, the Alibamu Conchatys lawyer who represents Auda, the sisters also "met Al Capp" before heading to Hollywood to act in several movie projects designed to capitalize on the myth surrounding the Wild West. Though it seems fair to suggest (as Battiste does) that there is much to celebrate about the energetic manner in which the aunts become free-wheeling proto-feminists and quite cavalierly inhabit the intercultural frontier spaces they find at the 101 Ranch and in Hollywood, the sum of their experiences comment on interactions between tribal and non-tribal spaces in interesting, often quite problematic, ways. To Auda's mind, their flight from Oklahoma represents a separation from Choctaw ways, a departure that endangers the tribe since "if all the Indians are off doing their own thing, tribalism will die."[57] To her mind "somebody's got to stay home. Maintain the land, maintain the community."[58] Rather than appearing as a commitment to the land, culture, and autonomy of the Choctaw people, Auda's charge appears as little more than narrow essentialism to Battiste, who fires back the rhetorical question: "You're saying that if Indians learn to play the piano, they can't be tribal any longer?"[59] At that point in the debate Auda

---

the headgear of a Red Indian, conspicuous barring of the back and broad wings, together with vinous head, neck and underparts make [... it] unmistakable" (http://www.birdsofbritain.co.uk/bird-guide/hoopoe.asp). As torrid as the association is, I can't help but think that Howe would relish the irony.

57   *Shell Shaker*, 110.
58   Ibid., 112.
59   Ibid.

clarifies her line of reasoning, and explains her conviction that "individual Indians can do whatever they want, but not without a price." She tells her lawyer "I want Indians to do whatever they're capable of," but insists that it would be "foolish to believe that tribes and tribalism don't suffer as a result."[60] Battiste rather grudgingly concedes the point, even though he hardly sounds convinced.

This dialectic is, to some extent, emblematic of a discussion about travel and trading that occur throughout Howe's book. On one hand, Battiste is keen to emphasize how the women were amongst a vanguard of Native artists who treated boundaries and borders as being—in the words of the late Paula Gunn Allen—"liminal and transformational," thereby creating, and inhabiting "site[s] [of] dynamic flux rather than a fixed point."[61] The sisters' vivaciousness and tenacity, when placed alongside their ability and readiness to recreate themselves as the ironically titled "Love Maidens of The Five Civilized Tribes," appears to Battiste as an instance where talent is met with tenacity in equal measure. Dovie and Delores are, then, akin to tribal leaders such as Standing Bear, who attended the federal school at Carlisle, Pennsylvania and later toured with Buffalo Bill's Wild West Show. Anishinaabe scholar Gerald Vizenor describes such persons as "postindian warriors of postmodern simulations," and argues that they "undermine and surmount, with imagination and the performance of new stories, the manifest manners of scriptural simulations and 'authentic' representations of the tribes in the literature of dominance."[62] In this context, the sisters are both wily survivors who knowingly subvert the representational image of tribal peoples, and emissaries who continue the Choctaw tradition of moving between towns, communities, and even cultures. On the other hand, Auda is concerned that her aunts' cross-cultural, transcontinental movement has resulted in a form of trading that sees spiritual, political, and geographical belonging bartered for a temporal, often thorny, version of fame and

---

60   Ibid., 113.
61   Paula Gunn Allen, *Off the Reservation: Reflections on Boundary-Busting, Border-Crossing Loose Canons* (Boston, MA: Beacon Press, 1998), 11.
62   Gerald Vizenor, *Manifest Manners: Narratives on Postindian Survivance* (Lincoln: University of Nebraska Press, 1994), 17.

freedom. Indeed, many readers will find it difficult to find the signs of an empowering hybridism in the Love Sisters' signature tune, which starts: "'Mid the wild and wooly prairies lived an Indian maid/Arrah Wanna, Queen of fairies of her tribe/Each night came an Irish laddie with a wedding ring/ He would sit outside her tent and with his bagpipes loudly sing."[63] Instead of symbolizing the putative richness arising from intercultural mingling on the American frontier, the Love Sisters' "act" hobbles together a series of stereotypes that arose out of dime novels, early American literature, and the Wild West shows, and marries these with some bowdlerized notion of Irish folk traditions; they become what Jacquelyn Kilpatrick describes as the "imaginary Indian [...] easily digested by the consumer [i.e. the American cinemagoer]."[64] Auda imagines her aunts appearing this way, and envisages, in her mind's eye, "how their long black hair must have whipped in the wind as they rode bareback on Paint ponies, parading their history in skimpy loincloths."[65] The sisters' real life doesn't seem much better to her; Auda recalls a "large poster-sized print of them with Will Rogers on the set of Life Begins at Forty" and thinks to herself that their success "came at a high price" even though it seems, on the face of it, as though "all three Oklahoma Indians [...] look as though they've attained the most American of ideals—wealth and fame."[66] This sentiment is corroborated at a later stage in the novel when the reader learns, via third-person narration, that "unlike the years she spent riding bareback in Wild West shows, or acting in the talkies, Delores believes her role as a modern foni miko, bone picker, is the only useful thing she's ever done."[67]

Rather than (metafictionally) rehearse what Christopher Taylor and others have described as a polarization between "theorists favoring an inward-facing nationalism and those insisting on an outward-facing cosmopolitanism," I would argue that Howe's novel disrupts, even transcends,

63   Shell Shaker, 153.
64   Jacquelyn Kilpatrick, Celluloid Indians: Native Americans and Film (Lincoln: University of Nebraska Press, 1999), 35.
65   Shell Shaker, 117.
66   Ibid.
67   Shell Shaker, 146.

tidy definitions of the "essentialist versus constructivist debate," and therefore challenges dictatorial views, Choctaw history, story, and people.[68]
Not unlike her short story "Choctalking on Other Realities," a work that
Womack describes as being about "intersecting and competing jurisdic-
tions, the tensions going in and out of borders," *Shell Shaker* deconstructs
the master narrative of American colonial history and contemporary race
relations. It does so by searching out sites of conflict or friction as well as
spaces of connection and association, thereby (re)telling the story in its fullest possible form. Thus instead of "looking outward and trying to establish
an understanding of how Native cultures interact with non-Native cultures"
on one hand, or "looking inward, establishing the relationship between
Native literatures and the tribal contexts from which they emerge" on the
other, Howe interrogates the very nature of the transactions that take place
along various intertribal and intercultural trade routes, questions various
modes of consumption, and considers the "price paid" in every instance.[69]

Throughout *Shell Shaker* the "price paid" is often mapped out through
sustained and affecting references to the corporeal. While making the claim
that the *Inkilish okla* "are somehow responsible for the [...] death" of the
Red Fox woman (most likely because they want to start a war between the
Chickasaw and the Choctaw), Nitakechi, Shakbatina's brother, remarks
that they "map their lands with the graves of women."[70] In doing so he
identifies a stark cultural difference between the English settlers and the
Choctaw; the former readily transplant their society's patriarchal authority
to the New World, while the latter believe that it is the "*Intek aliha*, the sisterhood, [who] controlled the rich fertile fields that sustained the people."
As well as drawing attention to the fraught nature of the exchanges that
arise out of colonial contact however, Nitakechi's account of the settlers'
involvement in the murder also reveals the deadly intent that lies behind
various acts of colonial cartography and imperialistic mapmaking. Here,

---

68   Christopher Taylor, "North America as Contact Zone: Native American Literary
      Nationalism and the Cross-Cultural Dilemma," *Studies in American Indian Literatures*
      22.3 (Fall 2010), 26.

69   Ibid., 29.

70   *Shell Shaker*, 10.

power relations between settler and indigene are literally mapped out with, and on, the bodies of indigenous women. This metaphor is extended at other points in the novel, perhaps most notably in Nowatima's account of the Trail of Tears. Here Auda's great-great-grandmother articulates the tribe's removal from their ancestral home beside Pearl River in Mississippi in terms of physical degradation and the consequent marking of the body: "it was very unsanitary as to our personage. No way to make a toilet. We all had fevers. Millions of flies ate from our flesh. *They left many scars on my body*."[71] Delores Love, to whom Nowatima tells the story, views a series of pockmarks on the old woman's forearm as she speaks, and decides that they are "cross-hatched scars where larvae once wriggled through the skin."[72] Reaching far beyond the realms of somatization or even traumatized remembrance, Nowatima's scars are a symbol of Choctaw continuance, but they also serve as a concrete reminder, indeed, *proof,* of the deep and troubling invasion into Choctaw "space" during the eighteenth and nineteenth centuries. In many ways, the description of the scars found on Nowatima's body literalizes the trauma suffered during removal and demonstrates how colonial greed and discordance between wildly divergent value systems were charted or sketched out on the female body. Howe's fiction assumes, therefore, the vital task of examining what Matthew Sparke describes as the way in which Native "bodies are variously mapped and left out of maps [...] are represented and dissimulated with political effect by different cartographies of colonialism."[73]

Importantly, in a moment of satire and poignancy Nowatima gestures toward the marks on her forearm and says to Delores, "See for yourself. I have been a good host."[74] By means of the play on the word "host," the reader might deduce that her scars are emblematic of the fact that the tribe has "hosted" parasitical organisms other than flies—that is to say, colonists.

---

71   *Shell Shaker*, 148 (emphasis added).

72   Ibid.

73   Matthew Sparke, "Mapped Bodies and Disembodied Maps: (Dis)placing Cartographic Struggle in Colonial Canada," in *Places Through the Body*, ed. Heidi J. Nast and Steve Pile (New York: Routledge, 1998), 305.

74   *Shell Shaker*, 148.

This possibility is made all the more significant by the fact that Nowatima's name translates into English as "She who walks and gives"; a name that seems to refer to both the movement enforced upon her during the Trail of Tears, and the giving of her lifeblood during the forced removal of her people from their homelands. The significance of the word "gives" and its association with a particular form of transaction or exchange deepens when one considers that Shakbatina, Nowatima's maternal ancestor, remembers that the *Inkilish okla* "traded me disease for [... the tribe's] corn."[75] Colonial contact and traffic is mapped out on her figure too, and in yet another passage of indirect discourse we hear of the "pockmarks on [... her] sagging breasts" and discover that the smallpox "epidemic has chewed [... her] to pieces."[76] Furthermore, the reference to the harboring of what, ultimately, turn out to be malevolent forces is foreshadowed by McAlester's contention that "America [...] has grown out of the mouths of ravenous white people [...] our lands, our foods, *our bodies have been the hosts the whites fed on*, until we're nearly all dead."[77] Isaac, meanwhile, regards a British reporter dispatched to cover the death of the chief for the BBC as a "Typical Brit [...]. Feeding off the misery of Indians."[78] Laced with irony, the reference to being a "good host" establishes a physical analog to the colonial relationship; (putatively) enriching opportunities for cultural exchange, economic trading, and political contact between Native and non-Native are shown to have dangerously debilitating consequences for the indigene. Howe's images of hosting and feeding serve as an effective reminder that Native bodies, Native lands, and, later, Native misery are integral to the colonial process. Accordingly, it becomes evident that even though the English and French settlers in Howe's novel have a craving to map their power and display their possession of the land in the first instance, they also seek out, and need, sustenance and a sense of purchase or rootedness in the second. The book subsequently appears to revisit Annette Kolodny's oft-cited

75   Ibid., 10.
76   Ibid., 14.
77   Ibid., 113 (emphasis added).
78   Ibid., 53.

argument that the early explorers displayed an "impulse to experience the
New World landscape not merely as an object of domination and exploitation, but [also] as a 'maternal garden,' receiving and nurturing human
children."[79] The purpose of Kolodny's scholarship was to scrutinize how
the "masculine appears to have taken power in the New World first," and
to consider the extent to which this domination precipitated and/or arose
out of "the continued repetition of the land-as-woman symbolization" in
the American context.[80] At first glance it may seem to the reader that the
Choctaw engage in a similar form of symbolization; Shakbatina's inner
narrative reminds the reader that "women were the land" and that "killing a woman for land would be like killing the future."[81] It is essential to
note, however, that Nitakechi's story distinguishes between the Choctaw
conception of a reciprocal relationship *between* the sisterhood and the land
on one hand, and the colonists' personification *of* the land as woman in
order to subjugate and control it on the other. In effect, one relationship is
predicated by symbiosis and trade between equals, the other by patriarchy,
consumption, and power.

Crucially, it is not only colonial men who vampirishly consume Native
bodies in the bid to establish new trade routes and map out a path to power.
According to Shakbatina, Red Shoes, the "renegade warrior," had "grown
into a giant *Osano* in the tradition of Hispano de Soto."[82] He "always hungered for more," she continues, and "would spy on [... Native] towns for
the *Inkilish okla* in return for trade and weapons."[83] Yet, it was not always
this way. As noted above, Red Shoe's original plan was to rid the land "of
both the *Filanchi okla* and the *Inkilish okla*" by obtaining "enough muskets and powder" for his warriors to fight the colonists with.[84] Choctaw

---

79 Annette Kolodny, *The Lay of the Land: Metaphor As Experience and History in
     American Life and Letters* (Chapel Hill: University of North Carolina Press, 1984),
     5.
80 Ibid., ix.
81 *Shell Shaker*, 10.
82 Ibid., 11.
83 Ibid.
84 Ibid., 128.

elder Divine Sarah explains that, as a child of a Chickasaw mother and a Choctaw father, the man once known as *Imatha Chitto* (the greatest giver) should have been ideally placed to act as "an interpreter" and "a messenger for both tribes."[85] In fact, his body—like Bienville's—even bears the sign of these linkages and networks of exchange as a result of the Choctaws having "tattooed Red Shoes' face with the intertribal sign of friendship." Despite his unique and privileged position, he transgresses, however, and does so in perhaps the most shocking way possible—he attacks his mother's people. Divine Sarah explains to Isaac and the two young men trying to find evidence that might exonerate Auda, Hoppy, and Nick, that the warrior chief "murdered two Chickasaw men [...] sold their scalps to a French officer" and, over time, became a "bloodsucker," a "ravenous man" who courted Anoleta "because he wanted her family's influence among the eastern Choctaws who controlled the rich bottom lands."[86] This is a story, then, of mendacity, malevolence, and despoiled interconnecting pathways.

Crucially, Howe's narrative stretches beyond suggesting that these troubled patterns of exchange existed throughout the colonial era and locates similar designs in contemporary times. This fact is made evident via Isaac's realization that "Divine Sarah's story spanned eons" and drew out a "dark pulsating energy between [... him] and his past," and countless similar moments in the novel. More importantly, it is also apparent in the elder's belief that Redford McAlester is a reincarnation of Red Shoes. The "*Osano* returns," Divine Sarah warns Isaac, and he will "continue consuming—it's his job."[87] Hence, even though McAlester is entirely cognizant of the pathways that link the past to the present and connect the Choctaw to other tribes' (inter)national territories and storied spaces, his greatest interest is in exploiting the "many strands of history and international commerce that are coming together in Southeastern Oklahoma" in order to amass wealth and power.[88] Howe deals with the chief's high-handed

85   Ibid., 71.
86   Ibid., 72.
87   Ibid., 73.
88   Ibid., 140.

account of his own double-dealings and his ability to "explain" his motives in terms of pseudo-historical, pseudo-corporate sound bite and cliché in a satirical, often cutting, usually hilarious, manner. During a derisive and despicable description of the long-standing connection between the Irish and the Choctaw, McAlester suggests sending a delegation to Ireland, not so much to celebrate or commemorate a donation sent from the tribe to that nation during the height of the Great Hunger, but rather to milk the public relations opportunity and "cry at all the international photo-ops."[89] "That potato famine anniversary has turned into one interest-bearing media account we can't let go of," Red tells Carl Tonica, the tribe's finance manager, adding "I'm so thankful the old chiefs donated several hundred dollars to the starving Irish in 1847, I could kiss all their graves."[90] Even though he seems to "remember himself" and draws a halt to his prattle by times, and even though his outrageous plans have fine comedic value, the Chief's attitude toward finance and history is enormously unsettling nevertheless. Not only is McAlester prepared to imperil the tribes' financial and political sovereignty by borrowing millions of dollars' worth of investment money from the Genovese family and the Mafia, but, as Auda explains to her sisters, the "payoff money he got from the Mafia. He was giving it to the IRA to bomb the Brits."[91] Although Red's regular off-loading of cash to a Provo bagman working under the moniker James Joyce seems highly implausible, and is described by Adair as resembling something like the "plot from a B movie," a deadly intent lurks behind the scheme nevertheless.[92] Suffice to say Joy Porter is undoubtedly correct in arguing that *Shell Shaker* is "at pains [...] to connect stories about the impact of colonialism across generations and across geographical divides."[93] I would add that the novel subsequently maps out the way in which continued trade, commerce, and contact across those same divides informs a highly complex, highly interconnected new world order.

89   Ibid., 25.
90   Ibid., 24.
91   Ibid., 93.
92   Ibid., 94.
93   Ibid., 78.

For that reason, it is entirely fitting that the Casino of the Sun should be at the center of the duplicity and violence that occurs in Howe's book (coincidentally, Casino del Sol is the name that the Pascua Yaqui Tribe chose for their casino, which opened in 1994 and has recently undergone extensive renovation). Auda explains that the casino fractured her relationship with Red, thereby sundering a partnership between "a popular Indian couple" that "led a ceremonial life" envied by many members of the wider community.⁹⁴ As well as there being a great irony about the fact that, architecturally and thematically, casinos often imitate ancient temples (to wit Las Vegas's Caesars Palace and the Luxor), there is also the simple reality that these structures have become important sites of commercial exchange. Internationally funded and visited by travelers from around the globe, these venues might playfully mimic and plastically reproduce the vista of a far-off El Dorado on one level, but, on another level, the financial, political, and geographical power that they generate is both serious and tangible—and, in Red's case, fatally so. As Gore Battiste points out to Auda "These are the new Indian Wars [...]. Redford McAlester was the first casualty."⁹⁵ In this context, the Casino of the Sun can be read as an intercultural meeting place that feeds a national and international marketplace—a marketplace that often consumes bodies, and therefore resembles a battlefield of sorts; it is undoubtedly one of the most important destinations on the trade routes mapped out in *Shell Shaker*. "Look where the Casino of the Sun is situated!" Auda tells her sisters and her lawyer, "Durant is just one hour from Dallas, a city with thousands of people who want to gamble. More important, the casino is less than an hour from I-35. Retirees from across the upper Midwest can stop and gamble on their way south to Mexico, or to the Texas coast for the winter."⁹⁶ More insidiously, when it comes to divvying up the "cost overruns" that were intentionally stitched into the deal that financed the construction of the casino, it had been "agreed to split the kickbacks equally; Indians fifty percent, white boys fifty percent"—a

94   Ibid., 89.
95   Ibid., 114.
96   Ibid., 90.

moment of mingling and symbiosis that sardonically comments on the notion that an intercultural "contact zone" informs, and enriches, both groups.[97]

Auda's growing awareness of the deceit that lies behind this trade relationship and her understanding of the way in which "customer traffic" flows across Choctaw lands, obviously ties in with the novel's motifs of exchange and consumption across political, cultural, and geographic borders. These elements of the story mesh together in a scene where Carl Tonica has a vision of a noisy protestor outside the casino. The protestor, who describes herself as a "descendant of the Grandmother of Birds" and is very possibly the spirit of Shakbatina, aims to reveal the immoral dealing that has made the casino development possible; addressing the crowd with a microphone, she makes public the fact that "Chief McAlester stole millions from the Mafia and gave it to the Irish Republican Army to kill Englishmen for crimes they committed against the Choctaw two hundred and fifty years ago."[98] Her words appear to do little to halt the flood of visitors to the casino however, and as Tonica watches a "busload of tourists from Dallas" arrive, it seems to him that the disembarking passengers "push past the old woman and ignore her sign." Then, in a clear moment of Swiftian satire, the indirect discourse informs the reader that the Choctaw finance director "isn't worried about" a drop in profits as a result of the descendant's presence; on the contrary, he knows that "the white people who frequent the casino [...] [w]ould rather eat their children than miss an opportunity to gamble."[99] This disturbing picture coalesces with countless images of parasitic trade and consumption throughout the novel. At one point Auda has a dream in which Red Shoes informs her that "everyone in the world will eat [Choctaw] foods—*Ahe, tanchi, tobi, isito, bapho*, but they will be called potatoes, corn, beans, squash, and peanut butter. Everything we have they will claim as theirs."[100] Accordingly, food is, by times, often associated not

97   Ibid., 139.
98   Ibid., 141.
99   Ibid.
100 Ibid., 81.

only with trade, but also with colonial greed, contemporary materialism, and the uneven, inequitable relationships that manifest as a result. Isaac describes the Irish interest in the Choctaw as being a result of two particular commonalities: "colonialism and potatoes."[101] Later Auda teases out the complexities of this association, reminding Gore and her sisters that in 1847 the "Irish were starving because English bureaucrats withheld food from them," and that during the Trail of Tears the "English, who would become the ruling class of Americans [...] withheld food and supplies from" the Choctaw.[102] For this reason, Red initially finds comfort in the belief that his donations to the provisional Irish Republican Army result in the "consumption" of English bodies through horrific terrorist attacks: "When I'd read about a building in London exploding or an English train derailing, I'd think 'that's Choctaw revenge, too.'"[103] Mercifully, this tragedy has been averted since "most of the money that McAlester paid" to the provos "didn't go toward killing other people," but went instead to "IRA bureaucracy."[104] The Choctaw community isn't quite as fortunate however; on the contrary, *Shell Shaker* reveals, in perhaps the most visceral fashion possible, how traditional values are replaced by a form of voraciousness that manifests as physical violence as well as moral and economic imbalance.

It is for this reason that many of Howe's characters seem to devour or be devoured. At the outset Shakbatina describes how "the Red Fox woman ran at my girl [Anoleta] like a rabid animal shouting, '*isht ahollo*,' witch, and throwing handfuls of rotting turkey heads" at her.[105] "Jealousy must have consumed her," she concludes. Much later, Nitakechi points out that "Red Shoes' mouth grows bigger" every day, a statement that leads his brother-in-law, Koi Chitto, to suggest that it "is time [... to] make sure that he never hungers again."[106] "Greed has conquered" the leader, Shakbatina's

---

101   Ibid., 53.
102   Ibid., 94.
103   Ibid., 191.
104   Ibid., 208.
105   Ibid., 9.
106   Ibid., 102.

spirit tells him, and has turned him into "the walking dead."[107] In response
to this developing situation, Anoleta attempts to satiate his appetite once
and for all, and prepares a meal that is laced with poison.[108] This plan fails
because Haya, Shakbatina's third daughter, warns Red Shoes of the danger.
It is not until Anoleta confronts her, that Haya recognizes her mistake.
Interestingly enough, her shame manifests physically: "Haya's face blanches
and swells. The scar on her cheek, a birthmark, rises like a red welt" and she
"nervously presses a forefinger against a sharp edge of her burden basket
until it splits her skin."[109] Thus, Haya "pays for her betrayal as blood oozes
down her figure." Just as Red Shoes "always hungered for more," McAlester
becomes, in Auda's words, "a predator of his own people."[110] Tellingly, Red's
hunger as an adult is, in ways, a continuation of appetites he developed in
childhood. Early in the novel he describes himself as "his mother's cake
and candy boy": "he said that his late mother had wanted him to become
a Southern Baptist preacher, but also follow the traditions of his ancestors.
'So when I'd go to church, I'd get cake; at Stomp Dances, candy,' he said,
grinning. It only made me fat as a kid.'"[111] More important than the childhood obesity is, of course, the fact that his childhood experiences not only
foreshadow a time when "McAlester's body was gorged with bad medicine"
and when "his assistants greeted him by asking, '*Chi niah katimi?*' 'How's
your fat,'" but that it also portends his willingness to play both sides; in one
simple anecdote about Red's upbringing we see how his appetites regulate
his actions and a dangerously self-motivated form of political expediency.

The illustrative value of food as an emblem of cultural and social
intermingling, and the novel's examination of the dangers that arise when
appetites grow exponentially, is underwritten at a later point in the novel.
Here, a feud between Susan Billy and Auda is figured in terms of pre- and
post-contact culinary dishes. Extremely displeased with her daughter's
relationship with McAlester, the matriarch of the Billy clan prepares a

107   Ibid., 172.
108   Ibid., 183.
109   Ibid., 183.
110   Ibid., 24.
111   Ibid., 20.

feast and serves "venison roast, mashed potatoes, fried squash, and red beans."[112] "For desert," Auda recalls, her mother had made "sunflower cakes and her favorite, *bahpo*, a nut pudding made from peanuts." It transpires that in designing the menu Susan had wittingly cooked "all the foods that Choctaws had eaten before contact with whites," a move that prepares the ground for the sudden directive that she issues to Auda during the meal: "Finish with that man [...]. McAlester is an *Osano*. End of story."[113] Susan's implicit (though some might argue that it is a rather *explicit*) means of expressing her displeasure signifies not so much a desire for cultural purity as it does a desire for cultural integrity and tradition within the tribe. The food she cooks—or, more properly, the *sharing* of it—is intended to remind her daughter of Choctaw values (as opposed to the exclusion of English or French influences). In other words, she is not harking back to an idealized pre-contact era, but is pointing out that McAlester's duplicitous deals and his willingness to disenfranchise members of the tribe effectively amounts to "starving his own people" and is therefore akin to the worst sins of colonization.[114] Crucially, Auda remembers that Susan's "comments became even" crueler after this stand-off between mother and daughter; at one point, the matriarch of the Billy clan had unkindly asked her eldest daughter if she was "'Still the Casino Chief's whipping girl ...?'"

The loaded term that Susan couches her censure in brings us back, once again, to body as a site of male violence, domination, and control. The potency of the phrase "whipping girl" is intensified by the fact that earlier in the narrative Auda recounts the vicious and terrifying attack that Red visited upon her just prior to his death, remembering "his bulging eyes, his knife at her throat."[115] During the course of that assault, he insists on knowing why she hasn't worn a particular dress that he has given her, and cuts her face with his pocket knife, telling her "I'm not hurting you. I'm marking you" as he does so. Context, complexity, texture, and

112 Ibid., 80.
113 Ibid.
114 Ibid., 84.
115 Ibid., 19.

tension are added to the scene as the action cuts between three settings and three places in time: Auda's bedroom on Sunday, September 22; Red's office on Saturday, September 21; and the story of the "Casino Chief's" rise to power during the 1980s. In allowing the story to range across these narrative spaces, Howe reveals that Auda, one of the "Billy women [who] were leaders in the community," worked tirelessly to "ensure he would be elected" and was crucial to his gaining the support of the women of Choctaw Country. Instead of creating a great leader, as Auda had hoped it would, the women's encouragement simply "fed [... Red's] hunger for power."[116] It is hardly surprising, then, that he is, figuratively speaking, seen to devour her and deplete her of her energy, and expend her political and personal resources. Even in good times, namely during the campaign, the Chief had used his lips "to feel his way down her neck and lingered there long enough to savor her pulse, measure the sweat and blood she would willingly give to his campaign."[117] On the day he died he did far worse, and "had clapped her left temple so hard that her head swam," "unzipped his pants and brought out a swollen penis," "ran off at the mouth, talked of tight dresses, of shooting off his gun, of pussy" and, significantly, "smacked his lips as if he were munching on something."[118] Auda then painfully recalls how he raped her and afterwards barked "'Wipe yourself off!'" before gruffly dismissing her. She confronts him before she leaves, however, by whispering "'what have you become.'"[119]

McAlester's response to this question is crucial to the events that unfold thereafter, since he is suddenly possessed by Red Shoes's spirit and launches a tirade ending with the definitive statement "I am *Imahata Chitto*, the greatest leader this nation has ever had! ... ALL I EVER ASKED IS THAT YOU SHOW ME SOME GODDAMN RESPECT AND WEAR THE GODDAMN DRESS I BOUGHT YOU."[120] Richly emblematic, the dress is an imported "short tight chemise" of "fresh blood color" that bears the

116   Ibid., 21.
117   Ibid.
118   Ibid., 19.
119   Ibid., 23.
120   Ibid., 24.

label "'*Prodotta in Italia*.'"[121] Like Red's precious Harvard tie, the dress is woven from a shade of vermillion that is in keeping with the "red [...] color [that Choctaw] warriors" wore only in times of dire need and strife. More importantly, it is both a totem of sexual and individual domination as well as being a sign of international trade and exchange; Red bets the D'Amato brothers that he can persuade Auda to wear the dress, thereby proving that he is "in control."[122] This confluence of imagery—the imported dress, Red's show of male authority and influence, the use of the body as a site of exchange and power—is emblematic of the novel's succinct commentary on the mapping out of international and intra-tribal trade routes. More specifically, it emphasizes the fraught nature of duplicitous or unequal patterns of trading, and contrasts the shenanigans surrounding the casino with more fruitful and more evenly balanced alliances. It is important to point out that in terms of cross-cultural and international relations we see strong and successful alliances on view in Tema's loving relationship with Borden, the Englishman she married, and Adair's take on the market sense that Mobile was named after ("*Mabilia*," the Indian root of the name, is "Choctaw for slick," Adair explains).[123]

In this context, the Italian dress is a stunning counterpoint to the mulberry cloth that an old woman encourages Koi Chitto to take to the *Inkilish okla* and *Filanchi okla*. "Its whiteness has been made by our beloved sun" she tells him, "if they wear it they will become hungry for peace."[124] However, Adair reminds her clients that in trade "balance is everything," and if greed distorts the equilibrium, relations quickly deteriorate.[125] The very fine balance between coalition and conflict is evident in the woman's guidance as to what Koi Chitto should do if the colonists reject the mulberry cotton: "If they refuse, be sure that you trade for muskets and gun powder."[126] Similarly, upon readying herself for her sacrificial death

121   Ibid., 25–26.
122   Ibid., 191.
123   Ibid., 42.
124   Ibid., 100.
125   Ibid., 39.
126   Ibid., 100.

Shakbatina is "dressed in white with [her] face painted red."[127] "I have split myself in two," she explains, before going on to say: "my message to my people is that we must fight to survive." Although her appearance is certainly dichotomous, it is in no way ambiguous; she forfeits her life so that "there will be no war between the Choctaws and the Chickasaws," but in doing so she insists that the tribes fight against nefarious forces in order to ensure their survival. And while Onatima once taught Shakbatina that wearing the vermillion is "a terrible fate for a granddaughter of peacemakers," the younger woman is quick to point out that "wars are more prevalent" in her own time than in her grandmother's.[128] It seems that Auda believes this is also the case in the twentieth century; a belief that, potentially, might have damaged the tribe. According to Adair, Auda used her position as a historian at the Southeastern Oklahoma State University to wage war on the master narrative of American history and became something of a "cultural agitator" who "focused on Indian warfare, instead of Indian commerce."[129] Although her challenge to the received historical record is entirely necessary and, on many levels, commendable, that abstract focus on the past causes the eldest Billy sister to lose sight of the contemporary issues facing the tribe; she becomes more concerned with correcting the historical record than the day-to-day task of securing adequate healthcare for the elderly or investing in the tribe's future. Auda's particular take on Choctaw history is possibly *as* damaging as Red's behaviour is. At one point:

> It occurs to her that most Indians in Oklahoma [...] didn't consider the details of their tribal history as she and Red did [...]. She wrote about Choctaw history as a means to correct the misinformation about the tribe, Red saw their history as a means to an end.[130]

In time, she realizes that their particular, sometimes skewed, sense of tribal history "might have been the disease that [...] consumed them both."[131]

127   Ibid., 15.
128   Ibid., 8.
129   Ibid., 44, 43.
130   Ibid., 113.
131   Ibid.

Ultimately, both characters use Choctaw history as a bargaining chip—
Auda to rectify historical inaccuracies and Red to seek revenge on the
British. Neither action has the intended cathartic effect, but ends, instead,
with "her body violated like the land, his shot clean through."[132]

Howe's novel doesn't just call attention to the ways in which trade,
travel, and contact leads to a destructive and adverse consumption or colonization of Native bodies however. On the contrary, *Shell Shaker* differentiates between necessary forms of exchange and expenditure on one hand,
and unscrupulous vampirism on the other. Perhaps the best example of
the former is the bone-picking ceremony mentioned above. In the wake of
Shakbatina's sacrifice (made so that her daughter might live) Koi Chitto
performs the sacred ritual of "rebirth" and "renewal."[133] After three days
of fasting and purification, the bereaved husband "heads to Shakbatina's
burial scaffold dressed only in a string cloth" where he "examines his wife's
decayed body" and notes how her "skin has been turned inside out by some
sharp-beaked, flesh-eating birds."[134] Finding the scent of her body "erotic"
Koi Chitto begins to dance on the burial scaffold, moving ever faster and
faster until he sees Shakbatina approach:

> Her skin is vibrant brown and she is half-naked. Her calf-length hair glistens in the
> moonlight. She comes very close, puts her hand on his penis. He puts his hands
> around her hands and together they stroke him, until he ejaculates on her body and
> screams, "Flesh of my flesh, I will be with you always. Flesh of my flesh I will return
> to you always [...]. I am the Bone Picker, dancer of death, transformer of life, the
> one who brings sex, the one who brings rebirth."[135]

Culminating in the "release" of Shakbatina's spirit as Koi Chitto "tears [her]
skull and spinal column from the rest of her bones," this scene centers, once
again, on the body of a Choctaw woman. It is crucial to note, however, that
images of death and consumption are mobilized to entirely different ends
at various points in Howe's novel. In this instance the body is consumed

132 Ibid., 192.
133 Ibid., 104 & 105.
134 Ibid., 105.
135 Ibid., 106–107.

by the elements, and picked apart by the husband in order to facilitate and guarantee regeneration and renewal. The mingling of the seed of life and the decomposing corpse completes the Choctaw life-circle in spiritual terms, and does so by emblematizing how "the people are ever living, ever dying, ever alive."[136] Liberated by the birds who scatter her skin across the countryside and by her husband, Shakbatina's corpse is welcomed back to the natural world, and her life-force is evermore "dancing the dance" between "life and rebirth."[137] On this level, the scene acts as a vital counterpoint to earlier moments in the novel. For instance, whereas Red once "spurted a million doomed Choctaws on the back of [Auda's] blue skirt," Koi Chitto frees his wife's spirit through a ritualized act of union that fuses life-forms and unites the living and dead. In this moment the material annihilation of the body comingles with, and enables, figurative and sacred forms of continuance; here, consumption is understood in terms of survivance and custom, rather than destruction and death.

The importance of differentiating between natural usage and rapacious or colonizing consumption is reiterated time and again in the novel. In Chapter 11, "Black Time," Red Shoes fallaciously and improvidently marshals Choctaw traditions in order to further his political and military ambitions. Upon arriving at Yanàbi Town he brags that he has "transformed [the severed heads of French soldiers] into something useful: food for birds" before posing a rhetorical question: "'Do not our traditions teach us that alive we are consumers, in death we are the consumed? We are life everlasting.'"[138] Shakbatina's spirit quickly reminds him that his decision to allow the crows to feast on the decapitated *Filanchi okla* has nothing to do with replenishment, but is, instead, a "painful" sign that his "greed has conquered" him.[139] Evidently enough, Red Shoes has subverted the traditional sense of rebirth, turning instead to far more gluttonous or avaricious practices. Other scenes in the novel interrogate the relation-

136   Ibid., 96.
137   Ibid., 107.
138   Ibid., 171.
139   Ibid., 172.

ship between certain forms of consumerism, colonial contact, and, most importantly, Choctaw lands. Just prior to Red Shoes's journey between the villages with the heads of the French soldiers, Delores Love has a vision of the "rosewood dining table that belonged to [her mother] Elizabeth Love."[140] Described as the family's "first attempt at buying colonial," the piece had been ordered from "a Sears Roebuck catalogue" and been carefully minded by the Loves. Notably, this treasured piece of furniture is a reproduction of a Queen Anne table; a fact that comments on both the historical relationship between the Choctaw and the British, *and* the extent to which capitalism and trade rely on simulation or imitation. For instance, not only was Anne the first English sovereign of a unified Great Britain, but the table is ordered from the Sears Roebuck & Co., the archetype of the mail-order houses that fuelled mass consumerism in America during the nineteenth and early twentieth centuries. On this level, the family's rather slavish attention to the dining table, the way in which "they all took turns polishing" it, and "applied a variety of homemade remedies to keep the finish looking new" seems to reflect a degree of subservience or near serfdom that refers to both their position as consumers *and* as historical subjects of the queen. They revere the queen, literally and metaphorically. Hence, Adair rather didactically describes the table as a symbol of "consumerism" and "internalized colonization," and explains to Delores and the assembled Billy women that "the English and the French taught the Indians [...] to love foreign things above all else" and to "think foreigners' things, ideas, and religions are better than what your own culture has."[141]

Yet, there is more to the table than Adair's slightly one-dimensional interpretation of its place in the Love family home or Delores's vision. In that vision Delores "fingers the edge of the table [...] thinks of her mother," and honors "her mother's teachings" by using "the hem of her black dress to wipe the surface clean."[142] On a basic level, the pride felt by the family when they bring it home from Fort Smith, Arkansas very possibly arises

140   Ibid., 158.
141   Ibid., 162.
142   Ibid., 159.

out of a powerful sense of financial independence. Despite its proximity to various forms of capital, both cultural and economic, the father's pet name for this piece of furniture, "'*Nam pisa*.' Something special," reflects the indigene's knack of re-interpreting extra-tribal, extra-cultural forms that usually operate within a decidedly formal symbolic structure. While the Queen Anne table might, strictly speaking, be "foreign" to the Oklahoma Choctaw, to the people (in this case the Loves) the essential meaning of the piece is very different to that experienced by other families, other cultures. The Loves' table is not simply a table or a fetishized commodity; it is "'*Nam pisa*.' Something special." In fact, the table is a site of connection that links Delores to her mother and, by association, the ancestors. In her vision, Delores sees "layers of dirt," "handfuls of earth" and, in time, a "lake of mud" form on its wooden surface. Adair's aunt is soon joined by "thoughts, voices and grandparents" who gather muster and finally succeed in opening "Mother Earth's beautiful body."[143] Although it could surely be argued that the "gigantic platform mound" that appears out of Mother Earth subsumes and buries the Queen Anne dining table—as Adair more or less argues is the case—it could just as easily be argued that the manifestation of Nanih Waiya, the "cradle of Choctawan civilization," arises out of Delores's contact with everything that her mother held sacred: the relatives, Grandmother of Birds, and even the table itself.[144] The point here is not that the Choctaw have become informed by, or reliant upon, cultural, material, or commercial presences originating from outside the tribe. Nor is the origin of the table the real issue here. Instead, the point seems to be that the tribe pays close attention to *how* things are consumed or used, *who* is using them, and to what ends. By extension, Howe's novel suggests that readers would do well by doing likewise. Accordingly, Delores's vision comments on consumption in a dynamic and arresting manner; the commercial artifact (the dining table) is reconfigured by its proximity to, and relationship with, tribal traditions—so much so that it transforms into the physical landscape that "feeds" the Choctaw soul. Crucially, this type of

143 Ibid.
144 Ibid., 161.

feeding is associated with nourishment and strength rather than gorging or devouring. Furthermore, within this process the commodity item is interpreted not just as a space associated with eating on one hand, or the cultural fallout associated with either historical colonization or the norms of American consumerist culture on the other. On the contrary, Elizabeth Love's much loved table is a *family* possession, prized by all.

Any possible connection between the Queen Anne table and cultural sustenance is made explicit through Howe's relation of a series of events that take place in the Billy kitchen immediately after Delores's vision. When she returns to the kitchen, the elder Love sister finds that the bowl of pastry she has been mixing by hand has turned, quite literally, to mud: "Delores raises her hands in the air and reveals black sticky fingers."[145] As soon as Dovie screeches and demands to know where the mud has come from, Delores replies matter-of-factly "'Mississippi,'" and goes on to tell the assembled family members about her revelation and her belief that the vision "'means we've got to bury McAlester in the soil of Mississippi, close to our Mother Earth.'" She concludes, to Adair's initial disgust, that it's necessary to give McAlester "'everything he ever wanted, and placate his troubled spirit.'" The manner in which the land symbolically appears in, and then grows out of, the pastry bowl provides a fairly obvious commentary on Choctaw sustenance. Meanwhile, the prospect of journeying to the mound and interring the dead Chief suggests a form of travel and mapping that focuses on homelands rather than conventional boundaries—legal, religious, municipal, and/or social. Tema points out that in order to take McAlester's body back to Mississippi, the family will have to effectively "steal his coffin" from the Durant funeral home.[146] As well as showing a disregard for extra-tribal limits or restrictions, the journey to the mound is based on a form of travel, trade, and contact that is very different to those on show earlier in the novel. That is to say, the trip to the mound countermands the notion that America's map is drawn in commercial and political terms that are purely defined by post-contact relations.

---

145   Ibid., 160.
146   Ibid., 161.

An "Okie caravan [...] stuffed with McAlester's clothes, ties, shoes, golf clubs, magazines, a computer, and an office copier" weaves its way across the countryside near the novel's end, and we learn that the Chief is to be buried in Mother Mound with his worldly goods and the "millions of dollars" he stole from the Mafia. By acting as a decisive counterpoint to the journey undertaken during the Trail of Tears, and possibly even evoking a memory of the Joad's pitiable passage across America, Howe's convoy highlights Choctaw continuance while deconstructing the American dream; the Billy's motorcade heads east toward the homelands, rather than west toward America's promised land.

Crucially, Red's return to Mississippi begins the process whereby the natural order can be restored, and the tribe's system of exchange and trade can finally supersede the mendacious and grasping structures on view for much of the novel. This return, the journey to inter him in Nanih Waiya, follows a road to recovery in two senses; his coffined body follows the physical route to Mississippi on September 26, 1991, while his spirit speeds along Talihina, Rocky Road. On this level, Howe's characters follow ancient routes which remain fundamental and intertwined in contemporary times. In fact, the extent to which these pathways are imbricated is reiterated time and again in the closing stages of the novel. In Chapter 12, "Suspended Animation," McAlester's spirit explains to Auda that he knew Nitakechi, Koi Chitto and Choucououlacta in a former existence. More than that, he states that it was at his "instigation that [his] warriors had stained the roads red, and that Nitakechi and Koi Chitto were killed."[147] Those "red roads" of the past are then directly associated with Choctaw lands in the present when Red says "Much later the council went along with the casino deal." The roads leading to Mother Mound serve a very different purpose during the gathering that precedes Red's burial, however. On this occasion, the many paths leading to Nanih Waiya carry Choctaw from several states and cities, thereby strengthening alliances and initiating deeper levels of accord and tribal union: "Delores begins shaking hands with [...] women from Zwolle, Louisiana; Homa, Louisiana; Lexington, Texas; and Mobile,

147   Ibid., 190.

Alabama" and, the narrator continues, "after a while, they decide to walk together around the sacred mound."[148] Importantly, their walk around the mound is accompanied by conversation, through which they map out the landscape and, with it, their experiences. This practice reminds me of the way in which "context—and [...] narrative—[once ...] accompanied each Native-made map."[149] In a particularly affecting moment that takes place during this walk around the embankment, Delores errs by recalling how the tribe had taken soil from the mound with them as they left. Although historically accurate, her tale omits one crucial piece of information that is then provided by a woman beside her—many Choctaws never left Mississippi. Following a brief moment of deep embarrassment for the elder Love sister, Edith LaHarve, the woman who initially corrected Delores, smoothes things over with her explanation that the tribe have "been separated for so long, that it's hard for us to remember that we once thought of ourselves as one body with different parts, but one heart."[150] In reference to the reunification that takes place at Mother Mound, LaHarve concludes: "However we always believed this day would come" and takes Delores's hands chanting "'*At chi hullo li*,'" which translates as "'I care for you.'"[151]

Although the final scene comes a full twenty-five pages after this one, and even though those pages include many developments in terms of plot and action (action which includes Delores's and Isaac's deaths at the hands of Hector d'Amato, the Mafioso's subsequent death in the Billy house, Auda's acquittal for the murder of McAlester, and a rather convoluted contribution to the story by the IRA man James Joyce), this exchange at the mound is very possibly Howe's *coup de grâce*. In this moment, the women's bodies are interlinked and female emissaries from various towns join forces to establish peace and unity. The compassion and reconciliation that is emblematized in the holding of hands, and the concomitant remapping of

148 Ibid., 196.
149 Kelli Lyon Johnson, "Writing Deeper Maps: Mapmaking, Local Indigenous Knowledges, and Literary Nationalism in Native Women's Writing," *Studies in American Indian Literatures* 19.4 (Winter 2007), 107.
150 *Shell Shaker*, 196.
151 Ibid.

corporeal and geographical space by the women, is coupled with an image of fruitful and balanced trading. This sacred site is somewhere that tribal stories can be retold or shared and the people can find succor and recover. In fact, just before she meets Edith LaHarve and the other women, Delores watches two herons and imagines that they see Nanih Waiya "as it once was [... an] earthen rampart [... with] wooden lookout posts [...] built at various intervals so the young men could watch for approaching visitors coming to trade their goods."[152] Like the "ancient trade route" that led to Yanàbi Town, the roads that lead to the mound end in a space that is "wide open."[153] This is a space where songs, stories, history, and land coalesce in what Howe calls "an integrated whole rather than individual parts."[154] At Mother Mound, uncle Isaac, a man who "should have been sitting on the tribal council all these years, but ... [who'd] preferred to take refuge at his ranch [...]. Hide out," finally takes responsibility for the tribe's future and passes on "the stone that once belonged to Grandmother of Birds" to Auda.[155] There, he and his erstwhile love, Delores—who Isaac believes is *truly* "Imataha Chitto, the prophesied leader"—sacrifice their lives in order to protect the people. The bodies of the old lovers are not so much consumed as they are offered; "Someone must remain with the chief and help him stay put," Isaac tells a grieving Auda.[156] With McAlester safely interred, the ancient stone is passed from Auda to Hoppy, the only son of Tema and her English husband Borden. Auda, meanwhile, inherits "the porcupine sash and the shells [that] once belonged to a descendent of Grandmother of Birds," and Tema and Adair take possession of Haya and Anoleta's burden baskets.[157] When they do so, Auda notices that the Billy home is "suddenly warm as wool, and alive with the ghosts of aunts and uncles, and future relatives."

152   Ibid., 194.
153   Ibid., 1.
154   Howe, "Blind Bread and the Business of Theory Making," 336.
155   *Shell Shaker*, 58, 212.
156   Ibid., 213.
157   Ibid., 220–221.

Shell Shaker is, then, a novel that exhibits a profound interest in what Howe describes as the process of "untangling the stories within stories within stories," thereby searching out the nexus between the teller, the tale, and the context in which the two co-exist.[158] In this way, story possesses far more than a figurative value, but is, instead, integral to the development and continuance of the people. Here, stories are the primary, most constructive, and handiest means through which to map out connections and relationships across centuries, territories, and generations. In this instance, Native fiction synthesizes and reveals the ways in which time, land, and family are tightly woven into a single entity or an imbricated whole. In charting this triad within her fiction, Howe certainly appears to put into practice her conviction that the discursive, and affective, power of "Native stories by Native authors" lies in the narrative's ability to "pull together all the elements of the storyteller's tribe and connect these in past, present, and future milieu."[159] Crucially, by "elements" she means "the people, the land, multiple characters, and *all* their manifestations and revelations." It should be no great surprise that we find in *Shell Shaker* a hectic, although never disorganized, narrative.

---

158   Howe, "Blind Bread and the Business of Theory Making," 338.
159   Ibid., 330 (emphasis added).

CHAPTER 7

"Not a Chaotic Wake, Not an Empty Space":[1] The Future of Art, Life, and Criticism in the Work of Craig Womack and Greg Sarris

> We could never write enough to say what stories are, how they function, or what methodologies might be best for considering them as primary critical tools, in a sort of meta-stories critical process. In fact stories may lead to, may have already led us to, theories and then back again to stories.[2]
>
> — GORDON D. HENRY, JR.

> This time [...] don't be daydreaming. Put your mind on the story.[3]
>
> — CRAIG WOMACK

> First a story.[4]
>
> — GREG SARRIS

Graham Swift's novel *Waterland*, which lends this final chapter its title, examines the manner in which stories are never fully complete, or definitive, but are instead skewed by eruptions or retellings that often challenge grand narratives and symbolic orders, be they historical, cultural, familial, or otherwise. Throughout the book, Tom Crick, Swift's narrator, struggles

1 Graham Swift, *Waterland* (New York: Vintage, 1992), 63.
2 Gordon Henry, Jr., Nieves Pascual Soler, and Silvia Martinez-Falquina, *Stories Through Theories/Theories Through Stories: North American Indian Writing, Storytelling, and Critique* (East Lansing: Michigan State University Press, 2009), 18.
3 Craig Womack, *Drowning In Fire* (Tucson: University of Arizona Press, 2001), 7.
4 Greg Sarris, *Keeping Slug Woman Alive: A Holistic Approach to American Indian Texts* (Los Angeles: University of California Press, 1993), 25.

to impose a sense of order through the act of storytelling, thereby trying to frame the historical past, to make sense out of it, to give it structure. Crick's quest is a futile one, however, primarily because he is unable to come to grips with the various fractures and disruptions that prevent him from framing a "complete and final version."[5] Although it is certainly a long way away from the indigenous contexts that inform this last chapter, I mention Swift's metafictional novel at the outset simply because *Waterland* is a superb example of fiction's ability to gesture toward the complex nature of the interplay between story, theory, the world, and the ancestors. As such, it provides something of a context for Craig Womack and Greg Sarris' metafictional and metacritical stories. Indeed, the plot of Swift's novel finds Tom Crick engaging with the philosophical vicissitudes of narrative itself, learning, as Gordon Henry, Jr., has argued, that "stories may lead to, may have already led us to, theories and then back again to stories." Thus, when reading *Waterland* one might feel that some sense of story's never-ending dimension is shared between writers as geographically distant and as culturally diverse as Swift and Henry. This is largely because Swift's work seems to mount a profound challenge to Westernized historical models. In the first instance, Tom Crick's stories point out the impossibility of a linear, chronological History that is described as "artificial" and which "dissolves" at one point in the narrative.[6] In the second instance, he idealizes a "Natural History" that "doesn't go anywhere," but "perpetually travels back to where it came from."[7]

However, there is a stark difference between Tom's "theory" that reality consists of "uneventfulness, vacancy, flatness," and the multidimensional realities Henry Jr. finds in the Anishinaabe world.[8] Thus, Swift's novel appears more concerned with the "wide empty space of reality" than with a connectedness between family or community members, or with the stories of the ancestors.[9] It is as though *Waterland*'s multidimensional

5   Ibid., 8.
6   Ibid., 206 & 265.
7   Ibid., 206 & 205.
8   Ibid., 40.
9   Ibid., 17.

stories have no place to take root, but are, instead, amorphous, floating, simultaneously submerged in and *lost to* the Ouze river and the Atlantic Sea, both of which are central to the plot. For that reason, one might argue that writers such as Henry Jr., Craig Womack, and Greg Sarris are working toward very different ends through their consideration of story, indigenous realities and metafiction. Obviously enough, the "death of History" may negate various forms of expression that are crucial for tribal writers like Womack and Sarris, both of whom have confronted the historical realities of indigenous dispossession and removal in fictional and critical narratives that deal with cultural and familial trauma. Similarly, *Waterland*'s description of "vast atavistic circles" would be problematic in a tribal context as well, not least because such imagery could appear to delimit Native identity or, worse still, feed into general assumptions concerning Native primitivism.[10]

Hence, even though Swift's idea of story, which uses metafiction as a narratological device and as a theme, can be compared with the aesthetic forms created by Womack and Sarris, it is surely necessary to consider the extent to which Womack and Sarris construct story in order to deal with the specific exigencies of life in Indian Country today. By moving freely between fictional/critical and metafictional/metacritical registers, both authors have become deeply engaged with historical and social contexts, political and cultural sovereignty, and the discourse surrounding Muscogee Creek and Pomo/Coast Miwok narrative and presence. As such, their "stories" create something other than the "chaotic wake" or the "empty space" that Tom Crick is haunted by, while at the same time playing with Westerns notions of history and time in much the same way as Swift's narrative does. The goal of this chapter is, then, to examine these authors' commitment to literary innovation and tribal realism, while also considering the manner in which both men have adapted their approach to literary studies in order to make a specific contribution to their tribal community.

10   Ibid., 204.

New Stories, New Times

Interestingly, Womack and Sarris have both taken stock of their professional (and personal) contribution to Native American Literary Studies and their tribes in recent times. Womack has revisited his earlier commentary on Muskogee Creek literature and culture. One of the main contributors to the movement now commonly known as American Indian Literary Nationalism, he recently explained: "*Red on Red* and *American Indian Literary Nationalism*, books I had written with great passion, at some point, began to haunt me."[11] The difficulty, as Womack explains it, is that he may have "closed down communication instead of opening it up."[12]

Meanwhile, at the very moment when Womack appeared to be undertaking a "spiritual journey" by searching for more enabling (some might say "less cutting") ways of "examining the material world and creating change", fellow writer and colleague Greg Sarris was embroiled in the latest stage of a fierce struggle over Indian Gaming Rights in Sonoma County, California.[13] As chairman of the Federated Indians of Graton Rancheria (FIGR)—which includes both Coast Miwok and Southern Pomo people—Sarris has been at the forefront of the tribe's bid to enter into a compact with the State of California and, thereafter, to open a casino under the auspices of the Indian Gaming Regulatory Act (1988). The operation proposed by the FIGR won approval at the California State Senate on May 7,

11   Craig Womack, "Cosmopolitanism and Nationalism in Native American Literature: A Panel Discussion," attended by Lisa Brooks, Michael Elliott, Arnold Krupat, Elvira Pulitano, and Craig Womack <http://www.southernspaces.org/2011/ cosmopolitanism-and-nationalism-native-american-literature-panel-discussion#sthash. LvCTUIpO. dpuf> accessed June 10 2012.

12   Keen to shake up the field, Womack made declaratory statements such as, "I do not write for everyone. I write for Muskogee Creek people," and warned tribal scholars not to give "away all [... their] power to a group of outsiders who then determine our aesthetics *for*" them: *Red on Red: Native American Literary Separatism* (Minneapolis: University of Minnesota Press, 1999), 10.

13   Womack, "Cosmopolitanism and Nationalism in Native American Literature: A Panel Discussion."

2012, and consists of a multimillion-dollar resort-style casino, including slot machines, a hotel, several bars, and disco. The project has been massively controversial since its inception, largely because of its scale, and the planning process has placed the tribe in a decade-long legal battle with environmental groups and local residents. As a result, the intended site for the casino was changed twice: first from the original southern Sonoma County site (the "Highway 37 Property") to a spot on Stony Point Road (the "Stony Point Road Property"), and then to its current off-reservation location in Rohnert Park, about fifty miles north of San Francisco. Objectors have, for the most part, resisted the development on grounds that the casino will cause environmental damage, consume excessive amounts of water, cause an exponential rise in the volume of traffic in the area, spawn addiction to gambling, and generally attract "undesirables" to the neighborhood.[14] These objectors have fought their case on three fronts: in the political arena, the court of law, and the court of public opinion, and have quite viciously attacked the tribe's sovereignty in various ways. The effect has been that Sarris—whose scholarship was once noted for its ability to initiate a "dialogue" that "opens and explores interpersonal and intercultural territories"—is, according to the media, reluctant to grant interviews, meet with members of the print media, or make appearances outside of a few book readings, conference events, or classroom settings.[15]

14   See: http://www.stopthecasino101.com/ id112.html.
15   Elvira Pulitano, *Toward a Native American Critical Theory* (Lincoln: University of Nebraska Press, 2003), 104. Regarding recent media comments, it is important to note that journalists and detractors routinely omit the final part of this quotation, in which Sarris adds: "But the moral part of me says, 'Don't fight fire with fire.'" (*San Diego Chronicle*, May 15, 2000). Recently, Sarris has explained that gaming is one of the only viable means of achieving economic independence and political sovereignty, and that by using "ancient ethics and aesthetics of place, bolstered by casino revenues, the 1,300 member tribe has partnered with county and state officials to secure and restore large tracts of open space, as well as to convert local farms to the production of organic produce for the low-income and needy, thus creating a model of local restoration and sustainability." <http://www.bioneers.org/conference/2012-schedule/ plenaries/friday/the-federated-indians-of-graton-rancheria> accessed September 24, 2012.

Whatever one thinks about Sarris's preparedness to talk to the press, it
is certainly the case that the tribal chairman has been riled into making
at least one uncharacteristically intemperate statement, telling reporters
that "Indians are making money off of white man's greed [...]. They gave
us alcohol that tore families apart, and we're giving them another addiction—gambling."[16] Although his annoyance is perhaps understandable, this
rather ill-advised statement is hardly in keeping with Sarris's initial search
for a form of "intercultural communication" that might allow "people [to]
see more than just what things seem to be."[17] A casual bystander might
even be forgiven for thinking that Sarris has vacated the dialogical space
he once sought out, and has now adopted a separatist, activist, and perhaps
even slightly protectionist, stance.

At first glance, both men appear to have made a dramatic volte-face—
Womack seems to have entered into a form of dialogue that he had previously shunned during the roundtable discussion at Emory; Sarris has given
the impression that he is withdrawing from all discussions.[18] Accordingly,

16   *San Diego Chronicle* (May 15, 2000).
17   Greg Sarris, *Keeping Slug Woman Alive: A Holistic Approach to American Indian Texts*
      (Los Angeles: University of California Press), 3. In a profile titled "The Enigmatic
      Leader Behind Rohnert Park Casino," *The Press Democrat*, a daily newspaper pub-
      lished in Sonoma County, claimed that Sarris has "has refused to discuss [the casino
      or the court cases] publicly for years." <http://www.pressdemocrat.com /article/
      20120 429/ARTICLES/ 120429494> accessed September 24, 2012. Despite these
      claims, it is possible to find details of several public appearances by the author—both
      before Hay's piece was published and since. Sarris participated in KQED's "Forum
      with Michael Krasny," and as well as speaking at Bioneers in 2012, he also posted
      responses to some of the casino's critics online at Waccob.net (http://www.kqed.
      org/a/forum/R20 1205090900; http://www.waccobb.net/forums/ showthread.
      php?91332-Greg-Sarris-at-Bioneers). I would argue that media descriptions of Sarris's
      "enigmatical" behavior are more closely related to adversarial and partisan coverage
      of the Rohnert Park development than they are related to the author's demeanor.
18   Significantly, Womack's "admission" came during a roundtable event, where he
      exchanged viewpoints with Abenaki scholar Lisa Brooks and non-Native literary
      critics Arnold Krupat and Elvira Pulitano. The meeting might have been somewhat
      unexpected because a few years prior, Pulitano had suggested, "Womack insists on
      a Native consciousness and a Native viewpoint out of which a Native American

there appears to be little connection between the first man's "mea culpa" and the second man's battle to open a casino (mind you, acerbic commentators will surely suggest that both men are "playing the odds"). Moreover, keen observers might argue that scholarly musings (to borrow a phrase that Womack has used recently) in the rarified environs of the university campus are of a somewhat different hue to the legal and political discourses arising out of the casino wars. Therefore, even though Sarris's influence on literary scholarship has been vast (Womack describes his 1993 work *Keeping Slug Woman Alive: A Holistic Approach to American Indian Texts* as "one of the most important books on tribal literature, ethnography, and reader response theory"), his role as tribal chairman has surely resulted in a different set of questions being applied to his work. In other words, the FIGR's dealings with state politicians, special interest groups, and the Station Casino group are all a long way from reader response theory. In much the same way, Womack's short story "The Song of Roe Náld" (2009), a text that—according to its author—"moves in and out of many worlds," and marks a "seeming departure from Muskogee Creek concerns," might seem distant from the "Creek stomp dance [...] a Creek casino [and] the tribal headquarters."[19] Indeed, in the wider collection of essays, Womack even goes as far as to pose some difficult rhetorical questions while re-examining his earlier bid to define literary and tribal presences and to identify Muskogee Creek values, writing in *Art as Performance*:

> Given [...] that nationalism is the most frightening phenomena of our time, maybe of any time, I might well wonder how I managed to create a body of work, acknowledged by others and myself, as a partisan forum for indigenous nationalism."[20]

---

critical theory should originate." (*Toward a Native American Critical Theory*, 79). She also charged that his brand of "Native American literary separatism [...] categorically excludes any possibility of encounter at the cultural crossroads." (96). Despite the potential for scholarly conflict, the roundtable brought about something of a reconciliation, and Womack soon turned his thoughts to "compassion," "listening," and intercultural dialogue.

19 Craig Womack, *Art as Performance, Story as Criticism: Reflections on Native Literary Aesthetics* (Norman: University of Oklahoma Press, 2010), 43.

20 Ibid., 331.

These are interesting times in Indian Country: it may well be the case that one or two of the main protagonists in the field of Native American Studies have entered new, perhaps somewhat divergent, phases of their career.

On closer inspection, however, it seems that Womack and Sarris' recent maneuvers are not only interrelated, but are, in fact, also in keeping with the basic tenets of their earlier methodological approaches and fictional works. In the first instance, Womack's blend of fiction and criticism, alongside his discussion of constitutional law and tribal autonomy, is an attempt to throw further light on the writer's understanding of, and engagement with, the rights and responsibilities of the Muskogee Creek. In so doing, he allows his reader to ponder the challenges and opportunities faced by other tribes and other writers, including the FIGR and Sarris. At the same time, Sarris's advocacy on behalf of the Pomo and Miwok has included his co-authoring of the Omnibus Indian Advancement Act (HR 5528) signed by President Clinton in 2000, and writing opinion pieces for newspapers, as well as contributing several forewords and introductions to books about tribal history, literature, and so on. These texts, along with the traditional stories told in *Keeping Slug Woman Alive*, and the fictional narratives that Sarris offers in *Grand Avenue* (1995), *Watermelon Nights* (1998), and elsewhere, are all part of that same continuum. Moreover, all of these texts, as well as the context that they inform and are informed by, speak directly to the complex heart of tribal sovereignty, aesthetics, expression, and autonomy in modern America. In truth, the fact that this level of interconnection exists between Womack's new book and the Rohnert Park Casino is itself testimony to the reality that the issues that inform tribal sovereignty and Native literatures are broader, and a great deal more complicated, than they might first appear to be. For that reason, we might do well to consider the unique praxis created by the stories, criticism, and activism of Womack and Sarris. I choose to do so because I think that these writers simultaneously address the consequences of various legal positions, cultural experiences, and artistic choices, and seek therefore to pre-empt some of the issues that may emerge within the field of reception. With that, Womack and Sarris have sought to engage the debate about insider/outsider stances in useful and dexterous ways throughout their careers, and have often forced critics (Native and non-Native alike) to be ever conscious of the particular spaces that they read from. No less significant is the fact that current "conversations" involving, and in some cases *about*, both scholars have often been engrossing for those of us concerned with the language used to frame and articulate tribal autonomy, tribal writers' involvement in sovereign acts, and the effect that both language and engagement have in the material world. Furthermore, recent events have crystallized the "in flux," "defined in motion" nature of Indian sovereignty while also revealing non-Native resistance to tribal self-determination in a fuller, often unflattering, light. These "conversations," and Womack and Sarris' handling of them, have much to tell us about the tribal storyteller's role in the ongoing definition of sovereignty. Whereas earlier chapters provided a close reading of exemplary novels (or, in the case of Sherman Alexie, a selection of poetry) in order to excavate interrelated questions about narrative and sovereignty, this final chapter takes a slightly different approach to the subject. Here, I want to track the interrelationship between modes of self expression and cultural narratives. More specifically, I am interested in the way in which narrative in its literary and formal sense maps on to the primacy of storytelling and stories as live(d) realities. This involves not only the study of fiction and criticism, but also the circumstances of daily life. Instead of searching for constructions of sovereignty in Womack's *Drowning in Fire* or Sarris's *Watermelon Nights*, as many others critics have already done, I wish to consider the broader set of stories and storied realities that each author tells and engages with.

Similar Stories

What recent developments reveal is the extent to which Womack and Sarris are profoundly engaged with a sovereignty that "protects homelands and jurisdiction" in the courtroom, while also "allow[ing] the evolution of cultures," art, and aesthetics.[21] Yet, those working in the field of Native American Literary Studies have not always aligned their values. As most people now know, in her book *Towards a Native American Critical Theory*, Elvira Pulitano attempted to draw a line of demarcation between Womack's "nativist approach" on one hand, and Sarris's "dialogic approach" on the other, thereby identifying a neat—but improbably neat, and therefore arguably untenable—distinction between what she saw as being two discrete methodological approaches to life and to letters. In a bid to identify, and reinforce, this division Pulitano refers to "such problematic categories as *self-determination, tribal*, and [...] *sovereignty*" during her discussion of Robert Warrior's phrase "intellectual sovereignty." The scholar clearly prioritized hybridity as the most useful and soundest of critical models.[22] However, this simplifying categorization gave rise to more problems than it solved. First, functional sovereignty and intercultural conversation are rarely as straightforward as Pulitano allows. Second, as Womack pointed out in his rebuttal of his colleague's view of things, Native scholars are constantly negotiating which theories might, at any one point in time, best facilitate a complex consideration of their own position and that of the tribe.[23] Thirdly, and following on from that point, even though Native scholars often take a slightly different approach, or arrive at slightly different conclusions, when assessing (and reassessing) the efficacy of certain terms, the usefulness of theoretical models, the experiences of their tribe, and so on, the fact remains that they often hold certain fundamental principles in common. To paraphrase Jace Weaver, there is more that holds indigenous scholars together than keeps them apart.[24] In that light, it is vital to acknowledge the simple reality that Womack's particular vision of literary

21   *Art as Performance*, 86.
22   Pulitano, *Toward a Native American Critical Theory*, 67.
23   Craig Womack, "The Integrity of American Indian Claims: (Or, How I Learned to Stop Worrying and love My Hybridity)," in *American Indian Literary Nationalism*, ed. Jace Weaver, Craig S. Womack, and Robert Warrior (Albuquerque: University of New Mexico Press, 2006), 125.
24   Jace Weaver, "Splitting the Earth: First Utterances and Pluralist Separatism," in *American Indian Literary Nationalism*, ed. Weaver, Womack, and Warrior, 73.

nationalism can accommodate, and make sense out of, the types of "transformation" through which Indians "adopt and adapt literary forms."[25] If anything, this sense of a friable, pluralistic nationalism that works across discernible borders between one tribal space and another, and between tribal and non-tribal spaces, is in keeping with—instead of being contrary to—Sarris's point that, "all of us [Native and non-Native ...] can inform and be informed by the other."[26] The trick, for those of us seeking to learn from these approaches—and hoping to conduct literary analysis in the wake of them—is to realize that there is a world of difference between methodologies which allow for alteration and conversation and those which lean toward incursion and dictation. We must be wary, then, of the dangerous slippage that might allow "dialogism" to be read as "hybridity" and sovereignty to read as isolationism.[27] It is this slippage that Womack refers to when he writes about non-Native scholars' "failed commitment to pluralism," a failure that has, in turn, led to the situation outlined by Niigaanwewidam James Sinclair, whereby:

> current uses of hybridity in Native literary criticism do not connote Native agency nor allow for sovereignty or self-determination ... In most notions of hybridity, Native-specific spaces must be cast away in favor of the contact zones where identities are impossible to articulate.[28]

Mikko Tuhkanen has also called attention to Abdul JanMohamed and Benita Parry's resistance to Homi K. Bhabha's "understanding of the hybridity of the colonial encounter," on the grounds that it possibly "disables all

---

25   Womack, "The Integrity of American Indian Claims," 160.

26   *Keeping Slug Woman Alive*, 7.

27   Womack tackles this question directly in *Art as Performance, Story as Criticism* when he writes: "Maybe, even, instead of being on the receiving end of contact, we can imagine ourselves as contactors rather than contactees, in ways that emphasize sharing instead of displacing" (338).

28   Niigaanwewidam James Sinclair, "Tending to Ourselves: Hybridity and Native Literary Criticism," in *Across Cultures/Across Borders: Canadian Aboriginal and Native American Literatures*, ed. Paul DePasquale, Renate Eigenbrod, and Emma LaRocque (Ontario: Broadview Press, 2010), 256.

oppositional politics of resistance."²⁹ In that context, it would be dangerous to take Womack's recent investigation into aesthetic play and artistic
deviance in *Art as Performance, Story as Criticism* as a definitive sign that
the author is now interested in the contact zone, or as an indication that
his earlier commitment to the Muskogee Creek people has somehow weak-
ened.³⁰ On the contrary, that book's inclusion of an introductory story
that "moves in and out of *many* worlds, tribal and non-tribal" can be read
as a part of an effort to think broadly about, conceptualize, and engage
what Sarris once described as "the *many* communities where [Native aca-
demics] live and work."³¹

Reflexively interrogating their position as writers from tribal communities, who produce work that non-tribal audiences often read, Sarris and
Womack turn to storytelling as a means to locate borders, stage intercultural
conversations, and illustrate cultural differences. Accordingly, they create
texts that are discursive in one or more contexts (the local, the global, the
tribal, the political, the academic, and so on). For both men, stories and
the performative aspect of storytelling inform important notions about
communication and listenership; storytelling suggests what it is to come
from a particular community, place, and people, and it also carries the possibility—the hope—that listeners, tribal and non-tribal alike, will make an
attempt to hear, to understand, and to respect. I would argue, then, that
Womack's clarification of his critical position and Sarris's work as tribal
chairman are sure signs that these scholars are not only committed to *both*
the study of "literature and art and other elements of culture" *and* to the
various forms of sovereignty that are "essential to Indian survival," but
also that these two elements are interlinked in vital and crucial ways.³²
For that reason, even though Pulitano provides an incisive and, by times,
sophisticated, analysis of Sarris's position as a cross-cultural mediator who
thoughtfully and instinctively considers his position(s), I would suggest

29   Mikko Tuhkanen, *The American Optic: Psychoanalysis, Critical Race Theory and
     Richard Wright* (Albany, NY: SUNY Press, 2009), 34.
30   *American Indian Literary Nationalism*, 143 & 144.
31   *Art as Performance*, 43; *Keeping*, 69 (emphasis added).
32   *Keeping*, 3; *Art as Performance*, 86.

that we might do well to place a little more emphasis on diversity and on boundary than we have done, thereby containing talk of hybridity and crossing.[33] It is not so much a case of seeing nationalism as being opposed to cosmopolitanism or sovereignty, as being in conflict with interculturalism. Rather, Native communities create their own realities, perform acts of sovereignty, and, above all, tell new stories.

"This Constitutes a Different Act, I Hope"

According to John Gamber, "Oklahoma becomes a sovereign home" for the Muskogee Creek characters in Womack's first novel, *Drowning in Fire*.[34] This is made possible by the author's interest in "the reconstruction of Creek/Muskogee identity in the specific landscape of" the state itself, and his "remarkably fluid reconstruction of culture."[35] Spanning almost three decades, from 1964 through to 1993, the plot of *Drowning in Fire* is primarily concerned with the life and experiences of Josh Henneha and Jimmy Alexander, two Creek boys who grow up together in rural Oklahoma and, after various trials and tribulations, eventually become lovers. Like LeAnne Howe's *Shell Shaker*, and, to some extent

---

33 Given that it is twenty years since the publication of *Keeping Slug Woman Alive* and a decade since *Toward a Native American Critical Theory* arrived on the scene, there has been ample time for Sarris and Pulitano to clarify their points. I will discuss Sarris's recent comments in the main body of the chapter. For her part, Pulitano refuses to finesse or reassess her take on hybridity as a term and a construct, writing: "I am not fully convinced that we *cannot* take a term so vested with negative connotations and transform it into something positive" ("Conclusion and Future Conversations," comments made during "Cosmopolitanism and Nationalism in Native American Literature: A Panel Discussion," at Emory University).

34 John Gamber, "Born out of the Creek Landscape: Reconstructing Community and Continuance in Craig Womack's *Drowning in Fire*," *MELUS* 34.2, "Ethnicity and Ecocriticism" (Summer 2009), 104.

35 Ibid., 103.

Treuer's *Little*, *Drowning in Fire* features a historical narrative that is closely intertwined with, and affects, the contemporary storyline featuring Josh and Jimmy. This story is set in the period when Oklahoma's statehood is decided, and features two historical characters, Tarbie and Seborn, Creek men who "live together back in the sand hills, away from everybody, without any women."[36] A source of amusement for "the young boys [who] giggle when they see them in two in the camp," Josh's great-aunt Lucy, explains, the men are valued by the elders, who respect their traditionalism and their refusal to partake in the allotment system and integrate with non-Native culture. Womack's characterization of Josh and Jimmy, as well as their historical predecessors Tarbie and Seborn, consequently raises issues concerning both traditionalism and colonization. As Mark Rifkin explains, the novel considers "relative knowledge of and commitment to Muskogee principles" in the context of the "social divisions inserted into Creek life by whites."[37] It can also be argued that Tarbie and Seborn's presence in the novel not only underlines the existence of Creek sovereignty and separatism, but that it also challenges a certain strand of homophobic orthodoxy found amongst non-Native Christians and which has been accepted by some members of the Creek community. By dealing with aspects of Creek life that might be considered deviant for one reason or another (and by one group or another), but were in fact routine, Womack's narrative serves to unsettle some of the accepted wisdom about old-time Muskogee traditionalism, and undermines one-dimensional perspectives that pit a morally superior "tribal past" against the "impurities" associated with contemporary living. The novel also deals with themes that were not often considered in earlier works of Native American fiction—tribal nationalism and homosexuality. By examining the vicissitudes of tribal *and* queer identities within the space of a single novel, Womack raises key issues. For instance, Josh and Jimmy must work through processes of sexual identification within a Muskogee context. This

---

36   Craig Womack, *Drowning in Fire* (Tucson: University of Arizona Press, 2001), 35.
37   Mark Rifkin, "Native Nationality and the Contemporary Queer: Tradition, Sexuality, and History in *Drowning in Fire*," *American Indian Quarterly* 32.4 (Fall 2008), 450.

is a crucial development, not least because Judith Halberstam reminds us, "Many young gays and lesbians think of themselves as part of a 'post-gender' world," and that "for them the idea of 'labeling' becomes a sign of oppression that they have happily cast off in order to move into the pluralistic world of infinite diversity."[38] However, as Halberstam argues, the cultural production and representation of queerness is more complex than the "post-gender" formulation allows, and there are concrete reasons for very carefully working through the consequences of moving from the heterosexual time of reproduction and linearity to a queer space. The same might be said of the theoretical shift from national and post-national spaces, and from tribalism to hybridity. The effect is that the author's first novel can be said to consider both the standards by which cultural traditions are defined and upheld, and art's ability to deviate from, or play with, values and conventions that are deemed normative in some way. As Lisa Tatonetti eloquently explains:

> Womack offer[s] an antidote to the historical erasures of queer-positive depictions of Native people by first acknowledging the problem—the assimilation of dominant narratives that cast homosexuality as illness or sin—and then providing a counter-narrative in the form of Tarbie and Seborn, who serve as a historically grounded example of Two-Spirit men accepted by their tribe.[39]

It is also important, Tatonetti continues, that the historical characters are "Creek nationalists who, stories reveal, just happen to be Two-Spirit," a move that allows Womack to balance "the men's racial, cultural, and sexual identities."[40]

This arresting consideration of tribal beliefs, convention, or expectation, and art's ability—if not its propensity—to subvert accepted standards continues apace in *Art as Performance, Story as Criticism*. Described

---

38 Judith Halberstam, *In a Queer Time and Place: Transgender Bodies, Subcultural Lives* (New York: New York University Press, 2005), 19.

39 Lisa Tatonetti, "The Emergence and Importance of Queer American Indian Literatures: Or, 'Help and Stories' in Thirty Years of *SAIL*," *Studies in American Indian Literatures* 19.4 (2007), 60.

40 Ibid.

by the author as a "fictional and critical mess," partly in jest and partly in recognition of his bid to destroy tidy definitions of "literature" and "criticism," this work is a collection of creative stories, close readings of literary criticism, survey-style essays relating to life, culture, and politics, as well as personal reverie. Womack continues his meditation on the degree of tension that might be said to exist between "the party line in Native Studies, [which] has to do with respect for cultural traditions" on one hand, and the autonomous nature of art and its concern with "deviance" on the other hand.[41] In essence, he does so by confronting the reader with a bricolage of criticism that links the fictional with the theoretical, and invention with critique—often blurring the lines between the two as he does so. Womack manages to weave trenchantly witty observances into a serious commentary on Native American fiction, Native American Studies, and international politics today. In doing so, he seems to produce "imaginative act[s]" that are similar to those created by LeAnne Howe—acts that show that: "Indians have something to say about the world beyond Indian country, that Native studies is not inherently parochial, [and] that tribally specific approaches have global implications."[42]

    Art as Performance, Story as Criticism opens with "The Song of Roe Náld" (2010), the short story mentioned above—which, in Womack's structure for this collection, is also his "First Mus(e)ing." While certainly punning—as he does throughout the collection—on his bi-fold position as both the ruminating critic and as an artist searching for a muse, Womack plays on the fact that the Native has long been the muse of non-Native artists working in various mediums and genres. Cleverly drawing attention to the fact that indigenous writers occupy a number of interlinked spaces, this structure alludes to the tribal author's position as a gifted commentator or artist, *and*, somewhat more problematically, as a continuing source of inspiration for those who hope to capture Indianness in some form or other. Roe Náld, the effete, affected, and solipsistic Wichita and Caddo

---

41 *Art as Performance*, 307–308.
42 Craig Womack, review of *Evidence of Red: Poems and Prose. Studies in American Indian Literatures* 17.4 (2005), 157.

auteur who is very much the star of Womack's story, draws attention to this fact in the final line when he says, simply: "We were being filmed."[43] This conclusion, and the story in general, speaks to the complexity of the position that tribal authors find themselves in—predominantly dreamers visited by the muse, but still objects of the non-Native gaze by times. Womack's discussion of aesthetics focuses, in part, on the slippage that occurs between "muse" as verb in the first instance and noun in the second, and considers the shifting ground between autonomy and artistic defiance (what he calls "deviance") and dependence and representation.

Hilarious, self-reflexive, challenging, and fantastic (in both senses of the word), "The Song of Roe Náld" is a first-person narrative that reveals the remarkably rich inner narrative of the eponymous protagonist—an independent filmmaker who hangs out on the University of Oklahoma campus. Roe Náld, known as Ronald until he adopted the "French pronunciation [... with a] throaty 'r,' nasalized long 'o' and accent on the second syllable" at age thirteen, is, in his own words, given over to "bitchy interior monologues" and diva-like strops.[44] He is also something of an Oklahoman aesthete, having graduated from the UCLA film school and returned to Norman by way of New York. Often hysterical and doing a super job of performing the role of the tormented artist, Womack's character comes across as a young man who possesses a rather endearing mixture of sincere naivety and calculated deviousness. Keenly observant but usually viewing life from his own slant perspective, the bold Roe Náld is besotted with Justin Crossman, the "un-Oklahoman looking" dance student with "an ethnic look of a Mediterranean sort" who he spots on "the carefully manicured lawns of the University of Oklahoma."[45] He is also unreliable or confused. Or both. The observant reader will recognize this fact from the very outset, largely because this self-portrait of the young artist begins with his recollection of:

43   *Art as Performance*, 36.
44   Ibid., 5.
45   Ibid., 10 & 4.

That […] summer of Oklahoma weirdness when each and every citizen of the state, from the panhandle to Sallisaw, should have fastened their seatbelts for a bumpy ride—what with frat boys getting drunk and naked and pissing on a ceremonial tipi set up for Native American Awareness Week at the University of Oklahoma [… and] a state legislator proposing a bill in the senate to publish a list by county that would "expose" all with HIV.[46]

Well-versed readers and curious researchers alike will be familiar with the fact that Tom Coburn (or "Dr. No" as he is known on Capitol Hill, an appellation that recognizes his preparedness to vote down virtually any bill or measure if it suits his own needs) co-authored the "HIV Prevention Act" (HR 1062) in 1997. These readers will also know that Coburn was elected junior senator for Oklahoma in 2004, and was re-elected with 70 percent of the vote in 2010. Coburn has upheld conservative Republican values during both of his terms, opposing gay rights and calling for a reduction of government spending on Medicare, in an often "hyperbolic rhetoric [that frames a] fervent social conservatism."[47] Interestingly, the *New York Times* profile of the junior senator also notes the fact that his public extremism belies a more moderate outlook often witnessed in private. Indeed, Coburn is a close friend of President Obama, with "whom he still speaks regularly and writes supportive notes, even while publicly ripping his performance as president."[48] This may well say something quite interesting about the donning of adversarial roles in contemporary America; it seems that folks like Coburn demonize folks like Roe Náld because it is politically expedient. Roe Náld, meanwhile, defines himself in polar opposition to Oklahoman "rednecks," the "white polyester trash [who] come by their stupidity naturally, having descended from a bunch of lowlifes, bootleggers, and convicts that (yes, that, not who) illegally entered Indian Territory or rushed in later on the heels of the land run at the end of the century."[49] In this

---

46   Ibid., 3.
47   Mark Leibovich, "A Senate Naysayer, Spoiling for Health Care Fight," *New York Times* (October 29, 2009) <http://www.nytimes.com/2009/10/30/health/policy/30coburn.html> accessed September 24 2012.
48   Ibid.
49   Womack, *Art as Performance*, 9 & 8–9.

story, as in American politics today, vilification and generalization have, rather dangerously, replaced sophisticated debate. The "tepee incident," which is how news organizations in Oklahoma referred to the Phi Kappa Psi fraternity's harassment of Native students during American Indian heritage week, took place in 1994 however, four years before Coburn's infamous bill. More significant, perhaps, is the red herring that Womack (or rather Justin) sells us in the form of Roe Náld's repeated references to "the Allan Houser sculpture of an Apache drummer" on the lawn outside the Fred Jones Museum of Art.[50] Although Houser made several sculptures of drummers, in bronze and in granite, and even though several of his pieces can be found on the University of Oklahoma campus, the "granite singer whose drumstick is raised in midair" is not one of them. In fact, the piece in question, which seems to be "Earth Song," actually sits outside the Heard Museum in Phoenix, Arizona. Given the public's familiarity with the Chiricahua Apache sculptor's extensive collection of sculptures, it is likely that many readers will spot the ploy straight away, and will realize that all is not as it seems. Consequently, the reader has every reason to suspect the narrator's reliability, and to question whether the startling event mentioned in the story's opening line—the death of the speaker's dance partner—actually occurred.

That said, the reader is, of course, aware that Roe Náld is spinning a yarn, and quickly realizes that Womack's "untoward artist" makes little or no bones about the fictional, or dramatic, aspects of his storytelling, nor does he attempt to hide his controlling influence over the tale that he is about to tell, or his exaggerated sense of self-importance. On the contrary, the narrator has a powerful, but misplaced, sense of his worldliness and his mastery, and dares to suggest that he is omnificent and God-like—this despite the fact that he is clearly neurotic and obsessed with his muse and his art. The allusion to Roe Náld's unlimited power within his own story is made via a dexterous veiled reference to N. Scott Momaday's classic *House*

---

50   Ibid., 4.

Made of Dawn.[51] "In the beginning was Justin," Roe Náld explains, adding, "Or, as a certain writer might say, in Justin was the beginning."[52] In this moment Womack references the complex relationship that can be found in moments of intertextual connection, and to the symbolic order in which narratives exist. On a fundamental level, Womack's biblical allusion creates a moment in which first stories—and stories about stories—are called to mind. On another, slightly more complex, level, Roe Náld calls the Old Testament to mind before summarily dismissing it. Here, the authority of a divinely ordered time is subjected to scrutiny and challenged by the parodic treatment of the sense of primacy and absolute beginning that the bible makes via its claim to authority. In sum, God's sovereignty is called into question as a result of this retelling, and Roe Náld replaces the Christian narrative with his new version.

Finally, on another level, it seems significant that these words echo, perhaps even mimic, the words of Tosamah, the peyote priest in Momaday's novel who tells his audience: "In the beginning was the Word, and the Word was with God, and the Word was God."[53] Channeling Momaday's *House Made of Dawn*, a text that contains decidedly modernist qualities and therefore challenges totalizing grand narratives, Womack's story becomes populous, layered; it brings a number of intertexts into play: the bible; *Red on Red*'s suggestion that tribal stories are the canon, the tree of story; Momaday's Pulitzer Prize winning novel; *and* Momaday's 1987 assertion that Monument Valley "is vast [...]. [It] does not occur to you that there is an end to it. You [...] imagine that you have come upon eternity [...] [Only in] the DINÉ BIZAAD, the Navajo language, which is endless, can this place be described."[54] In two short sentences, Roe Náld's narrative queers

---

51   Or "*House Maid at Dawn*," as an Irish university librarian once wrote whilst transcribing the list of novels that I intended to teach as part of a fledgling course on Native American writing during the late 1990s.

52   Ibid.

53   N. Scott Momaday, *House Made of Dawn* (New York: HarperCollins, 1999), 82.

54   N. Scott Momaday, "Landscape with Words in the Foreground," in *Old Southwest New Southwest: Essays on a Region and its Literature*, ed. Judy Nolte Lensink (Tucson: Tucson Public Library, 1987), 2.

Christian time, reconstitutes Momaday's work in order to gloss tribal fiction's long history, and places that history within the context of "endless" indigenous languages and stories. Finally, by calling attention to Momaday's disassembling of master narratives in his 1968 novel, Womack also suggests that new Indian characters must find new strategies of resistance.

Roe Náld's recycling of these words has a number of effects. Firstly, it positions him as God (at least in storytelling terms: in this figuration Justin, who has become "the word," is with Roe Náld, and therefore "with God"). Womack hammers home this point about artistic control in the expository critical essay that immediately follows the story and is titled "Art, Death, Desire." There he describes Roe Náld as a thwarted king who has been usurped by the presence, and ideas, of his muse: "Justin is the trusted loyal subject who betrays his King."[55] This point does, of course, raise some interesting questions about the artist's position as the sovereign ruler of the art form itself; the song is Roe Náld's, he calls the tune (or, at least in his mind he does). Secondly, it demonstrates a particular knowledge of Native American literature and the idiom that Roe Náld functions within as a tribal artist, albeit in a slightly cliquish manner that leaves those unversed in tribal fiction in the dark. Thirdly, and possibly *because* he leaves the reader in the dark, the eponymous narrator piques interest by refusing to reveal the identity of the unnamed "southern plains writer." This mysteriousness is itself a clue about the narrator's (un)reliability, and quite possibly the text's way of suggesting how knowledge or history is

---

55   *Art as Performance*, 39. Womack also has some interesting things to say about artistic sovereignty and originality here, and he explains that what might seem to be delusions of grandeur on Roe Náld's part may, in fact, be understood in terms of his position as director of the movie and storyteller in chief: "Those who do not like Roe Náld may wonder what ever made him think he could be King in the first place. Those who make films, however, might simply argue they call you the director for a reason" (39). Womack thus ponders the relationship between the artist, their tradition, and the muse, asking: "Are my ideas really my own? Or am I simply a pipeline through which flows all that came before me?" (ibid.). This question of "individual talent" and tradition obviously has particular relevance for the tribal writer.

acquired in the contemporary world—a series of fragments that spin out from cinematic and popular culture forms.

The various technical devices found in the story create, then, a semiotic situation that calls for a great deal of attention and care on the reader's part. This, in turn, calls attention to both the signs found in literature and culture, and creates a sense of suspense whereby the reader becomes eager to know what happens next. For instance, the revelation of how the central character's dance partner died is withheld from the reader for a full twenty-nine pages. At that point, a state game warden, who the Muskogee critic later describes as a "surreal cyclops" (with a small "c"), seems to bring the story's tension to an end when he intimates that the young Mr. Crossman has met his demise in a car crash.[56] However, the reader soon learns that all is not what it seems, and any growing sense that the story will move from artistic fancy to grim materiality with the news of Justin's tragic death is undercut by that character's sudden return "from the dead."[57] If the news of Justin's death in the opening line caused suspense, then his subsequent resurrection can most certainly be classified as a shock that conforms to the literary conventions surrounding mystery: "At first the congregation just sat in stunned silence, mouths agape."[58]

These are important developments for two reasons. Firstly, in this context, Womack's portrayal of Roe Náld's chaotic inner narrative, his characterization of the director's attraction to commotion and fuss, and his refusal to provide the reader with a clear or explicit conclusion, can each be read as a response to what Peter Vorderer once described as a "lack of

---

56   *Art as Performance*, 29. As well as containing a literary allusion, insofar as Roe Náld—
     our modern-day Odysseus—avoids the "cyclop's" threat to his wellbeing (that is, he
     avoids being fined for illegally poaching fish), this scene also gestures toward a pop-
     culture classic. The warden arrives in a "beautiful old Ford Fairlane," and his gung
     ho, almost comical, detective work might remind some readers of the spoof movie
     detective Ford Fairlane. A possible association between the two deepens with the
     reference to the textual "detective" having a "customized license plate [which] read
     'Sweetheart'"; his celluloid predecessor has a license plate that reads "bad ass" (*Art
     as Performance*, 27).
57   *Art as Performance*, 35.
58   Ibid.

[...] innovation, and ambiguity" in suspense writing.[59] Womack is playing with expectations and literary codes, thus challenging the assumptions surrounding both tribal fiction and fiction in general. You might even say that there is some genre-bending going on in Womack's story about the filming of *Transvestite Witches Take Revenge on a Redneck Farmer for Gay Bashing*. This simultaneously disrupts the ethnographic gaze that can inform non-Native perspectives, *and* demonstrates the means by which tribal writers challenge extant literary and critical precepts. Secondly, the fact that Justin remains "an impenetrable mystery" for much of the story, and is as "evasive in his resurrection as in life" would appear to suggest that, in this instance, readers must "be accomplished in actively generating meaning."[60] In short, this story calls for a degree of hermeneutic proficiency. Textual cues are embedded in the narrative; some of these are informative, others much more playful, but they are all concerned with eliciting an actively engaged reader. A good example of this is Roe Náld's reference to Justin as "young Ganymede."[61] Here, one cannot be sure whether the comparison draws a line of connection between the object of his affection and the beautiful Trojan prince of Greek mythology, the largest of Jupiter's moons, Christopher Marlowe's *Dido, Queen of Carthage* (which opens with the image of Ganymede being dangled upon Jupiter's knee), or, more obscurely, the plot of John Peyton Cooke's detective fiction *The Rape of Ganymede* (2008), a book set in late 1990s Manhattan and which features a gay private eye named Greg Quaintance. Indeed, Womack's subsequent allusion to Pope's "The Rape of the Lock" (1712), which is framed through the protagonist's dramatic severing of his own braids, could be said to establish a textual cross-pollination that places Belinda and Greg Quaintance in the same literary space, thus collapsing the gap between Pope's eighteenth-century aristocrats and Peyton Cooke's gay gumshoe. All of these characters are then brought into Roe Náld's Wichita

59   Peter Vorderer, *Suspense: Conceptualizations, Theoretical Analyses, and Empirical Explorations* (London: Routledge, 1996), 236.
60   *Art as Performance*, 35.
61   Ibid., 5.

and Caddo world—a move that may serve to remind the reader not only
of the creative richness within tribal fiction, but also the effort required
if one is to engage with this literature and recognize its specificity within
the broader literary canon. It does so by reminding its reader of the uses
of parody and intertextuality, high and low art, the real world (Jupiter)
and imaginary worlds. These observances, and the style in which they are
recorded, noted, and expressed, "constitutes a different [storytelling] act,"
both in terms of the short story form as it is mobilized by Native American
authors, and in terms of critical poses.[62] At once undermining the notion
that straightforward verisimilitude can exist within art, *and* considering
the real world situations in which art is read and interrogated, Womack
confronts his readership with challenging and entirely necessary questions.
By asking, "Is Roe Náld the critic [...] Or is [he] the performer who we
'pay' to lie to us" (and by then choosing to follow up that question with
yet another query, i.e. "What happens when you so thoroughly mix up
the two roles"), the Muskogee scholar scrutinizes the role of the Native
storyteller. He also reminds us of the dexterity shown by the tribal storyteller who negotiates her way through contemporary contexts and texts.[63]
Quite simply, the story thus provides a metalanguage for an examination
of storytelling in a Native American setting.

In many ways, the story seems to be focusing on medium as well. The
final line, "We were being filmed," introduces the medium of film to
the story. This seems to suggest that the story is consciously evaluating
the status of writing and written narrative through the medium of film.
This would appear to be a complex, albeit slightly imperfect, example
of what Jay David Bolter and Richard Grusin describe as remediation,
the process whereby one medium alludes to or even absorbs another and

62   The author makes this point quite forcefully when he poses the following rhetorical
     question in "Art, Death, Desire": "Is 'The Song of Roe Náld' liberatory because of
     its refusal to trot out the usual beads and feathers both [*sic*] non-Indian—and often
     even Indian—readers demand, or does it fail to maintain a minimal tribal integrity?
     How do you tell the difference?" (44).
63   *Art as Performance*, 49.

defines itself in relation to that medium.[64] A self-authenticating process, remediation challenges the (post)modernist assumption that new media, particularly virtual reality, and the internet, mark the development of entirely new aesthetic and new cultural principles, and therefore signal a complete and total break with the mediums that came before. Bolter and Grusin contend, persuasively enough, that new visual media gain their cultural significance primarily because they pay homage to, and adapt the most powerful elements of earlier media—photography remediated painting, film remediated stage production, and so on. One important result of this thesis is that everything is framed or remediated, and one medium is always informed by another medium. With regard to Womack's story, it seems to be staging some negotiation of very postmodern senses of reality in what might be described as a search for or perhaps leaning toward earlier, unmediated experience. In this way, the playfulness and reflexivity of the narrative's semiotic game quite possibly speaks to both the indigenous author's search for aesthetic and creative freedom on the one hand, while also demonstrating the extent to which the artistic performance ties in with, and develops, earlier Creek forms. This is, then, a poise (a pose?) or balance between literary fiction and tribal story, indigenous art and indigenous reality; the Pynchon-esque quality of Roe Náld's quest consequently ties in with Womack's earlier assertion that "tribal literatures are not some branch waiting to be grafted onto the main trunk (of American literature). Tribal literatures are the tree."[65]

One cannot help thinking that is itself a commentary on the proximate nature of artist and audience; here the "director" is also an observer, the "subject" shapes the artwork that is produced, and the audience reflexively plays a role by interpreting, even helping to create, the whole. Fourthly, and following on from this point, by reconstituting Momaday's seminal narrative, which itself quotes the "original" story (that is, the gospel), Roe Náld could also be said to be preparing us for an entirely changed context.

---

64   Jay David Bolter and Richard Grusin, *Remediation: Understanding New Media* (Cambridge, MA: MIT Press, 2000).
65   *Red on Red*, 6–7.

In effect, he suggests that the precepts have changed; in this way, his story could be said to be iconoclastic, insofar as as it serves as a dramatic shift away from Momaday's style of writing, which has become near gospel within Native American Literary Studies, *and* from the originary texts that Momaday subverted. If read this way, the film represents not an act of remediation, but rather a complete dissemblance of earlier Native American forms. The resulting form is not so much homage as it is desecration, and the sacred cows of the Native American art world are well and truly slaughtered (in fact, Justin's "shooting" of the Indians at the funeral might suggest as much).

Yet, this does not seem to be what is happening in the story. Although Roe Náld allows that his "storyline is [perhaps] too busy" by times, this crowdedness or busyness is not simply the result of a postmodern reflexivity. It is important to note that although the wonderfully crowded mind of Womack's narrator careers from references to Alfred Hitchcock, Andrew Lloyd Webber, and Cher, to Allan Houser, N. Scott Momaday, and Lynn Riggs, the Wichita Caddo director is, in fact, primarily following the example of his aunts in Indian Country. These women have a way of talking, he tells the reader, that goes "so far back in the past that they never get to the part they actually wanted to tell you about in the first place."[66] In this way, Roe Náld places a particular emphasis on tribal and familial roots and the stories that come from them, Thus, instead of simply adopting the self-reflexive narrative style of writers Don DeLillo and Lydia Davis, or the cinematography of Guy Maddin, and then using that style to produce some stylized version of the "new Indian," Womack's protagonist foregrounds his artistic maneuvers with an early reference to the ancestors. This contextualization—and the conversation(s) that come after it—initiate a conversation about voice and medium, and Roe Náld's story about stories possibly critiques postmodernism as being depthless; "I'm going to take you back [...] farther," he warns us on the second page of the story, before trundling us through hayfields and high art, movie plots and Mennonite beliefs.[67]

66   *Art as Performance*, 4.
67   Ibid.

In the critical essay that follows the story, Womack tells the reader something that she already knows: "every aspect of Roe Nåld's narration might occur only in his imagination," and points out that his character's "record of narrative inconsistencies, and the very narrative itself, stretch the limits of our belief."[68] That much is certainly true. Womack's narrator makes every effort to "take us" where he wishes us to go, and on his terms. The "mostly true" story that he tells, which is informed by a particularly fabulist bent, contains several "stretchers" that would make even Huck Finn blush. Not unlike the farcical, and in many ways unfulfilling, conclusion that awaits readers of Twain's novel, the final scene in "The Song of Roe Nåld" descends into apparent absurdity. So too is the reader of Roe Nåld's story likely to greet some of the narrator's histrionic outbursts and flights of fancy with a degree of incredulity and perhaps even irritation. (In fact, it is almost as though Womack's protagonist possesses the worst traits of Twain's characters Huck and Tom Sawyer combined; Huck's ability to ramble on and ensnare his listener with extraordinary stories about everyday life, and Tom's passion for narratological contrivance). This possible point of connection between Huck and Roe Nåld is copper fastened when Womack suggests that the latter's mother would like to see him "striking out, not for the territory but New York again, where he could further mature as an artist."[69] This rather explicit reference is important for reasons *other than* the fact that it contains a multitude of wistful ironies and has a delicious intricateness.[70]

Specifically, even though they are story bound figures that create their own, rather fantastic, stories, both characters are in fact central to the

68 Ibid., 49.
69 "Art, Death, Desire," *Art as Performance*, 46.
70 Womack sends Roe Nåld *away* from his home territory—which is of course the territory that Huck heads toward, possibly because he is excited by news of the "Indian wars." The image also highlights a link between Native and non-Native literary histories; Huck's storytelling relies on a set of influences that far exceeds biblical or classical literary references, and might well demonstrate Womack's point that "Tribal literatures are […] the most American of American literatures": *Red on Red*, 7.

process that ties stories and art to what Womack calls "social realities."[71] In
Twain's time, that may have meant producing a narrative that was, ostensibly, about the morality of slavery, but which might also have referred to
the horrors of Wounded Knee and Little Big Horn.[72] In our time, or, more
properly, in Roe Náld's time, human rights issues in America are played
out in slightly different arenas and in different ways, but the struggles take
place on the same hallowed ground, and the stakes are just as high. Hence,
the story's commentary on subjects such as gay rights, various sovereignties
(artistic, political, and/or tribal), Native/non-Native relations and alliances,
and so on is of profound importance. Here, it is not so much a question of
whether Roe Náld's narration or his art is "suspect" because of his affected
behavior, or whether or not Justin's death and resurrection has less of an
effect on us because it "might occur only in [Roe Náld's] imagination."[73]
So, even though the dancer's revivification echoes the Old Testament in a
manner that might playfully allude to the Providential ordering of man's
life as itself just another story, and even though his name might remind
readers of justin.tv (the website that allows anyone to broadcast online),
it is also the case that his name appears to pun on the question of what is
"just." This seems to suggest that we should concern ourselves with other
matters: for instance, the possibility that the film title chosen by Womack's
director responds, on some level, to incidents such as the Matthew Shepard
case in a biting, sharp manner; the simple reality that the story considers
the experiences of a young gay Indian in various settings—the University
of Oklahoma campus, New York, the tribal community, the white mainstream of American society, and so on; the point that this Wichita and
Caddo man, who has been educated in UCLA and New York, is "focused
on describing particular places, reflecting on their meaning, and considering
the aesthetic options available to him in depicting them."[74] Of course, we
also need to think about Womack's position as author and "creator" too;

---

71 *Art as Performance*, 49.
72 See: Sacvan Bercovitch, "Deadpan Huck: Or, What's Funny about Interpretation,"
    Kenyon Review 24.3/4 (Summer/Fall 2002), 90–134.
73 *Art as Performance*, 47 & 49.
74 *Art as Performance*, 45.

all the more so because the Muskogee critic points out that "Roe Náld is not Craig Womack" in his essay "Art, Death, Desire."[75]

As well as reminding us that we must differentiate between the author, implied author, and narrator, Womack underlines the simple fact that fictional characters often hold opinions or engage in acts that are wildly divergent from attitudes or dealings that can be associated with those of their creators. This point may seem self-evident, but many casual readers of tribal fiction often subscribe to the theory that the author uncomplicatedly and candidly reflects the tribe's worldview. This is not always the case, however, and readers may wish to allow for the kind of artistic deviance and cultural critique that Womack highlights in his fiction. "[M]yth and fiction are not the same thing," Womack writes in his essay "Resisting the Easy Connection."[76] Moreover, "To collapse the two literatures into a single genre [...] does disservice to both of them," namely because they do an edifying work on one another [...] not one of duplication."[77] Significantly enough, this argument would appear to run quite close to David Treuer's complaint that "readers and writers of Native American literature have made the mistake of assuming that writing and culture are interchangeable," and his subsequent warning that "We shouldn't interpret the book as myth."[78] Following on from that, the author also seems to encourage us to remember that fiction must not be read as fact, nor should the novel be seen as a medium that allows the curious reader direct, unmediated access to Native culture. Ultimately, then, Womack's fiction and criticism clearly demonstrates that we must formally consider the intricate relationship that can exist between tribal lifeways and literature in the first instance, and face up to the "frustrating challenge of relating literature to the real world in the hopes of seeing social change" in the second. The fact that Womack reiterates the point that he may not always see things the same way as Roe Náld does would suggest both a willingness to recognize a plurality of vision

75   Ibid., 43.

76   Ibid., 316.

77   Ibid.

78   David Treuer, *Native American Fiction: A User's Manual* (Minneapolis, MN: Graywolf, 2006), 201 & 149.

and also a willingness to constantly (re)consider his own position as tribal writer. Importantly enough, Roe Náld appears to be re-evaluating his role as impresario and aesthete by the time the story ends, largely because he is suddenly brought to the realization that the Indians attending Justin's funeral/resurrection/coming out "were being filmed."[79] The filmic reference seems all the more striking when we consider that the funeral scene marks a co-incidence of private and public spaces—spaces in which private grief and public funerary rites commingle. That is to say, the final scene seems to capture the particular tension that exists between immediacy and authenticity on the one hand, and a sense that such moments are impossible, that lived reality always already seems mediated, on the other. It also comments on the hyperreality of twentieth and twenty-first-century life; here members of the indigenous community are being placed on screen in order for non-Natives to watch, scrutinize, and possibly empathize with. Rather than bringing "The Song of Roe Náld" to an end, this final line marks a catching of breath that gives way to the next note in Womack's riff. In this moment, one is reminded of the way that Elizabeth Cook-Lynn's Aurelia "thinks of the story only if it goes on and on into the next story and the next and beyond."[80] One is also reminded of Frank Kermode's oft-quoted study *The Sense of an Ending: Studies in the Theory of Fiction* (1967), in which he argues that "in 'making sense' of the world we still feel a need [...] to experience that concordance of beginning, middle, and end which is the essence of our explanatory fictions."[81] Kermode's thesis is this hunger is driven by an approach to story that arises out of the structure of the bible and the classicist works that Cook-Lynn pits Aurelia's sense of continuance against. But, as Kermode counsels, we must "distinguish between myths and fictions" since "[m]yths are the agents of stability, fictions the agents

---

79   *Art as Performance*, 36.
80   Elizabeth Cook-Lynn, *Aurelia: A Crow Creek Trilogy* (Boulder: University Press of Colorado, 1999), 341.
81   Frank Kermode, *The Sense of an Ending: Studies in the Theory of Fiction* (Oxford: Oxford University Press, 2000), 35–36.

of change."[82] It is highly significant that there is no ending for Womack or for Roe Náld. Art and life continue. And so it goes.

Perhaps the most impressive aspect of Womack's tale and his critical reading of it is the tricky, oftentimes shrewd, manner in which he allows various narrative strands and contexts to proliferate and converge. By allowing a little of the hem to show beneath the artist's elaborate costume, he coaxes the reader into a worthwhile consideration of style and overall aesthetic effect *alongside* a deliberation on the function of storytelling and symbolism, the artist's position, her role, and her manipulation of the audience. On one level, this playfulness is a reminder that, for many observers, "Lying, the telling of beautiful untrue things, is the proper aim of Art."[83] On another level, Womack's story also reminds us that there are serious consequences arising out of the stories we tell. For instance, the performativity associated with acting and role-playing is a reminder of the "act" or performative gesture that, according to Judith Butler, "constructs the social fiction of its own psychological interiority."[84] On one hand, the events that we are privy to take place in a world in which "reality"—itself a social construct—is produced via limiting, heteronormative speech acts (effectively dangerous, controlling lies) that arise out of constantly repeated and cited social norms and contracts—be it the standards of Oklahoman society, the word according to the "Holy Roller crazies," or the "homophobes from [Roe Náld's] community."[85] Crucially, Roe Náld's auteurship and Justin's divaesque behavior can be read as code breaking, transgressive strategies that confound and disrupt the standards and principles of the hegemonic order. By mobilizing their own version of the Wildean lie of

---

82   Ibid., 39.

83   Oscar Wilde, "The Decay of Lying: An Observation," in *The Complete Writings of Oscar Wilde*, together with essays and stories by Lady Wilde, Volume 7 (New York: Aldine, 1910), 56.

84   Judith Butler, "Performative Acts and Gender Constitution: An Essay in Phenomenology and Feminist Theory," in *Performing Feminisms: Feminist Critical Theory and Theatre*, ed. Sue-Ellen Case (Baltimore, MD: Johns Hopkins University Press, 1990), 279.

85   *Art as Performance*, 18 & 32.

art, they disassemble the performative orthodoxy, thereby clearing a space in which other stories, other identities can flourish.

In this context, Womack's profession that he is not "Roe Náld's mother, *exactly*" seems significant as well.[86] While offering a comical nod to the fact that the writer metaphorically gives birth to each character, this throwaway comment summons a second image of cross-dressing or dragging out. That, in turn, re-emphasizes the possibility of subverting the codes, subverting gender performances. It is also important to note, however, that the short story's focus on performativity might also be said to engage and heavily critique Lacan's notion of the "Real," which was a major influence on Butler's theory of performativity. Arguing that "the real is impossible," Lacan insisted that our entrance into language separated us from our original state of nature in childhood. Yet, Roe Náld's suggestion that his story goes back "farther than" other fictional stories usually do, might serve to remind the reader that the tribal "Real" (and therefore the imaginary order, symbolic order, and narrative order) is different to that discussed by Lacan and the structural anthropologists, psychoanalysts, and phenomenologists that have followed in his footsteps. Finally, in a moment that brings these questions of art, pose, and reality together, Womack's use of the word "exactly" makes available a line of comparison between the author/mother of the fictional character in real time (Womack), and the mother figure in story time: Delia. Having "grown tired of the whole business" and decided to abandon the theatrical performance that is Justin's second coming, Delia stands up to leave and brings the whole story to a halt: "Everybody ceased talking and stared at her."[87] "Quit acting like Indians" she scolds them all, before walking "out of the church, head held high, [with] the novel *Vanity Fair* tucked under her arm."

Delia's sudden appearance on center stage and the fact that she is holding a copy of Thackeray's book is, in many ways, the story's *coup de grâce*. As Womack is very well aware, Thackeray's contemporaries often assumed, mistakenly, that the words and opinions of the narrator in *Vanity Fair* were

---

86   Ibid., 46 (emphasis added).
87   Ibid., 36.

those of the author—with the result that his satire was often misread or mis-interpreted. Yet, it is important to note that a closer analysis of Thackeray's novel reveals that the book is riddled with narrative inconsistencies, and that his seemingly hetrodiegetic, omniscient narrator is not only fallible but is even part of the action by times. Certain commentators, particularly Arnold Kettle and E.D.H. Johnson, have taken issue with these irregularities and narratological ambiguities, and have explained them in terms of the author's ill-judged attempt to blend satirical observations with aestheticized moralizing (Johnson), or his misplaced belief that he could draw attention to artifice and fantasy whilst retaining a powerful sense of imagination and wonderment (Kettle). Others, however, most notably Harold Bloom, H.M. Daleski, and Kathleen Tillotson, have argued that the shifting narrative per-spective and unsettling inconsistencies are Thackeray's greatest achievement, primarily because they interrogate totalizing viewpoints, accommodate all kinds of artistic and intellectual interventions, and challenge the (savvy) reader. Daleski even finds "a particularly flexible kind of omniscience," in the book, one that modulates "freely from the impersonal to the personal [...] from the detached to the self-conscious."[88] Importantly enough, he also argues that *Vanity Fair* "successfully encompasse[s] contradictions" and even accommodates "shifts [from] one order of reality to the other"—which is to say that it incorporates shifts from historical reality in one moment to imaginative reality in the next.[89] "The Song of Roe Nåld" makes some very similar moves, and gives rise to a similar set of questions about art and life. Just as readers of *Vanity Fair* may find themselves questioning Thackeray's characterization of the stage manager as masterful on the one hand and naive or helpless on the other, so will readers of Womack's story wonder whether Roe Nåld has complete omniscience as author, whether he is simply the teller/narrator, or whether he is, in fact, a luckless eyewitness. They might also ask if he is some mixture of all of these things. Regardless of the answers that this question is met with (and how it is answered will depend on each reader's subjective analysis of Womack's protagonist), we

88   H.M. Daleski, *Unities* (Athens: University of Georgia Press, 1985), 5.
89   *Art as Performance*, 7.

will still wonder whether the "you" that Roe Náld addresses is actually *us*, the real readers, or whether he is performing for an imaginary, implied audience? How that question is answered in turn will, of course, affect our understanding of the different levels of reality as they are constructed in the story, as well as inform the potential range of meanings within the field of reception. Deeper into the thicket we go, but if we are to consider Native American artistry as well as literature and its contexts deeply and fruitfully, then it is a very necessary journey that Womack brings us on.

Finally, there is Delia herself. Her name has a Greek etymology, meaning "of Delos," a reference to the floating island that, in Greek mythology, Zeus attached to the earth in order to provide Leto somewhere to give birth to his children, Artemis and Apollo. That relationship between Delos and earth seems rather important. In Womack's story, the floating, ephemeral signifiers found in artistic production have the potential to give real purchase and provide a definite sense of praxis. New spaces, new stories have a direct relationship to the tangible, material world. In fact, Womack emphatically argues that what is seen in the mind's eye has a profound effect on how we see the world *in toto*, and that one vision informs and inflects the other. Delia is central to all of this. The way in which Womack uses the word "exactly" in the critical essay that follows "The Song of Roe Náld," which is titled "Art, Death, Desire," seems to suggest that there is considerable propinquity between the author and this character. This proximity might arise out of a conceit mentioned above—explicitly, that the writer is the "parent" who brings forth characters and tales (and that it is often a painful and sometimes thankless process!) This reading is not entirely satisfying however, possibly because Delia's copy of *Vanity Fair* gestures toward a greater layer of complexity. We can pursue the potential semiotic significance of Thackeray's appearance in the story further. In a story that has several intertexts, Delia's copy of *Vanity Fair* may act as a visual cue to the reader to pursue deeper meanings.

When we do, we notice certain things, like the fact that the action stops the moment Delia speaks. Roe Náld explains how, at one point during Justin's funeral "Everyone in the line turned and looked at my mother, waiting for an explanation."[90] Delia, it seems, might be holding some answers. As well as being the narrator's mother (and being Roe Náld's mother is, in the protagonist's mind, probably akin to being the mother of God), Delia is the one person who prioritizes education and sees its value; she acquires, over time, "highly developed taste[s]" for cinematic and literary form. Delia is also an active member of the tribal community and is unafraid to challenge the orthodoxy within that community. At the same time, she revels in inappropriate—but sometimes necessary— humor and, most importantly, has a degree of control and comprehension that eludes her son and the story's other characters.[91] Indeed, it is only when his mother finally walks away that Roe Náld finally spots the camera and announces, outraged: "We were being filmed." Delia is, I would argue, the real auteur here, the one with the genuine knowledge and the best ideas. It is striking that the story comes to a sudden end with her departure, a turn of events that intimates that the director has just walked off set. Accordingly, rather than wonder whether Justin is a figment of Roe Náld's overdeveloped imagination, I find myself questioning whether the "son" isn't a figment of Delia's imagination. "I saw myself as Frankenstein's creation," Roe Náld confesses toward the story's end, thereby constructing a simile that has us wondering whether Justin has created a monster by thwarting his director's romantic advances. Even if that *is* what Roe Náld means, there is possibly another Dr. Frankenstein (or maybe even a Shelley) waiting in the wings: Delia. Read this way, as the imperfect offspring of his hard-working and sharply intelligent Wichita Caddo "mother," the flamboyant, naive, hysterical, and conceited (but ultimately amiable) protagonist makes sense of sorts: he is the result of Delia's artistic vision, her concern for the tribe's present-day concerns, and her dreaming about the future. Of course, like all children, she has to love him unconditionally and accept her son/character for what he is; in fact, the more Delia struggles with the aspects of his character that

90 *Art as Performance*, 34.
91 It could be argued that Justin—if "Justin" exists at all—is also aware of what is happening at all times (his dancing, acting, and even his staged funeral all take place with his consent and knowledge). No one looks to him for direction or advice however, unlike Delia.

don't make perfect sense to her, the more she will push herself outside of her conventional boundaries and learn through art. Delia does try to close down the production at one point during "Justin's funeral [which] wasn't exactly an art opening or a film preview."[92] At a certain stage, she suggests that they "get out of here" because she has heard that it is after the mass that Catholics "really start to make a scene." Rather than contradict my point that Delia is the auteur or director—an argument that might not appear to be in keeping with her desire to exit stage left—I would contend that she is actually struggling to contain the plot at this stage, and is searching for an ending. Like a rookie creative writer, Delia is panicking about the next "scene" and is confronting the very danger that Womack refers to when he explains "artistic projects [can] burgeon out of control. They can take on a life of their own, and this is both their power and their danger."[93]

Influenced by such diverse figures as Hitchcock and Houser, Harjo and Homer, this story is, above all, about the efficacy of Delia's position as director, the character who connects (and possibly creates) the crazy world of avant-garde, art-house cinema to the practical and concrete concerns of folk in Oklahoma. To be sure, Roe Náld makes a fair stab at changing the world through his art, but one feels that the world (or, more specifically, his *Oklahoman* world) may not be entirely ready for his work just yet. In making this point Womack explains that his character comes close to "breaking our trust when we hear how weird his actual films are."[94] For this author, a very fine balance exists between what is artistically challenging and what is purely artifice. Womack consequently points out that even though "we appreciate the disruptions that make us approach narrative skeptically by drawing attention to its own artifice [...] there is also a very human need for cohesive, entertaining storytelling."[95] *Vanity Fair* is of course a work that examines that balance. All this is made possible by the fact that, in terms of art appreciation and perception, Delia has "'graduated'" from her informal

92   Ibid., 33.
93   *Art as Performance*, 39.
94   Ibid., 47.
95   Ibid.

education, and she no longer needs Roe Náld "to recommend anything" since she has the "feelings and knowledge to make her own choices."[96] Delia searches out a particular form of praxis rather than becoming haughty or conceited because of her newfound knowledge, or resenting her time spent as an average Indian mom living in Carnegie, putting her kids through school, and doing casual work as a cleaner. For instance, she is as keen for the tribe to engage with avant-garde art forms as she is for her son to respect certain traditions and conventions. On one hand, she cultivates a "refined dignity" in order to stymie potentially homophobic responses to Roe Náld's art, while on the other hand she tells her son "We should have brought a gift or something" when they are about to view Justin's corpse in the funeral parlor. There is even a notable modification to Roe Náld's tone when he describes his mother to the reader; his entertaining but far-fetched delusions of grandeur, over-embellishments, and often contradictory account of things are now met with simple appreciation and calm unaffected narrative.

Stylistically speaking, this later section of the story has a near melancholia about it, and might therefore be associated with a certain timbre that is often found in life writing. Roe Náld's "flights of fantasy," as Womack calls them, have been enriched and complicated by this extra strand of less fanciful storytelling, which in turn allows us to see other dimensions of his character, and of his mother's character too. Above all else, "The Song of Roe Náld" is, then, about multiple layers, aspects, and standpoints, and in my mind, Delia may even be in control of the story throughout. At the risk of conjecture, or, worse still, a monocular interpretation of a story that has countless possible meanings, I like to imagine that Delia has "given birth" to Roe Náld in creative terms; that the story is told by her, and is perhaps the result of her having taken a creative-writing class.[97] In

---

96 Ibid., 32.
97 Like almost any story, "The Song of Roe Náld" generates multiple meanings and will therefore support a vast array of readings. Future work on the text might examine the significance of the water moccasin's appearance (27); Roe Náld's refiguring of an emergence story (21); the question of Justin's identity (who is named "Crossman" after all, 8); Womack's continued engagement with gay issues within

that context, the story's experimentation with form and perspective, its concomitant concern with community values and aesthetic judgments, the wealth of knowledge about Native American artistry and political experiences, and the often gentle treatment of a central protagonist who is, by times, sanctimonious and slightly unlovable, all make sense. The narrator concerns herself with the interaction between historical and imaginative realities, and is simultaneously interested in: forms of creative and artistic autonomy that might, on some level, revive ideas about tradition; the stories told by the "old ladies in [her] family, all [her] aunties and great aunties"; and the vast range of encounters that take place in Indian Country today. Crucially, there is no real way of separating these concerns, since they are all part of the same vast tapestry.

Changing Stories, Changing Contexts

As tribal chairman of the Federated Indians of Graton Rancheria and as holder of the Endowed Chair of Native American Studies at Sonoma State University, Greg Sarris is also interested in each constituent part of this rich tapestry. Like Womack, Sarris is an author who has mobilized oral and written storytelling in both political and cultural contexts. Interestingly, the Miwok-Pomo writer has, by times, sought other ways of intervening in current discourse and effecting change however. For instance, as noted above, Sarris has seemingly prioritized his work as tribal chairman above his work as a writer and critic. He has also chosen to enter into judicious

tribal and non-Native communities; the historical tensions—and recent attempts at reconciliation—between the Mennonites and Native American communities (see <http://www. themennonite. org/issues/13-11/articles/Mennonites_ apologize_to_Native_Americans>); the significance of the particular set of pop-culture images that Womack presents the reader with; and the various other allusions that the story teems with. In other words, this chapter is simply the beginning of the long critical conversation that is likely to surround the story.

silences on occasion, usually when dealing with non-Native media and detractors who have made despicable ad hominem attacks. And he has sought out the most viable means of supporting the tribe's quest for self-determination. It seems necessary, in light of these strategies, to consider not only the interaction that takes place between writing (both fiction and criticism) and *hors texte* indigenous experience, but also the efficacy that possibly arises out of Sarris's position as scholar, chairman, and leading figure in the development of economic and political initiatives. In doing so, one must consider Sarris's description of his own attempt to engage not only with tribal story, tribal community, and tribal knowledge, but also with the academic community and long established theoretical and critical precepts.

"'Here Greg,' Auntie Violet said. 'You can peel some potatoes.'"[98] By opening with this line, Sarris identifies a particular temporal and spatial setting that then serves to contextualize both the critical maneuvers that he will make throughout the book, and the storytelling that shapes and informs not only his scholarly activities, but his life as well. Like "The Song of Roe Náld," this work opens with the image of the "aunties and great-aunties" who are the family's storytellers, and examines the usefulness of reader-response theory within various settings: the classroom (both primary and university), the academy, and the wider world. "The stories mix and mingle," Sarris writes towards the end of his study, "I make sense of them, and this sense, of course, has much to do with my experience, my family, and my education."[99] Several critics have provided insightful and comprehensive analyses of the Miwok-Pomo writer's groundbreaking study of text, story, and mediation, not only in *Keeping Slug Woman Alive*, but also in the biographical work *Mabel McKay: Weaving the Dream*, the story cycle in *Grand Avenue*, and the novel *Watermelon Nights*.

For instance, Michelle Burnham argues that *Grand Avenue* is patently shaped by the "communitism" that Weaver speaks of, and argues that the book is a "a kind of literary Pomo basket whose intersubjective weave

98 *Keeping Slug Woman Alive*, 1.
99 Ibid., 193.

functions [...] to hold stories together [... and] ceremonially restore and heal Native community."[100] Moreover, Burnham argues, Sarris has a sense of storytelling and an understanding of the Western and Pomo narrative traditions that allows him to scrutinize the various spaces that are created via certain linguistic and cultural traditions, and via an exchange across the borders that exist between these traditions. Thus, Sarris introduces us to dynamic narrative spaces that can accommodate both synergies and demarcations, while also elaborating on tribal sovereignties and cultural exchanges. Meanwhile, Reginald Dyck reads *Watermelon Nights* as a novel that deals with the need for a "relational and pragmatic understanding of sovereignty," and which therefore captures Sarris's own propensity to see "institutional and cultural strategies [... for decolonization and tribal continuance] as mutually enhancing."[101] Dyck goes on to provide an elucidating analysis of the proximity between the fiction on one hand, and both the author's intercultural negotiation with the federal government during the restoration of the FIGR and the tribe's practice of sovereign rights in various aspects of daily life on the other. In this instance, all aspects of story—including various forms of fictional representation, oral narrative, and communal story—are part of an ongoing process of mediation and boundary setting.

In his estimation of the vital intervention that Sarris has made, both in the field of Native studies in general and Native American Literary Studies in particular, Womack underlines the significance of the Miwok-Pomo author's bid to widen the various critical lenses applied within Western literary theory, cultural studies, ethnography, and studies of tribal fiction. The most innovative and effective aspect of Sarris's work is, according to Womack, its ability to recast or reinterpret reader-response theory, primarily by telling his own story throughout his consideration of reception

---

100 Michelle Burnham, "Pomo Basketweaving, Poison, and the Politics of Restoration in Greg Sarris's *Grand Avenue*," *Studies in American Indian Literatures* 14.4 (2002), 20.

101 Reginald Dyck, "Practicing Sovereignty in Greg Sarris's *Watermelon Nights*," *Western American Literature* 45.4 (Winter 2011), 343.

aesthetics.[102] Consequently, what Womack deems to be "abstractions"— that is to say, theoretical paradigms that have little or no material effect—are "replaced with a reader and happenings."[103] The critical model is, in turn, modified in a way that both energizes modes of reading and interpretation that are extant within the academy, while also making those approaches relevant to tribal narratives and the communities that they come from.

It may be possible to link Sarris's originality in this area to the signifi- cant fact that many of his formative years were spent in the presence of the widely acclaimed Pomo basket weaver and medicine woman, Mabel McKay. As well as producing "feather baskets [that] are considered by many to be uniquely powerful and beautiful," Mabel McKay also had a "view of tradition" in which the weaver "dreamed the pattern. For her, tradition didn't mean that you were doing it the same way as the older generation or that you had been taught by a traditional weaver."[104] Importantly enough, Sarris and others have commented on the fact that Mabel's baskets are living entities, and therefore have a presence and a life-force as well as aesthetic beauty. They have also commented on the fact that the Pomo medicine woman could not distinguish between the stuff out of which the baskets are made (roots, her own dexterity, artistic vision, and so on), and her dreams, ability to doctor people, insight, and daily life.[105] These details, the particulars concerning aesthetics, departures from tradition, life-force, and the intermingling of the cultural artifact and experience, have much to tell us about Sarris's unique take on tribal life and tribal literature. Evidently enough, Sarris's role as both critic and practitioner is guided by a powerful sense of the relationship between writing and these particulars. In other words, it is possible to see the book as being *somewhat*

102 Craig Womack, "Book-Length Native Literary Criticism," *Reasoning Together*, 51 & 52.

103 Ibid., 52.

104 Brian Bibby, *The Fine Art of California Indian Basketry* (Berkeley, CA: Heyday Books, 1996), 83–84. Quoted in Sheridan Hough, "Phenomenology, Pomo Baskets, and the Work of Mabel McKay," *Hypatia* 18.2 (Spring 2003), 105.

105 Sheridan Hough, "Phenomenology, Pomo Baskets, and the Work of Mabel McKay," 106; Sarris, *Keeping Slug Woman Alive*, 51.

akin to the basket (as Burnham does), and to do so without corralling slightly dissimilar impulses, projects and experiences into one, or, worse still, seeming to somehow malign Mabel McKay's powers. While Sarris is honing artistic and critical perspectives and approaches that may deviate from the methodologies or attitudes of other members of the community, nonetheless his stories, narratives, and fictions are hugely informed by the specificities of a Miwok-Pomo worldview.

Elvira Pulitano's reading of Sarris's commitment to hybridization notwithstanding, the vast majority of scholars familiar with the logic expressed in *Keeping Slug Woman Alive* (and subsequent works) would argue that it is primarily the tribal perspective that shapes Sarris's work. Although Sarris combines critical methodology derived from academic study with personal narratives and perspectives, thereby refusing to "privilege an Indian's point of view regarding the texts and topics considered," his work is intended to facilitate a conversation across borders, to show that "each group can inform and be informed by the other."[106] Crucially, he treats "each group" as a discrete entity, and the book is not so much focused on a dialogism that leads to some form of creolization or hybridization, as it is on a form of dialogue that might help to cultivate understanding, empathy, and, just as importantly, autonomy. The careful and methodical work of Burnham, Dyck, and Womack, to name but a few of the scholars who are interested in Sarris's writing, bears this out.[107] Quite aside from the fact that others

106 Sarris, *Keeping Slug Woman Alive*, 7.
107 It must be noted that not everyone agrees that Sarris's 1993 work successfully facilitates dialogue, or that it serves either Native or non-Native communities well. The Lakota writer and critic Franci Washburn argues that "Sarris does not clearly explain what he is trying to say" throughout *Keeping Slug Woman Alive*, and, for that reason, the book "invites misunderstandings": "The Risk of Misunderstanding in Greg Sarris's *Keeping Slug Woman Alive: A Holistic Approach to American Indian Texts*," *Studies in American Indian Literatures* 16.3 (Fall 2004), 70 & 71. Her point is well taken, and there is certainly a risk that the reader will interpret Sarris's retelling of traditional stories through a non-Native lens, thereby misconstruing things. That would disserve both the reader's attempt to engage with Pomo storytelling and contexts in the first instance, and Sarris's bid to initiate the type of engagement that can facilitate meaningful cross-cultural understanding in the second. However, it seems to

have already paid significant and sustained attention to the various complex dimensions of the Miwok-Pomo author's approach to life and letters,
there is a need to examine Sarris's approach to writing since the turn of
the twenty-first century, and to consider his recent take on story, narrative,
dialogue, and intercultural contact. A necessary part of this process is the
consideration of both the legal challenges to tribal sovereignty in America
today and, lamentably enough, the resurgence of scurrilous representations
of Native peoples, the pedaling of assumptions about tribal experiences
and lives, and the bid to shore up glaring economic and political inequities.
Quite simply, I am calling for recognition of the relationship that exists
between Sarris's role as a teller of tales and the FIGR community's drive
for economic sovereignty and, by extension, recognition of the challenges
that face the writer as a consequence of his deep investment in tribal matters, and the seriousness of the conversations regarding Indian gaming.
In these closing pages, then, I want to reiterate the fundamental fact that
storytellers in Indian Country today are dreaming up new stories where
new challenges will be negotiated; narratives constructed by Sarris and
others remind us as readers of Native American writing that its stories
tell of both new and old sovereignties, map out ancestral territories, and
produce new(ly) imaginative spaces.

Significantly, in the recent past there have been occasions when Sarris's
keen ability to locate, consider, articulate, and emphasize the specificities
surrounding and informing tribal identity have been overlooked, and tribal
sovereignty challenged. For instance, on July 20, 2012, the board of the
Bioneers, "a collective of social and scientific innovators" whose goal it is
"to mimic 'nature's operating instructions' [... and] serve human ends without harming the web of life," were forced to issue a statement concerning

---

me that Washburn's fears—which emanate from a sensitive, and laudable, approach
to the narratives and their cultural context—might result in her being a little too
concerned with the goal of being "easily understood by the dominant majority" (81).
To my mind, non-Natives must do more to interpret, must work harder to interpret,
and, just as importantly, must accept that there will be moments when meaning is
not clear—either because they have failed to do enough to successfully interpret, or
because the fullest meaning is not available to those outside of the tribe.

the tribal chairman ahead of their annual conference, held in San Rafael, California, in October 2012.[108] Designed to assuage the objections of those members who had taken exception at the fact that Sarris had been invited to the conference as a guest speaker—and there must have been plenty of objections if a press release was warranted—the statement outlines some key facts. Firstly, it calls attention to the fact that the Bioneers' purpose is to "create a site of inquiry, respect and solidarity," in which people with diverse perspectives and objectives might come together in the hope of searching out ways of improving society, raise consciousness about ecological concerns, and generally broaden the horizons of those taking part.[109] Secondly, even though they acknowledge the fact that some Bioneers members are opposed to the Graton Rancheria Nation's plan to open a casino in Rohnert Park, and even signal their "deep appreciation for [those members'] willingness to challenge" the decision to invite Sarris to the conference, the authors are keen to outline their immense respect for the tribal chairman. Describing him as a leader who is "revitalizing the culture and livelihood of his people," and citing his status as both the elected leader of the FIGR and as an eminent academic, the statement issued by the Board refers to the "numerous social, cultural, environmental, and economic initiatives" that Sarris has been involved in, and refers to his "integrity." Overall, it is a glowing endorsement of the author's activism, and a powerful précis of his achievements. That fact notwithstanding, we must ask ourselves why such a summation is necessary.

It is necessary, in part, because Indian gaming continues to be such a controversial, and complex, matter. For instance, it is necessary to take into account the small number of intra-tribal disputes or disenrollments that have occurred in light of the per cap payment system, or to recognize the objections that many tribes have to gaming on moral, social, and spiritual grounds. There are also huge variations in the type and scale of gaming

---

108   The statement was co-authored by: "Melissa Nelson, A Native American Board Member, Cara Romero, Native American Director of [the Bioneers] Indigeneity Program, and Kenny Ausubel and Nina Simons, Co-CEOs and Founders [of Bioneers]."

109   <https://docs.google.com/file/d/0BxtT-CTV7S6uTWdMV2dYV1ZobkE/edit>.

run by the tribes, with geographical or regional differences playing a part in shaping the industry in many states (that is to say, population density, tourism infrastructure, and other elements often tend to shape the compacts drawn up between the tribes and the states). When the financial risks to the tribes are factored in, along with the complexities associated with drawing up legal agreements with the states and with financial backers, as well as environmental questions, Indian gaming is far from being a straightforward matter.[110] Regardless of how one feels about the issues surrounding large-scale casino developments, few commentators have denied that tribal communities are in chronic need of extensive economic investment. As well as enabling the provision of healthcare and education initiatives, profits from Indian gaming may also be used to fund language recovery projects, build cultural centers, guarantee food sovereignty, and support countless other badly needed programs. In the immediate short term, it is difficult to see where, exactly, the financial backing for these enterprises

110 It is a well-known fact that Indian gaming is an issue deserving of sustained and unbiased attention, largely because it has attracted much partisan commentary to date, and because it is so very controversial. Indeed, a *Los Angeles Times* editorial published on August 19, 2012, rehearses several of the key issues surrounding Indian gaming in the State of California: "A Bad Bet on Indian Casinos" <http://www.la times. com/news/opinion/editorials/la-ed-casinos-indian-northern-california-20120819,0,770034. story> accessed September 24 2012. Steven Andrew Light and Kathryn R.L. Rand, the founders and co-directors of the Institute for the Study of Tribal Gaming Law and Policy, which is part of the Northern Plains Indian Law Center at the University of North Dakota, maintain a web presence at www.indiangamingnow.com and this site provides useful, up-to-date information on Indian gaming. Their book *Indian Gaming and Tribal Sovereignty: The Casino Compromise* (Lawrence: University Press of Kansas, 2005) is recognized as being one of the most comprehensive and balanced studies of Indian gaming to date. Those interested in gaining a shorter, but no less detailed, overview of Indian gaming, its development, and the complex legal (as well as some of the social) issues involved should see Matthew L. Flether's essay "Bringing Balance to Indian Gaming," *Harvard Journal on Legislation* 44.1 (2007), 39–95. Eileen M. Luna-Firebaugh and Mary Jo Tippeconnic Fox's essay "The Sharing Tradition: Indian Gaming in Stories and Modern Life," *Wicazo Sa Review* 25.1 (2010), 75–86, makes a case for the tribes' ancestral connection to gaming and further explains Indian communities' sovereign rights in this area.

will come from if not from the proceeds earned via Indian gaming. In fact, when faced with large-scale social and fiscal challenges, many tribal leaders and their people are likely to come to the same conclusion as the poet protagonist in Sherman Alexie's short story "Love, Hunger, Money": "Now/we've got our own game/of Reservation Roulette/and I'd advise the faithful/to always bet on red."[111] Indian gaming is also one of the most dynamic and hotly contested arenas in which legal issues surrounding tribal sovereignty are being tested, clarified, and enacted today.[112] Moreover, the Supreme Court's ruling in the case of *Match-E-Be-Nash-She-Wish Band of the Pottawatomi Indians v. David Patchak et al.*, and similar cases has guaranteed that this will continue to be the situation for some time to come.[113] In that context, it is hardly surprising that the board of Bioneers

111   Sherman Alexie, "Love, Hunger, Money," *High Country News* (September 19, 1994).
112   I am not for a second suggesting that various cases concerning environmental justice and tribal sovereignty are less significant. On the contrary, the case of the Haudenosaunee Passport and land claims by the Oneida Indian Nation, the Seneca, the Cheyenne, and several other tribes are obviously crucial. However, these cases often have a lower profile in terms of media interest and reporting. There is also the argument that victory in the cases concerning casinos and gaming would help to support other legal battles and social initiatives—partly because the revenue generated in the wake of these victories can then be used to support land claims and so on. See: Daniel I.S.J. Rey-Bear, "The Flathead Water Quality Standards Dispute: Legal Bases for Tribal Regulatory Authority over Non-Indian Reservation Lands," *American Indian Law Review* 20.1 (1995/1996), 151–224; A. Cassidy Sehgal, "Indian Tribal Sovereignty and Waste Disposal Regulation," *Fordham Environmental Law Review* 5.2 (2011), 431–458; the case of Joyce M. King, director of the Akwesasne Justice Department for the Mohawk Council of Akwesasne, whose Haudenosaunee passport was confiscated when she attempted to cross the Canadian border on June 18, 2011.
113   In an 8–1 ruling released on June 18 2012 (Justice Sotomayor was the sole dissenter), the Supreme Court found that a private landowner, David Patchak, had the right to file a suit against the Secretary of the Interior in response to the Secretary's 2009 decision to take land into trust on behalf of the tribe at Gun Lake. Patchak contends that he has been adversely affected by the Secretary of the Interior's decision, which cleared the way for a casino that, in turn, led to an intolerable "increase in traffic and crime and irreversible change [to] the area's rural quality." Although the Quiet Title Act of 1972 prevents suits that challenge title to Indian lands in these

thought it wise to address these complexities, and to explain them to an audience that may not have a deep understanding of the issues at hand, or an appreciation of the work that Sarris and the FIGR are currently involved in. On that level, the organizers' decision to issue a statement can, perhaps, be viewed as a logical move.

Unfortunately, aside from glossing the complexities of the issue at hand, the Bioneers organizers also encountered "racist stereotypes about Native Americans" once Sarris's lecture was announced.[114] It is entirely lamentable that the board found it necessary, as a result, to point out that it was unfair and illogical to argue that casinos cause a greater amount of environmental damage than other, similarly scaled, developments, or that tribal communities are "held to impossible standards of being 'traditional Indians' and modern people simultaneously."[115] It is also a great shame that some Bioneers members needed to be reminded of the historical legacies of colonization, tribes' sovereign right to broker economic deals with fellow sovereigns (particularly the states), and the simple reality that several tribes are dexterously balancing landscape traditions with new forms of land use. Significantly, plans for the Rohnert Park casino have generated—or, more properly, *unmasked*—a great deal of trite commentary about Indian sovereignty and thinly veiled racism. Much of this is evident in the bruising, often invidious, allegations that have been made by the various special interest groups who protested against the FIGR's proposed development. The most vocal, and troubling, of these claims have come from a group calling itself "Stop the Casino 101 Coalition" (STC101C), and can be found on a website of the same name.[116] As well as challenging the casino

---

circumstances, Patchak has been allowed to sue simply because he was not claiming to have any competing interest in the land at Gun Lake. The case is ongoing and the ramifications are not yet known as a result.

114 <http://www.waccobb.net/forums/showthread.php?91332-Greg-Sarris-at-Bioneers> accessed September 24 2012.

115 Ibid.

116 The group describes itself as follows: "Stop the Casino 101 Coalition (STC101) is a non-sectarian, multicultural organization created in 2003 to address the serious social and environmental issues of the Federated Indians of Graton Rancheria's Las

on environmental grounds, STC101C has also argued that the State of California was deprived of "jurisdiction to govern gambling on the land." This claim was made on the basis that the Highway 37 property remained "under state jurisdiction even *after* title to the land [was] transferred by a private owner to the federal government in trust for an Indian tribe," and was therefore bound by state law, which prohibits gambling.[117] The group has also taken issue with the Memorandum of Understanding between the City of Rohnert Park and the FIGR, solely because the MOU referred to the second proposed site for the casino, and not its current location. To date, none of these challenges have derailed the tribe's compact with the state, nor stood in the way of the revenue sharing agreement that has been worked out between the FIGR and the Sonoma County supervisors.[118]

Vegas-style casino proposed for Rohnert Park" <http://rohnertpark-cotati.patch. com/users/stop-the-casino-101-coalition> accessed October 24 2012.

117 *Stop the Casino 101 Coalition, Marilee Montgomery, Pam Miller and Fred Soares v. Edmund G. Brown Jr., Governor of the State of California, in his official capacity, and DOES 1 through 100.* Case Number SCV-251712.

118 The revenue sharing compact is an extremely interesting agreement in its own right. Involving limited waivers on tribal sovereignty, this compact includes a clause that obliges the FIGR to pay a cash advance to Sonoma county in the event that the state of California fails to pass along monies that the tribe will pay to the state in the first instance, but which are actually destined for county coffers. The sums in question are considerable; Sonoma County is guaranteed $9 million each year, which is to be used to offset the various impacts made by the casino. That figure could rise to $38 million if the casino is very successful in years to come. The amount paid to the county is on top of the money promised to Rohnert Park by the tribe (a figure that has been reported as being approximately $200 million over twenty years), a further $8 million a year earmarked for Sonoma's Indian Health Project and Sonoma County tribes who do not have Indian gaming on their lands. Moreover, a separate figure of $30 million per annum that will support farming initiatives, county parks, and environmental conservation. Two aspects of these deals are striking: firstly, and most importantly, by agreeing to waive its sovereignty, albeit in a limited manner, the FIGR invoked the "right *to exercise* [their] sovereignty" as they see fit: FIGR website <http://www.gratonrancheria.com/news092906_6.htm> accessed October 20 2012 (emphasis in original). Secondly, as well as providing some sense of the sheer amount of social projects that will be developed as a result of casino profits, the various compacts and arrangements agreed between the FIGR, the state, the county,

No more successful, but certainly more corrosive, rancorous, and, I would say, hateful, have been STC101C's attempts to cast aspersions on the tribe's long history and their ad hominem attack on Tribal Chairman Sarris. In seeking to undermine the historical evidence that led to President Clinton's restoration of the FIGR on December 27, 2000, the grand webmasters behind the site interpret historical documents in a rather bizarre and self-serving manner.[119] Implicitly suggesting that intermarriage or intercultural mixing have somehow displaced the authority inherent within the FIGR's sovereignty (the final paragraph on this page of the website concludes that "the residents [...] at Graton Rancheria in 1952, were a mixed bag"), STC101C seek to define various resident's blood-quantum and to construe some meaning from that. As well as quite unfairly placing the burden of proof on the tribe, this strategy aims to parse tribal history in a manner that is invasive, divisive, and invidious enough to be deemed paracolonial at best, and profoundly racist at worst.[120] Tied in with this

---

and Station Casinos, are all products of the tribe's right to enter into negotiations as sovereigns, *and* their willingness to deal with non-Native groups in an amicable and fair manner. Whatever one thinks about the morals of casino money or about the state and county's deal with the tribe, one fact remains clear: the tribes are reaching mutually beneficial agreements with non-tribal political leaders and policy makers.

119 For instance, they cite Special Indian Agent John J. Terrell's letter of June 14, 1920, to the Commissioner of Indian Affairs: "I have in mind that this 15.45 acre tract should be set aside, in event of purchase, for the village home of the Marshall, Bogeda [*sic*] and Tomales Bay Indians." On their website STC101 then write: "Note that Terrell's letter confirms that it was Washington's original intent to use this land for landless or homeless Indians from the vicinity of Marshall and Sebastopol, not as a village home," thereby entirely disregarding the fact that Terrell wrote "this 15.45 acre tract should be set aside, in event of purchase, *for the village home of*" (emphasis added).

120 The issue of blood-quantum is an especially difficult one, and, at the moment, many "Indian communities are torn between losing members through intermarriage, and the real or perceived role of blood quantum in keeping the remaining cultures pure and strong": "How Indian Are You?," Minnesota Public Radio (April 2001) <http://news.minnesota.publicradio.org/projects/2001/04/brokentrust/horwichj_quantum-m/index.shtml> accessed October 20 2012. Mark Rifkin has recently sought to remind his readers that: "the concept of having a 'quantum' of Indianness became institutionalized in the late-nineteenth and early-twentieth-century censuses of Native groups

move, and equally as troubling, is the line of attack taken in the section of
the website which, until recently, bore the snappy title "Biography Material
of Greg Sarris Ancestry."[121] Here, the coalition offers its version of Sarris's
genealogy, disputes the writer's story about his ancestry, and makes public
a set of convictions that had previously been made known in a letter sent
to the Bureau of Indian Affairs. The letter in question had called on the
BIA to "de-certify Mr. Greg Sarris as Chairman," on the basis that he "possesses no Native American blood, and specifically, no Coast Miwok and/
or Southern Pomo blood."[122]

---

     conducted by the federal government, and such designations became an administra-
     tive tool of federal Indian policy starting in the 1910s as the basis for decisions about
     'competence' to own land, determinations made as part of the allotment program
     that sought to break up Native landholding and eliminate Native sovereignty. The
     current efforts to determine the contours and limits of Native governance by invok-
     ing the apparently biologically self-evident figure of the *Indian*, therefore, have a
     long history as part of attempts to dismantle Native peoplehood and to bring Native
     lands into the regular jurisdiction of the US. It is hardly the place of Stop the Casino
     101 to decide who belongs in the Federated Graton Ranchera Nation. Instead, the
     communities themselves will decide on how best to reform blood quantum rules,
     balance these issues with enrollment rights and responsibilities, and negotiate with
     federal government as sovereigns thereafter": "Reauthorizing Indianness [or Acts of
     Violence Against Native Self-Determination]" <http://www.firstpeoples newdirec-
     tions.org/blog/?p=5446> accessed October 20 2012.
121   STC101 have recently amended this to read "Biography: Greg Sarris Ancestry."
122   "Anti-casino group says leader of rival tribe not Indian," *Capitol Weekly* <www.capi-
     tol weekly.net/article.php?xid=ymeu28afca9np1> accessed October 20, 2012. On
     September 15, 2012, Velia A. Navarro, a sixty-eight-year-old third cousin of Sarris's,
     signed a declaration stating that her ancestors were not of Indian descent. Navarro's
     statement outlines her particular version of the family history, and pays special atten-
     tion to the life of Reinette Sarragossa, the woman who was her great-grandmother
     (and therefore Sarris's great-grandmother too). The statement would appear to have
     been prepared at the behest of STC101C (although that fact is, for rather obvious
     reasons, never stated). Publication of this document raises several questions. Navarro
     contradicts the memory of her "younger half-sister" Linda Trujillo, who works at
     the tribe's headquarters. Section 7 of the statement also seems to suggest that the
     family history might have been amended in order to "whitewash" the family story;
     Navarro remembers that asking about possible mulatto heritage "got me in trouble,

As well as being entirely unpalatable, undeserving of any real attention, and alien to any meaningful discussion about tribal sovereignty (to say nothing of literary criticism), the coalition's anti-tribal rhetoric is horribly misdirected and destructive, while also making a mockery of their call for justice, fairness, or useful debate. Regardless of what opinions one holds on Indian gaming (and, as noted above, there are many), it is shocking to think that a group that includes a Pentecostal minister (Pastor Chip Worthington), a city councilman (Mike Healy), and other "community leaders" can abide by this attempt to undermine the FIGR right to Californian homelands. Yet, this is exactly the path that they have chosen to take. The fact that the STC101C is a mainstream organization—according to their own website at least—is possibly the most disconcerting detail of all; although these tactics are more in keeping with those of the Far Right, in this case they are being deployed by a group that allies itself with the Rohnert Park Families group and various Christian churches. That point alone acts as a serious reminder of the degree of resolve that is required in the ongoing battle against hidebound assaults on Indian cultures, communities, and rights today. Most significantly, perhaps, the STC101C's scurrilous attempt to target Sarris personally, rather than the wider political questions concerning land and space is, quite simply, blind to the realities of tribal sovereignty.[123] Vice-chair of the FIGR, Lorelle W.B. Ross, pointed this out in a letter to the BIA that was sent after the coalition's call for Sarris's decertification. In that letter Ross explained that the assault on the chairman was "deeply offensive to" communities who have contended with continuous

---

so I never asked about it again." This statement seems to be in keeping with the story that Sarris tells in *Keeping Slug Woman Alive*, in which he recounts his grandmother, Evelyn (Reinette's daughter), did not wish to identify as Indian.

123 The *Press Democrat* newspaper pointed to both of these facts in an editorial published on February 20, 2010, in which the editor noted that this "ersatz challenge only introduces ugly issues of race into a debate that should focus on public policy [...]. [And] should be withdrawn": "About Sarris" <http://www.pressdemocrat.com/ article/20100220/OPINION/100219340/0/SEARCH> accessed October 20 2012. Significantly, the editorial also stated "by federal law, tribal membership is determined by tribal members. And the Graton tribe has spoken clearly."

attempts "to deny or delegitimize the American Indian identity, experience, and history." Significantly, she went on to note that as well as being
morally reprehensible, the coalition's correspondence had, quite simply,
disregarded the "exclusive right" of every Indian tribe "to determine its
own membership."[124] That determination is key. Despite various attempts
to reignite anachronistic debates about identity politics, despite the vexed
exchanges that some parties seek, and despite the (sometimes necessary)
legal and political challenges to tribal developments, one truth shines
through: sovereignty is both recognized in, and enacted through, various
tribes' sovereign-to-sovereign negotiations with counties, states, and the
federal government. In short, the FIGR have successfully negotiated with
a compendium of administrative and business interests, and have reached
agreements that have, to date, cleared the way for new initiatives.

What, we might ask, has any of this to do with Sarris's work as a scholar
and as a fictionist? Well, quite a lot actually. In the Prologue to *Keeping
Slug Woman Alive*, Sarris cites his interest in the work of ethnographers
arguing for receptive and useful cross-cultural dialogue, through which the
various parties involved might recognize "personal and cultural [bounda-
ries]" and, by extension, "the limits on and possibilities for understanding
one another in the exchange."[125] He then takes the image of "ongoing [...]
continued communication" and meshes it with critical patterns emerging
from reader response theory, before finally describing his personal desire
to focus on, and record, the "scholar's interaction with a text [... and] the
scholar's autobiography." My point is *not* that we should take the story of
the FIGR casino development as being akin to the stories that Sarris tells
in the pages that follow this Prologue (even though the author has spoken
about his experiences during several lectures, book readings, conference
gatherings, and so on). Instead, I would like to suggest that we might read
the discourse surrounding the casino in two ways. In the first instance, the
various compacts worked out between the FIGR and various sovereigns

---

124   Letter to The Honorable Larry Echo Hawk, Assistant Secretary—Indian Affairs,
       Department of the Interior, dated February 12, 2010 <http://www.gratonrancheria.
       com/index.htm> accessed September 18 2012.
125   *Keeping Slug Woman Alive*, 6.

are, in effect, material examples of the types of conversation and exchange that can take place if Native and non-Native groups choose to seek out a mutually acceptable agreement. In the second instance, the unfortunate turn taken by objectors to the casino is a reminder of the fact that dialogue can occur if, and *only* if, both groups are prepared to respect the borders, engage honorably, and listen to one another. The STC101C's particular method of attack is to attempt dissolution of the tribe's borders by negating the community's claim to village lands and to the ancestors. Some Bioneers followers have taken a less direct—some might even say a slightly less offensive approach—by questioning the moral and environmental costs, but their resistance is often dependent upon and informed by the same set of stereotypical and clichéd images that the STC101C employ.[126] Fundamentally, both of these responses reveal an inability to comprehend or acknowledge either the complex circumstances that modern Native communities exist within, or the exigencies of tribal self-government and economic autonomy. As a result, it seems that many non-Native commentators are either unwilling or unable to appreciate the ways in which tribes such as the Kashaya Pomo "make and remake the culture as they negotiate and mediate a range of cultural and intercultural phenomena in a variety of ways to fashion a sense of identity and self."[127] Like many of the audiences who listened to—and misunderstood—Mabel McKay's talks, these folks

---

126 I do not wish to make too much out of the personal opinions of a small number of respondents who contributed to the forum. It is nevertheless important to note the appearance of commonly held assumptions about tribal communities and/or American race relations. One poster made reference to "the native regard and respect for the land, the critters on the land, and the natural life cycle," and called on the FIGR to find "a more noble way of Native Americans reclaiming and embracing their land," and to "honor the spirit of a beautiful people." Another stated, baldly: "I have a problem with the entire notion of granting one group of people rights that the rest of society does not have. We all are Americans, like it or not, all created equal, but because Native Americans were screwed in the (now) distant past, they are entitled to special treatment, an unfair advantage, not available to anyone else" (ibid.). It is also worth noting that Sarris responded to these opinions directly <WaccoBB.net> accessed October 24 2012.

127 *Keeping Slug Woman Alive*, 179.

want answers, often very *specific* answers to their questions, but are unwilling to take the time to listen to the fullest story, to engage with a value system that is not theirs, to examine their own value system and cultural referents.

In all of this, there is Sarris's crucial position as fictionist, scholar, storyteller, and tribal chairman of the Federated Indians of Graton Rancheria. His creative writing, his autographically informed scholarship, and, more recently, his forays into journalism and constitutional literature, frame existing narratives and open out new realities, new worlds, and new stories to every reader who cares to seek out his prose. In much the same way as Gerald Vizenor and Jill Doerfler pooled their skills as researchers and writers with the constitutional delegates and the members of the proposal team who drafted the constitution of the White Earth Nation, Sarris's authorship—and his citizenship—has had a profound effect that reaches far beyond the classroom, the library, and the academy.[128] His goal, it seems, is to create stories that make sense of the world by dealing with its tensions and fractures, while also forging/ pursuing the possibility of greater unities within its lived realties. With this in mind, future work might situate the various stories Sarris has told in relation to his scholarly writing. For instance, his authoring of the Omnibus Indian Advancement Act (HR 5528) could be interestingly explored in relation to his 2009 "Guest Opinion" piece in the *Press Democrat* in order to arrive at a deeper understanding of the close association between tribal self-determination, political activism, and various forms of writing. The forewords to Betty Goerke's *Chief Marin: Leader, Rebel and Legend* (2007) and Lois Crozier-Hogle and Darryl Babe Wilson's *Surviving in Two Worlds: Contemporary Native American Voices* (1997) could be read in these terms as well.[129] These pieces followed the introduction that Sarris wrote for a special edition of *Studies in America Indian Literatures* in 1994, and all three pieces underline the importance of *storied* sovereignty.

---

128 I am indebted to Jill for her explanation of the process that resulted in the White Earth Constitution.

129 Lois Crozier-Hogle and Darryl Babe Wilson, *Chief Marin: Leader, Rebel and Legend* (Berkeley, CA: Heyday Books, 2007), ix–x; *Surviving in Two Worlds: Contemporary Native American Voices* (Austin: University of Texas Press, 1997), ix–x.

Sarris's life and work seems worthy of a book-length investigation, and I am sure we will not wait long for that publication, or several like it, to appear. Indeed, considering the tribal chairman's connections to Robert Redford and his penchant for the dramatic, there may even be a biopic. More importantly, the story about Sarris's leadership of the FIGR and the tribe's expression of its sovereign right to self-determination in the face of stiff opposition is about more than story or literary criticism alone. Hence, Sarris's position as fictionist and activist, academic and leader has revealed, in crystal clarity, the crucial interweave and imbrications that mesh scholarship and fiction to real-world or *hors-texte* concerns. It is that fact and that fact alone that I want to have as my focus in these closing pages to *Sovereign Stories*. It is hoped that this brief examination of the writer's close involvement in the tribe's efforts to initiate important economic, political, and social change, will complement and further those excellent readings of *Grand Avenue* and *Watermelon Nights* mentioned above. But more importantly, instead of "reading" Sarris's stories here, thereby attempting to make sense out of them, put some shape on them, or construe meaning, I would rather emphasize their essentially unlimited nature and the overall significance of that for Sarris, the Federated Indians of Graton Ranchera, and those of us who read and listen to the stories. If, as readers, we listen to these stories in the spirit in which they are told, a spirit of sharing across defined narratological, cultural, and spiritual spaces, then we might "learn lessons about what has gone wrong, what is right and healthful, and what we must do to connect with what is right and healthful."[130] We might also begin to appreciate the simple reality that the voices of the spirits, and tribal voices in general, "aren't going away. They aren't going to disappear and hide someplace."[131] By listening, by being *good* listeners, by being *good* neighbors, and by earning the trust and respect of the tellers of the tales that we are so interested in, non-Native readers will come to realize that there is nothing more important than the stories themselves; fundamentally, "the stories go round and round, on and on."[132]

---

130 *Surviving in Two Worlds*, x.
131 Ibid.
132 *Chief Marin*, x.

Bibliography

Agnew, David, "Nationalism," in *A Companion to Cultural Geography*, ed. James S. Duncan, Nuala C. Johnson, and Richard H. Schein, London: Blackwell, 2004, 223–237.

Aldama, Frederick Luis, review of *Red Matters: Native American Studies* by Arnold Krupat and *Grave Concerns, Trickster Turns: The Novels of Louis Owens* by Chris LaLonde, *American Literature* 75.3 (2003), 663–665.

Alexie, Sherman, *The Business of Fancydancing*, New York: Hanging Loose Press, 1992.

——, *First Indian on the Moon*, New York: Hanging Loose Press, 1993.

——, *Old Shirts and New Skins*, Los Angeles: American Indian Studies Center, University of California, 1993.

——, "In Response to Elizabeth Cook-Lynn's Pronouncement That I One of the New, Angry (Warriors) Kind of like Norman Schwarzkopf and Rush Limbaugh," *Wicazo Sa Review* 9.2 (Autumn 1993), 9.

——, *One Stick Song*, New York: Hanging Loose Press, 2000.

——, "What Sacagawea Means to Me [and Perhaps to You]," *Time* (July 8, 2002). <http://www.time.com/time/magazine/article/0.9171.1002814.00.html>

——, *The Toughest Indian in the World*, New York: Atlantic Monthly Press, 2000.

——, *Ten Little Indians*, New York: Grove Press, 2004.

——, "The World's Toughest Indian: Sherman Alexie: Author, Screenwriter, Trash-talker," interview by Jon Lurie, *Rake Magazine* (May 29, 2007). <http://archives.secretsofthecity.com/ magazine/ reporting/straight-talk/ world-s-toughest-indian>

——, *Conversations at KCTS 9*, directed by Enrique Cerna, Seattle: PBS—KCTS, 2008.

——, *Face*, New York: Hanging Loose Press, 2009.

——, *War Dances*, New York: Grove/Atlantic, 2009.

——, "The Lost Colony of Roanoke, 1587," *Guernica: A Magazine of Art and Politics*, <http://www.guernicamag.com/poetry/sherman_alexie_lost_colony_of_roa-noke_1587_ 8_1_11>

——, "Writers and Company," interview with Eleanor Wachtel, CBC radio (December 26, 2010). <http://www.cbc.ca/player/Radio/Writers+and+Company/2010/ ID/1720854498/>

——, "Sherman Alexie in Conversation with Ross Frank PhD," interview with Ross Frank. <http://www.youtube.com/watch?v=ZWolPAoDk3g>

Alfred, Taiaiake, "Sovereignty," in *Sovereignty Matters: Locations of Contestation and Possibility in Indigenous Struggles for Self-Determination*, ed. Joanne Barker, Lincoln: University of Nebraska Press, 2005, 33–50.

——, *Peace, Power, Righteousness: An Indigenous Manifesto*, Oxford: Oxford University Press, 2008.

Allen, Chadwick, *Blood Narrative: Indigenous Identity in American Indian and Maori Literary and Activist Texts*, Durham, NC: Duke University Press, 2002.

Allen, Paula Gunn, "Special Problems in Teaching Leslie Marmon Silko's *Ceremony*," *American Indian Quarterly* 14.4 (1990), 379–386.

——, *Off the Reservation: Reflections on Boundary-Busting, Border-Crossing Loose Canons*, Boston, MA: Beacon Press, 1998.

Anderson, Benedict, *Imagined Communities: Reflections on the Origins and Spread of Nationalism*, London: Verso, 1991.

Appleford, Rob, "A Response to Sam McKegney's 'Strategies for Ethical Engagement: An Open Letter Concerning Non-Native Scholars of Native Literatures'," *Studies in American Indian Literatures* 21.3 (Fall 2009), 58–65.

Barker, Joanne, "For Whom Sovereignty Matters," in *Sovereignty Matters: Locations of Contestation and Possibility in Indigenous Struggles for Self-Determination*, ed. Joanne Barker, Lincoln: University of Nebraska Press, 2005, 1–32.

Barthes, Roland, "Myth Today," in *A Barthes Reader*, ed. Susan Sontag, New York: Hill and Wang, 1982, 93–149.

Baudrillard, Jean, *Simulations*, Cambridge, MA: MIT Press, 1983.

Belsey, Catherine, *Critical Practice*, London: Routledge, 2002.

Bercovitch, Sacvan, *Nathanael West: Novels and Other Writings*, New York: Library of America, 1997.

——, "Deadpan Huck: Or, What's Funny about Interpretation," *The Kenyon Review* 24.3/4 (Summer 2002), 90–134.

Berger, John, *Ways of Seeing*, London: BBC/Penguin, 1972.

Berlo, Janet C., and Ruth B. Phillips, *Native North American Art*, Oxford: Oxford University Press, 1998.

Bevis, William, "Native American Novels: Homing In," in *Recovering the Word: Essays in Native American Literature*, ed. Brian Swann and Arnold Krupat, Berkeley: University of California Press, 1987, 580–619.

Bhabha, Homi K., *The Location of Culture*, London: Routledge, 1994.

Bibby, Brian *The Fine Art of California Indian Basketry*, Berkeley, CA: Heyday Books, 1996.

Bird, Gloria, "Towards a Decolonization of the Mind and Text 1: Leslie Marmon Silko's *Ceremony*," *Wicazo SA Review* 9.2 (1993), 1–8.

Blewster, Kelly, "Tribal Visions," *Biblio* (March 1999), 22–29.

Bolter, Jay David, and Richard Grusin, *Remediation: Understanding New Media*, Cambridge, MA: MIT Press, 2000.

Bradley, David, "March 1989 Interview by Dorothee Peiper-Riegraf." <www.peiper-riegraf-collection.com>

Brehm, Victoria, "The Metamorphoses of an Ojibwa *Manido*," *American Literature* 68 (1996), 677–706.

Brooks, Lisa, "Digging at the Roots: Locating an Ethical, Native Criticism," in *Reasoning Together: The Native Critics Collective*, ed. Craig S. Womack, Daniel Heath Justice, and Christopher B. Teuton, Norman: University of Oklahoma Press, 2008, 234–264.

——, *The Common Pot: The Recovery of Native Space in the Northeast*, Minneapolis: University of Minnesota Press, 2008.

Bruyneel, Kevin, *The Third Space of Sovereignty: The Postcolonial Politics of US–Indigenous Relations*, Minneapolis: University of Minnesota Press, 2007.

Burnham, Michelle, "Pomo Basketweaving, Poison, and the Politics of Restoration in Greg Sarris's *Grand Avenue*," *Studies in American Indian Literatures* 14.4 (2002), 18–36.

Butler, Judith, "Performative Acts and Gender Constitution: An Essay in Phenomenology and Feminist Theory," in *Performing Feminisms: Feminist Critical Theory and Theatre*, ed. Sue-Ellen Case, Baltimore, MD: Johns Hopkins University Press, 1990, 270–282.

Camille, Michael, "Simulacrum," in *Critical Terms for Art History*, ed. Robert S. Nelson and Richard Shiff, Chicago, IL: University of Chicago Press, 1996, 31–32.

Campbell, Duncan, "Voice of the New Tribes," *The Guardian* (January 4, 2003). <http://www.guardian.co.uk/ books/2003/jan/04/artsfeatures.fiction>

Carlson, David J., "Trickster Hermeneutics and the Postindian Reader: Gerald Vizenor's Constitutional Praxis," *Studies in American Indian Literatures* 23.4 (2011), 13–47.

Caruth, Cathy, "Trauma and Experience," in *The Holocaust: Theoretical Readings*, ed. Neil Levi and Michael Rothberg, Edinburgh: Edinburgh University Press, 2003, 192–198.

Chakraborty, Mridula Nath, "Wa(i)ving It All Away Producing Subject and Knowledge in Feminisms of Colours," in *Third Wave Feminism: A Critical Exploration*, ed. Stacy Gillis, Gillian Howie, and Rebecca Munford, London: Palgrave Macmillan, 2011, 101–113.

Charles, Ron, "Love in the Time of Bitterness," review of *Shadow Tag* by Louise
    Erdrich, *Washington Post* (February 3, 2010). <http://articles.washingtonpost.
    com/2010-0203/news/36852962_1_shadow-tag-louise-erdrich-irene>
Christie, Stuart, *Plural Sovereignties and Contemporary Indigenous Literature*, New
    York: Palgrave Macmillan, 2009.
Cihlar, James, review of *Shadow Tag* by Louise Erdrich, *Prairie Schooner* 85.1 (Spring
    2011), 173–176.
Cixous, Hélène, "The Laugh of the Medusa," trans. Keith Cohen and Paula Cohen,
    in *The New French Feminisms*, ed. Elaine Marks and Isabelle de Courtivron,
    Amherst: University of Massachusetts Press, 1980.
Cohen, Dorrit, *Transparent Minds: Narrative Modes for Presenting Consciousness in
    Fiction*, Princeton, NJ: Princeton University Press, 1978.
Colum, Padraic, "With James Joyce in Ireland," *New York Times* (June 11, 1922).
    <http://www.nytimes.com/books/00/01/09/specials/joyce-colum.html>
Cook-Lynn, Elizabeth, "The Radical Conscience in Native American Studies," *Wicazo
    Sa Review* 7.2 (Autumn 1991), 9–13.
——, "American Indian Intellectualism and the New Indian Story," *American Indian
    Quarterly* 20.1, "Special Issue: Writing about (Writing about) American Indians"
    (Winter 1996), 57–76.
——, *Aurelia: A Crow Creek Trilogy*, Boulder: University of Colorado Press, 1999.
——, "Reclaiming American Indian Studies," in Elizabeth Cook-Lynn, Tom Holm,
    John Red Horse, and James Riding, *Wicazo Sa Review* 20.1, "Colonization/
    Decolonization, II" (Spring 2005), 169–177.
——, *Anti-Indianism in Modern America: A Voice from Tatekeya's Earth*, Champaign:
    University of Illinois Press, 2007.
——, *A Separate Country: Postcoloniality and American Indian Nations*, Lubbock:
    Texas Tech University Press, 2012.
Cox, James H., *Muting White Noise: Native American and European American Novel
    Traditions*, Norman: University of Oklahoma Press, 2005.
——, "The Past, Present, and Possible Futures of American Indian Literary Studies,"
    Studies in American Indian Literatures 20.2 (Summer 2008), 102–112.
Crawford, Suzanne J., and Dennis F. Kelley, *American Indian Religious Traditions:
    An Encyclopaedia*, Santa Barbara, CA: AB-CLIO, 2005.
Crozier-Hogle, Lois and Darryl Babe Wilson, *Surviving in Two Worlds: Contemporary
    Native American Voices*, Austin: University of Texas Press, 1997.
Daleski, H.M., *Unities: Studies in the English Novel*, Athens: University of Georgia
    Press, 1985.
d'Errico, Peter, "American Indian Sovereignty: Now you see it, Now you Don't."
    <http://www.umass.edu/legal/derrico/nowyouseeit.html>

de Man, Paul, *Blindness and Insight: Essays in the Rhetoric of Contemporary Criticism*, Oxford: Routledge, 1996.

de Lauretis, Theresa, 1986, "Feminist Studies/Critical Studies: Issues, Terms, and Contexts," in *Feminist Studies/Critical Studies*, ed. Teresa de Lauretis, Bloomington: Indiana University Press, 1986.

Deane, Seamus, "Joyce the Irishman," in *The Cambridge Companion to James Joyce*, ed. Derek Attridge, Cambridge: Cambridge University Press, 2004.

Deloria Jr., Vine, review of *Anti-Indianism in Modern America: A Voice from Tatekeya's Earth* by Elizabeth Cook-Lynn, *Pacific Historical Review* 71.3 (August 2002), 487–489.

Dennis, Helen May, *Native American Literature: Towards a Spatialized Reading*, London: Routledge, 2007.

Derrida, Jacques, *Of Grammatology*, trans. Gayatri Chakravorty Spivak [1974], Baltimore, MD: Johns Hopkins University Press, 1997.

Doerfler, Jill, "An Anishinaabe Tribalography: Investigating and Interweaving Conceptions of Identity during the 1910s on the White Earth Reservation," *American Indian Quarterly*, 33.3 (2009), 295–324.

Dreyfus, Hubert L., and Paul Rainbow, *Michel Foucault: Beyond Structuralism and Hermeneutics*, ed. Hubert L. Dreyfus and Paul Rainbow, Chicago, IL: University of Chicago Press, 1983.

Durham, Jimmie, and Jean Fisher, "The Ground has been Covered," *Art Form* (Summer 1988).

Dyck, Reginald, "Practicing Sovereignty in Greg Sarris's *Watermelon Nights*," *Western American Literature* 45.4 (Winter 2011), 340–361.

Erdrich, Louise, *Tracks*, New York: Flamingo, 1994.

——, *Books and Islands in Ojibwe Country*, Washington DC: National Geographic Society, 2003.

——, review of "Louis Riel, A Comic Strip Biography" by Chester Brown, *The Circle: Native American News and Arts* (February 8, 2009). <http://thecirclenews.org/index.php?option=com_content&task=view&id=68&Itemid=50>

——, "Interview with Louise Erdrich," Bill Moyers, PBS (April 9, 2010). <http://www.pbs.org/ moyers/journal/04092010/watch2.html>

——, *Shadow Tag*, New York: Harper Perennial, 2011.

Eckermann, Elizabeth, "Foucault, Embodiment and Gender Subjectivities: The Case of Voluntary Self-Starvation," in *Foucault, Health and Medicine*, London: Routledge, 1997, 151–172.

Egan, Timothy, "An Indian Without Reservations," *New York Times* (January 18, 1998).

Fagan, Kristina, "Tewatatha:wi: Aboriginal Nationalism in Taiaiake Alfred's *Peace, Power, Righteousness: An Indigenous Manifesto*," *American Indian Quarterly* 28.1–2 (Winter/Spring 2004), 12–29.

Fall, Juliet, *Drawing the Line: Nature, Hybridity, and Politics in Transboundary Spaces*, London: Ashgate, 2005.

Ferrari, Rita, "'Where the Maps Stopped': The Aesthetics of Borders in Louise Erdrich's *Love Medicine* and *Tracks*," *Style* 33.1 (1999), 144–165.

Fitz, Karsten, review of *Little*, by David Treuer, *American Indian Culture and Research Journal* 22.1–2 (1998), 271–275.

Fletcher, Matthew L.M., "*Native American Fiction* Tough on Indian Culture," *Indian Country Today* (August 3, 2007). <http://works.bepress.com/cgi/viewcontent, cgi?article=1021&context=matthew_fletcher>

Foucault, Michel, *The Use of Pleasure*, trans. Robert Hurley, London: Vintage Books, 1990.

Freedman, Diane P., "Border Crossing as Method and Motif in Contemporary American Writing, or, How Freud Helped Me Case the Joint," in *The Intimate Critique: Autobiographical Literary Criticism*, ed. Diane P. Freedman, Olivia Frey, and Frances Murphy Zauhar, Durham, NC: Duke University Press, 1993, 13–22.

Gamber, John, "Born out of the Creek Landscape: Reconstructing Community and Continuance in Craig Womack's *Drowning in Fire*," *MELUS* 34.2, "Ethnicity and Ecocriticism" (Summer 2009), 103–123.

Gates, Henry Louis, *Figures in Black: Words, Signs, and the "Racial" Self*, Oxford: Oxford University Press, 1987.

——, "'Ethnic and Minority' Studies," in *Introduction to Scholarship in Modern Languages and Literatures*, ed. Joseph Gibaldi, 2nd edn, New York: Modern Language Association, 1992, 288–302.

Gaudio, Michael, *Engraving the Savage*, Minneapolis: University of Minnesota Press, 2008.

Gellner, Ernst, and John Breuilly, *Nations and Nationalisms: New Perspectives on the Past*, Ithaca, NY: Cornell University Press, 2009.

Geniusz, Wendy Djinn, *Our Knowledge is Not Primitive: Decolonizing Botanical Anishinaabe Teachings*, Syracuse, NY: Syracuse University Press, 2009.

Genocchio, Benjamin, "Art Review: A Horse Trader's Daughter, With Visions of Injustice," *New York Times* (November 12, 2006).

Gillan, Jennifer, "Reservation Home Movies: Sherman Alexie's Poetry," *American Literature* 68.1, "Write Now: American Literature in the 1980s and 1990s" (March 1996), 91–110.

Goerke, Betty, *Chief Marin: Leader, Rebel and Legend*, Berkeley: Heyday Books, 2007.

Grassian, Daniel, *Understanding Sherman Alexie*, Columbia: University of South Carolina Press, 2005.

Greene, Graham, *The End of the Affair* [1951], London: Vintage, 2004.

Green, Michelle, "The Final Chapter: Facing Divorce and Sex-Abuse Allegations, Author Michael Dorris Takes His Own Life," *People Magazine* (April 28, 1997). <http://www.people.com/people /archive/article/0.20121946.00.html>

Gross, Lawrence, "The Comic Vision of Anishinaabe Culture and Religion," *American Indian Quarterly* 26.3 (Summer 2002), 436–459.

Gubar, Susan and Joan Hoff, *For Adult Users Only: The Dilemma of Violent Pornography*, Bloomington: University of Indiana Press, 1989.

Hagen Cohen, Leah, "Cruel Love," review of Louise Erdrich's *Shadow Tag*, *New York Times* (February 5, 2010). <http://www.nytimes.com/2010/02/07/books/ review/Cohen-t.html?pagewanted=all&_r=0>

Halberstam, Judith, *In a Queer Time and Place: Transgender Bodies, Subcultural Lives*, New York: New York University Press, 2005.

Hardack, Richard, "'A Music Seeking Its Words': Double-Timing and Double-Consciousness in Toni Morrison's *Jazz*," *Callaloo* 18.2 (1995), 451–471.

Heider, Karl G., "The Rashomon Effect: When Ethnographers Disagree," *American Anthropologist* 90.1 (1988), 73–81.

Henry Jr., Gordon, Nieves Pascual Soler, and Silvia Martinez-Falquina, *Stories Through Theories/Theories Through Stories: North American Indian Writing, Storytelling, and Critique*, East Lansing: Michigan State University Press, 2009.

Herman, Matthew D., "'The Making of Relatives': Sovereignty and Cosmopolitan Democracies," in *Foundations of First People's Sovereignty: History, Education and Culture*, ed. Ulrike Wiethaus, New York: Peter Lang, 2008, 21–42.

——, *Politics and Aesthetics in Contemporary Native American Literature: Across Every Border*, New York: Routledge, 2009.

Holland, Sharon P., "The Revolution, 'In Theory'," *American Literary History* 12.1–2 (Spring–Summer 2000), 327–336.

Hollrah, Patrice, "Decolonizing the Choctaws: Teaching LeAnne Howe's *Shell Shaker*," *American Indian Quarterly* 28.1–2 (2004), 73–85.

Hough, Sheridan, "Phenomenology, Pomo Baskets, and the Work of Mabel McKay," *Hypatia* 18.2 (Spring 2003), 103–113.

Houston, Robert, "Stealing Cattle and a Way of Life," *New York Times Book Review* (September 8, 1991), 35.

Howe, LeAnne, "Tribalography: The Power of Native Stories," *Journal of Dramatic Theory and Criticism* 14 (1999), 117–126.

——, "My Mothers, My Uncles, Myself," in *Here First: Autobiographical Essays by Native American Writers*, ed. Arnold Krupat and Brian Swann, New York: Modern Library, 2000, 212–228.

——, *Shell Shaker*, San Francisco: Aunt Lute Books, 2001.

——, "Blind Bread and the Business of Theory Making: By Embarrassed Grief," in *Reasoning Together: The Native Critics Collective*, ed. Craig S. Womack, Daniel Heath Justice, and Christopher B. Teuton, Norman: University of Oklahoma Press, 2008, 325–339.

Jaggi, Maya, "All Rage and Heart," interview with Sherman Alexie, *The Guardian* (May 3, 2008). <http://www.guardian.co.uk/books/2008/may/03/featuresreviews. guardianreview13>

Jahner, Elaine, *Spaces of the Mind: Narrative and Community in the American West*, Lincoln: University of Nebraska Press, 2004.

Johnson, Kelli Lyon, "Writing Deeper Maps: Mapmaking, Local Indigenous Knowledges, and Literary Nationalism in Native Women's Writing," *Studies in American Indian Literatures* 19.4 (Winter 2007), 103–120.

Justice, Daniel Heath, "Seeing (and Reading) Red," in *Indigenizing the Academy: Transforming and Empowering Communities*, ed. Devon Abbott Mihesuah and Angela Cavender Wilson, Lincoln: University of Nebraska Press, 2004, 100–123.

——, *Our Fire Survives the Storm: A Cherokee Literary History*, Minneapolis: University of Minnesota Press, 2006.

——, "'Go Away, Water!': Kinship Criticism and the Decolonization Imperative," in *Reasoning Together: The Native Critics Collective*, ed. Craig S. Womack, Daniel Heath Justice, and Christopher B. Teuton, Norman: University of Oklahoma Press, 2008, 147–168.

Kalb, John D., review of *Native American Fiction: A User's Manual* and *The Translation of Dr Apelles: A Love Story* by David Treuer, *Studies in American Indian Literatures* 20.2 (Summer 2008), 113–116.

Kermode, Frank, *The Sense of an Ending: Studies in the Theory of Fiction* [1967], Oxford: Oxford University Press, 2000.

Kilpatrick, Jacquelyn, *Celluloid Indians: Native Americans and Film*, Lincoln: University of Nebraska Press, 1999.

King, Thomas, *The Truth About Stories*, Minneapolis: University of Minnesota Press, 2005.

Kirwan, Padraig, "Language and Signs: An Interview with Ojibwe Novelist David Treuer," *Journal of American Studies* 43.1 (2009), 71–88.

Kolodny, Annette, *The Lay of the Land: Metaphor as Experience and History in American Life and Letters*, Chapel Hill: University of North Carolina Press, 1984.

Konigsberg, Eric, "In His Own Literary World, a Native Son without Borders," *New York Times* (October 20, 2009). <http://www.nytimes.com/2009/10/21/ books/21alexie.html?_r=0>

Konkle, Maureen, "Indian Literacy, US Colonialism, and Literary Criticism," in *Postcolonial Theory and the United States: Race Ethnicity, and Literature*, ed.

Amritjit Singh and Peter Schmidt, Jackson: University of Mississippi Press, 2000, 151–174.

Krupat, Arnold, "Scholarship and Native American Studies: A Response to Daniel Littlefield, Jr.," *American Studies* 34.2 (1993), 81–100.

——, "Nationalism, Indigenism, Cosmopolitanism: Critical Perspectives on Native American Literatures," *Centennial Review* 42.3 (1998), 617–626.

——, *The Turn to the Native: Studies in Criticism and Culture*, Lincoln: University of Nebraska Press, 1998.

——, "Culturalism and Its Discontents: David Treuer's *Native American Fiction: A User's Manual*," *American Indian Quarterly* 33.1 (Winter 2009), 131–160.

Ladino, Jennifer K., "'A Limited Range of Motion?' Multiculturalism, 'Human Questions,' and Urban Indian Identity in Sherman Alexie's *Ten Little Indians*," *Studies in American Indian Literatures* 21.3 (Fall 2009), 36–57.

Laub, Dori, "Bearing Witness or the Vicissitudes of Listening," in *The Holocaust: Theoretical Readings*, ed. Neil Levi and Michael Rothberg, Edinburgh: Edinburgh University Press, 2003, 221–226.

Lazarus, Neil, *The Postcolonial Unconscious*, Cambridge: Cambridge University Press, 2011.

Leibovich, Mark, "A Senate Naysayer, Spoiling for Health Care Fight," *New York Times* (October 29, 2009). <http://www.nytimes.com/2009/10/30/health/policy/30coburn.html>

Levin, Amy K., *Gender Sexuality and Museums: A Routledge Reader*, Oxford: Routledge, 2010.

Levine, George, "Literary Realism Reconsidered: 'The world in its length and breadth,'" in *Adventures in Realism*, ed. Matthew Beaumont, London: Blackwell, 2007, 13–32.

Lincoln, Kenneth, "Red Stick Lit Crit," review of *Red on Red: Native American Literary Separatism* by Craig S. Womack, *Indian Country Today* 26.44.

Loomba, Ania, *Colonialism/Postcolonialism*, London: Routledge, 2005.

Lyons, Scott Richard, "Rhetorical Sovereignty: What Do American Indians Want from Writing?" *College Composition and Communication* 51.3 (2000), 447–468.

——, "Battle of the Bookworms," *Indian Country Today* (August 10, 2007). <http://groups.yahoo.com/group/NatNews/message/45678?var=1>

——, *X-marks: Native Signatures of Assent*, Minneapolis: University of Minnesota Press, 2010.

Lyotard, Jean-François, *The Differend: Phrases in Dispute*, trans. Georges Van Den Abbeele, Manchester: Manchester University Press, 1988.

Mermann-Jozwiak, Elizabeth, "Re-membering the Body: Body Politics in Toni Morrison's *The Bluest Eye*," *Literature Interpretation Theory* 12.2 (2001), 189–204.

Michael, John, *Anxious Intellects: Academic Professionals, Public Intellectuals, and Enlightenment Values*, Durham, NC: Duke University Press, 2000.

Milesi, Laurent, "Introduction: Language(s) with a Difference," *James Joyce and the Difference of Language*, ed. Laurent Milesi, Cambridge: Cambridge University Press, 2004.

Millet, Larry, *AIA Guide to the Twin Cities*, Minneapolis: Minnesota Historical Society Press, 2007.

Milofsky, David, "A Hard Look at American Indian Writers," *Denver Post* (September 3, 2006). <http://denverpost.com/bookbeat/ci_4269459#ixzz1R9eiUWfI>

Miscevic, Nenad, "Nationalism," In *The Stanford Encyclopedia of Philosophy*. <http://plato.stanford.edu/archives/fall2008/entries/nationalism>

Momaday, N. Scott, *House Made of Dawn* (1968), New York: Harper Collins, 1999.

——, "Landscape with Words in the Foreground," in *Old Southwest New Southwest: Essays on a Region and its Literature*, ed. Judy Nolte Lensink, Tucson: Tucson Public Library, 1987.

Montague, John, "The Unpartitioned Intellect," in *Irish Writers and Society at Large*, ed. Masaru Sekine, Totowa, NJ: Barnes and Noble Imports, 1985.

Moore, David L., "Sherman Alexie: Irony, Intimacy, and Agency," in *The Cambridge Companion to Native American Literature*, ed. Joy Porter and Kenneth M. Roemer, Cambridge: Cambridge University Press, 2005, 297–310.

Morley, Catherine "Plotting against America: 9/11 and the Spectacle of Terror in Contemporary American Fiction," *Gramma/Γράμμα: Journal of Theory and Criticism* 16 (2008), 293–312.

Morrison, Toni, *Playing in the Dark: Whiteness and the Literary Imagination*, Cambridge, MA: Harvard University Press, 1992.

Morse, John D., "Oral History interview with Edward Hopper" (June 17, 1959), Archives of American Art. <http://www.aaa.si.edu/collections/interviews/oral-history-interview-edward-hopper-11844>

Moss, Laura, "'The Plague of Normality': Reconfiguring Realism in Postcolonial Theory," *Jouvert: A Journal of Postcolonial Studies* 5.1 (Autumn 2000). <social.chass.nesu.edu/jouvert/v5i1/moss.htm>

Murray, David, *Forked Tongues: Speech, Writing and Representation in North American Indian Texts*, London: Pinter, 1991.

Neary, Lynn, "From Erdrich, a Page Turner with Deceit at Heart," review of *Shadow Tag* by Louise Erdrich (February 7, 2010). <http://www.npr.org/templates/story/story.php?storyId=123420779>

Nelson, Joshua, "'Humor Is My Green Card': A Conversation with Sherman Alexie, *World Literature Today* (July–August 2010), 37–43.

New, W.H., "Learning to Listen," in *Native Writers and Canadian Writing*, ed. W.H. New, Vancouver: University of British Columbia Press, 1990, 4–10.

Niatum, Duane, "On Stereotypes," in *Recovering the Word: Essays on Native American Literature*, ed. Brian Swann and Arnold Krupat, Berkeley: University of California Press, 1987, 552–562.

Nolan, Emer, *James Joyce and Nationalism*, London: Routledge, 1995.

Novak, Amy, "'A Marred Testament': Cultural Trauma and Narrative in Danticat's *The Farming of Bones*," *Arizona Quarterly* 62.4 (2006), 93–120.

Nygren, Åse, "A World of Story-Smoke: A Conversation with Sherman Alexie," *MELUS* 30.4, "Home: Forged or Forged?" (Winter 2005), 149–169.

O'Brien, Eugene, "The Question of Theory," *Other Voices* 2.2 (2002). <http://www. othervoices.org/2.2/obrien>

O'Connor, Flannery, *Mystery and Manners: Occasional Prose*, New York: Farrar, Straus, & Giroux, 1969.

Owens, Louis, *Mixedblood Messages: Literature, Film, Family, Place*, Norman: University of Oklahoma Press, 1998.

Page, Philip, "Traces of Derrida in Toni Morrison's *Jazz*," *African American Review* 29 (1995), 55–66.

Paperno, Irina, "What Can Be Done with Diaries?" *Russian Review* 63.4 (October 2004), 561–573.

Parker, Robert Dale, *The Invention of Native American Literature*, Ithaca, NY: Cornell University Press, 2003.

Peach, Linden, *Toni Morrison*, New York: Palgrave, 1998.

Pease, Donald E., "Author," in *Critical Terms for Literary Study*, ed. Frank Lentricchia and Thomas McLaughlin, Chicago, IL: University of Chicago Press, 1995, 105–121.

Peterson, Nancy J., "History, Postmodernism, and Louise Erdrich's *Tracks*," *PMLA* 109.5 (October 1994), 982–994.

——, "Introduction: On Incendiary Art, the Moral Imagination, and Toni Morrison," *Modern Fiction Studies* 52 (2006), 261–269.

Philpott, Dan, "Sovereignty," in *The Stanford Encyclopedia of Philosophy*. <http:// plato.stanford.edu/entries/sovereignty>

Pinsker, Sanford, "The Tortoise and the Hare: Or, Philip Roth, Cynthia Ozick, and the Vagaries of Fiction Writing," *Virginia Quarterly Review* 81 (2005), 214–224.

Pinter, Harold, "Art, Truth & Politics" (Nobel Lecture, 2005). <http://www.nobel-prize.org/nobel_prizes/literature/laureates/2005/pinter-lecture.html>

Porter, Joy, "'Primitive' Discourse: Aspects of Contemporary North American Indian Representations of the Irish and of Contemporary Irish Representations of North American Indians," *American Studies* 49.3/4 (Fall/Winter 2008), 63–85.

Powell, Malea, "Blood and Scholarship: One Mixed Blood's Story," in *Race, Rhetoric, and Composition*, ed. Keith Gilyard, Portsmouth, NH: Boynton/Cook, 1999, 1–16.

Pulitano, Elvira, *Toward a Native American Literary Theory*, Lincoln: University of Nebraska Press, 2004.

——, "Crossreading Texts, Crossreading Identity: Hybridity, Diaspora and Transculturation in Louis Owens' *Mixedblood Messages*," in *Louis Owens: Literary Reflections on his Life* and *Work*, ed. Jacquelyn Kilpatrick, Norman: University of Oklahoma Press, 2004, 79–102.

Purdy, Anthony, "Introduction," in *Literature and the Body*, ed. Anthony Purdy, Amsterdam: Rodopi, 1992.

Rabinowitz, Sima, review of *Little* by David Treuer, *Hungry Mind Review* (August 14, 2001).

Rader, Dean, *Engaged Resistance: American Indian Art, Literature, and Film from Alcatraz to the NMAI*, Austin: University of Texas Press, 2011.

Raheja, Michelle H., "Reading Nanook's Smile: Visual Sovereignty, Indigenous Revisions of Ethnography, and Atanarjuat (The Fast Runner)," *American Quarterly* 59.4 (2007), 1159–1185.

Reid, E. Shelley, "The Stories We Tell: Louise Erdrich's Identity Narratives," *MELUS* 25.3/4, "Revising Traditions" double issue (Autumn–Winter 2000), 65–86.

Rifkin, Mark, "Native Nationality and the Contemporary Queer: Tradition, Sexuality, and History in *Drowning in Fire*," *American Indian Quarterly* 32.4 (Fall 2008), 443–470.

Roberson, Susan L., "Translocations and Transformations: Identity in N. Scott Momaday's *The Ancient Child*," *American Indian Quarterly* 22.1/2 (1998), 31–45.

Roth, Wendy D., and Jal D. Mehta, "The Rashomon Effect: Combining Positivist and Interpretivist Approaches in the Analysis of Contested Events," *Sociological Methods Research* 31.2 (November 2002), 131–173.

Rothberg, Michael, "A Failure of the Imagination: Diagnosing the Post-9/11 Novel: A Response to Richard Gray," *American Literary History* 21.1 (2009), 152–158.

Rozelle, Page, "The Teller and the Tale: History and the Oral Tradition in Elizabeth Cook-Lynn's *Aurelia: A Crow Creek Trilogy*," *American Indian Quarterly* 25.2 (Spring 2001), 203–215.

Ruppert, James, "Mediation and Multiple Narrative in Contemporary Native American Fiction," *Texas Studies in Literature and Language* 28 (1986), 209–225.

Said, Edward, *Reflections on Exile and Other Essays*, Cambridge, MA: Harvard University Press, 2000.

Sanders, Karla, "A Healthy Balance: Religion, Identity, and Community in Louise Erdrich's *Love Medicine*," *MELUS* 23.2 (Summer 1998), 129–155.

Sands, Kathleen M., "Louise Erdrich's Love Medicine," *Studies in American Indian Literatures* 9.1 (1985), 12–24.

Sandoz, Devin, "simulation / simulacrum." <http://lucian.uchicago.edu/blogs/mediatheory/keywords/simulation-simulacrum>

Sarris, Greg, *Keeping Slug Woman Alive: A Holistic Approach to American Indian Texts*, Los Angeles: University of California Press, 1993.

Scholder, Fritz, "Fritz Scholder," Academy of Achievement interview (July 29, 1996). <http://www.achievement.org/autodoc/page/sch1int-1>

——, "Fritz Scholder: Indian/not Indian," exhibition brochure, Washington DC: National Museum of the American Indian, 2008.

Semmel, K.E., "An Interview with Sherman Alexie," *The Writer's Chronicle* 43.6 (May/Summer 2011). <https://www.awpwriter.org/library/writers_chronicle_issues/maysummer_2011>

Sequoya Magdaleno, Jane, "How (!) is an Indian? A Contest of Stories, Round 2," in *Postcolonial Theory and the United States: Race Ethnicity, and Literature*, ed. Amritjit Singh and Peter Schmidt, Jackson: University of Mississippi Press, 2000, 279–299.

Shackleton, Mark, "'June Walked over It like Water and Came Home': Cross-Cultural Symbolism in Louise Erdrich's *Love Medicine* and *Tracks*," in *Transatlantic Voices: Interpretations of Native North American Literatures*, ed. Elvira Pulitano, Lincoln: University of Nebraska Press, 2007, 188–205.

Shanley, Kathryn, "'Born from the Need to Say': Boundaries and Sovereignties in Native American Literary and Cultural Studies," in *Native American Literature: Boundaries and Sovereignties*, a special edition of *Paradoxia: Studies in World Literary Genres* (2001), 3–16.

Shklovsky, Victor, "Art as Technique," in *Russian Formalist Criticism: Four Essays*, ed. Lee T. Lemon and Marion J. Reis, Lincoln: University of Nebraska Press, 1965, 3–24.

Showalter, Elaine "Killing the Angel in the House: The Autonomy of Women Writers," *Antioch Review* 50.1/2 (Winter/Spring 1992), 207–220.

Smith, Dinitia, "Heroes Now Tend to Be More Hard Edged, Urban, and Pop Orientated," *New York Times* (April 21, 1997). <http://www.nytimes.com/1997/04/21/books/heroes-nowtend-to-be-more-hard-edged-urban-and-pop-oriented.html>

Smyth, Gerry, "The Politics of Hybridity: Some Problems with Crossing the Border," in *Comparing Post-Colonial Literatures: Dislocations*, ed. Patricia Murray and Ashok Bery, London: Macmillan, 2000, 43–58.

Sparke, Matthew, "Mapped Bodies and Disembodied Maps: (Dis)placing Cartographic Struggle in Colonial Canada," in *Places Through the Body*, ed. Heidi J. Nast and Steve Pile, New York: Routledge, 1998, 305–336.

Squint, Kirstin, "Choctawan Aesthetics, Spirituality, and Gender Relations: An Interview with LeAnne Howe," *MELUS* 35.3 (Fall 2010), 211–224.

Steinmetz, Paul "Sherman Alexie shakes up university crowd," March 22, 2011. <http://blog. ctnews.com/steinmetz/2011/03/22/sherman-alexie-shakes-up-university-crowd>

Stirrup, David, "Life after Death in Poverty: David Treuer's *Little*," *American Indian Quarterly* 29.3–4 (Summer–Fall 2005), 651–72.

Stokes, Karah, "What About the Sweetheart?: The 'Different Shape of Anishinabe Two Sisters Stories in Louise Erdrich's Love Medicine and Tales of Burning Love," *MELUS* 24.2 (Summer 1999), 89–105.

Stripes, James, "'We Think in Terms of What Is Fair': Justice versus 'Just Compensation' in Elizabeth Cook-Lynn's *From the River's Edge*," *Wicazo Sa Review* 12.1 (Spring 1997), 165–187.

Suleiman, Susan Rubin, *The Female Body in Western Culture: Contemporary Perspectives*, Cambridge, MA: Harvard University Press, 1986.

Swift, Graham, *Waterland* [1983], New York: Vintage, 1992.

Tatonetti, Lisa, "The Emergence and Importance of Queer American Indian Literatures: Or, 'Help and Stories' in Thirty Years of *SAIL*," *Studies in American Indian Literatures* 19.4 (2007), 143–170.

Taylor, Christopher, "North America as Contact Zone: Native American Literary Nationalism and the Cross-Cultural Dilemma," *Studies in American Indian Literatures* 22.3 (Fall 2010), 26–44.

Terry, Don, "From '80 Crime, White–Sioux Tension Today," *New York Times* (February 20, 1996). <http://www.nytimes.com/1996/02/20/us/from-80-crime-white-sioux-tension-today.html?pagewanted=all&src=pm>

Teuton, Christopher B., "Theorizing American Indian Literature: Applying Oral Concepts to Written Traditions," In *Reasoning Together: The Native Critics Collective*, ed. Craig S. Womack, Daniel Heath Justice, and Christopher B. Teuton, Norman: University of Oklahoma Press, 2008, 193–215.

Teuton, Sean, "Placing the Ancestors: Postmodernism, 'Realism,' and American Indian Identity in James Welch's *Winter in the Blood*," *American Indian Quarterly* 25 (2001), 626–650.

——, *Red Land, Red Power: Grounding Knowledge in the American Indian Novel*, Durham, NC: Duke University Press, 2008.

——, "The Callout: Writing American Indian Politics," in *Reasoning Together: The Native Critics Collective*, ed. Craig S. Womack, Daniel Heath Justice, and Christopher B. Teuton, Norman: University of Oklahoma Press, 2008, 105–125.

Tobin, Dan, *Awake in America: On Irish American Poetry*, Notre Dame, IN: Notre Dame University Press, 2011.

Treuer, David, *Little*, London: Granta, 1997.

——, "Reading Culture," *Studies in American Indian Literatures* 14.1 (Spring 2002), 51–64.

——, *Native American Fiction: A User's Manual*, Minneapolis, MN: Graywolf, 2006.

——, "A Language Too Beautiful to Lose," *Los Angeles Times* (February 3, 2008). <http://articles.latimes.com/2008/feb/03/books/bk-treuer3>

——, "Little Doesn't Wear Feathers," interview. <http://www.pioneerplanet.com/columnists/docs/GROSSMAN/docs/009265.htm>

Tuhkanen, Mikko, *The American Optic: Psychoanalysis, Critical Race Theory and Richard Wright*, Albany, NY: SUNY Press, 2009.

Van Houtum, Henk, Olivier Kramsch and Wolfgang Zierhofer, *B/ordering Space*, London: Ashgate, 2005.

Vizenor, Gerald, "The Ruins of Representation: Shadow Survivance and the Literature of Dominance," *American Indian Quarterly* 17.1 (Winter 1993), 7–30.

——, *Manifest Manners: Narratives on Postindian Survivance*, Lincoln: University of Nebraska Press, 1994.

——, "George Morrison: Anishinaabe Expressionist Artist," *American Indian Quarterly* 30.3–4 (Summer/Fall 2006), 646–660.

Vorderer, Peter, *Suspense: Conceptualizations, Theoretical Analyses, and Empirical Explorations*, London: Routledge, 1996.

Warren, Kenneth W., "Delimiting America: The Legacy of Du Bois," *American Literary History* 1 (1989), 172–189.

Warrior, Robert, *Tribal Secrets: Recovering American Indian Intellectual Traditions*, Minneapolis: University of Minnesota Press, 1995.

Washburn, Franci, "The Risk of Misunderstanding in Greg Sarris's *Keeping Slug Woman Alive: A Holistic Approach to American Indian Texts*," *Studies in American Indian Literatures* 16.3 (Fall 2004), 70–82.

Watson, Bruce, "George Catlin's Obsession," *Smithsonian* (December 2002). <http://www.smithsonianmag.com/arts-culture/catlin.html?c=y&page=3>

Weaver, Jace, Craig S. Womack, and Robert Warrior, *American Indian Literary Nationalism*, Albuquerque: University of New Mexico Press, 2006.

——, *That the People Might Live: Native American Literatures and Native American Community*, New York: Oxford University Press, 1997.

——, *Other Words: American Indian Literature, Law, and Culture*, Norman: University of Oklahoma Press, 2001.

——, "Splitting the Earth: First Utterances and Pluralist Separatism," in *American Indian Literary Nationalism*, ed. Jace Weaver, Craig S. Womack, and Robert Warrior, Albuquerque: University of New Mexico Press, 2006, 1–90.

West, Shearer, *Portraiture*, Oxford: Oxford University Press, 2004.

Wiebe, Robert H., *Who We Are: A History of Popular Nationalism*, Princeton, NJ: Princeton University Press, 2002.

Wiethaus, Ulrike, *Foundations of First People's Sovereignty: History, Education and Culture*, New York: Peter Lang, 2008.

Wilde, Oscar, "The Decay of Lying: An Observation," in *The Complete Writings of Oscar Wilde*, together with essays and stories by Lady Wilde, vol. 7, New York: Aldine, 1910.

Williams, Sarah T., "Man of Many Tribes," *Star Tribune* (March 23, 2011). <http://www.startribune.com/entertainment/ books/11435616.html>

Wilkins, David E., "Indigenous Self-Determination: A Global Perspective," in *Foundations of First People's Sovereignty: History, Education and Culture*, New York: Peter Lang, 2008, 11–20.

Wilson, Mary Louise Defender, NEA National Heritage Fellow website bio. <http://www.nea.gov/honors/heritage/fellows/fellow.php?id=1999_05&type=bio>

Womack, Craig S., *Red on Red: Native American Literary Separatism*, Minneapolis: University of Minnesota Press, 1999.

——, *Drowning In Fire*, Tucson: University of Arizona Press, 2001.

——, review of *Anti-Indianism in Modern America: A Voice from Tatekeya's Earth*, by Elizabeth Cook-Lynn, *American Indian Quarterly* 28.1/2, Special Issue: Empowerment Through Literature (Winter–Spring 2004), 130–141.

——, review of *Evidence of Red: Poems and Prose* by LeAnne Howe, *Studies in American Indian Literatures* 17.4 (2005), 157–161.

——, "The Integrity of American Indian Claims (Or, How I Learned to Stop Worrying and love My Hybridity)," in *American Indian Literary Nationalism*, ed. Jace Weaver, Craig S. Womack, and Robert Warrior, Albuquerque: University of New Mexico Press, 2006, 91–178.

——, "A Single Decade: Book-Length Native Literary Criticism," in *Reasoning Together: The Native Critics Collective*, ed. Craig S. Womack, Daniel Heath Justice, and Christopher B. Teuton, Norman: University of Oklahoma Press, 2008, 3–104.

——, *Art as Performance, Story as Criticism: Reflections on Native Literary Aesthetics*, Norman: University of Oklahoma Press, 2010.

——, "Cosmopolitanism and Nationalism in Native American Literature: A Panel Discussion," attended by Lisa Brooks, Michael Elliott, Arnold Krupat, Elvira Pulitano, and Craig Womack. <http://www.southernspaces.org/2011/cosmopolitanism-and-nationalism-native-american-literature-panel-discussion#sthash.LvCTUIpO.dpuf>

Wood, Gabby, "Man and Muse," *The Observer* (April 25, 2004).

Woolf, Virginia, *A Room of One's Own* [1929], Orlando: First Harvest, 1989.

Index

American Studies: Culture, Society and the Arts

Series editor:
Shamoon Zamir
New York University, Abu Dhabi

The series aims to publish studies of the American achievement in the literary and non-literary arts, of American intellectual history and of American cultural and social history, from the period of discovery to the present. It invites disciplinary pluralism and comparative approaches extending beyond national boundaries, as well as explorations which work within more conventional frameworks. The series is not confined to a particular critical or theoretical orientation. It welcomes contributions by scholars working both within and outside the academy and seeks to support work of intellectual independence and imaginative scope. Publications in a variety of formats will be considered: critical, historical and theoretical studies, essay collections, conference proceedings, annotated editions, anthologies, as well as work which may cross critical and creative borders.

Volume 1   Clive Bush:
Holding the Line. Selected Essays in American Literature and Culture.
376 pages. 2009. ISBN 978-3-03911-571-6

Volume 2   Gerd Hurm and Ann Marie Fallon (eds):
Rebels without a Cause? Renegotiating the American 1950s.
292 pages. 2007. ISBN 978-3-03910-936-4

Volume 3   Mick Gidley (ed.):
Writing with Light. Words and Photographs in American Texts.
299 pages. 2010. ISBN 978-3-03911-572-3

Volume 4   Michael Stone-Richards:
Logics of Separation. Exile and Transcendence in Aesthetic Modernity.
450 pages. 2011. ISBN 978-3-03911-008-7

Volume 5   Joy Porter (ed.):
Place and American Indian History and Culture.
392 pages. 2007. ISBN 978-3-03911-049-0